BARRON'S

NYSTCE
LAST · ATS-W · CST

3RD EDITION

Dr. Robert D. Postman
Professor, Mercy College,
Westchester County, New York

BARRON'S

To my wife
Liz
and my children
Chad, Blaire, and Ryan
and my grandson Quinn
This book is dedicated to you.

All inquiries should be addressed to:
Barron's Educational Series, Inc.
250 Wireless Boulevard
Hauppauge, New York 11788
www.barronseduc.com

Library of Congress Catalog Card No. 2010006254

ISBN-13: 978-0-7641-4298-7
ISBN-10: 0-7641-4298-4

Library of Congress Cataloging-in-Publication Data

Postman, Robert D.
    Barron's NYSTCE / Robert D. Postman. — 3rd ed.
        p. cm.
    Includes bibliographical references and index.
    ISBN-13: 978-0-7641-4298-7
    ISBN-10: 0-7641-4298-4
    1. Teachers—Certification—New York (State) 2. Teaching—New York
(State)—Examinations—Study guides.   I. Title. II. Title: NYSTCE.
    LB1763.N7P66 2010
    371.1209747—dc22

                                                    2010006254

PRINTED IN THE UNITED STATES OF AMERICA

9 8 7 6 5 4 3 2 1

FSC
Mixed Sources
Product group from well-managed
forests and other controlled sources
Cert no. SW-COC-002507
www.fsc.org
© 1996 Forest Stewardship Council

Contents

Preface   v

PART 1: YOUR REVIEW PLAN   1

1 Passing the LAST, ATS-W, and CST   3

The Tests   3
Passing Scores, Raw Scores, and Scale Scores   5
How to Prepare for the Tests   6

2 Test Preparation Techniques and Test-Taking Strategies   9

Preparing for the LAST, ATS-W, and CST   10
What College Students Say About the Tests   11
Proven Test-Taking Strategies   14
Selected-Response Strategies   15
Constructed-Response Strategies   17

PART 2: LAST PREPARATION   19

3 LAST Objectives   21

Objectives   21

4 Diagnostic LAST   29

Diagnostic LAST   33
Answer Key   58
Answer Explanations   59
Constructed Response   70
Diagnostic LAST Scoring   72

5 Reading Comprehension   75

Vocabulary Review   75
Types of Selected-Response Items   83
Five Steps for Answering Selected-Response
 Questions   88

6 Writing   113

Nouns and Verbs   113
Be Sure Subjects and Verbs Agree   116
Sentences   117
Steps for Writing Passing Essays   118
Constructed-Response Assignment   119

7 Practice LAST   127

Practice LAST   131
Answer Key   154
Answer Explanations   155
Constructed Response   165

PART 3: ATS-W PREPARATION   169

8 ATS-W Objectives

Objectives for the ATS-W—Elementary   171
Objectives for the ATS-W—Secondary   182

9 ATS-W Diagnostic Quiz and Review   195

Using This Chapter   195
ATS-W Diagnostic Review Quiz   196
Practice Written Assignment   199
ATS-W Review   206

10 Practice ATS-W— Elementary   245

Practice ATS-W—Elementary   249
Answer Key   272
Answer Explanations   273
Constructed Response   285

11 Practice ATS-W— Secondary 289

Practice ATS-W—Secondary 293
Answer Key 312
Answer Explanations 313
Constructed Response 325

PART 4: CST PREPARATION 329

12 CST: Multiple Subjects Objectives 331

Objectives 331

13 CST: Multiple Subjects Preparation Guide 349

Preparation Steps 349

14 CST: Multiple Subjects Practice Test 359

Practice CST: Multiple Subjects 363
Answer Key 384
Answer Explanations 385
Constructed Response 397

PART 5: JOB SEARCH 401

15 Finding a Teaching Job 403

How Can I Find a Job? 403
Teacher Certification and Job Search Links 406

Preface

This book shows you how to get a passing score on the LAST, ATS-W, and CST. The book has been field-tested by college students and prospective teachers and reviewed by experienced teachers and subject matter specialists.

My wife, Liz, a teacher and a constant source of support, made significant contributions to this book. I hope she accepts my regrets for the lost months. My children Chad, Blaire, and Ryan have also been supportive as I worked on this and other books over the years.

Kristen Girardi did a masterful job with this manuscript. Many special touches in the book are due to her caring attention.

Thanks also to my colleagues Bill Prattella, Andy Peiser, Reggie Marra, and Mary Ellen Hoffman for their suggestions and insight. Thanks also to Esther Wermuth, Mary Lou Pagano, Susan Oliver, Demetra Keane, Larry Ashley, Bessie Ford, and Olga De Jesus for their contributions.

Special thanks to the undergraduate and graduate students and those changing careers, and to those at the Metropolitan Museum of Art for their assistance. I am also grateful to those at the New York Education Department for taking the time to talk with me, and to those at other New York colleges who talked to me about their experiences with the testing.

The next generation awaits. You will help them prepare for a vastly different, technological world.

PART 1

YOUR REVIEW PLAN

CHAPTER 1

Passing the LAST, ATS-W, and CST

TEST INFO BOX

The New York State Teacher Certification Tests are offered by National Evaluation Systems (NES).

Go to *www.nystce.nesinc.com* for a registration form, test dates, Internet registration, score reports, and test guides.

THE TESTS

The LAST consists of 80 selected-response items and a constructed response.

The ATS-W consists of 80 selected-response items and a constructed response. There is an elementary and a secondary version of the ATS-W.

The CST Multiple Subjects consists of 90 selected-response items and a constructed response.

The Tests

The NYSTCE Liberal Arts and Sciences Test (LAST), the Elementary or Secondary versions of Assessment of Teaching Skills—Written (ATS-W), and a Content Specialty Test (CST) are required for most New York State teaching certificates.

This book is about the LAST, the ATS-W and the CST Multiple Subjects. It contains five full-length practice tests with answer explanations as well as appropriate review help.

The LAST, ATS-W, and CST are not exclusionary tests. That means they are not specifically designed to make earning a teaching certificate exceptionally hard. However, they are real tests and a little unusual in their structure. So spend a reasonable amount of time preparing for them.

There are two test sessions on each test day—morning and afternoon. The ATS-W and the CST Multiple Subjects are given only in the morning. The LAST is given only in the afternoon. That means you may take a maximum of two tests on one test day, but you cannot take the ATS-W and the CST Multiple Subjects on the same day.

Some students like to take two tests on one test day and a single other test on a second day. The LAST should be taken first. However, scheduling all three tests in time to graduate can be difficult. Students report that if they are going to take two tests, they usually take the LAST and the ATS-W. Other students like to take one test at a time. The order in which you take the tests is up to you.

LAST

TIP

Reading comprehension and essay writing are the keys to the LAST. You do not have to know about teaching.

- Four hours to complete the entire test.
- 80 selected-response items. Most items involve reading comprehension.
- One constructed-response essay scored 1, 2, 3, or 4 by two readers with a combined score range of 2 to 8. Blank or completely inappropriate essays are scored U.
- The essay asks you to choose one of two sides to an argument and to defend your choice.
- The selected-response items are 80% of your score.
- The constructed-response is 20% of your score.
- You decide when you complete each part of the test.

ATS-W

TIP

A blend of education coursework and some classroom experience helps most with ATS-W.

- Four hours to complete the entire test.
- 80 selected-response items. Most items involve classroom or school situations.
- One constructed-response essay scored 1, 2, 3, or 4 by two readers with a combined score range of 2 to 8. Blank or completely inappropriate essays are scored U.
- The essay is based on your discussion of appropriate instructional practices or decisions.
- The selected-response items are 80% of your score.
- The constructed-response is 20% of your score.
- You decide when you complete each part of the test.

CST Multiple Subjects

- Four hours to complete the entire test.
- 90 selected-response items. Items cover a wide range of subjects, including reading instruction, English, mathematics, science, social studies, physical education, and careers.

TIP

Having a broad knowledge of elementary school subjects, of teaching school subjects, and experience teaching about literacy helps most with the CST.

- One constructed-response essay scored 1, 2, 3, or 4 by two readers with a combined score range of 2 to 8. Blank or completely inappropriate essays are scored U.
- The essay is very focused. You must write about specific examples of phonics or grammar issues demonstrated by the writing of or discussions among elementary school students.
- The selected-response items are 90% of your score.

- The constructed response is 10% of your score.
- You decide when you complete each part of the test.

Passing Scores, Raw Scores, and Scale Scores

The passing score for each test is a scale score of 220.

Your raw score is the number of items you answer correctly or the number of points you earn. Your scale score shows your raw score on a single scale compared with others who took the same version of the test. Items on different versions of the test have different difficulty levels. To make up for this difference in difficulty, the harder items earn more scale points while easier items earn fewer scale points. To allow for the difference in the difficulty of each version of a test, the passing scores are given as scale scores. The scale scores for the selected-response items on each test and for the constructed-response essay range from 100 to 300.

Raw Scores That Lead to Passing

First, here is a warning. We have anecdotal information about the raw scores that have led to a passing scale score of 220. This can change at any time. A simple statistical rearrangement can make it harder or easier to get a passing scale score. Your Test Report will show your scale scores but not the number correct that earned you that score.

Generally speaking, a raw score of a little over 65% of the selected-response items and an essay score in the upper half (5–8) has usually earned a passing score. Better scores on one part of the test may offset lower scores on the other part.

Possible Passing Raw Scores

	Selected Response	Constructed Response
LAST	53–57 correct	Combined score of 5, 6, 7, 8
ATS-W	53–57 correct	Combined score of 5, 6, 7, 8
CST	54–59 correct	Combined score of 5, 6, 7, 8

Please be careful. There is also anecdotal information that higher raw scores have been required for passing scale scores. Do not use the scores shown in the table as goals but, rather, as indicators of what was needed in the past. We can't and don't say that these scores will be the same in the future.

Simply do your best. Remember that you can pick up raw score points by using the fundamental test strategies. Think strategically! If you know 45 of 80 answers on the LAST, you need to find some way to answer 10 or 12 of the remaining 35 items correctly.

TIP

Fundamental Test Strategies
- Always write a brief outline before you write your essay.
- Eliminate every answer choice you know is incorrect.
- Always guess if you have to.
- Never leave an answer blank.

Registration, Test Scores, and Study Guides

Your first stop should be the NYSTCE website *http://www.nystce.nesinc.com/*. The site features full information about the tests. You register online at the website, and you can quickly receive your scores through that some site. The site also has test information guides for each test with some examples of practice questions. The website does not include full-length tests. You should access those study guides first to get sample test questions and answers.

How to Prepare for the Tests

Review enough so you will pass. Do not spend a lot of extra time on things you do not need help with. Many, many people do not need more than a standard preparation. You may be one of them.

I meet people all the time who would have passed if they had a little more practice with test-taking strategies and practice writing essays. The amount of time you spend properly preparing for the tests is significantly less than the amount of time you will spend if you fail and have to register again, prepare again, and take the tests again. For most people, just retaking a single test again can take 6 to 8 hours on the day of the test.

Standard Review

A standard review is sufficient for most people. A reasonable goal is to spend about 7 hours preparing for each test, 21 hours in all. You might go under or over that time, but it is a good guideline.

- Spend 1 hour to review the Test Objectives in this book, the test guide from the website, and to review the test overview and test-taking strategies in this book.
- Spend 4 hours to take one each of the full-length tests in the book. Time yourself carefully. It is tedious, but getting used to that tedium is a big part of preparing for these tests.
- Spend 1 additional hour or so to score your test and review the answer explanations and the sample essays. You will learn a lot at this stage.
- Spend 1 hour or so per test for any last-minute review and to talk to some of your friends who have just taken the test. They may have a few extra pointers.

Extended Review

You may find you have difficulty with one of the tests—answering the questions or writing the essays. If that happens, you need to do an extended review. Additional help with reading comprehension, writing essays, and reviewing AST-W content is available in this book. Take the time to review those sections.

The constructed-response essays make a big difference in your score. If you are not good at writing them, get some help from the writing center or a person experienced with holistic grading. The help is worth the effort.

Crisis Review

If you have procrastinated, you may have to do a crisis review. You may have less than a week until test day or maybe even less than a few days. Your time and your options are limited. Choose the one or two tests you will take on test day. Take the test(s) found in this book. Review the answers and answer explanations. If you have time, go over the relevant review material in this book and look at the sample questions from the NYSTCE website.

How to Prepare for the Tests

Your Preparation Plan

This section shows you how to prepare for each test.

☑ Review this chapter and Chapter 2 about test strategies	Page 9
☑ Review the LAST Objectives in Chapter 3	Page 21

LAST Preparation

Diagnostic LAST I

☑ Take the Diagnostic LAST I	Page 33
☑ Mark your test and review the answer explanations	Page 58
☑ Review the scoring guide and recommendations for further study	Page 73
☑ Decide if additional review is necessary	Page 73

LAST Review

Check a box to indicate your additional LAST Review.

Complete the LAST review based on your LAST diagnostic results

❏ Reading comprehension, Chapter 5	Page 75
❏ Writing, Chapter 6	Page 113
❏ Practice LAST	Page 127
❏ Mark your test and review the answer explanations	Page 154

ATS-W Preparation

☑ Review the ATS-W Objectives, Chapter 8	Page 171
☑ Complete Diagnostic ATS-W quiz, Chapter 9	Page 195
❏ Review the Diagnostic Checklist	Page 202
☑ Review the ATS-W preparation material based on your diagnostic results	Page 206
☑ Take the appropriate ATS-W	

Check the box for your test.

❏ Practice ATS-W–Elementary, Chapter 10	Page 245
❏ Practice ATS-W–Secondary, Chapter 11	Page 289
❏ Mark your test and review the answer explanations	

Elementary, Page 272   Secondary, Page 312

❏ You may take the other ATS-W for additional practice if you wish

How to Prepare for the Tests

CST Multiple Subjects Preparation

☑ Review the CST: Multiple Subjects Objectives, Chapter 12   Page 331

☑ Review the CST: Multiple Subjects Preparation Guide, Chapter 13   Page 349

☑ Take the CST Multiple Subjects Test, Chapter 14   Page 359

☑ Mark your test and review the answer explanations   Page 384

Test Preparation Techniques and Test-Taking Strategies

CHAPTER 2

TEST INFO BOX

This chapter shows you essential test-taking strategies. It includes steps for constructed-response items and scored constructed-response examples. The most important strategies are discussed below.

SELECTED RESPONSE

Eliminate and then guess. There is no penalty for wrong answers. Never leave any answer blank.

Suppose you eliminate just one incorrect answer choice on all the items and you guess every answer. On average you would get about 26 correct. Suppose you eliminate two incorrect answer choices on all the items and you guess every answer. On average, you would get 40 correct.

CONSTRUCTED RESPONSE

Write an outline first, then complete the constructed-response essay.

Topic Paragraph: Begin the constructed response with an introduction to orient the reader to the topic. The first paragraph should clearly state the main idea of your entire constructed response.

Topic Sentence: Begin each paragraph with a topic sentence that supports the main idea.

Details: Provide details, examples, and arguments to support the topic sentence.

Grammar, Punctuation, Spelling: Edit sentences to conform to standard usage. Avoid passive construction; write actively and avoid the passive voice. That is, write "I passed the test," rather than "The test was passed."

Conclusion: End the constructed response with a paragraph that summarizes your main points.

Words Matter: In general, longer essays tend to receive higher scores.

Preparing for the LAST, ATS-W, and CST

By now you've sent in the registration form and the test is at least four to nine weeks away. This section describes how to prepare for the LAST and the ATS-W. The next chapter describes test-taking strategies. Before we go on, let's think about what you are preparing for.

Wait! Why Test Me? I'm a Good Person!

Why indeed? Life would be so much easier without tests. If anyone tells you that they like to take tests, don't believe them. Nobody does. Tests are imperfect. Some people pass when they should have failed, while others fail when they should have passed. It may not be fair, but it is very real. So sit back and relax. You're just going to have to do it, and this book will show you how.

Who Makes Up These Tests and How Do They Get Written?

Consider the following scenario. It is late in the afternoon. Around a table sit teachers, deans of education, parents, and representatives of the state education department. In front of each person is a preliminary list of skills and knowledge that teachers should possess. The list comes from comments by an even larger group of teachers and other educational professionals.

Those around the table are regular people just like the ones you might run into in a store or on the street. They all care about education. They also bring to the table their own strengths and weaknesses—their own perspectives and biases. What's that? An argument just broke out. People are choosing up sides and, depending on the outcome, one item on the list will stay or go.

The final list goes to professional test writers to prepare test items. These items are tried out, refined, and put through a review process. Eventually the test question bank is established, and a test is born. These test writers are not geniuses. They just know how to write questions. You might get a better score on this test than some of them would.

Keep those people around the table and the test writers in mind as you use this book. You are preparing for their test. Soon, you will be like one of those people around the table. You may even contribute to a test like this one.

Get Yourself Ready for the Test

Most people feel at least a little bit uncomfortable about tests. You are probably one of them. No book is going to make you feel comfortable. But here are some suggestions.

Most people are less tense when they exercise. Set up a reasonable exercise program for yourself. The program should involve exercising in a way that is appropriate for you 30 to 45 minutes each day. This exercise may be just as important as other preparation.

Prepare with another person. You will feel less isolated if you have a friend or colleague to study with.

GET READY

- Exercise
- Prepare with a friend
- Be realistic about the outcome

Accept these important truths. You are not going to get all the answers correct. You don't have to. You can take this test over again if you have to. There is no penalty for taking the test again. This is not a do or die, life or death situation.

What College Students Say About the Tests

More than 500 students were surveyed just after they took the LAST, ATS-W, and the CST. Their reactions to the tests and their advice to future test takers are summarized below.

What College Students Say About the LAST

Students say you should take the LAST after the sophomore year. Most students say to write the essay first and then answer the selected-response items. But other students report success when they answered the selected-response items first. Even the best test takers say that time pressure can be a real issue on the LAST. They advise using a watch or clock to monitor your time and to leave an hour for the essay. Check with your education advisor for advice about when to take the LAST.

SELECTED RESPONSE

Students say the LAST is primarily a reading comprehension test. The test consists mainly of passages followed by items about the passage. Some passages are difficult and some items are tricky. Passages and items may integrate liberal arts concepts.

Students say you may see some graphs, charts and maps, and English usage items. The visual arts items often show a picture and ask for some common sense interpretation. Items related to these topics are not reading comprehension items.

Students say that almost all of the items can be answered just from the information in the passage.

CONSTRUCTED RESPONSE

Students say the most important thing is to write an outline before you start to write. They say to be sure to write about the topic. The constructed response can be about anything. It is how you write, not your point of view that matters.

> **STUDENTS' ADVICE TO YOU ABOUT PREPARING
> FOR THE LAST**
> 1. Learn how to answer reading comprehension items and how to write an essay under time pressure.
> 2. Take practice tests in realistic situations.
> 3. Practice reading in the content areas of science, history, and social studies.
> 4. Get a broad overview of reading graphs, charts, maps, and English.

What College Students Say About the ATS-W

Students say you should take the ATS-W after you finish most of your education courses and after you have field experience. Most students say to write the essay first and then answer the selected-response items. Check with your education advisor about when to take the ATS-W.

SELECTED RESPONSE

Students say the ATS-W is just as much about your teaching experience as about your college education courses. Most of the test consists of passages describing teaching or other education-related situations followed by items about the passage.

Students say most of the information needed to answer the items is found in the passage.

Students say you need to use common sense based on your education experience as you answer the questions. They say that between 35 percent and 55 percent of the items can be answered using informed common sense.

Students say you should have a broad general background in education related areas.

CONSTRUCTED RESPONSE

Students say the most important thing is to write at least a brief outline before you start to write the assignment. They say to be sure to write about the topic. The constructed response will be about a teaching or school-related situation. It is how well you respond to the education-related situation, not your writing ability, that matters on this constructed response.

**STUDENTS' ADVICE TO YOU ABOUT PREPARING
FOR THE ATS-W**

1. Get lots of teaching experience.
2. Take practice tests in a realistic situation.
3. Get a broad overview of education-related areas.
4. Learn how to answer reading comprehension items and how to write essays and curricula. Practice reading and writing.

What College Students Say About the CST Multiple Subjects

Students say you should take the CST Multiple Subjects near the end of your elementary and/or early childhood program. Most students say to do the selected-response items first, but there have been many successful students who did the constructed-response essay first. Some students have been surprised that although 4 hours seemed a long time for a test, they still felt time pressure.

SELECTED RESPONSE

Students say there are a lot of subject matter questions about the subjects taught in elementary school. Much of this test is a test of knowledge. However, some questions are about teaching reading and some questions are about teaching the school subjects. You actually have to know something to take the test. Although some questions can be difficult and cover unexpected information, students said that most questions covered topics learned in high school. Students felt that test-taking strategies can be particularly helpful on the CST because some answers are easy to eliminate.

CONSTRUCTED RESPONSE

Students say that the constructed-response essay is always going to be about phonics or grammar. You will see some student work or read a discussion between students. Then you usually have to figure out what problem the student is having, come up with some ways of dealing with the problem, and support the remedial steps you recommend. Students remark that the constructed-response essay is less important in the scoring than the selected-response items.

STUDENTS' ADVICE ABOUT PREPARING FOR THE CST

1. Read up on reading and phonics instruction.
2. Review the information about history, English, reading, social studies, and math. Most of the questions are not extremely difficult. However, a few will be challenging.
3. Really get the rhythm of how to answer questions you are not really sure of. You can often eliminate several incorrect answers, which will help your score.

FOLLOW THIS FINAL WEEK PLAN

MONDAY

Make sure you have your admission ticket.
Make sure you know where the test is given.
Make sure you know how you're getting there.

TUESDAY

Visit the test site, if you haven't done it already. You don't want any surprises this Saturday.

WEDNESDAY

Get some sharpened No. 2 pencils, a digital watch or clock, and a good big eraser and put them aside.

THURSDAY

Take a break from preparing for the test, and relax.

FRIDAY

Complete any forms you have to bring to the test.
Prepare any snacks or food you want to bring with you.
Talk to someone who makes you feel good or do something enjoyable and relaxing.
Have a good night's sleep.

SATURDAY—TEST DAY

Dress comfortably. There are no points for appearance.
Eat the same kind of breakfast you've been eating each morning.
Don't stuff yourself. You want your blood racing through your brain, not your stomach.
Get together things to bring to the test including: registration ticket, identification forms, pencils, calculator, eraser, and snacks or food.

Get to the test room, not the parking lot, about 10 to 15 minutes before the start time.
Remember to leave time for parking and walking to the test site.
Hand in your forms—you're in the door. You're ready. This is the easy part.
Follow the test-taking strategies in the next section.

Proven Test-Taking Strategies

Testing companies like to pretend that test-taking strategies don't help that much. They act like that because they want everyone to think that their tests only measure your knowledge of the subject. Of course, they are just pretending; knowing test-taking strategies can make a big difference.

However, there is nothing better than being prepared for the material on this test. If you are prepared, then these strategies can make a difference. Use them. Other people will be. Not using them may very well lower your score.

Be Comfortable

Get a good seat. Don't sit near anyone or anything that will distract you. Stay away from your friends. If you don't like where you are sitting, move or ask for another seat. You paid money for this test, and you have a right to favorable test conditions.

You Will Make Mistakes

You are going to make mistakes on this test. The people who wrote the test expect you to make them.

You Are Not Competing with Anyone

Don't worry about how anyone else is doing. Your score does not depend on theirs. When the score report comes out it doesn't say, "Nancy got a 661, but Blaire got a 670." You just want to get the score required for your certificate. If you can do better, that's great. Stay focused. Remember your goal.

Selected-Response Strategies

It's Not What You Know That Matters, It's Just Which Circle You Fill In

No one you know or care about will see your test. An impersonal machine scores all selected-response questions. The machine just senses whether the correct circle on the answer sheet is filled in. That is the way the test makers want it. If that's good enough for them, it should be good enough for you. Concentrate on filling in the correct circle.

Do Your Work in the Test Booklet

You can write anything you want in your test booklet. The test booklet is not used for scoring and no one will look at it. You can't bring scratch paper to the test so use your booklet instead.

Some of the strategies we recommend involve writing in and marking up the booklet. These strategies work and we strongly recommend that you use them.

Do your work for a question near that question in the test booklet. You can also do work on the cover or wherever else suits you. You may want to do calculations, underline important words, mark up a picture, or draw a diagram.

You Can Be Right but Be Marked Wrong

If you get the right answer but fill in the wrong circle, the machine will mark it wrong. We told you that filling in the right circle was what mattered. We strongly recommend that you follow this strategy.

Write the letter for your answer big in the test booklet next to the number for the problem. If you change your mind about an answer, cross off the "old" letter and write the "new" one. At the end of each section, transfer all the answers together from the test booklet to the answer sheet.

EXAMPLE

What number times 0.00708 is equal to 70.8?

B

(A) 100,000 × 0.00708 = 708
(B) 10,000 × 0.00708 = 70.8
(C) 1,000
(D) 0.01

The correct answer is (B) 10,000.

TIP

Watch That Answer Sheet
Remember that a machine is doing the marking. Fill in the correct answer circle completely. Don't put extra pencil marks on the answer section of the answer sheet. Stray marks could be mistaken for answers.

Some Questions Are Traps

Some questions include the words *not*, *least*, or *except*. You are being asked for the answer that doesn't fit with the rest. Be alert for these types of questions.

Save the Hard Questions for Last

You're not supposed to get all the questions correct, and some of them will be too difficult for you. Work through the questions and answer the easy ones. Pass the other ones by. Do these more difficult questions the second time through. If a question seems really hard, draw a circle around the question number in the test booklet. Save these questions until the very end.

They Show You the Answer

Every selected-response test shows you the correct answer for each question. The answer is staring right at you. You just have to figure out which one it is. There is a 20 or 25 percent chance you'll get it right by just closing your eyes and pointing.

Some Answers Are Traps

When someone writes a test question, they include distracters. Distracters are traps—incorrect answers that look like correct answers. It might be an answer to an addition problem when you should be multiplying. It might be a correct answer to a different question. It might just be an answer that catches your eye. Watch out for this type of incorrect answer.

Eliminate the Incorrect Answers

If you can't figure out which answer is correct, then decide which answers can't be correct. Choose the answers you're sure are incorrect. Cross them off in the test booklet. Only one left? That's the correct answer.

Guess, Guess, Guess

If there are still two or more answers left, then guess. Guess the answer from those remaining. Never leave any item blank. There is no penalty for guessing.

Constructed-Response Strategies

Here's How They Score You

Constructed responses are rated 1–4. The raters use these general guidelines.

4   A well developed, complete constructed response. Shows a thorough response to all parts of the topic. Clear explanations that are well supported. An assignment that is free of significant grammatical, punctuation, or spelling errors.

3   A fairly well developed, complete constructed response. It may not thoroughly respond to all parts of the topic. Fairly clear explanations that may not be well supported. It may contain some significant grammatical, punctuation, or spelling errors.

2   A poorly developed, incomplete constructed response. It does not thoroughly respond to most parts of the topic. Contains many poor explanations that are not well supported. It may contain some significant grammatical, punctuation, or spelling errors.

1   A very poorly developed, incomplete constructed response. It does not thoroughly respond to the topic. Contains only poor, unsupported explanations. Contains numerous significant grammatical, punctuation, or spelling errors.

> **UNSCORABLE CONSTRUCTED RESPONSES**
>
> A constructed response is rated unscorable (U) if it is blank; unrelated to the topic, no matter how well written; not long enough to score; written in a language other than English; or illegible. A rating of U means the test is a failure regardless of the score on the selected-response section.

Your Responses Are Graded Holistically

Holistic rating means the raters assign a score based on their informed sense about your writing. Raters have a lot of essays to look at and they do not do a detailed analysis.

After each test date, National Evaluation Systems gets together a group of readers in Albany, New York. These readers typically consist of teachers and college professors. They put these readers up in an Albany area motel. At first, representatives of NES show the readers the topics for the recent test and review the types of responses that should be rated 1, 2, 3, or 4. The readers are trained to evaluate the responses according to the NES guidelines.

Each written assignment is evaluated twice, without the second reader knowing the evaluation given by the first reader. If the two evaluations differ significantly, other readers review the assignment. Your score is the sum of the evaluations.

Your essay may also be graded online. Whatever the case, make it easy for these readers to give you a high score.

PART 2

LAST PREPARATION

CHAPTER 3

LAST Objectives

> ## TEST INFO BOX
>
> The following pages contain the official list of LAST Objectives. Review these objectives to develop a sense of the kind of information you will encounter on LAST test items. However, remember that all LAST selected-response items are reading comprehension items.
>
> Following your review of these objectives, take the Diagnostic LAST in Chapter 4 on page on page 29. Depending on your diagnostic score, additional reading comprehension help is available in Chapter 5 on page 75, and additional writing help is available in Chapter 6 on page 113. There is a second practice LAST on page 131.
>
> ### SUBAREAS
>
> ### SELECTED RESPONSE
>
> I. Scientific, Mathematical, and Technological Processes
> II. Historical and Social Scientific Awareness
> III. Artistic Expression and the Humanities
> IV. Communication and Research Skills
>
> ### CONSTRUCTED RESPONSE
>
> V. Written Analysis and Expression

Objectives

SUBAREA I—SCIENTIFIC, MATHEMATICAL, AND TECHNOLOGICAL PROCESSES

1. Use mathematical reasoning in problem-solving situations to arrive at a logical conclusion and to analyze the problem-solving process.

EXAMPLES

- Analyze problem situations for logical flaws.
- Examine problems to determine missing information needed to solve them.
- Analyze a partial solution to a problem to determine an appropriate next step.

- Evaluate the validity or logic of an argument or advertising claim that is based on statistics or probability.

2. Understand connections between mathematical representations and ideas, and use mathematical terms and representations to organize, interpret, and communicate information.

EXAMPLES

- Analyze data and make inferences from two or more graphic sources (e.g., diagrams, graphs, equations).

- Restate a problem related to a concrete situation in mathematical terms.

- Use mathematical modeling/multiple representations to present, interpret, communicate, and connect mathematical information and relationships.

- Select an appropriate graph or table summarizing information presented in another form (e.g., a newspaper excerpt).

3. Apply knowledge of numerical, geometric, and algebraic relationships in problem-solving and mathematical contexts.

EXAMPLES

- Represent and use numbers in a variety of equivalent forms (e.g., integer, fraction, decimal, percent).

- Apply operational algorithms to add, subtract, multiply, and divide fractions, decimals, and integers.

- Use scales and ratios to interpret maps and models.

- Use geometric concepts and formulas to solve problems (e.g., estimating the surface area of a floor to determine the approximate cost of floor covering).

- Solve problems using algebraic concepts and formulas (e.g., calculating wages based on sales commission).

- Apply appropriate algebraic equations to the solution of problems (e.g., determining the original price of a sale item given the rate of discount).

4. Understand major concepts, principles, and theories in science and technology, and use that understanding to analyze phenomena in the natural world and to interpret information presented in illustrated or written form.

EXAMPLES

- Use an appropriate illustration, graphic, or physical model to represent a scientific theory, concept, or relationship presented in an excerpt.

- Relate a major scientific principle, concept, or theory to a natural phenomenon.

- Use design processes or procedures to pose questions and select solutions to problems and situations.

- Apply technological knowledge and skills to evaluate the degree to which products and systems meet human and environmental needs.

- Analyze excerpts describing recent scientific discoveries or technological advances in relation to underlying scientific principles, concepts, or themes.

  5. Understand the historical development and cultural contexts of mathematics, science, and technology; the relationships and common themes that connect mathematics, science, and technology; and the impact of mathematics, science, and technology on human societies.

EXAMPLES

- Analyze the historical, societal, or environmental effects of given developments in science and technology (e.g., computerization).

- Recognize how mathematical models can be used to understand scientific, social, or environmental phenomena.

- Evaluate how historical and societal factors have promoted or hindered developments in science and technology.

- Analyze how the developments in scientific knowledge may affect other areas of life (e.g., recognizing types of scientific data likely to affect government policy-making regarding pollution control).

  6. Understand and apply skills, principles, and procedures associated with inquiry and problem solving in the sciences.

EXAMPLES

- Apply scientific methods and principles (including nonquantitative methods such as case studies) to investigate a question or a problem.

- Formulate questions to guide research and experimentation toward explanations for phenomena and observations.

- Infer the scientific principles (e.g., reliance on experimental data, replication or results) or skills (e.g., observation, inductive reasoning, familiarity with statistics and probability) that contributed to a scientific development as described in an excerpt.

- Demonstrate familiarity with electronic means of collecting, organizing, and analyzing information (e.g., databases, spreadsheets).

- Analyze components of a given experimental design (e.g., dependent and independent variables, experimental groups, control groups).

- Demonstrate an understanding of the nature of scientific inquiry (including ethical dimensions) and the role of observation and experimentation in science.

SUBAREA II—HISTORICAL AND SOCIAL SCIENTIFIC AWARENESS

  7. Understand the interrelatedness of historical, geographic, cultural, economic, political, and social issues and factors.

EXAMPLES

- Assess the likely effects of human activities or trends (described in written or graphic form) on the local, regional, or global environment.

- Assess ways in which major transformations related to human work, thought, and belief (e.g., industrialization, the scientific revolution, the development of various religions and belief traditions) have affected human society.

- Infer aspects of a society's social structure or group interactions based on information presented in an excerpt.

- Analyze ways in which social, cultural, geographic, and economic factors influence intergroup relations and the formation of values, beliefs, and attitudes.

- Assess the social or economic implications of political views presented in an excerpt.

8. Understand principles and assumptions underlying historical or contemporary arguments, interpretations, explanations, or developments.

EXAMPLES

- Infer the political process (e.g., popular sovereignty, separation of powers, due process of the law) illustrated in given situations or arguments.

- Recognize assumptions (e.g., regarding the nature of power relationships) that inform the positions taken by political parties.

- Analyze assumptions on which given U.S. policies (e.g., national health insurance, foreign relations) are based.

- Recognize concepts and ideas underlying alternative interpretations of past events.

- Infer the economic principles (e.g., supply and demand, redistribution of wealth) upon which a given explanation is based.

9. Understand different perspectives and priorities underlying historical or contemporary arguments, interpretations, explanations, or developments.

EXAMPLES

- Identify the values (e.g., commitment to democratic institutions) implicit in given political, economic, social, or religious points of view.

- Recognize the motives, beliefs, and interests that inform differing political, economic, social, or religious points of view (e.g., arguments related to equity, equality, and comparisons between groups or nations).

- Analyze multiple perspectives within U.S. society regarding major historical and contemporary issues.

- Recognize the values or priorities implicit in given public policy positions.

- Analyze the perceptions or opinions of observers or participants from different cultures regarding a given world event or development.

10. Understand and apply skills, principles, and procedures associated with inquiry, problem solving, and decision making in history and the social sciences.

EXAMPLES

- Analyze a description of research results to identify additional unanswered questions or to determine potential problems in research methodology.

- Determine the relevance or sufficiency of given information for supporting or refuting a point of view.

- Assess the reliability of sources of information cited in historical or contemporary accounts or arguments and determine whether specific conclusions or generalizations are supported by verifiable evidence.

- Evaluate the appropriateness of specific sources (e.g., atlas, periodical guide, economic database) to meet given information needs (e.g., the distribution of natural resources in a given region, the political philosophy of a presidential candidate).

- Distinguish between unsupported and informed expressions of opinion.

11. Understand and interpret visual representations of historical and social scientific information.

EXAMPLES

- Translate written or graphic information from one form to the other (e.g., selecting an appropriate graphic representation of information from an article on historical changes in global populations).

- Relate information provided in graphic representations (e.g., regarding population or economic trends) to public policy decisions.

- Interpret historical or social scientific information provided in one or more graphs, charts, tables, diagrams, or maps.

- Infer significant information (e.g., geographic, economic, sociological) about a historical or contemporary society based on examinations of a photograph, painting, drawing, cartoon, or other visual representation.

SUBAREA III—ARTISTIC EXPRESSION AND THE HUMANITIES

12. Understand and analyze elements of form and content in works from the visual and performing arts from different periods and cultures.

EXAMPLES

- Recognize important elements in a given work of the visual or performing arts (e.g., focal point, symmetry, repetition of shapes, perspective, motif, rhythm).

- Determine how a sense of unity or balance is achieved in a given work from the visual or performing arts.

- Characterize the theme, mood, or tone of a given work from the visual or performing arts.

- Determine how specific elements in a given work of the visual or performing arts (e.g., color, composition, scale, instrumentation, set design, choreography) affect audience perceptions of the content of the work.

13. Analyze and interpret works from the visual and performing arts representing different periods and cultures and understand the relationship of works of art to their social and historical contexts.

EXAMPLES

- Identify similarities and differences in forms and styles of art from different movements or periods of time.

- Compare and contrast two or more works from the visual or performing arts in terms of mood, theme, or technique.

- Demonstrate an understanding of art as a form of communication (e.g., conveying political or moral concepts, serving as a means of individual expression).

- Analyze ways in which the content of a given work from the visual or performing arts reflects a specific cultural or historical context.

14. Understand forms and themes used in literature from different periods and cultures.

EXAMPLES

- Identify characteristic features of various genres of fiction and nonfiction (e.g., novels, plays, essays, autobiographies).

- Distinguish the dominant theme in a literary passage.

- Recognize common literary elements and techniques (e.g., imagery, metaphor, symbolism, allegory, foreshadowing, irony) and use those elements to interpret a literary passage.

- Determine the meaning of figurative language used in a literary passage.

15. Analyze and interpret literature from different periods and cultures and understand the relationship of works of literature to their social and historical contexts.

EXAMPLES

- Analyze how the parts of a literary passage contribute to the whole.

- Compare and contrast the tone or mood of two or more literary passages.

- Analyze aspects of cultural or historical context implied in a literary passage.

- Distinguish characteristic features of different literary genres, periods, and traditions reflected in one or more literary passages.

- Make inferences about character, setting, author's point of view, etc., based on the content of a literary passage.

- Recognize how a text conveys multiple levels of meaning.

16. Analyze and interpret examples of religious or philosophical ideas from various periods of time and understand their significance in shaping societies and cultures.

EXAMPLES

- Distinguish the religious and philosophical traditions associated with given cultures and world regions.

- Recognize assumptions and beliefs underlying ideas presented in religious or philosophical writing.

- Analyze societal implications of philosophical or religious ideas.

- Compare and contrast key concepts presented in two excerpts reflecting different philosophical or religious traditions.

SUBAREA IV—COMMUNICATION AND RESEARCH SKILLS

17. Derive information from a variety of sources (e.g., magazine articles, essays, websites).

EXAMPLES

- Identify the stated or implied main idea of a paragraph or passage.

- Select an accurate summary or outline of a passage.

- Organize information presented on a website or other electronic means of communication.

- Comprehend stated or implied relationships in an excerpt (e.g., cause-and-effect, sequence of events).

- Recognize information that supports, illustrates, or elaborates the main idea of a passage.

18. Analyze and interpret written materials from a variety of sources.

EXAMPLES

- Recognize a writer's purpose for writing (e.g., to persuade, to describe).

- Draw conclusions or make generalizations based on information presented in an excerpt.

- Interpret figurative language in an excerpt.

- Compare and contrast views or arguments presented in two or more excerpts.

19. Use critical-reasoning skills to assess an author's treatment of content in written materials from a variety of sources.

EXAMPLES

- Analyze the logical structure of an argument in an excerpt and identify possible instances of faulty reasoning.

- Distinguish between fact and opinion in written material.

- Determine the relevance of specific facts, examples, or data to a writer's argument.

- Interpret a content, word choice, or phrasing of a passage to determine a writer's opinion, point of view, or position on an issue.

- Evaluate the credibility, objectivity, or bias of an author's argument or sources.

20. Analyze and evaluate the effectiveness of expression in a written paragraph or passage according to the conventions of edited American English.

EXAMPLES

- Revise text to correct problems relating to grammar (e.g., syntax, pronoun-antecedent agreement).

- Revise text to correct problems relating to sentence construction (e.g., those involving parallel structure, misplaced modifiers, run-on sentences).

- Revise text to improve unity and coherence (e.g., eliminating unnecessary sentences or paragraphs, adding a topic sentence or introductory paragraph, clarifying transitions between and relationships among ideas presented).

- Analyze problems related to organization of a given text (e.g., logical flow of ideas, grouping of related ideas, development of main points).

21. Demonstrate the ability to locate, retrieve, organize, and interpret information from a variety of traditional and electronic sources.

EXAMPLES

- Demonstrate familiarity with basic reference tools (e.g., encyclopedias, almanacs, bibliographies, databases, atlases, periodical guides).

- Recognize the difference between primary and secondary sources.

- Formulate research questions and hypotheses.

- Apply procedures for retrieving information from traditional and technological sources (e.g., newspapers, CD-ROMs, the Internet).

- Interpret data presented in visual, graphic, tabular, and quantitative forms (e.g., recognizing levels of statistical significance).

- Organize information into logical and coherent outlines.

- Evaluate the reliability of different sources of information.

SUBAREA V—WRITTEN ANALYSIS AND EXPRESSION

22. Prepare an organized, developed composition in edited American English in response to instructions regarding audience, purpose, and content.

EXAMPLES

- Take a position on an issue of contemporary concern and defend that position with reasoned arguments and supporting examples.

- Analyze and respond to an opinion presented in an excerpt.

- Compare and contrast conflicting viewpoints on a social, political, or educational topic, as presented in one or more excerpts.

- Evaluate information and propose a solution to a stated problem.

- Synthesize information presented in two or more excerpts.

Diagnostic LAST

<hr/>

TEST INFO BOX

This diagnostic test helps you decide if you need further review. It contains the types of items you will encounter on the real test. The distribution of items varies from one test administration to another.

Take this test in a realistic, timed setting.

The setting will be most realistic if another person times the test and ensures that the test rules are followed exactly. But remember that many people do better on a practice test than on the real test. If another person is acting as test supervisor, he or she should review these instructions with you and say "Start" when you should begin and "Stop" when time has expired.

You have 4 hours to complete the 80 selected-response questions and the written assignment. Keep the time limit in mind as you work.

Each selected-response question or statement in the test has four answer choices. Exactly one of these responses is correct. Mark your response on the answer sheet provided for this test.

Use a pencil to mark the answer sheet. The actual test will be machine scored so completely darken in the answer space.

Once the test is complete, review the answers and explanations for each item.

When you are ready, turn the page and begin.

Review the Diagnostic LAST Scoring that immediately follows the test for helpful advice.

Answer Sheet

DIAGNOSTIC LAST

1 Ⓐ Ⓑ Ⓒ Ⓓ	21 Ⓐ Ⓑ Ⓒ Ⓓ	41 Ⓐ Ⓑ Ⓒ Ⓓ	61 Ⓐ Ⓑ Ⓒ Ⓓ
2 Ⓐ Ⓑ Ⓒ Ⓓ	22 Ⓐ Ⓑ Ⓒ Ⓓ	42 Ⓐ Ⓑ Ⓒ Ⓓ	62 Ⓐ Ⓑ Ⓒ Ⓓ
3 Ⓐ Ⓑ Ⓒ Ⓓ	23 Ⓐ Ⓑ Ⓒ Ⓓ	43 Ⓐ Ⓑ Ⓒ Ⓓ	63 Ⓐ Ⓑ Ⓒ Ⓓ
4 Ⓐ Ⓑ Ⓒ Ⓓ	24 Ⓐ Ⓑ Ⓒ Ⓓ	44 Ⓐ Ⓑ Ⓒ Ⓓ	64 Ⓐ Ⓑ Ⓒ Ⓓ
5 Ⓐ Ⓑ Ⓒ Ⓓ	25 Ⓐ Ⓑ Ⓒ Ⓓ	45 Ⓐ Ⓑ Ⓒ Ⓓ	65 Ⓐ Ⓑ Ⓒ Ⓓ
6 Ⓐ Ⓑ Ⓒ Ⓓ	26 Ⓐ Ⓑ Ⓒ Ⓓ	46 Ⓐ Ⓑ Ⓒ Ⓓ	66 Ⓐ Ⓑ Ⓒ Ⓓ
7 Ⓐ Ⓑ Ⓒ Ⓓ	27 Ⓐ Ⓑ Ⓒ Ⓓ	47 Ⓐ Ⓑ Ⓒ Ⓓ	67 Ⓐ Ⓑ Ⓒ Ⓓ
8 Ⓐ Ⓑ Ⓒ Ⓓ	28 Ⓐ Ⓑ Ⓒ Ⓓ	48 Ⓐ Ⓑ Ⓒ Ⓓ	68 Ⓐ Ⓑ Ⓒ Ⓓ
9 Ⓐ Ⓑ Ⓒ Ⓓ	29 Ⓐ Ⓑ Ⓒ Ⓓ	49 Ⓐ Ⓑ Ⓒ Ⓓ	69 Ⓐ Ⓑ Ⓒ Ⓓ
10 Ⓐ Ⓑ Ⓒ Ⓓ	30 Ⓐ Ⓑ Ⓒ Ⓓ	50 Ⓐ Ⓑ Ⓒ Ⓓ	70 Ⓐ Ⓑ Ⓒ Ⓓ
11 Ⓐ Ⓑ Ⓒ Ⓓ	31 Ⓐ Ⓑ Ⓒ Ⓓ	51 Ⓐ Ⓑ Ⓒ Ⓓ	71 Ⓐ Ⓑ Ⓒ Ⓓ
12 Ⓐ Ⓑ Ⓒ Ⓓ	32 Ⓐ Ⓑ Ⓒ Ⓓ	52 Ⓐ Ⓑ Ⓒ Ⓓ	72 Ⓐ Ⓑ Ⓒ Ⓓ
13 Ⓐ Ⓑ Ⓒ Ⓓ	33 Ⓐ Ⓑ Ⓒ Ⓓ	53 Ⓐ Ⓑ Ⓒ Ⓓ	73 Ⓐ Ⓑ Ⓒ Ⓓ
14 Ⓐ Ⓑ Ⓒ Ⓓ	34 Ⓐ Ⓑ Ⓒ Ⓓ	54 Ⓐ Ⓑ Ⓒ Ⓓ	74 Ⓐ Ⓑ Ⓒ Ⓓ
15 Ⓐ Ⓑ Ⓒ Ⓓ	35 Ⓐ Ⓑ Ⓒ Ⓓ	55 Ⓐ Ⓑ Ⓒ Ⓓ	75 Ⓐ Ⓑ Ⓒ Ⓓ
16 Ⓐ Ⓑ Ⓒ Ⓓ	36 Ⓐ Ⓑ Ⓒ Ⓓ	56 Ⓐ Ⓑ Ⓒ Ⓓ	76 Ⓐ Ⓑ Ⓒ Ⓓ
17 Ⓐ Ⓑ Ⓒ Ⓓ	37 Ⓐ Ⓑ Ⓒ Ⓓ	57 Ⓐ Ⓑ Ⓒ Ⓓ	77 Ⓐ Ⓑ Ⓒ Ⓓ
18 Ⓐ Ⓑ Ⓒ Ⓓ	38 Ⓐ Ⓑ Ⓒ Ⓓ	58 Ⓐ Ⓑ Ⓒ Ⓓ	78 Ⓐ Ⓑ Ⓒ Ⓓ
19 Ⓐ Ⓑ Ⓒ Ⓓ	39 Ⓐ Ⓑ Ⓒ Ⓓ	59 Ⓐ Ⓑ Ⓒ Ⓓ	79 Ⓐ Ⓑ Ⓒ Ⓓ
20 Ⓐ Ⓑ Ⓒ Ⓓ	40 Ⓐ Ⓑ Ⓒ Ⓓ	60 Ⓐ Ⓑ Ⓒ Ⓓ	80 Ⓐ Ⓑ Ⓒ Ⓓ

Diagnostic LAST

Directions: Each item on this test includes four answer choices. Select the best choice for each item and mark that letter on the answer sheet.

The country of Mexico and the settlers in Texas, then a part of Mexico, had been at war since 1835. After a Texican victory at the Battle of San Jacinto in 1836, Texas became a sovereign country. Texas was admitted as a state of the United States in 1845. Mexico objected. The Mexican-American War, which was different from the earlier strife between Mexico and Texas, started in 1846.

1. According to the passage, just before Texas became a state, it was

   (A) a part of Mexico.
   (B) a part of the United States.
   (C) a nation.
   (D) a part of the Louisiana Purchase.

School officials were trying to decide how students arrived to school each morning. This information was important because those at the school had to decide how many bike stands to have and how much space to set aside for parents to drop off their children at school.

At first they estimated the percent of students who walked to school and those who arrived by bike, car or bus. Their original estimates were that 60 percent of students walked to school or rode a bike to school, while 40 percent of students arrived by car or by bus. But then they realized that these estimates were not accurate enough. So they conducted a survey to gather this information directly from the students.

On Monday, the principal found out how students arrived at school that morning. The graph is shown at right. The principal also took the survey on each day that week.

On Tuesday, the graph for walking shrank by half, while the graph for biking doubled. On Wednesday the results for walking and biking stayed the same as Monday, but the numbers for car and bus were reversed.

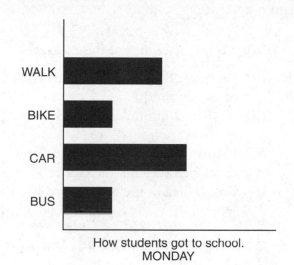

How students got to school.
MONDAY

2. Which of the following statements accurately describes the graph on that Wednesday?

   (A) There were about twice as many walkers as bikers.
   (B) There were about three times as many car riders as bus riders.
   (C) There were about three times as many car riders as bikers.
   (D) There were about half as many car riders as bike riders.

Use this passage to answer items 3–4.

We use language, including gestures and sounds, to communicate. Humans first used gestures but it was spoken language that opened the vistas for human communication. Language consists of two things. First we have the thoughts that language conveys and then the physical sounds, writing and structure of the language itself.

Human speech organs (mouth, tongue, lips, and the like) were not developed to make sounds, but they uniquely determined the sounds and words humans could produce.

Human speech gradually came to be loosely bound together by unique rules for grammar.

Many believe that humans developed their unique ability to speak with the development of a specialized area of the brain called Broca's area. If this is so, human speech and language probably developed in the past 100,000 years.

3. What is the main idea of this passage?

   (A) Language consists of thoughts and physical sounds.
   (B) Human communication includes gestures.
   (C) Human speech and language slowly developed through the years.
   (D) Broca's area of the brain controls speech.

4. What is the first component of language development?

   (A) gestures
   (B) thoughts
   (C) sound
   (D) writing

5. What power of 10 would you multiply times 3.74 to get 374,000,000?

   (A) 10^6
   (B) 10^7
   (C) 10^8
   (D) 10^9

Use this passage to answer items 6–9.

There was very little oxygen in the earth's atmosphere about 3.5 billion years ago. We know that molecules (much smaller than a cell) can develop spontaneously in this type of environment. This is how life probably began on earth about 3.4 billion years ago.

Eventually these molecules linked together to form complex groupings of molecules. These earliest organisms must have been able to ingest and live on nonorganic compounds. Over a period of time, these organisms adapted and began using the sun's energy.

The organisms began to use photosynthesis, which released oxygen into the oceans and the atmosphere. The stage was set for more advanced life forms.

The first cells were prokaryotes (bacteria), which created energy (respired) without oxygen (anaerobic). Next these cells developed into blue-green algae prokaryotes, which were aerobic (creating energy with oxygen) and used photosynthesis. The advanced eukaryotes were developed from these primitive cells.

Algae developed about 750 million years ago. Even this simple cell contained an enormous amount of DNA and hereditary information. It took about 2.7 billion years to develop life to this primitive form. This very slow process moved somewhat faster in the millennia that followed as animal and plant forms slowly emerged.

Animals developed into vertebrate (backbone) and invertebrate (no backbone) species. Mammals became the dominant vertebrate species and insects became the dominant invertebrate species. As animals developed, they adapted to their environment. The best adapted survived. This process is called natural selection. Entire species have vanished from earth.

Mammals and dinosaurs coexisted for more than 100 million years. During that time, dinosaurs were the dominant species. When dinosaurs became extinct 65 million years ago, mammals survived. Freed of dinosaurian dominance, mammals evolved into the dominant creatures they are today. Despite many years of study, it is not known what caused the dinosaurs to become extinct or why mammals survived.

6. This passage suggests

   (A) that mammals were the more intelligent species.
   (B) how life evolved on earth.
   (C) that mammals and dinosaurs were natural enemies.
   (D) the environment did not affect evolution.

7. The author's purpose for writing this passage is to

   (A) entertain.
   (B) narrate.
   (C) persuade.
   (D) inform.

8. The tone of this passage is best described as

   (A) objective.
   (B) depressed.
   (C) nostalgic.
   (D) cynical.

9. The main idea of the second paragraph is

   (A) Molecules can only ingest nonorganic compounds.
   (B) Evolution is based on adaptation.
   (C) Photosynthesis allowed organisms to exist without the need of sunlight.
   (D) Oxygen is more important to life than the sun's energy.

Use this passage to answer items 10–13.

Many anthropologists believe the first inhabitants of South America crossed over the Bering Strait land bridge. These native South Americans traveled down the west coast of what is now Canada, the United States, Mexico, and Central America to South America.

The crossing may have begun 15,000 to 20,000 years ago, and continued for thousands of years. Some of these Native South Americans reached the Islands of Terra del Fuego off the tip of South America about 8,000 years ago. Two major native civilizations developed in South America. The Incan empire developed in the highlands near the Andes mountains, while the Chibcha empire became dominant in what is now Colombia. Other native civilizations developed throughout South America.

Early voyages by Columbus and Amerigo Vespucci never reached South America. European colonizing nations introduced

**Languages of
South American Countries**

African slaves into South America, primarily into northeastern Brazil and into the Caribbean Islands. Most slaves were forced into labor on sugar plantations. Historians believe that the number of slaves brought to these regions may be 25 times the 500,000 African slaves brought into the United States.

The importation of slaves stopped before 1850 and European immigration increased about this same time. Most Europeans came to the east coast of South America, primarily to southern Brazil and to Argentina. By 1950 about 8,000,000 Europeans had immigrated to South America.

Most South Americans with European origins trace their roots to Portugal, Spain, and Italy.

10. The non-Spanish languages spoken in western South America result from

(A) early Incan influence.
(B) the primitive nature of the countries.
(C) immigration by Mayan Indians.
(D) proximity to Central America.

11. What accounts for the use of Italian as an official language in southeastern South America?

(A) The voyages of Christopher Columbus
(B) The exploration of the Americas by Amerigo Vespucci
(C) Italian and German immigration following World War II
(D) Italian and German immigration in the eighteenth century

12. The only French-speaking South American nation is associated with

(A) the French government in exile during World War II.
(B) exiles from French-speaking Quebec.
(C) the revolt of the Foreign Legion during the Algerian crisis.
(D) the French penal colony Devil's Island.

13. According to the map, about what percent of South American countries have Spanish as an official language?

(A) 80 percent
(B) 70 percent
(C) 50 percent
(D) 40 percent

Use this passage to answer items 14–18.

The War of 1812

The War of 1812 is one of the least understood conflicts in American his-tory. However, many events associated
Line with the war are among the best remem-
(5) bered from American History. The war began when the United States invaded British colonies in Canada. The invasion failed, and the United States was quickly put on the defensive. Most Americans
(10) are not aware of how the conflict began. During the war, the *USS Constitution* (Old Ironsides) was active against British ships in the Atlantic. Captain William Perry, sailing on Lake Erie, was famous
(15) for his yelling to his shipmates, "Don't give up the ship." Most Americans remember Perry, and his famous plea but not where, or in which war, he was engaged.
(20)   Most notably, British troops sacked and burned Washington, D.C. during this conflict. Subsequent British attacks on Fort McHenry near Baltimore were repulsed by American forces. It was during
(25) this battle that Francis Scott Key wrote the "Star-Spangled Banner" while a prisoner on a British ship. The "rockets' red glare, bombs bursting in air" referred to ordi-nance used by the British to attack the
(30) fort. Many Americans mistakenly believe that the "Star-Spangled Banner" was written during or shortly after the Revolutionary War.

14. All the following statements can be implied from the passage EXCEPT

   (A) The British did not start the war.
   (B) Francis Scott Key was not at Fort McHenry when he wrote the "Star-Spangled Banner."
   (C) The rockets referred to in the "Star-Spangled Banner" were part of a celebration.
   (D) The British army entered Washington, D.C., during the war.

15. Which of the following words is the most appropriate replacement for "sacked" in line 20?

   (A) entered
   (B) ravished
   (C) invaded
   (D) enclosed

16. Which of the following statements best summarizes the difference referred to in the passage between Perry's involvement in the War of 1812 and the way many Americans remember his involvement.

   (A) Perry was a drafter of the Constitution and later served on the *Constitution* in the Atlantic, although many Americans don't remember that.
   (B) Perry served in the Great Lakes, but many Americans don't remember that.
   (C) Perry served in the Great Lakes, and many Americans remember that.
   (D) Perry served on the *Constitution* at Fort McHenry during the writing of the "Star-Spangled Banner," although many Americans do not remember that.

17. What can be inferred about Francis Scott Key from lines 25–27 of the passage?

   (A) He was killed in the battle.
   (B) All his papers were confiscated by the British after the battle.

   (C) He was released by or escaped from the British after the battle.
   (D) He returned to Britain where he settled down.

18. What main point is the author making in this passage?

   (A) The Americans fought the British in the War of 1812.
   (B) The Revolutionary War continued into the 1800s.
   (C) The British renewed the Revolutionary War during the 1800s.
   (D) Many Americans are unaware of events associated with the War of 1812.

19. This painting incorporates which of the following techniques?

   (A) It uses three-dimensional space.
   (B) It uses only circles and semicircles.
   (C) The curved lines of the three-dimensional figures contrast with the straight lines of the two-dimensional figures.
   (D) It uses mainly overlapping circles.

20. A scientist cuts in half a just fallen hailstone and finds a series of rings much like tree rings. What could be found from counting the approximate number of rings?

    (A) how long the hailstone was in the atmosphere before falling to earth
    (B) how far from the surface the hailstone was before it started falling
    (C) how much precipitation fell during the hailstorm
    (D) how many times the hailstone was blown above the freezing level

$$(123 + 186 + 177) \div (3) =$$

21. Which of the following statements could result in the number sentence given above?

    (A) The athlete wanted to find the median of the three jumps.
    (B) The athlete wanted to find the average of the three jumps.
    (C) The athlete wanted to find the quotient of the product of three jumps.
    (D) The athlete wanted to find the sum of the quotients of the three jumps.

Use this graph to answer item 22.

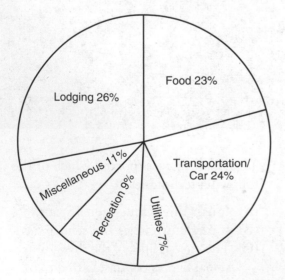

Jane's Monthly Budget

22. Jane spends $2,600 in May. She needs $858 that month for transportation/car expenses, which is more than the budget allows. Any needed money will come from miscellaneous. When she recalculates her budget chart, what percent is left for miscellaneous?

    (A) 2 percent
    (B) 6 percent
    (C) 9 percent
    (D) 11 percent

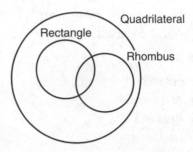

23. The above diagram shows the relationship among quadrilaterals, rectangles, and rhombuses. What conclusion can we draw from this diagram?

    (A) All quadrilaterals are rhombuses.
    (B) All quadrilaterals are rectangles.
    (C) All rectangles are not rhombuses.
    (D) Some rhombuses are not rectangles.

An experiment usually tries to test the effect of one thing on something else. The thing the experiment is testing the effect *of* is the independent variable. The thing the experiment is testing the effect *on* is the dependent variable. For example, the experimenter may test the effect of a particular hamster food. In that experiment, the independent variable is the type of food. The dependent variable is the growth of the hamster.

An experimental design should include both experimental and control groups. The experimental group consists of hamsters that get the new food—HF2. The control group consists of hamsters that get the current food—HF1.

The experimental and control groups must be very similar. You don't want one of the groups to grow more because the hamsters in that group are healthier, younger or more likely to grow for some other reason.

You can take some steps to ensure that the two groups of hamsters will be as identical as possible. One way is to randomly assign hamsters to the two groups. Random assignment means that the experimenter has no role in assigning the hamsters, and ensures that hamsters are assigned to either the experimental group or the control group in an unbiased way.

Some experiments establish a correlation. Correlation is a way of showing how strongly two variables are related. But correlation does not mean cause and effect. For example, a correlation of 1 between two variables means they are perfectly related. However, this correlation does not mean that one necessarily causes the other. For example, economists report that there is a high positive correlation between the amount of snowfall in Colorado and the size of the state budget. The snowfall does not cause the higher state budget. But there is a strong correlation between the two.

Average Ounces Gained Per Animal

Week #	HF1	HF2
1	4	9
2	3	4
3	2	3
4	1	2
5	1	2
6	1	1

24. An experiment is set up to determine the effects of a new hamster food HF2 as compared to the effects of a current hamster food HF1. Each group receives the same quantity of food and the same attention. From the above data choose the best conclusion for the experiment.

 (A) HF2 group gained more weight.
 (B) HF1 group lived longer.

 (C) HF2 group got more protein.
 (D) HF1 group got better nutrition.

25. What appropriate criticism might a scientist have of the experiment in the previous question?

 (A) Averages should not be used in this type of experiment.
 (B) The null hypothesis is not stated in the appropriate form.
 (C) Hamsters are not found as pets in enough homes for the experiment to be widely applicable.
 (D) The experiment does not describe sufficient controls to be valid.

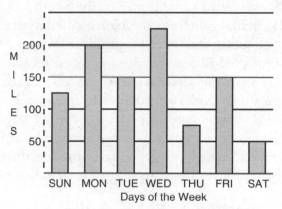

Miles Traveled Each Day on a Family Camping Trip

26. In total, how many miles were traveled Wednesday through Friday?

 (A) 150
 (B) 225
 (C) 300
 (D) 450

An earthquake is a sudden movement of the Earth, caused by the abrupt release of strain that has accumulated over a long time. Earthquakes are usually measured on the Richter scale. This scale is based on exponents, which are powers of 10. A quake measured on the Richter scale at 2 actually has a strength of 10^2 or 100. An earthquake measured at 4 has a strength of 10^4 or 10,000. Obviously, a small difference in the Richter scale number actually means a large difference in the strength of an earthquake.

27. One earthquake registers 2 on the Richter scale. A second earthquake registers 8 on the scale. Approximately how much more powerful is the second earthquake?

    (A) 6 times more powerful
    (B) 600 times more powerful
    (C) 100,000 times more powerful
    (D) 1,000,000 times more powerful

Item 28 refers to this passage.

After the Civil War, Confederate states slowly returned to the Union. However, Union troops stayed in the South until 1877. During this period of reconstruction, former slaves gained some power in the South. Carpetbaggers from the North collaborated with white scalawags (Southerners who supported Reconstruction) and former slaves to keep Confederates out of power. In turn, the Black Codes and the KKK emerged as ways to subjugate and terrorize former slaves. Grandfather clauses, you can't vote if your grandfather did not vote, were used to deny former slaves the vote.

28. Which of the following is the most accurate statement about carpetbaggers?

    (A) Carpetbaggers worked indirectly with the KKK.
    (B) Carpetbaggers moved south to improve slaves' conditions.
    (C) Carpetbaggers helped fill a power vacuum.
    (D) Carpetbaggers joined with Confederates to suppress slaves.

29.   ah autumn coolness
           hand in hand paring away

    Which of the following could be the third line in the haiku poem above?

    (A) in the wetness
    (B) branches and leaves
    (C) eggplants cucumbers
    (D) til the end of day

Items 30 and 31 refer to the following poem.

My love falls on silence nigh
I am alone in knowing the good-bye
For while a lost love has its day
A love unknown is a sadder way

30. The word *nigh* in line 1 means

    (A) clear.
    (B) complete.
    (C) near.
    (D) not.

31. This passage describes
    (A) loving someone and being rebuffed.
    (B) being loved by someone you do not love.
    (C) loving someone who loves another person.
    (D) loving someone without acknowledgment.

On July 4, 1776, the Continental Congress approved the United States Declaration of Independence. The Declaration includes four "self-evident" truths:

1. Equality of all persons
2. Inalienable rights of life, liberty, and the pursuit of happiness
3. The rights of the government come from the governed
4. The right of the people to alter or abolish a destructive government

32. Which of the following is NOT an example of a self-evident truth found in the Declaration of Independence?

    (A) Being treated equal to someone else
    (B) Being free from taxation without representation
    (C) Being able to have a say in the government
    (D) Being able to change a government that is hurting society

Items 33–38 refer to this passage.

Computer-based word processing programs have spelling checkers and even a thesaurus to find synonyms for highlighted words. To use the thesaurus, the student just types in the word, and a series of synonyms and antonyms appears on the computer screen. The program can also show recommended spellings for misspelled words. I like having a computer program that performs these mechanical aspects of writing. However, these programs do not teach about spelling or word meanings. A person could type in a word, get a synonym and have not the slightest idea what either meant.

Relying on this mindless way of checking spelling and finding synonyms, students will be completely unfamiliar with the meanings of the words they use. In fact, one of the most common misuses is to include a word that is spelled correctly but used incorrectly in the sentence.

It may be true that a strictly mechanical approach to spelling is used by some teachers. There certainly is a place for students who already understand word meanings to use a computer program that relieves the drudgery of checking spelling and finding synonyms. But these computer programs should never and can never replace the teacher. Understanding words—their uses and meanings—should precede this more mechanistic approach.

33. What is the main idea of this passage?

   (A) Mechanical spell checking is one part of the initial learning about spelling.
   (B) Programs are not effective for initially teaching about spelling and synonyms.
   (C) Teachers should use word processing programs as one part of instruction.
   (D) Students who use these programs won't learn about spelling.

34. Which of the following information is found in the passage?

   I. The type of computer that runs the word processor

II. The two main outputs of spell-checking and thesaurus programs
III. An explanation of how to use the word-processing program to teach about spelling and synonyms

   (A) I only
   (B) II only
   (C) I and II only
   (D) II and III only

35. Which aspect of spell-checking and thesaurus programs does the author like?

   (A) That you just have to type in the word
   (B) That the synonyms and alternative spellings are done very quickly
   (C) That the difficult mechanical aspects are performed
   (D) That you don't have to know how to spell to use them

36. Which of the following questions could be answered from the information in the passage?

   (A) When is it appropriate to use spell-checking and thesaurus programs?
   (B) How does the program come up with recommended spellings?
   (C) What type of spelling learning experiences should students have?
   (D) Why do schools buy these word processing programs?

37. Which of the following statements could be used in place of the first sentence of the last paragraph?

   (A) It may be true that some strict teachers use a mechanical approach.
   B) It may be true that a stringently mechanical approach is used by some teachers.
   (C) It may be true that inflexible mechanical approaches are used by some teachers.
   (D) It may be true that some teachers use only a mechanical approach.

38. According to this passage, what could be the result of a student's unfamiliarity with the meanings of words or synonyms?

    (A) using a program to display the alternative spellings

    (B) relying on mindless ways of checking spelling and finding synonyms

    (C) strictly mechanical approaches

    (D) using microcomputers to find synonyms for highlighted words

Use this map to answer items 39 and 40.

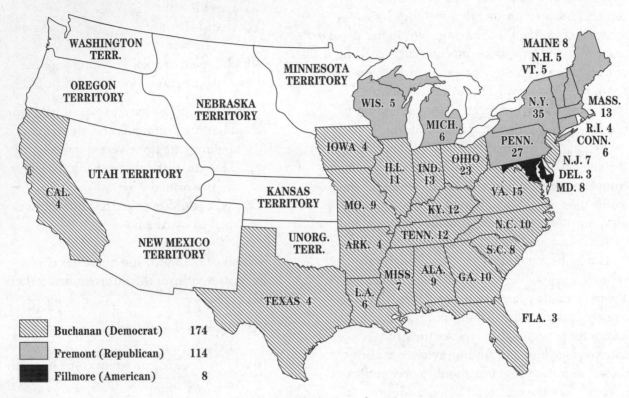

Buchanan (Democrat)   174
Fremont (Republican)   114
Fillmore (American)   8

Presidential Election of 1856

39. The numbers in each state on this map show

    (A) the number of counties in each state.
    (B) the number of representatives from each state.
    (C) the electoral votes in each state.
    (D) the number of representatives won by the victorious party in each state.

40. What conclusion might you reasonably draw from this map?

    (A) Were it not for Texas and California, Fremont would have won the election.
    (B) Buchanan supported the rebel cause.
    (C) Fremont was favored by the northernmost states.

    (D) Fremont was favored by the states that fought on the Union side in the Civil War.

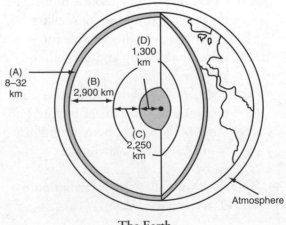

The Earth

41. In the diagram, what letter labels the mantle?

(A) A
(B) B
(C) C
(D) D

Items 42–44 refer to this passage.

Most of the world's religions emerged in Africa and Asia. About two billion people follow some Christian religion, and one billion Christians are Roman Catholics. There are about one billion Muslims, 800 million Hindus and 350 million Buddhists. There are fewer who follow tribal religions or who are Sikhs, Jews, Shamanists, Confucians, and followers of other religions. About one billion people are nonreligious and about 250 million people are atheists.

Hinduism emerged in India about 2500 B.C. Hindu beliefs are a mixture of the religious beliefs of invaders of India and the religious beliefs of native Indians. Hinduism embraces a caste system with religious services conducted by members of the priestly caste. Most Hindus worship one of the gods Vishnu and Shiva, and the goddess Shakti.

Hindus believe that a person's *karma*, the purity or impurity of past deeds, determines a person's ultimate fate. A karma can be improved through pure acts, deeds, and devotion.

Judaism developed from the beliefs of the Hebrew tribes located in and around Israel before 1300 B.C. From about 1000 B.C. to 150 B.C. a number of different authors wrote a series of books describing the religion, laws, and customs which are now known as the Old Testament of the Bible. The Old Testament describes a single just God. Judaism is an important world religion because elements of Judaism can be found in both Islam and Christianity.

Hebrews trace their ancestry to Abraham and his grandson Jacob, whose 12 sons are said to have founded the 12 tribes of Israel. About 1000 B.C. David is believed to have united these 12 tribes into a single religious state. Modern Jews refer to the Talmud, a book of Jewish law and tradition written around 400 A.D.

Buddhism was founded around 525 B.C. in India. The religion was founded by Buddha, Siddhartha Gautama, who lived from about 560 B.C. to about 480 B.C. The Triptika contains Buddha's teachings. A large number of *Sutras* contains a great body of Buddhist beliefs and teachings. Monastic life provides the main organizational and administrative structure for modern-day Buddhism.

It is said that Buddha achieved his enlightenment through meditation, and meditation is an important Buddhist practice. Buddhism holds that life is essentially meaningless and without reality. Buddhists seek to achieve Nirvana, a great void of perfection, through meditation and just acts.

Jesus was probably born about 5 B.C. He acquired a small following of Jews who believed he was the Messiah. Later this belief was developed into a worldwide religion known as Christianity. Christianity was generally tolerated in Rome, although there were periods of persecution. The Emperor Constantine converted to Christianity about 300 A.D. In the mid-300s Christianity was decreed the state religion of Rome. Augustine (St. Augustine) converted to Christianity in the late 300s.

In the Byzantine Era, starting after the Visigoths looted Rome, there was an Eastern and Western emperor. Constantinople was the capital in the East. This division led in 1054 to the great schism of the Catholic church, which survives to this day. The Crusaders captured Constantinople and defeated the Eastern Byzantines in 1204. In 1453 Constantinople was captured by the Turks and renamed Istanbul.

Mohammed was born in 570 A.D. and went into Mecca in 630 and founded Islam. The Koran contains the 114 chapters of Islamic religion and law. Around 640 A.D. the Omar, religious leader, established an Islamic empire with Damascus as the capital. The capital was eventually moved to Baghdad. The Muslims enjoyed a prosperous economy, and in the late days of the empire Omar Khayyam wrote the *Rubaiyat.*

Muslim armies conquered Spain and much of France by about 730. A series of Caliphs ruled from 750 until 1250 when an army originally led by Genghis Khan sacked Baghdad and killed the last caliph.

42. According to the passage, a Sutra would be best described as which of the following?

   (A) It contains just teachings.
   (B) It contains just a list of tribes.
   (C) It contains both beliefs and teachings.
   (D) It contains both law and tradition.

43. According to the passage, which of the following is correct?

   I. Siddhartha Gautama is said to have achieved enlightenment through karma.
   II. Jews today do not rely on the Old Testament for religious law.
   III. Christians were usually persecuted in the Holy Roman Empire.

   (A) II only
   (B) II and III
   (C) I and III
   (D) I, II, and III

44. Which of the following best paraphrases the first sentence in the fourth paragraph?

   (A) Judaism led to beliefs of the Hebrew tribes located near Israel before 1300 B.C.
   (B) The beliefs of Hebrew tribes located near Israel before 1300 B.C. provided the basis for Judaism.
   (C) Hebrew tribes in and around Israel before 1300 B.C. developed their beliefs from Judaism.

   (D) The area in and around Israel before 1300 B.C. had Hebrew tribes with Judaic beliefs.

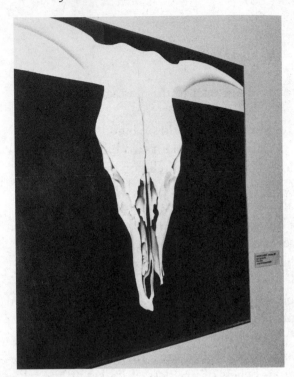

45. This picture could be best described by saying

   (A) it is an abstract figure on a rectangular background.
   (B) the nearly symmetrical shape of the figure suggests that its completion is expected.
   (C) the Rorschach-like image suggests an underlying psychological theme.
   (D) the real life object has an abstract quality.

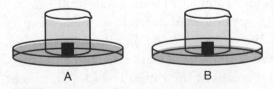

46. Identical beakers (above) were filled with water. Overflow was caused by the different solid objects placed in the beakers. The size of the objects cannot be determined. What is the most likely explanation of the differing amounts of overflow?

   (A) The object in beaker A is heavier.
   (B) The object in beaker B is heavier.

(C) The object in beaker A has more mass.

(D) The object in beaker B has more mass.

Cellular phones, once used by the very rich, are now available to almost everyone. With one of these phones, you can call just about anywhere from just about anywhere. Since the use of these phones will increase, we need to find legal and effective ways for law enforcement agencies to monitor calls.

47. Which of the following choices is the best summary of this passage?

(A) Criminals are taking advantage of cellular phones to avoid legal wiretaps.

(B) The ability to use a cellular phone to call from just about anywhere makes it harder to find people who are using the phones.

(C) The increase in cellular phone use means that we will have to find legal ways to monitor cellular calls.

(D) Cellular phones are like regular phones with a very long extension cord.

Occasionally, college students will confuse correlation with cause and effect. Correlation just describes the degree of relationship between two factors. For example, there is a positive correlation between poor handwriting and intelligence. However, writing more poorly will not make you more intelligent.

48. The authors main reason for writing this passage is to

(A) explain the difference between correlation and cause and effect.

(B) encourage improved penmanship.

(C) explain how college students can improve their intelligence.

(D) make those with poor penmanship feel more comfortable.

The way I look at it, Robert E. Lee was the worst general in the Civil War—he was the South's commanding general, and the South lost the war.

49. What assumption does the writer of this statement make?

(A) War is horrible and should not be glorified.

(B) Pickett's charge at Gettysburg was a terrible mistake.

(C) A general should be judged by whether he wins or loses.

(D) The South should have won the Civil War.

1	②	③	4	⑤	6	⑦	8	9	10
11	12	13	14	15	16	17	18	19	20
21	22	23	24	25	26	27	28	29	30
31	32	33	34	35	36	37	38	39	40
41	42	43	44	45	46	47	48	49	50
51	52	53	54	55	56	57	58	59	60
61	62	63	64	65	66	67	68	69	70
71	72	73	74	75	76	77	78	79	80
81	82	83	84	85	86	87	88	89	90
91	92	93	94	95	96	97	98	99	100

50. Cross off the multiples of 2, 3, 5, and 7 that are greater than these numbers in the above hundreds square. Which numbers in the 80s are not crossed off?

(A) 83, 87

(B) 81, 89

(C) 83, 89

(D) 81, 87

Use this graph to answer items 51 and 52.

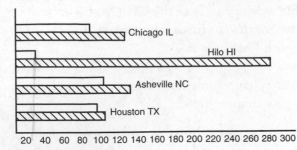

Chicago IL

Hilo HI

Asheville NC

Houston TX

20 40 60 80 100 120 140 160 180 200 220 240 260 280 300

☐ Clear Days
▨ Days with Precipitation

51. A correct interpretation of this graph is, on average,

    (A) most days in Houston have precipitation.
    (B) less than 10 percent of the days in Hilo have no precipitation.
    (C) most days in Asheville have no precipitation.
    (D) most days in Chicago have precipitation.

52. A business may be moved to one of the four cities on the graph. What conclusion can be drawn from the graph to help make the final decision?

    (A) On average, most precipitation in Hilo is from brief afternoon thundershowers.
    (B) On average, Asheville, North Carolina, gets only a few inches of snow.
    (C) On average, Asheville and Chicago receive about the same amount of precipitation.
    (D) On average, Houston has the most days without precipitaton.

53. You add the first 5 odd numbers (1, 3, 5, 7, 9) and find that the answer is 25. What is the sum of the first 90 odd numbers?

    (A) 450
    (B) 8,100
    (C) 179
    (D) 4,500

54. The steplike appearance of the buildings in this photograph is created by

    (A) the setbacks that occur every three or four stories.
    (B) the photographer's position when the picture was taken.
    (C) the proximity of the buildings to the street.
    (D) the relationship between the symmetric appearance of the windows and the horizontal lines indicating new floors.

The computers in the college dormitories are actually more sophisticated than the computers in the college computer labs, and they cost less. It seems that the person who bought the dormitory computers looked around until she found powerful computers at a low price. The person who runs the labs just got the computers offered by the regular supplier.

55. The best statement of the main idea of this paragraph is

    (A) it is better to use the computers in the dorms.
    (B) it is better to avoid the computers in the labs.
    (C) the computers in the dorms are always in use so, for most purposes, it is better to use the computers in the labs.
    (D) it is better to shop around before you buy.

The college sororities are "interviewed" by students during rush week. Rush week is a time when students get to know about the different sororities and decide which ones they want to join. Each student can pledge only one sorority. Once students have chosen the three they are most interested in, the intrigue begins. The sororities then choose from among the students who have chosen them.

56. Which of the following strategies will help assure a student that she will be chosen for at least one sorority and preferably get into a sorority she likes?

   I. Choose at least one sorority she is sure will choose her
  II. Choose two sororities she wants to get into
 III. Choose her three favorite sororities
 IV. Choose three sororities she knows will choose her

   (A) I and II
   (B) I and III
   (C) I only
   (D) III only

In response to my opponent's question about my record on environmental issues, I want to say that the real problem in this election is not my record. Rather the problem is the influence of my opponent's rich friends in the record industry. I hope you will turn your back on his rich supporters and vote for me.

57. Which of the following statements best illustrates the author's primary purpose?

   (A) clearing the author's name
   (B) describing the problems of running for office
   (C) informing the public of wrongdoing
   (D) convincing the voting populous

58. A boat costs $5 more than half the price of a canoe. Which of the following expressions shows this relationship?

   (A) $B + \$5 = C/2$
   (B) $B = 1/2C + \$5$
   (C) $B + \$5 = 2C$
   (D) $B + \$5 > C/2$

59. The primary function of the central building in this photograph is to

   (A) contrast with the cloudy sky.
   (B) emphasize the symmetry of the roadways on either side.
   (C) complete a collection of geometric shapes with the other structure shown behind it.
   (D) contrast with the traditional building behind it.

60. All the following items in this photograph suggest symmetry EXCEPT

   (A) the clouds.
   (B) the central building.
   (C) the main building on the left part of the picture.
   (D) the structure on the right part of the picture.

Recycling Rate by City
(Per Hundred Thousand Pounds Per Year from 1988–1993)

	1988	1989	1990	1991	1992	1993
Chicago, Illinois	*	52	67	120	302	485
St. Louis, Missouri	20	80	175	360	420	650
Seattle, Washington	15	70	98	136	243	358
San Francisco, California	*	23	75	124	285	402
New York, New York	*	10	56	250	370	590
Miami, Florida	*	25	98	145	290	370

*The recycling rate is less than one per hundred thousand pounds.

61. Which of the following statements is supported by the data given in the above table?

   (A) St. Louis increased the capabilities of its recycling plants by 50 percent during the years 1990 and 1991.
   (B) Since 1991 the recycling rate increased significantly in each city.
   (C) People living in Miami are not recycling as they should be.
   (D) The population of all these cities has increased significantly since 1988.

Items 62–64 refer to these three paragraphs.

I

   (1) Of course, I have never gotten too involved in my children's sports. (2) I have never yelled at an umpire at any of my kid's games. (3) I have never even—_____, I didn't mean it.

II

   (4) Before long, the umpire's mother was on the field. (5) There the two parents stood, toe to toe. (6) The players and the other umpires formed a ring around them and looked on in awe.

III

   (7) Sometimes parents are more involved in little league games than their children. (8) I remember seeing a game in which a player's parent came on the field to argue with the umpire. (9) The umpire was not that much older than the player.

62. Which of the following shows the correct order for these three paragraphs?

   (A) I, II, III
   (B) I, III, II
   (C) II, I, III
   (D) III, II, I

63. Which of the following best fits in the blank in sentence 3?

   (A) Well
   (B) Being a parent
   (C) How come I
   (D) Repeat after me

64. What other "sporting" event is the author trying to recreate in paragraph II?

   (A) bullfight
   (B) wrestling match
   (C) boxing match
   (D) football game

Use this excerpt from Washington Irving's *The Legend of Sleepy Hollow* to answer item 65.

About two hundred yards from the tree a small brook crossed the road and ran into a marshy and thickly wooded glen, known by the name of Wiley's swamp. A few rough logs, laid side by side, served for a bridge over this stream. On that side of the road where the brook entered the wood, a group of oaks and chestnuts, matted thick with wild grapevines, threw a cavernous gloom over it. To pass this bridge was the severest trial. It was at this identical spot that the unfortunate Andre was captured, and under the covert of those chestnuts and vines were the sturdy yeomen concealed who surprised him. This has ever since been considered a haunted stream, and fearful are the feelings of the schoolboy who has to pass it alone after dark.

65. Which of the following is discussed in this passage?

(A) the thing that frightened Ichabod
(B) how trees affected the road
(C) the sounds a horse makes
(D) Ichabod nearly being thrown from a horse

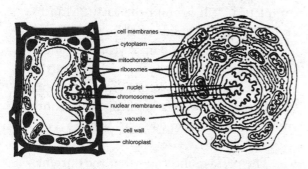

Plant Cell   **Animal Cell**

Plant cells and animal cells have many common components. All cells have a cell membrane at the outer edge of the cell. A nucleus, the cell's "brain," inside the cytoplasm is protected by a nuclear membrane. The nucleus contains chromosomes. The Golgi apparatus makes, stores, and distributes hormone and enzyme materials. Plant cells have a cell wall outside the membrane. Plant cells also contain chloroplasts where photosynthesis takes place.

66. According to the passage and the diagram, the cell wall

(A) is narrower in animal cells than in plant cells.
(B) is found in only plant cells.
(C) is one of the features found in all cells.
(D) is narrower in plant cells than the cell walls of animal cells.

Some scientists say that it is possible to estimate the temperature by counting the number of times a cricket chirps in a minute. One method is to count the number of cricket chirps and add 40 to estimate the temperature.

Only male crickets make a chirping sound. They do it by rubbing their front wings together. Generally speaking, crickets chirp faster as the temperature increases and slower as the temperature cools. If you are out at night in a field full of crickets, the sound of the chirping can be almost deafening.

A scientist decides to try an experiment. The scientist measures the temperature and writes a prediction of the number of cricket chirps that will be heard in 15 seconds. The scientist plans to go into a field full of crickets at night and count one cricket's chirps for 15 second to check the accuracy of the formula.

67. What is the most fundamental assumption the scientist makes?

(A) The scientist can actually count the number of cricket chirps in 15 seconds.
(B) The field will contain chirping crickets.
(C) The formula used to predict temperature from the number of cricket chirps is correct.
(D) The scientist will be listening to the chirps of only one cricket.

Items 68–69 refer to this paragraph.

I think women are discriminated against; however, I think men are discriminated against just as much as women. It's just a different type of discrimination. Consider these two facts: Men die about 6 years earlier than women, and men are the only people who can be drafted into the armed forces. That's discrimination!

68. What is the author's main point in writing this passage?

    (A) Men are discriminated against more than women are.

    (B) Both sexes are discriminated against.

    (C) Women are not discriminated against.

    (D) On average, men die earlier than women.

69. Which of the following could be substituted for the word *drafted* in the second to last sentence?

    (A) inducted against their will

    (B) signed up

    (C) pushed in by society

    (D) drawn in by peer pressure

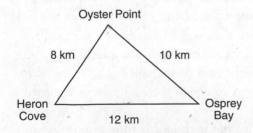

70. The diagram shows three towns, the roads connecting them, and the distance between each town. Which of the following is the shortest distance?

    (A) Osprey Bay to Heron Cove to Oyster Point and then halfway to Osprey Bay

    (B) Halfway between Oyster Point and Heron Cove, to Heron Cove to Osprey Bay to Oyster Point

    (C) Quarter-way from Heron Cove to Osprey Bay, to Osprey Bay to Oyster Point to Heron Cove

    (D) Heron Cove to Oyster Point to Osprey Bay, then halfway to Heron Cove

71. Which of the following best describes how this picture shows the results of effort?

    (A) The determination in the reaper's stance

    (B) The fallen stalks of wheat

    (C) The curved scythe handle

    (D) The solitude of the reaper

The moon takes about 28 days to complete a cycle around the earth. Months, 28 days long, grew out of this cycle. Twelve of these months made up a year. But ancient astronomers realized that it took the earth about 365 days to make one revolution of the sun. Extra days were added to some months and the current calendar was born.

72. The passage indicates that the current calendar

    (A) describes the moon's movement around the earth.

    (B) is based on the sun's position.

    (C) is based on the earth's rotation and position of the moon.

    (D) combines features of the moon's cycle and the earth's revolution.

Items 73–74 refer to the following.

Confederate Major General W. H. C. Whiting was recuperating in a prisoner-of-war camp in New York. Not long before, Whiting had been in charge of the Confederate forces in Wilmington, North Carolina. In the later years of the Civil War, Wilmington had become the gateway to the Confederacy. He said, "I do not know now that there is another place, excepting perhaps Richmond, we should not sooner see lost than this." Whiting died unexpectedly of his wounds in the prison camp.

Blockade runners coming to Wilmington traveled over the ocean, past Cape Fear into the Cape Fear River, and up the river to Wilmington. Blockade runners had to pass through either the new inlet or the old inlet. The old inlet took ships one way around Smith Island into the Cape Fear River, while the new inlet took ships another way around the island and then into the river.

Whichever inlet that arriving blockade runners took, they passed by Fort Fisher. Fort Fisher was the key to protecting these ships, and the key to defending Wilmington. Blockade runners were just about immune from Union attack once they came under the fort's protection. No fewer than ten other fortifications protected the Cape Fear River.

Fort Holmes was on Smith Island, which was west across the new inlet from Fort Fisher. Fort Caswell was west across the Old Inlet from Fort Holmes, and Fort Johnson was across the Cape Fear River from Fort Fisher.

73. A blockade runner approached Wilmington with goods from Nova Scotia. As the blockade runner passed through the new inlet, Fort Fisher was generally to the

(A) east of Fort Holmes.
(B) west of Fort Caswell.
(C) west of Fort Holmes.
(D) east of Fort Caswell.

74. In the next to last sentence of the first paragraph, Whiting means

(A) I do not know which city is more important to the Confederacy, Richmond or Wilmington.
(B) The only place more important to the Confederacy than Richmond was Wilmington.
(C) Richmond is the most important city in the Confederacy and I do not know how important Wilmington is.
(D) I do not know if losing Richmond will be worse than losing the supply line between Wilmington and Bermuda, Nassau, and Nova Scotia.

Items 75–76 refer to this poem.

The Sullen Sky
I see the sullen sky;
Dark, foreboding sky.
Swept by dank and dripping clouds;
Like ominous shrouds.

A sky should be bright,
Or clear and crisp at night.
But it hasn't been that way;
Oh, a dungenous day.

That has been my life,
And that has been my strife.
I wish the clouds would leave;
Ah, a sweet reprieve.

75. Which of the following best describes the author's message?

(A) The author doesn't like rainy, cloudy weather.
(B) The author wants people to be free of worry.
(C) The author is hoping his life will get better.
(D) The author lives in an area where it is often cloudy and rainy.

76. The last two lines in the first stanza reflect which of the following?

    (A) simile
    (B) hyperbole
    (C) metaphor
    (D) euphemism

77. The school is planning a class trip. They will go by bus. There will be 328 people going on the trip, and each bus holds 31 people. How many buses will be needed for the trip?

    (A) 9
    (B) 10
    (C) 11
    (D) 18

Items 78–79 refer to this passage.

Using percentages to report growth patterns can be deceptive. If there are 100 new users for a cereal currently used by 100 other people, the growth rate is 100 percent. However if there are 50,000 new users for a cereal currently used by 5,000,000 people, the growth rate is 1 percent. It seems obvious that the growth rate of 1 percent is preferable to the growth rate of 100 percent. So while percentages do provide a useful way to report growth patterns, we must know the initial number the growth percentage is based on before we make any conclusions.

78. According to this passage,

    (A) lower growth rates mean higher actual growth.
    (B) higher growth rates mean higher actual growth.
    (C) the growth rate depends on the starting point.
    (D) the growth rate does not depend on the starting point.

79. Which of the following can be implied from this passage?

    (A) Don't believe any advertisements.
    (B) Question any percentage growth rate.
    (C) Percentages should never be used.
    (D) Any growth rate over 50 percent is invalid.

80. Say that Company A and Company B try to raise money by selling bonds to the public. Which of the following could cause the interest rate for Company A's bonds to be much higher than the rates for Company B's bonds?

    (A) The bonds for Company A have a higher risk.
    (B) The bonds for Company B have a higher risk.
    (C) The management of Company A wants to reward its investors.
    (D) The management of Company B wants to reward its investors.

Written Assignment

> **Directions:** Write an essay on the topic below. Use the lined pages that follow. Write your essay on this topic only. An essay on another topic will be rated Unscorable (U).

Was it better to have a maximum speed limit of 55 miles per hour, or is it better to have speed limits as high as 70 mph?

The maximum 55 mph speed limit was better. The national speed limit was set at 55 mph for two reasons: to conserve gasoline and to reduce accidents. These reasons are just as important today as they were when this speed limit was established. Why risk a single life so that people can go 10 or 15 miles per hour faster. If you have 60 miles to drive, then going 65 mph instead of 55 mph, you'll arrive ten minutes sooner—ten minutes; even if its 360 miles you'll arrive just 60 minutes sooner. Ten minutes or 60 does not justify losing a single life.

Speed limits as high as 70 mph are better. First it's important to note that speed limits as high as 70 mph do not mean there's a 70 mph speed limit everywhere. In fact, in most places the speed limit is 55 mph or less. But there are stretches of Interstate highways in rural areas where it does not make sense to limit the speed to 55 mph. Many people drive 500 or 600 miles a day on an Interstate trip and driving 70 mph instead of 55 shortens the trip by almost three hours. That means people will be less tired and less likely to be involved in an accident.

Was it better to have a maximum speed limit of 55 miles per hour, or is it better to have speed limits as high as 70 mph?

Review and evaluate the opposing positions presented above.

Choose one of these positions.

Write an essay that supports your position following the guidelines presented above.

Answer Key
DIAGNOSTIC LAST

1. C	21. B	41. B	61. B
2. A	22. A	42. C	62. D
3. C	23. D	43. A	63. A
4. B	24. A	44. B	64. C
5. C	25. D	45. D	65. B
6. B	26. D	46. C	66. B
7. D	27. D	47. C	67. D
8. A	28. C	48. A	68. B
9. B	29. C	49. C	69. A
10. A	30. C	50. C	70. D
11. D	31. D	51. C	71. B
12. D	32. B	52. D	72. D
13. B	33. B	53. B	73. A
14. C	34. B	54. A	74. B
15. B	35. C	55. D	75. C
16. B	36. A	56. A	76. A
17. C	37. D	57. D	77. C
18. D	38. B	58. B	78. C
19. D	39. C	59. D	79. B
20. D	40. C	60. A	80. A

Answer Explanations

1. **(C)** The passage indicates that Texas became a sovereign nation in 1836, and that status remained unchanged until Texas became a state in 1845. (A) and (B) are incorrect because although Texas had once been a part of Mexico, Texas became a nation before it became a state. The passage does not mention the Louisiana Purchase.

2. **(A)** The graphs for walkers and bikers remained unchanged from Monday to Wednesday, so this statement is true for both Monday's graph and Wednesday's graph. (C) and (D) are incorrect because they are only true for Monday's graph. (D) is incorrect because there were approximately the same number of car and bike rides.

3. **(C)** The author gradually traces the evolution of speech and language. That is the main idea. (A) is false. The passage does not indicate that language consists of thoughts. (B) and (D) are true, but they are details and do not reflect the main idea of the passage.

4. **(B)** The author clearly states in the first paragraph that thought precedes speech as language develops. (A) gestures, (C) sound, and (D) writing are all language, but not the first component of language, according to the passage.

5. **(C)** To multiply by a positive power of 10, move the decimal point to the right the number of places shown in the power.

    (A) $3.74 \times 10^6 = 3,740,000$
    (B) $3.74 \times 10^7 = 37,400,000$
    (C) $3.74 \times 10^8 = 374,000,000$

    Stop here—this is the correct answer.

    (D) $3.74 \times 10^9 = 3,740,000,000$

6. **(B)** The passage does not explicitly describe how life evolved, but it does suggest a chain of evolution. (A) is incorrect because the passage says mammals survived after dinosaurs became extinct, not that mammals were more intelligent. (C) is incorrect because there is no mention in the passage about conflict between dinosaurs and mammals. (D) is incorrect because the first paragraph indicates that the earliest stages of evolution happened because of the particular environment that existed on earth billions of years ago.

7. **(D)** The passage states facts, clarifies, and explains and the author's intent is to inform. (A) is incorrect because the author is not trying to entertain us. (B) is incorrect because the author does not intend to tell a story. A passage about a day in the life of a dinosaur might be a narration if the main purpose was to tell the story, not convey the facts. (C) is incorrect because the author is not trying to convince us of a particular point of view. This passage contains facts.

8. **(A)** The author's purpose for writing the passage dictates the tone. The author objectively states information that (B) is incorrect because the author displays no particular emotion. (C) is incorrect because, while the author is describing things from the past, he or she shows no interest in returning to these "good old days." (D) is incorrect because the passage is objective, and the author displays no particular emotion.

9. **(B)** The entire paragraph describes ways in which animals adapted to the environment. The other choices are generally too detailed to be the main idea. Besides, the other choices are false. (A) is false; the second paragraph says groupings of molecules "must have been able" to ingest nonorganic compounds. (C) and (D) are also false. The third paragraph mentions photosynthesis and that it releases oxygen into the atmosphere. However, the paragraph never mentions that photosynthesis allows plants to exist without sunlight nor that oxygen is more important to life than the sun's energy.

10. **(A)** The passage indicates that the Incas had an early culture near the Andes mountains on the west coast of South America, which is where the native dialects are shown on the map. (B) is incorrect because there is nothing about the primitive nature of a country that would explain the presence of a language. (C) is incorrect because the Mayans were primarily located on the east coast of Mexico. (D) is incorrect because Central America is several countries away and just being near Central America would not account for the languages.

11. **(D)** You can eliminate (A) and (B) because as the passage says, Columbus and Vespucci never reached South America. (C) and (D) are the only choices remaining, and it is just more reasonable that immigration 200 years ago would have more impact on a spoken language than immigration 55 years ago.

12. **(D)** The French penal colony of Devil's Island was located off the coast of French Guyana. (A) is incorrect because this French exile government was located in England. (B) is incorrect because there were no exiles from French-speaking Quebec. (C) is incorrect because Algeria is located in north Africa, not in South America.

13. **(B)** Nine of thirteen South American countries have Spanish as a language.

$9 \div 13 = 0.69$, which is about $0.7 = 70\%$.

Another approach is to work from the answers.

(A) $80\% = 0.8 \times 13 = 10.4$
(B) $70\% = 0.7 \times 13 = 9.1$. We can stop here—this is the correct answer.
(C) 50%
(D) 40%

14. **(C)** (C) *cannot* be implied from the passage. Lines 26–28 state that rockets refer to ordinance or weapons used by the British. You might also be struck that this is an unlikely answer. (A) can be implied from lines 5–7, which mention that the war started with an American invasion of Canada. (B) can be implied from lines 24–26, which mentions that Francis Scott Key was a prisoner on a British ship. (D) can be implied from the passage because lines 19–20 state that the British troops sacked and burned Washington.

15. **(B)** You can tell from the context that damage is being done. In this context, sacked means looting a city. Ravished is the best choice and describes what happens when a town is sacked. The words in (A) and (D) have entirely different meanings than sacked. (C), "invaded," is incorrect because a city is sacked after it is invaded.

16. **(B)** The last sentence in the first paragraph says that most Americans remember Perry, but not where he served. (A) is incorrect because the ship *U.S.S. Constitution* and the Constitution of the United States are different. (C) is incorrect because the passage indicates that most Americans don't remember that he served in the Great Lakes. (D) is incorrect because Perry was not at Fort McHenry.

17. **(C)** Francis Scott Key was able to distribute his "Star-Spangled Banner" in America, so he must have been released by or escaped from the British. (A) and (B) are incorrect because the "Star-Spangled Banner" would not have been published if these choices were true. (D) is incorrect because there is nothing in the passage to indicate that Key returned to Britain, nor that he came from Britain for that matter.

18. **(D)** The author signals in the first sentence this main point of unawareness of events associated with the War of 1812. (A) is incorrect because, while this statement is true, it is not the main idea of this paragraph. (B) is incorrect because the Revolutionary War ended 25 years earlier. (C) is incorrect because, according to the passage, the British did not start the conflict.

19. **(D)** The painting does mainly use overlapping circles, although there are exceptions. (A) is incorrect because the painting is two dimensional. (B) is incorrect because some of the shapes are not circles or semicircles. (C) is incorrect because there are no three-dimensional figures.

20. **(D)** A new layer of water is added below the freezing level of the atmosphere and then the layer is frozen when the hailstone is blown above the freezing level. (A), (B), and (C) are incorrect because, while these events might impact the size of the hailstone, none of them would produce rings.

21. **(B)** The number sentence corresponds to finding an average. To find an average, you add the scores and divide by the number of scores. (A) is incorrect because the median is the middle number after the numbers are arranged in

order. (C) is incorrect because the number sentence shows a "sum," not a "product." (D) is incorrect because the number sentence shows the "quotient of the sum," not the sum of the quotients.

22. **(A)** Divide to find the percent for transportation.

    $858 \div \$2600 = 0.33 = 33\%$

    Subtract the current transportation percentage from 33% to find the percent to be taken from miscellaneous

    $33\% - 24\% = 9\%$.

    Subtract to find the percent left for miscellaneous.

    $11\% - 9\% = 2\%$

    (B), (C), and (D) are incorrect because they do not result from the calculation shown above.

23. **(D)** The overlap of the rhombus and the rectangle rings shows that some (not all) rhombuses are rectangles. This means that some rhombuses are not rectangles. (A) is incorrect because the quadrilateral ring is not inside the rhombus ring. (B) is incorrect because the quadrilateral ring is not inside the rectangle ring. (C) is incorrect because the rhombus and rectangle rings overlap.

24. **(A)** The table shows that each animal in the HF2 group gained more weight each week than the HF1 group and more weight overall. (B), (C), and (D) are incorrect because there are no experimental results about which group lived longer, got more protein, or got better nutrition.

25. **(D)** The experiment does not describe how the experimenters ensured that group HF2 did not receive special attention, nor does it describe any other experimental controls. (A) is incorrect because averages are fine for this type of comparison. (B) is incorrect because the form of the hypothesis does not affect the validity of the experiment. (C) is incorrect because the statement is obviously false, and even if it were true, it is not an appropriate criticism of the experiment itself.

26. **(D)** Add 225 (W), 75 (TH), and 150 (F): $225 + 75 + 150 = 450$. (A) is incorrect because this is just the distance on Friday. (B) is incorrect because this is just the distance on Wednesday. (C) is incorrect because this is the sum of the Wednesday and Thursday distances.

27. **(D)** The first quake measures 10^2, which is 100. The other quake measures 10^8, which is 100,000,000. Divide to find how much more powerful the second quake is; 10^8 divided by 10^2 is 10^6. The second quake is; 10^6 times more powerful. The number 10^6 means 1 followed by 6 zeros, which is 1,000,000.

    You could also just divide 100,000,000 by 100 to get 1,000,000.

Eliminate (A) and (B) immediately. It does not make much sense that a quake measuring 100,000,000 would be just 6 times more powerful or 600 times more powerful than a quake measuring 100.

The second quake is 1,000,000 times more powerful than the second quake.

28. **(C)** As the fourth sentence indicates, the carpetbaggers, white scalawags, and former slaves collaborated to keep the confederates out of power and thus helped to fill a power vacuum. (A) and (B) are incorrect because there is no indication in the passage that carpetbaggers either worked with the KKK or were interested in improving slaves' conditions. (D) is incorrect because the passage indicates the carpetbaggers worked to keep the Confederates out of power.

29. **(C)** In general, haiku follows a 5-7-5 syllabic scheme with *no* rhyming. (C) alone meets these criteria. (A) and (B) are incorrect because they each include lines with four syllables, not the required five. (D) is incorrect because the last word "day" rhymes with the word "away."

30. **(C)** The word *nigh* means near in space or time. (A) is incorrect because "clear" means obvious or transparent. (B) is incorrect because "complete" means finished or total. (D) is incorrect because "not" is a modifier that means opposite.

31. **(D)** The passage indicates that love falls on silence and that love unknown is sad. This leads to the conclusion that the passage is about loving without acknowledgment. (A) is incorrect because rebuffed means rejected and there is no mention of rejection in the passage. (B) is incorrect because there is no indication of love from another person. (C) is incorrect because there is no mention of a third person.

32. **(B)** Choices (A), (C), and (D) are specifically referred to in the list as self-evident truths, so eliminate them as correct answers. Even though freedom from taxation without representation was a basis for the American Revolution, the Declaration of Independence does not include (B), freedom from taxation without representation, as a self-evident truth.

33. **(B)** The next to the last sentence in the first paragraph indicates that these programs do not teach about spelling or word meanings. (A) is incorrect because this statement is contrary to the last sentence in the passage. (C) is incorrect; while true, it is not the main idea of this passage. (D) is incorrect because the passage never makes this claim.

34. **(B)** The types of computers used and teaching methods are not mentioned in the passage. To answer Roman numeral items, decide first which of the Roman numeral statements are true. Then find the answer that matches.

    I. Incorrect. The type of computer is never mentioned in the passage.

   II. Correct. The main outputs—spelling suggestions and synonyms—are in the passage.

  III. Incorrect. These approaches are specifically omitted.

Only II is correct—(B).

35. **(C)** The fourth sentence in the first paragraph explains that the author likes having a program to perform the mechanical aspects. (A), (B), and (D) are incorrect because, while they are mentioned in the passage, they are not mentioned as something the author likes.

36. **(A)** This question can be answered from the information in the passage's last paragraph. (B), (C), and (D) are never directly addressed in the passage.

37. **(D)** This choice paraphrases the first sentence in the last paragraph. In that sentence the word "strictly" means exclusively or only. The word "only" appears in this choice. (A) is incorrect because there is no synonym for "strictly," and strict teachers may not strictly use this approach. (B) is incorrect because "stringently" means severe or harsh and it is not a synonym for "strictly." (C) is incorrect because "inflexible" means rigid and is not a synonym for "strictly."

38. **(B)** This choice paraphrases the first sentence in the second paragraph. (A), (C), and (D) are incorrect because these could not *result from* "unfamiliarity with meanings . . . ."

39. **(C)** Presidential elections are decided by electoral votes, and the caption clearly indicates that the map shows the results of a presidential election. (A), (B), and (D) are incorrect because the map clearly shows presidential election results, and not the number of representatives or the number of counties.

40. **(C)** Refer to the map shading, which shows that Fremont won all northernmost states. (A) is incorrect because Buchanan would have lost the 8 votes that Fremont gained, leaving a winning margin of 42 votes for Buchanan. (B) and (D) are incorrect because these conclusions are not supported by the shading patterns in the map. Just because a candidate won most of the Southern states does not *guarantee* that the candidate supported the rebel cause.

41. **(B)** The earth's mantle is the first part of the earth beneath the earth's surface. (A) indicates the earth's crust, (C) indicates the earth's outer core, (D) indicates the earth's inner core.

42. **(C)** This choice is the best answer because the third paragraph describes Sutras as containing beliefs and teachings. (A) is incorrect because the passage describes the Triptika as containing teachings. (B) is incorrect because the passage does not identify anything as containing just religious tribes. (D) is incorrect because the passage identifies the Talmud as containing both law and tradition.

43. **(A)** Consider each Roman numeral choice and then choose your answer.

    I. Incorrect. The passage indicates that Siddhartha Gautama (Buddha) is said to have achieved enlightenment through meditation.
    II. Correct. Jews today do not rely on the Old Testament for religious law; they rely on the Talmud.
    III. Incorrect. The passage indicates Christianity was generally tolerated in Rome.

    Only II is correct—(A).

44. **(B)** This sentence correctly reflects the essential point that Judaism developed from the beliefs of these tribes. (A) and (C) are incorrect because these choices make it seem that the tribes developed their beliefs *from* Judaism. (D) is incorrect because it makes it seem that the tribes already had Judaic beliefs.

45. **(D)** The title of this painting by Georgia O'Keeffe is "Cow's Skull." (A) and (B) might be reasonably correct answers, were it not for the most correct answer in (D). (C) is incorrect because the figure does not resemble a Rorschach inkblot.

46. **(C)** More mass means there is more of the object, that is, it takes up more space. Diagram A shows the most overflow, indicating that the object in that beaker has more mass. (A) and (B) are incorrect because a heavier object would not necessarily take up more space. For example, two ounces of gold would take up less space than one ounce of iron. (D) is incorrect because the overflow in Diagram B is less than the overflow in Diagram A.

47. **(C)** This choice paraphrases the conclusion found in the last sentence of the passage. (A) and (B) are incorrect because, while a person may draw this conclusion, it is not in the paragraph and would not be in the summary. (D) is incorrect because the passage does not contain this information.

48. **(A)** The author explains the difference between correlation and cause and effect with an explanation and an example. Choices (B), (C), and (D) are incorrect because they are not in the passage.

49. **(C)** The writer believes that generals should be judged by results. Even if you do not agree, that is the view of this writer. (A), (B), and (D) are incorrect because the writer does not base the paragraph on any of these statements.

50. **(C)** This process crosses all the numbers but the prime numbers. The numbers in (C) are the prime numbers in the 80s. (A), (B), and (D) are incorrect because they contain multiples of 3.

    81 is a multiple of 3 so $3 \times 17 = 81$

    87 is a multiple of 3 so $3 \times 19 = 87$

51. **(C)** On average, Asheville has 235 days without precipitation. Note that the graph does not show days that are cloudy and have no precipitation. (A) is incorrect because Houston has only 100 out of 365 days with precipitation. (B) is incorrect because Hilo has 285 days with precipitation, which leaves 85 days without precipitation. That's about 25 percent of the days without precipitation. (D) is incorrect because only about one-third of the days in Chicago have precipitation.

52. **(D)** On average, Houston has 259 days without precipitation. Notice this item is different from the previous one because this correct choice is the one city that has the most days without precipitation. (A) and (B) are incorrect because this information is not included in the graph. (C) is incorrect because the days with precipitation are not the same as the amount of precipitation.

53. **(B)** Investigate the pattern to find that the sum of the first n numbers is n^2. The sum of the first 90 odd numbers is 90^2 or 8,100. (A) is incorrect because it follows the incorrect pattern of multiplying 90 by 5. (C) is incorrect because it is too small to be the sum of the first 90 odd numbers. (D) is incorrect because it follows the incorrect pattern of multiplying 90 by 50.

54. **(A)** The setbacks create the steplike appearance. (B), (C), and (D) are incorrect because none of these choices *creates* the steplike appearance.

55. **(D)** The paragraph describes how careful shopping can result in lower prices. (A), (B), and (C) are all conclusions that could be drawn from the passage, but none of them is the main idea.

56. **(A)** Consider each Roman numeral choice and then choose your answer.

    I. Yes. This choice guarantees that she will be accepted to at least one sorority.
    II. Yes. This choice means she will preferably get into a sorority she wants.
    III. No. This choice eliminates the guarantee that she will be chosen for at least one sorority.
    IV. No. This choice makes it unlikely she will be chosen for a sorority she likes.

    Strategies I and II guarantee she will be chosen by at least one sorority and preferably the sorority that she likes—Choice (A).

57. **(D)** The author is denying one accusation, making another and trying to convince others. (A) is incorrect because the author never tries to clear his or her name. (B) is incorrect because the problems of running for office are not discussed. (C) is incorrect because the reference to "rich supporters" is not an accusation of wrongdoing.

58. **(B)** This expression correctly shows the relationship.

$$\underset{\underset{B \quad = \quad \$5 \qquad + \qquad \frac{1}{2} \qquad \times \qquad c}{}}{\underline{\text{Boat}\; \text{costs}\; \$5\; \text{more than}\; \text{half the price}\; \text{of a canoe}}}$$

$$B = \tfrac{1}{2}\,c + 5$$

(A) and (C) are incorrect because they do not correctly show the equality. (D) is incorrect because it is an inequality.

59. **(D)** The central building, the Louvre Pyramid, serves as a contrast with the traditional building behind it. (A) is incorrect because the contrast with the clouds is insignificant compared to (D). (B) is incorrect because the building does not emphasize the symmetry of any roads. (C) is incorrect because the building does not complete a collection of geometric shapes.

60. **(A)** The clouds do not suggest symmetry. (B), the rectangular central building, (C) and (D) the geometric buildings to the left and right, and the placement of the geometric buildings all suggest symmetry.

61. **(B)** The recycling amounts in the table increase for each city after 1991. (A) is incorrect because there is no data in the table to support recycling capability. (C) is incorrect because there is no basis for knowing how much recycling should be going on in Miami. (D) is incorrect because, while certainly true, it is not supported by data in the table.

62. **(D)** The paragraphs are most naturally ordered as shown in (D). III is the introductory passage, II follows directly from the last sentence in III, I follows directly from II.

63. **(A)** The author is saying, "You caught me or I caught myself. I'm guilty, but I didn't mean it." (B) and (C) make no sense in this context. (D) makes sense in this context but it is not as good a fit as (A).

64. **(C)** Boxers stand toe to toe in a boxing match. (A) is incorrect because a bull-fight involves an animal and a person. (B) is incorrect because a wrestling match does not feature toe-to-toe action. (D) is incorrect because a football game involves teams.

65. **(B)** The third sentence tells us that "oaks and chestnuts [trees] . . . threw a cavernous gloom over it [the road]." (A) is incorrect because we don't learn of Ichabod's fears until the second paragraph. The "sturdy yeomen" described in the first paragraph were waiting for Andre. (C) and (D) are incorrect because these descriptions appear in the second paragraph.

66. **(B)** The last paragraph of the passage mentions that a cell wall is found in plant cells. No mention is made of a cell wall in animal cells. The diagram confirms this because the line denoting a cell wall points to only a plant cell.

67. **(D)** For the experiment to be successful, the scientist must listen to or record the chirps of only one cricket. This is the fundamental assumption the scientist must make. (A) might be a problem because a cricket can chirp 3 or 4 times per second on a warm evening. However, the scientist could always make a sound recording. (B) is not really an assumption about the experiment. If crickets are not chirping, the scientist will not count the chirps. (C) is not the answer. Since the scientist is checking the accuracy of the formula, there is no significant assumption that the formula is correct.

68. **(B)** The author says that men are discriminated against just as much as women and gives an example to support his view. (A) is incorrect because the passage reads "discriminated against just as much." (C) is incorrect because the passage indicates that women are discriminated against. (D) is incorrect because, while true, this is a fact the author uses to support the main point, not the main point itself.

69. **(A)** Drafted, in the sense used here, means to be inducted into the armed forces against your will. (B) is incorrect because it does not show the lack of agreement that drafting carries with it. (C) is incorrect because society itself does not push someone into a draft. (D) is incorrect because peers do not draw a person into being drafted.

70. **(D)** Add to find the distances. The totals for each answer choice are as follows:

    (A) 25
    (B) 26
    (C) 27
    (D) 24

    (D) is the shortest.

71. **(B)** The *results* of the farmer's effort can be seen only in the stalks of wheat already cut. (A), (C), and (D) are incorrect because neither determination, nor the shape of the handle, nor the reaper's solitude shows results.

72. **(D)** The passage identifies both the moon's cycle and the earth's revolution as factors contributing to the development of the current calendar. (A) is incorrect because, it does not mention the sun's revolution. (B) is incorrect because the calendar is not based on only the sun's position. (C) is incorrect because the current calendar is not based on the position of the moon.

73. **(A)** The first sentence in the fourth paragraph reads, "Fort Holmes was on Smith Island, which was west across the New Inlet from Fort Fisher." This means that Fort Fisher must be on the east side of the new inlet.

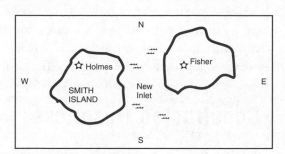

74. **(B)** General Whiting's words are a little convoluted, but this choice is what he meant. You can eliminate answers to confirm this choice. (A) is incorrect because Whiting thinks Richmond is more important. (C) is incorrect because Whiting thinks Wilmington is second in importance to Richmond. (D) is incorrect because, while Whiting does not want to lose the supply line, he is specifically discussing the loss of Wilmington.

75. **(C)** This poem is not to be taken literally. The poet is describing his or her life and expressing the hope that his or her life will improve. (A) and (D) are incorrect because these are literal interpretations. (B) is incorrect because the poet does not express concern about other people's lives.

76. **(A)** The last two lines in the first stanza compare clouds to shrouds. The comparison shows that the figure of speech must be a metaphor or a simile. The poem uses the word "like," so the figure of speech must be a simile. (B) is incorrect because a hyperbole is a drastic overstatement. (C) is incorrect because a metaphor is a comparison in which the word "like" is not used. (D) is incorrect because a euphemism is an inoffensive term substituted for an offensive term.

77. **(C)** Divide 328 ÷ 31 = 10 R 18. You will need ten buses and another bus for the 18 remaining people. That is a total of 11 buses. (A) and (B) are incorrect because 9 or 10 buses are not enough. (D) is incorrect because 18 are more buses than you need.

78. **(C)** The rate, alone, does not provide enough information. You must know the starting point. (A) and (B) are incorrect because the passage gives examples that directly contradict each of these choices. (D) is incorrect because the growth rate does depend on the starting point.

79. **(B)** You should question any growth rate when only the percentage is given. (A) is incorrect because the word "any" makes this answer too general. (C) is incorrect because this general statement is not supported by the paragraph. (D) is incorrect because nothing in the paragraph sets over 50 percent growth rate as invalid.

80. **(A)** The main reason a company pays a much higher rate than another company is because that company's bonds are riskier. (B) is incorrect because riskier bonds for Company B means the rates for those bonds would be higher. (C) is incorrect because a company may pay higher rates to attract investors, but the main reason a company pays a much higher rate than another company is because that company's bonds are riskier. (D) is incorrect because that would make the interest rates higher for Company B's bonds.

Constructed Response

Show your essay to an English professor or a high school English teacher. Ask him or her to rate your essay 1–4 using this scale.

4   A well developed, complete written assignment.
    Shows a thorough response to all parts of the topic.
    Clear explanations that are well supported.
    An assignment that is free of significant grammatical, punctuation, or spelling errors.

3   A fairly well developed, complete written assignment.
    It may not thoroughly respond to all parts of the topic.
    Fairly clear explanations that may not be well supported.
    It may contain some significant grammatical, punctuation, or spelling errors.

2   A poorly developed, incomplete written assignment.
    It does not thoroughly respond to most parts of the topic.
    Contains many poor explanations that are not well supported.
    It may contain some significant grammatical, punctuation, or spelling errors.

1   A very poorly developed, incomplete written assignment.
    It does not thoroughly respond to the topic.
    Contains only poor, unsupported explanations.
    Contains numerous significant grammatical, punctuation, or spelling errors.

Diagnostic LAST Essay Scoring

Your goal is to write an essay that scores 3 or 4. Score your essay using the scale above and the sample essay that follows. Scoring your own essay can be difficult. Showing your essay to a scoring expert will probably help you evaluate your performance.

Your goal is to write an essay with a score in the upper half. If you have not achieved that goal on this essay, you can try the essay in the chapter "Practice LAST" in this book. You can also get more help now about writing high-scoring essays before you take the LAST practice test.

Sample Essay

This is an example of a strong essay. The essay states a clear position, discusses the pros and cons mentioned in the prompt, and then reaches a conclusion. There are no meaningful errors in grammar or punctuation. Nothing about the writing style interferes with the reader's ability to understand the author's position.

The 502 words in this essay also indicates that it is worthy of a score in the upper half. The number of words itself is not enough to earn a high score. However, an essay of about this length will likely be required for a high score.

Let's Have a Reasonable Speed Limit

The speed limit should be a maximum of 55 miles per hour. Even though I have a long commute each day on the New York State Thruway, I believe that the speed limit should not be increased to 70 miles per hour. Many people disagree with me. However, my position has compelling arguments that support my conviction.

I am going to begin by discussing the some of the opposing views presented in the description of this task. Then I'll reflect on the views that favor my proposition for a lower speed limit. Finally, I'll use this information to support my position and then present some additional thoughts.

Those who want the speed limit raised to 70 miles per hour say that people would arrive at their destinations more quickly. They also state that getting somewhere in as little time as possible is a good thing. However, those arguments fail. If raising the speed limit to 70 is good, why not raise it even higher? How about raising it to 110 miles per hour? Travel time would be significantly reduced. However, I do not know of anyone who believes that the speed limit should be 110 miles per hour. Arriving quickly is not a compelling reason to raise the speed limit.

The speed limit should be 55 miles per hour primarily because higher speed limits result in more accidents and more deaths. I recently read several reports indicating that higher speed limits lead to more traffic-related deaths. Is arriving at a destination more quickly worth the lives lost, the disabling injuries, and the monetary costs resulting from high-speed accidents? No. A speed limit of 55 miles per hour saves lives.

Not raising the speed limit makes good economic sense. Cars traveling at 55 miles per hour make better gas mileage than those traveling at 70 miles per hour. The slower speed limit saves fuel. A speed limit of 55 miles per hour will help this nation decrease its gasoline usage and dependence on foreign oil. It will also help individual drivers keep more of their hard-earned cash in their wallets. Driving slower saves both gas and money.

No one actually drives at or below the speed limit, especially on interstates. While driving here today, the speed limit on the road I took was 65 miles per hour. However, no one was driving less than 75 miles per hour. Most people drive approximately 10 miles per hour above the posted limit. If the speed limit was raised to 75 miles per hour, most people would probably drive 85 miles per hour which is just too crazy for me.

The speed limit should be set at a reasonable 55 miles per hour. Since most people drive faster than the posted limit, the actual speed limit would be 65 miles per hour. Lives will be saved. Injuries and property damage will be avoided. Gasoline will be conserved. A 55-mile-per-hour speed limit seems like a winning proposition to me.

See pages 58–70 at *http://www.nystce.nesinc.com/PDFs/NY_fld001_prepguide.pdf* for a scoring guide and additional samples of weak and strong essays.

Diagnostic LAST Scoring

This diagnostic LAST scoring helps you decide whether you need some additional review and whether you should take the Practice LAST II.

The scoring information from any practice test is an estimate. Passing raw scores on these tests vary widely, and this test will likely not have same the difficulty level of the actual test you take. That is why this scoring information is advisory only, as a guide to further study. You should NOT try to predict your scale score on the actual LAST from these test results.

I just want to emphasize again that these recommendations are informed estimates. Test writers could raise the raw score required for a passing score.

The decision to pursue additional review is up to you. You must decide if the time spent on that additional review and the additional practice test is likely to help. You can always decide to use only parts of the review.

Step 1—Score Your Test

Selected response _____ Number correct out of 80

Constructed-response essay _____ Number of points out of 8 from two scorers.

If just one person scores your essay, multiply that single score by two. This will not be the best indication of your constructed-response score.

Step 2—Consider Your Additional Review Options

SELECTED RESPONSE

These scoring ranges indicate whether you need some or all of the additional reading comprehension review in Chapter 5. These score ranges are only advisory.

_____ Less than 40 correct   Additional review is strongly indicated

_____ 41 to 52 correct   Additional review is advised

_____ 53 to 59 correct   Consider some additional review

_____ More than 60 correct   Additional review not indicated but is available

CONSTRUCTED-RESPONSE ESSAY

These scoring ranges presume two scorers have accurately scored your essay. They help you decide whether you need some or all of the additional writing review and the additonal practice essay in Chapter 6. These score ranges are only advisory.

_____ 2 or 3 points   Additional writing review is strongly indicated

_____ 4 points   Additional writing review is indicated

_____ 5 points   Additional writing review may be indicated

_____ 6 to 8 points   Additional writing is not indicated but is available

Step 3

Decide whether to take the Practice LAST in Chapter 7. If you spent time on extra review, you should probably take Practice LAST. However, you may also elect to take Practice LAST even if you did not pursue further review. You can also decide to complete only a portion of the test if you just want more questions or an additional essay topic.

Reading Comprehension

Vocabulary Review

You can't read if you don't know the vocabulary. But you don't have to know every word in the dictionary. Follow this reasonable approach to understand the vocabulary on these tests.

Context Clues

Many times you can figure out a word from its context. Look at these examples. Synonyms, antonyms, examples, or descriptions may help you figure out the word.

1. The woman's mind wandered as her two friends *prated* on. It really did not bother her though. In all the years she had known them, they had always *babbled* about their lives. It was almost comforting.
2. The wind *abated* in the late afternoon. Things were different yesterday when the wind had *picked up* toward the end of the day.

3. The argument with her boss had been her *Waterloo*. She wondered if the *defeat* suffered by Napoleon *at this famous place* had felt the same.

4. The events swept the politician into a *vortex* of controversy. The politician knew what it meant to be spun around like a toy boat in the *swirl of water* that swept down the bathtub drain.

Passage 1 gives a synonym for the unknown word. We can tell that *prated* means babbled. *Babbled* is used as a synonym of *prated* in the passage.

Passage 2 gives an antonym for the unknown word. We can tell that *abated* means slowed down or diminished because *picked up* is used as an antonym of *abated*.

Passage 3 gives a description of the unknown word. The description of *Waterloo* tells us that the word means *defeat*.

Passage 4 gives an example of the unknown word. This example of a *swirl of water* going down the bathtub drain gives us a good idea of what a *vortex* is.

Roots

A root is the basic element of a word. The root is usually related to the word's origin. Roots can often help you figure out the word's meaning. Here are some roots that may help you.

Root	Meaning	Examples
bio	life	biography, biology
circu	around	circumference, circulate
frac	break	fraction, refract
geo	earth	geology, geography
mal	bad	malicious, malcontent
matr, mater	mother	maternal, matron
neo	new	neonate, neoclassic
patr, pater	father	paternal, patron
spec	look	spectacles, specimen
tele	distant	telephone, television

Prefixes

Prefixes are syllables that come at the beginning of a word. Prefixes usually have a standard meaning. They can often help you figure out the word's meaning. Here is a list of prefixes that may help you figure out a word.

Prefix	Meaning	Examples
a-	not	amoral, apolitical
il-, im-, ir-	not	illegitimate, immoral, incorrect
un-	not	unbearable, unknown
non-	not	nonbeliever, nonsense
ant-, anti-	against	antiwar, antidote
de-	opposite	defoliate, declaw
mis-	wrong	misstep, misdeed
ante-	before	antedate, antecedent
fore-	before	foretell, forecast
post-	after	postfight, postoperative
re-	again	refurbish, redo
super-	above	superior, superstar
sub-	below	subsonic, subpar

The Vocabulary List

Here is a list of a few hundred vocabulary words. This list includes everyday words and a few specialized education terms. Read through the list and visualize the words and their definitions. After a while you will become very familiar with them.

Of course, this is not anywhere near all the words you need to know for the exams. But they will give you a start. These words also will give you some idea of the kinds of words you may encounter on the examinations.

abhor To regard with horror
I abhor violence.

abstain To refrain by choice
Ray decided to abstain from fattening foods.

abstract Not related to any object, theoretical
Mathematics can be very abstract.

acquisition An addition to an established group or collection
The museum's most recent acquisition was an early Roman vase.

admonish To correct firmly but kindly
The teacher admonished the student not to chew gum in class.

adroit Skillful or nimble in difficult circumstances
The nine year old was already an adroit gymnast.

adversary A foe or enemy
The wildebeest was ever-alert for its ancient adversary, the lion.

advocate To speak for an idea; a person who speaks for an idea
Lou was an advocate of gun control.

aesthetic Pertaining to beauty
Ron found the painting a moving aesthetic experience.

affective To do with the emotional or feeling aspect of learning
Len read the Taxonomy of Educational Objectives: Affective Domain.

alias An assumed name
The check forger had used an alias.

alleviate To reduce or make more bearable
The hot shower helped alleviate the pain in her back.

allude To make an indirect reference to, hint at
Elaine only alluded to her previous trips through the state.

ambiguous Open to many interpretations
That is an ambiguous statement.

TIP

A great way to develop a vocabulary is to read a paper every day and a news magazine every week, in addition to the other reading you are doing. There are also several inexpensive books, including *1100 Words You Need to Know, Pocket Guide to Vocabulary,* and *Vocabulary Success* from Barron's, which may help you develop your vocabulary further.

apathy Absence of passion or emotion
The teacher tried to overcome their apathy toward the subject.

apprehensive Fear or unease about possible outcomes
Bob was apprehensive about visiting the dentist.

aptitude The ability to gain from a particular type of instruction
The professor pointed out that aptitude alone was not enough for success in school.

articulate To speak clearly and distinctly, present a point of view
Chris was chosen to articulate the group's point of view.

assess To measure or determine an outcome or value
There are many informal ways to assess learning.

attest To affirm or certify
I can attest to Cathy's ability as a softball pitcher.

augment To increase or add to
The new coins augmented the already large collection.

belated Past time or tardy
George sent a belated birthday card.

benevolent Expresses good will or kindly feelings
The club was devoted to performing benevolent acts.

biased A prejudiced view or action
The judge ruled that the decision was biased.

bolster To shore up, support
The explorer sang to bolster her courage.

candid Direct and outspoken
Lee was well known for her candid comments.

caricature Exaggerated, ludicrous picture, in words or a cartoon
The satirist presented world leaders as caricatures.

carnivorous Flesh eating or predatory
The lion is a carnivorous animal.

censor A person who judges the morality of others; act on that judgment
Please don't censor my views!

censure Expression of disapproval, reprimand
The senate acted to censure the congressman.

cessation The act of ceasing or halting
The eleventh hour marked the cessation of hostilities.

chronic Continuing and constant
Asthma can be a chronic condition.

clandestine Concealed or secret
The spy engaged in clandestine activities.

cogent Intellectually convincing
He presented a cogent argument.

cognitive Relates to the intellectual area of learning
Lou read the Taxonomy of Educational Objectives: Cognitive Domain.

competency Demonstrated ability
Bert demonstrated the specified mathematics competency.

complacent Unaware self-satisfaction
The tennis player realized she had become complacent.

concept A generalization
The professor lectured on concept development.

congenital Existing at birth but non-hereditary
The baby had a small congenital defect.

contemporaries Belonging in the same time period, about the same age
Piaget and Bruner were contemporaries.

contempt Feeling or showing disdain or scorn
She felt nothing but contempt for their actions.

contentious Argumentative
Tim was in a contentious mood.

corroborate To make certain with other information, to confirm
The reporter would always corroborate a story before publication.

credence Claim to acceptance or trustworthiness
They did not want to lend credence to his views.

cursory Surface, not in depth
Ron gave his car a cursory inspection.

daunt To intimidate with fear
Harry did not let the difficulty of the task daunt him.

debacle Disastrous collapse or rout
The whole trip had been a debacle.

debilitate To make feeble
He was concerned that the flu would debilitate him.

decadent Condition of decline/decay
Joan said in frustration, "We live in a decadent society."

deductive Learning that proceeds from general to specific
He proved his premise using deductive logic.

demographic Population data
The census gathers demographic information.

denounce To condemn a person or idea
The diplomat rose in the United Nations to denounce the plan.

deter To prevent or stop an action, usually by some threat
The president felt that the peace conference would help deter aggression.

diligent A persistent effort; a person who makes such an effort
The investigator was diligent in her pursuit of the truth.

discern To perceive or recognize, often by insight
The principal attempted to discern which student was telling the truth.

discord Disagreement or disharmony
Gail's early promotion led to discord in the office.

discriminate To distinguish among people or groups based on their characteristics
It is not appropriate to discriminate based on race or ethnicity.

disdain To show or act with contempt
The professional showed disdain for her amateurish efforts.

disseminate To send around, scatter
The health organization will disseminate any new information on the flu.

divergent Thinking that extends in many directions, is not focused
Les was an intelligent but divergent thinker.

diverse Not uniform, varied
Alan came from a diverse neighborhood.

duress coercion
He claimed that he confessed under duress.

eccentric Behaves unusually, different from the norm
His long hair and midnight walks made Albert appear eccentric.

eclectic Drawing from several ideas or practices
Joe preferred an eclectic approach to the practice of psychology.

eloquent Vivid, articulate expression
The congregation was spellbound by the eloquent sermon.

emanate To flow out, come forth
How could such wisdom emanate from one so young?

embellish To make things seem more than they are
Art loved to embellish the truth.

empirical From observation or experiment
The scientist's conclusions were based on empirical evidence.

employment A job or professional position (paid)
You seek employment so you can make the big bucks.

enduring Lasting over the long term
Their friendship grew into an enduring relationship.

enhance To improve or build up
The mechanic used a fuel additive to enhance the car's performance.

enigma A mystery or puzzle
The communist bloc is an "enigma wrapped inside a mystery." (Churchill)

equity Equal attention or treatment
The workers were seeking pay equity with others in their industry.

equivocal Uncertain, capable of multiple interpretations
In an attempt to avoid conflict, the negotiator took an equivocal stand.

expedite To speed up, facilitate
Hal's job at the shipping company was to expedite deliveries.

exploit Take maximum advantage of, perhaps unethically
Her adversary tried to exploit her grief to gain an advantage.

extrinsic Coming from outside
The teacher turned to extrinsic motivation.

farce A mockery
The attorney objected, saying that the testimony made the trial a farce.

feign To pretend, make a false appearance of
Some people feign illness to get out of work.

fervent Marked by intense feeling
The spokesman presented a fervent defense of the company's actions.

fiasco Total failure
They had not prepared for the presentation, and it turned into a fiasco.

formidable Difficult to surmount
State certification requirements can present a formidable obstacle.

fracas A noisy quarrel or a scrap
The debate turned into a full-fledged fracas.

gamut Complete range or extent
Waiting to take the test, her mind ran the gamut of emotions.

glib Quickness suggesting insincerity
The glib response made Rita wonder about the speaker's sincerity.

grave Very serious or weighty
The supervisor had grave concerns about the worker's ability.

guile Cunning, crafty, duplicitous
When the truth failed, he tried to win his point with guile.

handicapped Having one or more disabilities
The child study team classified Loren as handicapped.

harass Bother persistently
Some fans came to harass the players on the opposing team.

heterogeneous A group with normal variation in ability or performance
Students from many backgrounds formed a heterogeneous population.

homogeneous A group with little variation in ability or performance
The school used test scores to place students in homogeneous groups.

hypocrite One who feigns a virtuous character or belief
Speaking against drinking and then driving drunk make him a hypocrite!

immune Protected or exempt from disease or harm
The vaccination made Ray immune to measles.

impartial Fair and objective
The contestants agreed on an objective, impartial referee.

impasse Situation with no workable solution
The talks had not stopped, but they had reached an impasse.

impede To retard or obstruct
Mason did not let adversity impede his progress.

implicit Understood but not directly stated
They never spoke about the matter, but they had an implicit understanding.

indifferent Uncaring or apathetic
The teacher was indifferent to the student's pleas for an extension.

indigenous Native to an area
The botanist recognized it as an indigenous plant.

inductive Learning that proceeds from specific to general
Science uses an inductive process, from examples to a generalization.

inevitable Certain and unavoidable
After the rains, the collapse of the dam was inevitable.

infer To reach a conclusion not explicitly stated
The advertisement sought to infer that the product was superior.

inhibit To hold back or restrain
The hormone was used to inhibit growth.

innovate To introduce something new or change established procedure
Mere change was not enough, they had to innovate the procedure.

inquiry Question-based Socratic learning
Much of science teaching uses inquiry-based learning.

intrinsic inherent, the essential nature
The teacher drew on the meaning of the topic for an intrinsic motivation.

inundate To overwhelm, flood
It was December, and mail began to inundate the post office.

jocular Characterized by joking or good nature
The smiling man seemed to be a jocular fellow.

judicial Relating to the administration of justice
His goal was to have no dealings with the judicial system.

knack A talent for doing something
Ron had a real knack for mechanical work.

languid Weak, lacking energy
The sunbather enjoyed a languid afternoon at the shore.

liaison An illicit relationship or a means of communication
The governor appointed his chief aid liaison to the senate.

lucid Clear and easily understood
The teacher answered the question in a direct and lucid way.

magnanimous Generous in forgiving
Loretta is magnanimous to a fault.

malignant Very injurious, evil
Crime is a malignant sore on our society.

malleable Open to being shaped or influenced
He had a malleable position on gun control.

meticulous Very careful and precise
Gina took meticulous care of the fine china.

miser A money hoarder
The old miser had more money than he could ever use.

monotonous Repetitive and boring
Circling the airport, waiting to land, became monotonous.

mores Understood rules of society
Linda made following social mores her goal in life.

motivation Something that creates interest or action
Most good lessons begin with good motivation.

myriad Large indefinite number
Look skyward and be amazed by the myriad of stars.

naive Lacking sophistication
Laura is unaware, and a little naive, about the impact she has on others.

nemesis A formidable rival
Lex Luthor is Superman's nemesis.

novice A beginner
Her unsteady legs revealed that Sue was a novice skater.

nullified Removed the importance of
The penalty nullified the 20-yard gain made by the running back.

objective A goal
The teacher wrote an objective for each lesson.

oblivious Unaware and unmindful
Les was half asleep and oblivious to the racket around him.

obscure Vague, unclear, uncertain
The lawyer quoted an obscure reference.

ominous Threatening or menacing
There were ominous black storm clouds on the horizon.

palatable Agreeable, acceptable
Sandy's friends tried to make her punishment more palatable.

panorama A comprehensive view or picture
The visitors' center offered a panorama of the canyon below.

pedagogy The science of teaching
Part of certification tests focus on pedagogy.

perpetuate To continue or cause to be remembered
A plaque was put up to perpetuate the memory of the retiring teacher.

pompous Exaggerated self-importance
Rona acted pompous, but Lynne suspected she was very empty inside.

precarious Uncertain, beyond one's control
A diver sat on a precarious perch on a cliff above the water.

precedent An act or instance that sets the standard
The judge's ruling set a precedent for later cases.

preclude To act to make impossible or impracticable
Beau did not want to preclude any options.

precocious Very early development
Chad was very precocious and ran at six months.

prolific Abundant producer
Isaac Asimov was a prolific science fiction writer.

prognosis A forecast or prediction
The stock broker gave a guarded prognosis for continued growth.

provoke To stir up or anger
Children banging on the cage would provoke the circus lion to growl.

psychomotor Relates to the motor skill area of learning
I read the Taxonomy of Behavioral Objectives: Psychomotor Domain.

quagmire Predicament or difficult situation
The regulations were a quagmire of conflicting rules and vague terms.

qualm Feeling of doubt or misgiving
The teacher had not a single qualm about giving the student a low grade.

quandary A dilemma
The absence of the teacher aide left the teacher in a quandary.

quench To put out, satisfy
The glass of water was not enough to quench his thirst.

rancor Bitter continuing resentment
A deep rancor had existed between the two friends since the accident.

rationale The basis or reason for something
The speeder tried to present a rationale to the officer who stopped her.

reciprocal Mutual interchange
Each person got something out of their reciprocal arrangement.

refute To prove false
The lawyer used new evidence to refute claims made by the prosecution.

remedial Designed to compensate for learning deficits
Jim spent one period a day in remedial instruction.

reprove Criticize gently
The teacher would reprove students for chewing gum in class.

repudiate To reject or disown
The senator repudiated membership in an all male club.

resolve To reach a definite conclusion
A mediator was called in to resolve the situation.

retrospect Contemplation of the past
Ryan noted, in retrospect, that leaving home was his best decision.

revere To hold in the highest regard
Citizens of the town revere their long time mayor.

sanction To issue authoritative approval or a penalty
The boxing commissioner had to sanction the match.

scrutinize To inspect with great care
You should scrutinize any document before signing it.

siblings Brothers or sisters
The holidays give me the chance to spend time with my siblings.

skeptical Doubting, questioning the validity
The principal was skeptical about the students' reason for being late.

solace Comfort in misfortune
Her friends provided solace in her time of grief.

solitude Being alone
Pat enjoyed her Sunday afternoon moments of solitude.

stagnant Inert, contaminated
In dry weather the lake shrank to a stagnant pool.

stereotype An oversimplified generalized view or belief
We are all guilty of fitting people into a stereotype.

subsidy Financial assistance
Chris received a subsidy from her company so she could attend school.

subtle Faint, not easy to find or understand
Subtle changes in the teller's actions alerted the police to the robbery.

subterfuge A deceptive strategy
The spy used subterfuge to gain access to the secret materials.

superficial Surface, not profound
The inspector gave the car a superficial inspection.

tacit Not spoken, inferred
They had a tacit agreement.

taxonomy Classification of levels of thinking or organisms
I read each Taxonomy of Educational Objectives.

tenacious Persistent and determined
The police officer was tenacious in pursuit of a criminal.

tentative Unsure, uncertain
The athletic director set up a tentative basketball schedule.

terminate To end, conclude
He wanted to terminate the relationship.

transition Passage from one activity to another
The transition from college student to teacher was not easy.

trepidation Apprehension, state of dread
Erin felt some trepidation about beginning her new job.

trivial Unimportant, ordinary
The seemingly trivial occurrence had taken on added importance.

ubiquitous Everywhere, omnipresent
A walk through the forest invited attacks from the ubiquitous mosquitoes.

ultimatum A final demand
After a trying day, the teacher issued an ultimatum to the class.

usurp To wrongfully and forcefully seize and hold, particularly power
The association vice president tried to usurp the president's power.

vacillate To swing indecisively
He had a tendency to vacillate in his stance on discipline.

valid Logically correct
The math teacher was explaining a valid mathematical proof.

vehement Forceful, passionate
The child had a vehement reaction to the teacher's criticism.

vestige A sign of something no longer there or existing
Old John was the last vestige of the first teachers to work at the school.

vicarious Experience through the activities or feelings of others
He had to experience sports in a vicarious way through his students.

virulent Very poisonous or noxious
The coral snake has a particularly virulent venom.

vital Important and essential
The school secretary was a vital part of the school.

waffle To write or speak in a misleading way
The spokesperson waffled as she tried to explain away the mistake.

wary Watchful, on guard
The soldiers were very wary of any movements in the field.

Xanadu An idyllic, perfect place
All wished for some time in Xanadu.

yearned Longed or hoped for
Liz yearned for a small class.

zeal Diligent devotion to a cause
Ron approached his job with considerable zeal.

Types of Selected-Response Items

The LAST is primarily a test of reading comprehension. A few math-related questions are thrown in, and a few are about interpreting pictures. However, very little knowledge is required to answer these questions. You mainly need common sense. In fact, very little specific knowledge is required beyond the information on the LAST. This section gives an integrated approach to answering the literal and figurative reading items on the LAST and some exposure to the other questions you might run across.

The LAST consists mainly of reading passages followed by multiple-choice items. You do not have to understand the entire passage to answer the questions. In fact, the most common error is to read the entire passage before reading the questions. Do not do that. It just wastes time. You just have to know enough to get the correct answer. Less than half, often less than 25 percent, of the details in a passage are needed to answer a question.

Let me repeat again this essential reading strategy. Do not begin by reading the passage in detail. In fact, that kind of careful reading will almost certainly get you into trouble. Read in detail only after you have read a question and are looking for the answer. This section shows you how to do that.

Reading Comprehension Questions

The LAST contains two general types of reading comprehension questions—literal comprehension and figurative comprehension. Literal questions typically ask directly about the passage. Figurative questions typically ask you to infer, interpret, extend, and apply ideas in the passage.

The correct answer will be the best choice available among the choices listed. The correct answer will be based on the passage, not on something not in the passage that you may know is true or think is true.

LITERAL COMPREHENSION—MAIN IDEA (MAIN PURPOSE)

These questions ask about the main focus of the reading passage. You have to identify the main idea or main purpose of the passage. In other words, what is the main reason why the author wrote the passage?

- Main idea questions often include the words "main idea."
  For example,
  Which of the following describes the main idea of the passage?

- Main purpose questions often include the words "primary purpose."
  For example,
  What is the primary purpose of this passage?

Find the central idea of the passage to answer these questions. What was the author really trying to get at? Why did the author write the passage?

Some main ideas may not be directly stated in the passage. However, the main idea or purpose must be from the passage. It cannot be what you think the author might have in mind.

LITERAL COMPREHENSION—SUPPORTING DETAILS

Authors give details to support the main idea. These details may be facts, opinions, experiences, or discussions. The following are some examples of supporting details questions.

- Which of the following does the author use to support the main idea in the passage?

- Which of the following details is not found in this passage?

- How did the author explain (a statement) in the passage?

- At which line number(s) does the passage describe the outcomes of (an event) it mentions?

The answer choices will usually include statements or summaries of statements found in the passage. Read the question carefully to be sure what details you are asked to find.

Answer choices frequently include details you know to be true but are not explicitly found in the passage. Eliminate those. The correct answer will be found in the passage.

LITERAL COMPREHENSION—VOCABULARY QUESTIONS

A passage has lots of words and phrases. Vocabulary questions typically ask you to show that you know the meaning of one of those words or phrases. The following are some examples of vocabulary questions.

- Which of the following words is a synonym for (the word) in line 99 of the passage?

- Which of the following gives the best definition of (word) in line 99 of the passage?

- All of the following gives the best meaning for the (phrase/word) in line 99 EXCEPT.

The vocabulary section of this book (pages 75–83) gives a vocabulary review. It also includes ways to identify words from their context. A word in context is not always a strict dictionary definition.

Word meaning can be literal or figurative. For example, the author may write, "Stand up for what you believe in." The question asks about the meaning of "stand up." One of the choices is "stand up straight." Another choice is "take a position." The main dictionary definition is "stand up straight." However, that is not what these words mean in context. The words mean "take a position," which is the correct answer.

TIP

A literal definition may sometimes be right and may sometimes be wrong. You should think about the word's meaning in context when answering the question.

LITERAL COMPREHENSION—ORGANIZATION

These questions ask you about the way a passage is organized. Although this sounds hard, the answer choices are simply descriptive language. Using common sense will better help you answer these questions than will having any specialized knowledge.

Organization questions are just what you think they are. For example,

Which of the following choices best describes the way the passage is organized?

Some moderately difficult words may appear in the choices. Use the vocabulary skills shown on pages 75–77 to tackle those words if they occur.

FIGURATIVE COMPREHENSION—INFERENCE

An inference question asks you to identify something that can be reasonably implied or inferred from a passage. The answers to inference questions will not be directly stated in the passage. Inference questions look like the following.

- Which choice below can be inferred from this passage?

- What can be inferred about (name or event) from lines XXX–XXX in the passage?

Test writers try to write five choices for which only one is clearly the most correct inference. They usually do a good job. However, sometimes other apparently reasonable inferences slip in. Choose the inference a test writer would choose.

Choose an inference based on the passage. Do not make a choice just because it is true, even though you will find choices like that. Do not make a choice because it has some other emotional appeal. The inference has to be based exclusively on information in the passage.

FIGURATIVE COMPREHENSION—EVALUATE SUPPORTING DETAILS

Some of these questions may ask you to decide if details support the main idea. At other times, the questions introduce other details and ask you to determine if the details would strengthen or weaken the author's argument. The following are examples of this type of question.

- Which of the following statements, if added to the passage, would best support (weaken) the author's argument?

- Which of the following would be needed to support the author's claim fully?

A main idea, a position, or a claim need appropriate support from details. Think about the author's claim or argument. What does the argument convinces you of? What information is questionable or missing?

Strengthening or weakening an argument does not mean to prove or disprove that argument. Here is an example.

An author wrote, "All my shoes are black." Then a character said, "Did I see you wearing brown shoes the other day?" The second statement does weaken the first but does not disprove it. The second statement may be wrong, or it may be meant as a joke. Whether or not it is accurate, the second statement is enough to make us think and is enough to weaken the author's statement.

FIGURATIVE COMPREHENSION—FACT OR OPINION

These questions usually ask you to identify whether a part of the passage is a fact or an opinion. All of the answer choices come from the passage. Let's review a little bit about facts and opinions.

> **FACT**
> A fact can be either true or false. Do not think that a fact must always be true.

Something is true only if it is always true. The statement "trees shed their leaves in fall and winter" sounds true. However, it is not. Several trees native in the southern climates, such as live oak trees, never shed their leaves. Any statement is false if just one counterexample exists.

1. **True fact**—Most of Africa is in the Northern Hemisphere.
   A map shows that over 60% of Africa is in North America.

2. **False fact**—Mexico is in South America.
   A map shows that Mexico is actually in North America.

> **OPINION**
> An opinion is a personal belief not based on proof. An opinion cannot be proven true or shown to be false.

1. **Opinion**—It is great to vacation near the ocean.
   This is someone's personal view. There is no way to prove it is always true or always false. It is an opinion.

2. **Opinion**—Swimming is most fun when the air temperature is cold.
   This just does not seem right, and most people would probably disagree with it. However, there is no way to prove it true or false. It is an opinion.

The following is an example of a fact or opinion question.

Which of these statements from the passage is a fact rather than an opinion?

The best way to approach this question is to think about a fact. Remember that a fact can always be proven true or shown to be false. If a statement cannot be proven true or shown to be false, it is an opinion.

FIGURATIVE COMPREHENSION—MAKING PREDICTIONS

A prediction is a statement about something that may happen. These questions may ask you to identify predictions that can be made from the information in the passage. They may also ask you to identify something that a person may say or do based on information in the passage. The following is an example that could lead to a prediction.

EXAMPLE

Derek loves to go out on his boat. However, he did not go out yesterday because the waves were over 3 feet. It is reasonable to predict that Derek would not go out on his boat in the future if the waves were over 3 feet.

Making predictions questions look like the following.

Which of the statements below is the author most likely to agree with?

Do not choose an answer because it is correct or because you agree with it. The answer must be predictable from information in a passage.

Making a prediction is not the same as saying you are absolutely sure. In the example above, Derek might go out on the boat in special circumstances. For instance, if the waves were over 3 feet but a friend on another boat needed help, Derek might go out on his boat under those circumstances. However, we would not predict that situation based only on the information in the passage.

FIGURATIVE COMPREHENSION—DRAWING CONCLUSIONS

These questions ask you to assume that everything in the passage is correct and then to draw a conclusion from that information. You need to draw a logical conclusion based on two pieces of information. These two pieces of information do not have to appear near one another in the passage. Here is a simple example that could lead to a conclusion.

EXAMPLE

Whenever Liz meets someone she knows, she always talks to them. When Liz talks to someone she knows, she always shakes hands.

We can conclude that if Liz meets someone she knows, she shakes that person's hand. We cannot conclude that if she shakes hands with someone, she already knows that person. This second conclusion is not supported by the passage.

Drawing conclusions questions look like the following.

> Based on the information in the passage, which of the following is the most reasonable conclusion?

Do not choose an answer just because it is correct or because you agree with it. The answer must flow logically from information in the passage.

Other Question Types

You will come across a few questions that involve math, but seldom if ever is real math knowledge needed. The same is true for the questions you will see about graphs, maps, or art images. Advanced knowledge is not required. You may also come across some questions about grammar errors in a passage or about the correct order of sentences or paragraphs.

Five Steps for Answering Selected-Response Questions

TIP

You do not have to read the passage in detail. In fact, careful slow reading will almost certainly get you into trouble. Strange as it seems follow this advice—avoid careful, detailed reading at all costs.

Most of the LAST consists of passages followed by selected-response questions. You do not have to know what an entire reading passage is about. You just have to know enough to get the answer correct. Less than half, often less than 25 percent, of the information in any passage is needed to answer all the questions.

Buried among all the false gold in the passage are a few valuable nuggets. Follow these steps to hit pay dirt and avoid the fool's gold.

Reading About Reading

Reading seems to be a natural process. Reading about reading and about steps to taking reading tests can seem contrived and confusing. However, we know that these steps and techniques work. Once you apply the steps to the practice exercises, your reading ability and scores will improve.

Five Steps To Taking A Reading Test

During a reading test follow these steps.

1. Skim to find the topic of each paragraph.
2. Read the questions and answers.
3. Determine what the question is really asking.
4. Eliminate incorrect answers.
5. Scan the details to find the answer.

1. SKIM TO FIND THE TOPIC OF EACH PARAGRAPH

Your first job is to find the topic of each paragraph. The topic is what a paragraph or passage is about.

The topic of a paragraph is usually found in the first and last sentences. Read the first and last sentences just enough to find the topic. You can write the topic in the margin next to the passage. Remember, the test booklet is yours. You can mark it up as much as you like.

Reading Sentences

Every sentence has a subject that tells what the sentence is about. The sentence also has a verb that tells what the subject is doing or links the subject to the complement. The sentence may also contain a complement that receives the action or describes what is being said about the subject. The words underlined in the following examples are the ones you would focus on as you preview.

1. The famous educator <u>John Dewey founded</u> an educational movement called <u>progressive education.</u>
2. Sad to say, we have learned <u>American school children</u> of all ages <u>are poorly nourished.</u>

You may occasionally encounter a paragraph or passage in which the topic can't be summarized from the first and last sentences. This type of paragraph usually contains factual information. If this happens, you will have to read the entire paragraph.

2. READ THE QUESTIONS AND THE ANSWERS

Now read the questions—one at a time. Read the answers for the question you are working on. Be sure that you understand what each question and its answer, mean.

3. DETERMINE WHAT THE QUESTION IS REALLY ASKING

Summarize the essense of the question to help identify the correct answer choice.

Before you answer a question, be sure you know whether it is asking for a fact or an inference. If the question asks for a fact, the correct answer will identify a main idea or supporting detail. We'll discuss more about main ideas and details later. The correct answer may also identify a cause-and-effect relationship among ideas or be a paraphrase or summary of parts of the passage. Look for these.

If the question asks for an inference, the correct answer will identify the author's purpose, assumptions, or attitude and the difference between fact and the author's opinion. Look for these elements.

4. ELIMINATE INCORRECT ANSWERS

Read the answers and eliminate the ones that you absolutely know are incorrect. Read the answers literally. If you know it's wrong, cross it off.

Distracters

Test writers try to fool you. They deliberately write incorrect answer choices designed to distract your attention from the correct answer choice. These distracters can be tempting and you should be aware of them as you take the LAST, the ATS-W, and the CST. Use them to help you eliminate incorrect answers.

There are four main types of distracters described below. You can frequently arrive at the correct answer by just eliminating incorrect answers.

Misstatement

This distracter occurs most commonly, and more often on the LAST than on the ATS-W or the CST. A misstatement distracter often looks like it came right from the passage. But it changes ever so slightly the meaning of the passage, turns words around, or uses words out of context. The slightest change from the original passage may make the answer choice incorrect.

Look at these examples.

Passage: The area near the coast had deciduous and evergreens. The evergreens included a live oak and some magnolia trees. The evergreens had crowded out the deciduous trees as time went on.

Here are some examples of misstatements about this passage that might be incorrect answer choices.

(A) The area near the ocean had both deciduous and evergreen trees.

This misstates the passage. The passage mentions only the coast and not an ocean.

(B) The area is crowded with deciduous and evergreen trees.

The word "crowded" is taken out of context because nothing in the passage indicates that the area was crowded with trees.

(C) The area near the coast had some magnolia trees that were deciduous.

All of these words are from the passage but they are "turned around" to completely misstate the passage.

Right Answer—Wrong Question

This distracter gives a correct answer from the passage, but not a correct one for the question you are trying to answer. This distracter appears on the LAST, ATS-W, and the CST.

Passage: The area near the coast had deciduous and evergreens. The evergreens included a live oak and some magnolia trees. The evergreens had crowded out the deciduous trees as time went on.

Question: What best describes the trees near the coast?

(A) A live oak and some magnolias.

This answer is directly from the passage. And it is the correct answer to "What are some of the evergreen trees near the coast?" But it does not answer the question above. It also does not answer the question "What evergreen trees are near the coast?" because the passage just says what the evergreens included. There may have been more.

Appealing Language

This distracter draws your attention because it has very appealing language or appears to be fundamentally true. This distracter appears on the LAST and the ATS-W, but is a particular favorite on the ATS-W and the CST.

Passage: Stan Gozeki is a physical education teacher with a very unruly student in the class. The student has refused to follow instructions and challenged authority many times in the past and school officials have indicated that if he continues in this way he may have to be removed from school.

1. Suddenly the student acts out and verbally challenges Mr. Gozeki's authority causing Mr. Gozeki to correctly

(A) use corporal punishment because this is an emergency case, and if Mr. Gozeki does not quiet the student down administrators may hear of the incident and the student may be suspended from school and forced to go home where there is no one to watch over him.

Everything in the answer choice after "use corporal punishment" is appealing language. The language seeks to make it seem that Mr. Gozeki is well motivated and is doing the right thing. But a teacher in New York may not employ corporal punishment and all of these words are just meant to distract.

Always—Never

This distracter uses extreme words such as "always" and "never." Appealing language can make an incorrect answer seem correct; always-never distracters can make a seemingly correct answer incorrect. If you can think of one exception, or if the answer is debatable, then the extreme answer choice is incorrect. Not every extreme answer choice is incorrect, but you should be aware when you see them. This distracter appears on the LAST, ATS-W, and the CST.

Passage: Stan Gozeki is a physical education teacher with a very unruly student in the class. The student has refused to follow instructions and challenged authority many times in the past and school officials have indicated that if he continues in this way he may have to be removed from school.

2. Mr. Gozeki discusses the student with the school guidance counselor and the counselor gives this appropriate advice:

(A) Never go in the locker room when this student is there.

That's unrealistic. There are just too many things that might cause Mr. Gozeki to go into the locker room when the student is in there. This extreme answer is incorrect. A correct choice might be "Do your best not to go into the locker room when this student is there."

5. SCAN THE DETAILS TO FIND THE ANSWER

Once you have eliminated incorrect answers, compare the other answers to the passage. When you find the answer that is confirmed by the passage—stop. That is your answer choice. Follow these other suggestions for finding the correct answer.

You will often need to read details to find the main idea of a paragraph. The main idea of a paragraph is what the writer has to say about the topic. Most questions are about the main idea of a paragraph. Scan the details about the main idea until you find the answer. Scanning means skipping over information that does not answer the question.

Look at this paragraph.

There are many types of boats. Some are very fast while others could sleep a whole platoon of soldiers. I prefer the old putt-putt fishing boat with a ten-horsepower motor. That was a boat with a purpose. You didn't scare many people, but the fish were sure worried.

The topic of this paragraph is boats. The main idea is that the writer prefers small fishing boats to other boats.

Some Answers Are Not Related to the Main Idea

Some answers are not related to the main idea of a paragraph. These questions may be the most difficult to answer. You just have to keep scanning the details until you find the correct answer.

Who Wrote This Answer?

People who write tests go to great lengths to choose a correct answer that cannot be questioned. That is what they get paid for. They are not paid to write answers that have a higher meaning or include great truths.

Test writers want to be asked to write questions and answers again. They want to avoid valid complaints from test takers like you who raise legitimate concerns about their answers.

They usually accomplish this difficult task in one of two ways. They may write answers that are very specific and based directly on the reading. They may also write correct answers that seem very vague.

A Vague Answer Can Be Correct

How can a person write a vague answer that is correct? Think of it this way. If I wrote that a person is 6 feet 5 inches tall, you could get out a tape measure to check my facts. Since I was very specific, you are more likely to be able to prove me wrong.

On the other hand, if I write that the same person is over 6 feet tall you would be hard pressed to find fault with my statement. So my vague statement was hard to argue with. If the person in question is near 6 feet 5 inches tall, then my vague answer is most likely to be the correct one.

TIP

Don't choose an answer just because it seems more detailed or specific. A vague answer may be just as likely to be correct.

Applying the Steps

Let's apply the five steps to this passage and question.

Many vocational high schools in the United States give off-site work experience to their students. Students usually work in local businesses part of the school day and attend high school the other part. These programs have made American vocational schools world leaders in making job experience available to teenage students.

1. According to this paragraph, American vocational high schools are world leaders in making job experience available to teenage students because they

   (A) have students attend school only part of the day.
   (B) were quick to move their students to schools off-site.
   (C) require students to work before they can attend the school.
   (D) involve their students in cooperative education programs.

Step 1: Skim to find the topic of each paragraph. Both the first and last sentences tell us that the topic is vocational schools and work experience.

Step 2: Read the questions and answers.

Step 3: Determine what the question is really asking. Why are American vocational education high schools the world leaders in offering job experience?

Step 4: Eliminate incorrect answers. Answer (C) is obviously wrong. It has to do with work before high school. Answer (B) is also incorrect. This has to do with attending school off-site. This leaves answers (A) and (D).

Step 5: Scan the details to find the answer. Scan the details and find that only parts of answer (A) are found in the passage. In the correct answer (D), note that cooperative education is another name for off-site work during school.

Here's how to apply the steps to the following passage.

Problem Solving

Problem solving has become the main focus of mathematics learning. Students learn problem-solving strategies and then apply them to problems. Many tests now focus on problem solving and limit the number of computational problems. The problem-solving movement is traced to George Polya who wrote several problem-solving books for high school teachers.

Problem Solving Strategies

Problem-solving strategies include guess and check, draw a diagram, and make a list. Many of the strategies are taught as skills, which inhibits flexible and creative thinking. Problems in textbooks can also limit the power of the strategies. However, the problem-solving movement will be with us for some time, and a number of the strategies are useful.

Step 1: Skim to find the topic of each paragraph. The topic of the first paragraph is problem solving. You find the topic in both the first and last sentences. Write the topic next to the paragraph. The topic for the second paragraph is problem-solving strategies. You can write the topic next to each paragraph.

Now we are ready to look at the question. If the question is about problem solving "in general" we start looking in the first paragraph for the answer. If the question is about strategies, we start looking in the second paragraph for the answer.

Step 2: Read the questions and answers.

1. According to this passage, a difficulty with teaching problem-solving strategies is:

    (A) The strategies are too difficult for children.
    (B) The strategies are taught as skills.
    (C) The strategies are in textbooks.
    (D) The strategies are part of a movement.

Step 3: Determine what the question is really asking. The question is asking you to find a difficulty teaching problem-solving strategies.

Step 4: Eliminate incorrect answers. Answer (A) can't be right because difficulty is not mentioned in the passage. That leaves (B), (C), and (D) for us to consider.

Step 5: Scan the details to find the answer. The question asks about strategies so we look immediately to the second paragraph for the answer. The correct answer is (B). Choice (C) is not correct because the passage does not mention strategies in textbooks. There is no indication that (D) is correct.

Try Them Out

The following passages test your abilities to answer the different types of reading comprehension questions. You will probably see completely different questions on the PPST you take.

Remember that you are looking for the best answer from among the ones listed, even if you can think of a better answer. The answer must be supported by the passage. Do not pick an answer choice just because it is true or because you agree with it.

Apply the five steps. Do not look back to remind yourself what question type it is. Do not look ahead at the answers. Looking ahead at the answers will deny you important experiences, and it may well hurt your performance.

Cross off the answers you know are incorrect. Circle the answer. The correct answers to these questions are found on pages 102–112. Do not look at the answers until you complete your work.

Directions: Read the following passage. After reading the passage, choose the best answer to each question from among the four choices. Answer all the questions following the passage on the basis of what is stated or implied in the passage.

Today's students have hand-held calculators that can graph one or even many equations. Students can even type in several equations and the calculator will "solve" them. This is the best way just to see a plotted graph quickly.

This is the worst way to learn about graphing and equations. The calculator can't tell the student anything about the process of graphing and does not teach them how to plot a graph.

Left to this electronic graphing process, students will not have the hands-on experience patterns needed to see the patterns and symmetry that characterize graphing and equations. They may become too dependent on the calculator and be unable to reason effectively about equations and the process of graphing.

It may be true that graphing and solving equations is taught mechanically in some classrooms. There is also something to be said for these electronic devices, which give students the opportunity to try out several graphs and solutions quickly before deciding on a final solution.

For all their electronic accuracy and patience, these graphing calculators cannot replace the process of graphing and solving equations on your own. For mastery of equations and graphing comes not just from seeing the graph automatically displayed on a screen; it also comes from a hands-on involvement with graphing.

1. The main idea of the passage is that

   (A) a child can be good at graphing equations only through hands-on experience.
   (B) teaching approaches for graphing equations should be improved.
   (C) accuracy and patience are the keys to effective graphing instruction.
   (D) the new graphing calculators have limited ability to teach students about graphing.

2. According to this passage, what negative impact will graphing calculators have on students who use them?

   (A) They will not have experience with four-function calculators.
   (B) They will become too dependent on the calculator.
   (C) They can quickly try out several graphs before coming up with a final answer.
   (D) They will get too much hands-on experience with calculators.

3. According to the passage, which of the following is a major drawback of the graphing calculator?

   (A) It graphs too many equations with their solutions.
   (B) It does not give students hands-on experience with graphing.
   (C) It does not give students hands-on experience with calculators.
   (D) This electronic method interferes with the mechanical method.

4. The passage includes information that would answer which of the following questions?

   (A) What are the shortcomings of graphing and solving equations as it sometimes takes place?
   (B) How many equations can you type into a graphing calculator?
   (C) What hands-on experience should students have as they learn about graphing equations?
   (D) What is the degree of accuracy and speed that can be attained by a graphing calculator?

5. The description of a graphing calculator found in this passage tells about which of the following?

   I. The equations that can be graphed
   II. The approximate size of the calculator
   III. The advantages of the graphing calculator

   (A) I only
   (B) II only
   (C) I and II only
   (D) II and III only

Use this passage to answer items 6–9.

> On July 2, 1937 during her famed journey across
> the Pacific Ocean to complete flying around the
> world, noted aviator Amelia Earhart disappeared.
> *Line* Speculation remains about the cause and validity of
> (5) her elusive disappearance. Earhart's whereabouts
> remain a mystery. As one of the first female aviators
> to attempt an around-the-world flight, Earhart
> solidified her reputation as one of the most daring
> women of her day. She achieved a series of
> (10) record-breaking flights, such as surpassing the
> women's altitude record of 14,000 feet (4.3 km) in 1922
> and venturing solo across the Atlantic Ocean
> in 1932. This trailblazer not only paved the way
> for women aviators but advocated independence,
> (15) self-reliance, and equal rights for all women.
>
> Billed as the First Lady of the Air or Lady Lindy
> (Charles A. Lindbergh's female counterpart),
> Earhart challenged gender barriers. She influenced
> women's position in the nascent aviation industry.
> (20) She was a founding member and president of the
> Ninety-Nines, an international organization of
> women pilots. In 1932 after completing her solo
> flight across the Atlantic Ocean, President Herbert
> Hoover presented Earhart with the National
> (25) Geographic Society's gold medal, an honor never
> before bestowed on a woman. She was also the
> first woman to receive the National Aeronautical
> Association's honorary membership.

6. Which of the following is most likely an assumption made by the author of the paragraph?

   (A) Amelia Earhart was an American spy captured by Japanese forces.
   (B) Charles Lindbergh would not have disappeared had he been the pilot on this mission.

(C) Amelia Earhart's daring nature caused her to crash on her flight.
(D) Amelia Earhart may not have died when she disappeared.

7. Which of the following statements, if added to the passage, would weaken the author's statement that Amelia Earhart's whereabouts are unknown?

(A) A strong storm was reported by a ship along the flight route that Amelia Earhart was following.
(B) The last person to see Amelia Earhart's plane reported that the plane seemed very heavy as it lifted off.
(C) A search pilot reported signs of recent human habitation on a deserted island along the flight route that Amelia Earhart took.
(D) Further research on the radio in Amelia Earhart's plane revealed that all the radios in that version of the Lockheed Vega often failed.

8. The author's attitude toward Amelia Earhart can best be described as

(A) condescending.
(B) reverential.
(C) unsettled.
(D) abhorrent.

9. This passage indicates that Earhart would most likely have agreed with which of the following?

(A) Good planning is the secret to any successful endeavor.
(B) Experience is the quality most likely to serve you well in times of trouble.
(C) Life is full of unexpected events and outcomes.
(D) The recognition of America's leaders is the best reward for effort.

Use this passage to answer items 10–16.

    Thousands of different types of rocks and minerals
    have been found on Earth. Most rocks on the planet's
    surface formed from only eight elements (oxygen,
Line silicon, aluminum, iron, magnesium, calcium, potassium,
(5) and sodium). However, these elements combined in a number
    of ways to make rocks that are very different.

    Rocks are continually changing. Wind and water wear
    them down and carry bits of rock away. The tiny particles
    accumulate in a lake or ocean and harden into rock again.
(10) Scientists say the oldest rock ever found is more than
    3.9 billion years old. Earth itself is at least 4.5 billion
    years old. However, rocks from the beginning of Earth's history
    have changed so much from their original form that they
    have become new kinds of rock.

(15) Rock-forming and rock-destroying processes have been active for billions of years. Today in the Guadalupe Mountains of western Texas, you can find limestone, a sedimentary rock, that was a coral reef in a tropical sea about 250 million years ago. Half Dome in Yosemite
(20) Valley, California, which is about 8,800 feet (2.7 km) above sea level, is composed of quartz monzonite, an igneous rock that solidified several thousand feet within Earth. A simple rock collection captures the enormous sweep of the history of our planet.

10. What is the main purpose of this passage?

    (A) To provide information that rocks are continually changing
    (B) To emphasize that Earth is made of rock from areas as diverse as the tallest mountains and the floor of the deepest ocean
    (C) To examine the thousands of different types of rocks and minerals that have been found on Earth
    (D) To prove that in a simple rock collection containing a few dozen samples, one can capture an enormous sweep of the history of our planet and the processes that formed it

11. Which of the following words or phrases is the best substitute for the word "accumulate" in Line 9?

    (A) disperse
    (B) renew
    (C) break down
    (D) gather

12. According to the passage, most rocks at Earth's surface are formed from

    (A) oxygen, silicon, calcium, and potassium.
    (B) aluminum, iron, and magnesium.
    (C) one of eight elements.
    (D) elements combined in a number of ways.

13. Why does the author mention that rocks are continually changing?

    (A) To make the reading more technical
    (B) To provide a visual description
    (C) To provide the reader with a physical description of rocks
    (D) To provide information to the reader as to why all rocks look different

14. Which of the following is the best description of the organization of this passage?

    (A) An overall description is followed by some specific examples.
    (B) A discussion of one topic ends with a discussion of an entirely different topic.
    (C) Specific examples are given, followed by an explanation of those examples.
    (D) A significant question is raised, followed by possible answers to that question.

15. What can be reasonably inferred from the passage? That the author

    (A) believes only what he or she can personally observe.
    (B) is open to accepting theories presented by others. —
    (C) believes science is a mixture of fact and fiction.
    (D) knows how Earth itself was created.

16. Which of the following statements from the paragraph is *most* convincingly an opinion as opposed to a fact?

    (A) A simple rock collection captures the enormous sweep of the history of our planet.
    (B) Thousands of different types of rocks and minerals have been found on Earth.
    (C) Today in the Guadalupe Mountains of western Texas, you can find limestone, a sedimentary rock, that was a coral reef in a tropical sea about 250 million years ago.
    (D) Wind and water wear them down and carry bits of rock away. The tiny particles accumulate in a lake or ocean and harden into rock again.

Use this passage to answer item 17.

The potential for instruction provided by cable in the classroom is eclipsed by the number of educational practitioners who remain uninformed

Line about the concept or who lack proficiency in the

(5) use of protocols and strategies necessary to optimize its benefits. Teachers, trainers, and educational administrators nationwide would benefit from structured opportunities, rather than trial and error, to learn how to maximize

(10) the potential of the medium. Cable in the classroom can introduce real events into instruction by reporting the news from a perspective with which young people are familiar. Broadcasts received by television

(15) satellite can present issues as opportunities in which young people can play an active role rather than as overwhelming problems no one can solve. By incorporating current events and televised symposia, learners are exposed to

(20) perspectives beyond their teachers' own views and can explore truth without sensationalism or condescension. Cable television access to the classroom thus allows learners to make informed judgments about the content under study.

17. Which of the following conclusions can be reasonably drawn from this passage?

    (A) The potential for television in the classroom is more important than the opposition against it.
    (B) A lack of understanding of appropriate strategies is the reason cable in the classroom has not been fully implemented.
    (C) The reason cable in the classroom has not been accepted goes beyond being informed about this instructional tool.
    (D) Cable in the classroom ensures that teachers' views will receive the appropriate attention.

Use this graph to answer item 18.

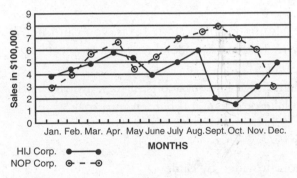

Sales for Two Companies During the Year

18. This graph *best* demonstrates which of the following?

    (A) NOP has more employees.
    (B) From August to September, the differences in sales grew by about $450,000.
    (C) In October, NOP had over $600,000 more in sales than HIJ.
    (D) In total, HIJ had more sales this year than NOP.

Use this picture to answer item 19.

19. Which of the following best describes the picture?

    (A) A brick plaza sweeping by open latticed rectangles
    (B) A surreal world visited by real people
    (C) A visitors center at a spaceport
    (D) A central spire framed by sphere, semicircle, and sky

Use this map to answer items 20–21.

Western cattle trails and railroads about 1875

20. Which cattle trail passes through the fewest states or territories?

    (A) Chisholm
    (B) Sedalia
    (C) Goodnight-Loving
    (D) Western Trail

21. If drovers move a herd of cattle about 25 kilometers per day, about how many days would it take to move a herd from Fort Smith to Sedalia on the Sedalia Trail?

    (A) 8
    (B) 16
    (C) 24
    (D) 32

22. At the shipping center, the coordinator is planning to send 87 cartons containing electronics equipment to Rochester, New York. The shipments will go in trucks specifically designed to carry the cartons containing these parts. Exactly

16 cartons will fit in each truck. What is the fewest number of trucks the coordinator can use to ship the cartons?

(A) 5
(B) 6
(C) 7
(D) 8

Practice Passage Answers

Don't read this section until you have completed the practice passage.

Here's how to apply the steps.

Step 1: Skim to find the topic of each paragraph. You may have written a topic next to each paragraph. Suggested topics are shown next to the following selection. Your topics don't have to be identical, but they should accurately reflect the paragraph's content.

Graphing Calculators

Today's students have hand-held calculators that can graph one or even many equations. Students can even type in several equations and the calculator will "solve" them. This is the best way to see a plotted graph quickly.

This is the worst way to learn about graphing and equations. The calculator can't tell the student anything about the process of graphing and does not teach them how to plot a graph.

Problem with Graphing Calculators

Left to this electronic graphing process, students will not have the hands-on experience needed to see the patterns and symmetry that characterize graphing and equations. They may become too dependent on the calculator and be unable to reason effectively about equations and the process of graphing.

It may be true that graphing and solving equations is taught mechanically in some classrooms. There is also something to be said for these electronic devices, which give students the opportunity to try out several graphs and solutions quickly before deciding on a final solution.

Why its a Problem

For all their electronic accuracy and patience, these graphing calculators cannot replace the process of graphing and solving equations on your own. For mastery of equations and graphing comes not just from seeing the graph automatically displayed on a screen; it also comes from a hands-on involvement with graphing.

Good Points

Apply Steps 2 through 5 to each of the questions.

1. The main idea of the passage is that

   (A) a child can be good at graphing equations only through hands-on experience.
   (B) teaching approaches for graphing equations should be improved.

(C) accuracy and patience are the keys to effective graphing instruction.

(D) the new graphing calculators have limited ability to teach students about graphing.

Step 2: Read the question and answers.

Step 3: Determine what the question is really asking. You have to identify the main idea of the passage. This is a very common question on reading tests. Remember that the main idea is what the writer is trying to say or communicate in the passage.

Step 4: Eliminate incorrect answers. Answers (B) and (C) are not correct. Answer (C) is not at all correct based on the passage. Even though (B) may be true, it does not reflect what the writer is trying to say in this passage.

Step 5: Scan the details to find the answer. As we review the details we see that both answer (A) and answer (D) are both stated or implied in the passage. A scan of the details, alone, does not reveal which is the main idea. We must determine that on our own.

2. According to this passage, what negative impact will graphing calculators have on students who use them?

(A) They will not have experience with four-function calculators.

(B) They will become too dependent on the calculator.

(C) They can quickly try out several graphs before coming up with a final answer.

(D) They will get too much hands-on experience with calculators.

Step 2: Read the questions and answers.

Step 3: Determine what the question is really asking. This is a straightforward comprehension question. What negative impact will calculators have on students who use them? The second and third paragraphs have topics related to problems with calculators. We'll probably find the answer there.

Step 4: Eliminate incorrect answers. Answer (C) is not a negative impact of graphing calculators. Scan the details to find the correct answer from (A), (B), and (D).

Step 5: Scan the details to find the answer. The only detail that matches the question is in paragraph 3. The authors says that students may become too dependent on the calculators. That's our answer.

3. According to the passage, which of the following is a major drawback of the graphing calculator?

(A) It graphs too many equations with their solutions.

(B) It does not give students hands-on experience with graphing.

(C) It does not give students hands-on experience with calculators.

(D) This electronic method interferes with the mechanical method.

Step 2: Read the question and answers.

Step 3: Determine what the question is really asking. This is another straightforward comprehension question. This question is somewhat different from Question 2. Notice that the question asks for a drawback of the calculator. It does not ask for something that is wrong with the calculator itself. The topics indicate that we will probably find the answer in paragraph 1 or paragraph 2.

Step 4: Eliminate incorrect answers. Answer (C) is obviously wrong. Graphing calculators do give students hands-on experience with calculators. Be careful! It is easy to mix up (C) and (B). Answer (A) is a strength of the calculator and is also incorrect. Let's move on to the details.

Step 5: Scan the details to find the answer. Choices (B) and (D) remain. The details in paragraph 2 reveal that the correct answer is (B).

4. The passage includes information that would answer which of the following questions?

   (A) What are the shortcomings of teaching about graphing equations as it sometimes takes place?
   (B) How many equations can you type into a graphing calculator?
   (C) What hands-on experience should students have as they learn about graphing equations?
   (D) What is the degree of accuracy and speed that can be attained by a graphing calculator?

Step 2: Read the question and answers.

Step 3: Determine what the question is really asking. This is yet another type of reading comprehension question. You are asked to identify the questions that could be answered from the passage.

Step 4: Eliminate incorrect answers. Choices (B) and (D) are not correct. None of this information is included in the passage. This is not to say that these questions are not important. Rather it means that the answers to these questions are not found in this passage.

Step 5: Scan the details to find the answer. Both (A) and (C) are discussed in the passage. However, a scan of the details reveals that the answer to (C) is not found in the passage. The passage mentions hands-on experience, but it does not mention what types of hands-on experience students should have. There is an answer for (A). Graphing is taught mechanically in some classrooms.

5. The description of a graphing calculator found in this passage tells about which of the following?

   I. The equations that can be graphed
   II. The approximate size of the calculator
   III. The advantages of the graphing calculator

   (A) I only
   (B) II only
   (C) I and II only
   (D) II and III only

Step 2: Read the question and answers.

Step 3: Determine what the question is really asking. This is another classic type of reading comprehension question. You are given several choices. You must decide which combination of these choices is the absolutely correct answer.

Step 4: Eliminate incorrect answers. If you can determine that Statement I, for example, is not addressed in the passage, you can eliminate ALL answer choices that include Statement I.

Step 5: Scan the details to find which of the original three statements are true.

  I. No, there is no description of which equations can be graphed.
 II. Yes, paragraph 1 mentions that the calculators are hand-held.
III. Yes, paragraph 4 mentions the advantages.

Both II and III are correct.

Answers to items 6–9. Refer to passage on page 96.

6. Which of the following is most likely an assumption made by the author of the paragraph?

   (A) Amelia Earhart was an American spy captured by Japanese forces.
   (B) Charles Lindbergh would not have disappeared had he been the pilot on this mission.
   (C) Amelia Earhart's daring nature caused her to crash on her flight.
   (D) Amelia Earhart may not have died when she disappeared.

Step 2: Read the question and answers.

Step 3: Determine what the question is really asking. The correct answer will be an assumption reflected in the passage.

Step 4: Eliminate incorrect answers. Always try to eliminate at least one answer. Eliminate (A) because nothing in the passage discusses either the Japanese or American spies.

Step 5: Scan to find the answer. (D) is the correct answer. The author assumes that Amelia Earhart may not have died when she disappeared. The author never states it. However, the author questions the validity of Earhart's disappearance and calls her whereabouts a mystery. Eliminate choice (B) because nothing indicates anything about Lindbergh, except for Earhart's nickname. (C) is incorrect because nothing in the passage indicates any reason for her disappearance.

7. Which of the following statements, if added to the passage, would weaken the author's statement that Amelia Earhart's whereabouts are unknown?

   (A) A strong storm was reported by a ship along the flight route that Amelia Earhart was following.
   (B) The last person to see Amelia Earhart's plane reported that the plane seemed very heavy as it lifted off.
   (C) A search pilot reported signs of recent human habitation on a deserted island along the flight route that Amelia Earhart took.
   (D) Further research on the radio in Amelia Earhart's plane revealed that all the radios in that version of the Lockheed Vega often failed.

Step 2: Read the question and answers.

Step 3: Determine what the question is really asking. The correct answer will be the one that would weaken the author's argument that Amelia's whereabouts are unknown. Remember that weaken does not mean disprove. This is a question about evaluating supporting details.

Step 4: Eliminate incorrect answers. Eliminate (B) and (D) because each contains information about why her plane may have encountered trouble but not about her whereabouts.

Step 5: Scan to find the answer. The reports of human habitation on a deserted island choice (C), is the only statement that would weaken that argument, although it would not by itself disprove the statement. The other statements are incorrect. Choice (A) a strong storm, choice (B) a heavy plane, and choice (D) a malfunctioning radio do not provide any information about her whereabouts. Do not be tempted by the specific information about Earhart's plane found in choice (D).

8. The author's attitude toward Amelia Earhart can best be described as

   (A) condescending.
   (B) reverential.
   (C) unsettled.
   (D) abhorrent.

Step 2: Read the question and answers.

Step 3: Determine what the question is really asking. The correct answer will be the one that best describes how the author feels about Amelia Earhart.

Step 4: Eliminate incorrect answers. Eliminate (D) abhorrent. It is a negative word, and the author has a very positive attitude toward Amelia Earhart.

Step 5: Scan to find the answer. Choice (B) is correct. Reverential means to honor and respect, which is obviously how the author feels toward Earhart. Choice (A) is incorrect because condescending means to look down on. Choice (C) is incorrect because the author was settled in his opinion of Amelia Earhart. Abhorrent means to have strong negative feelings.

9. This passage indicates that Earhart would most likely have agreed with which of the following?

   (A) Good planning is the secret to any successful endeavor.
   (B) Experience is the quality most likely to serve you well in times of trouble.
   (C) Life is full of unexpected events and outcomes.
   (D) The recognition of America's leaders is the best reward for effort.

Step 2: Read the question and answers. You have to identify what Amelia Earhart would have probably said.

Step 3: Determine what the question is really asking. The correct answer is the one that correctly predicts what Earhart would have probably said.

Step 4: Eliminate incorrect answers. Eliminate (D) because this passage is mainly about Earhart's disappearance, not about recognition or rewards.

Step 5: Scan to find the answer. Choice (C) is correct. This passage is about Amelia's disappearance. If she were able to draw anything from that today, it would be the uncertainty of life. The other choices, (A) and (B), are incorrect because none of them meant anything on that fateful day that she likely crashed into the Pacific Ocean.

Answers to items 10–16. Refer to passage on page 97.

10. What is the main purpose of this passage?

    (A) To provide information that rocks are continually changing
    (B) To emphasize that Earth is made of rock from areas as diverse as the tallest mountains and the floor of the deepest ocean
    (C) To examine the thousands of different types of rocks and minerals that have been found on Earth
    (D) To prove that in a simple rock collection containing a few dozen samples, one can capture an enormous sweep of the history of our planet and the processes that formed it

Step 2: Read the question and answers.

Step 3: Determine what the question is really asking. The correct answer will best summarize passage. Why did the author write it? You can save lots of time by reading the questions and answer choices before reading the passage.

Step 4: Eliminate incorrect answers. Answer (D) is clearly wrong. The main purpose is not about rock collections. You might be able to eliminate more, but you can be sure of this one. If you had to guess, eliminating just this one answer would increase the odds that you will guess correctly.

Step 5: Scan to find the answer. The answer to this question is (C) because most of the passage describes that thousands of different types of rocks and minerals have been found on Earth. (A) is incorrect because the passage was not written primarily to discuss that rocks continually change. (B) is incorrect because it states facts found in the passage that are too detailed to be the main purpose.

11. Which of the following words or phrases is the best substitute for the word "accumulate" in Line 9?

    (A) disperse
    (B) renew
    (C) break down
    (D) gather

Step 2: Read the question and answers.

Step 3: Determine what the question is really asking. The correct answer will be the choice that best defines the meaning of "accumulate" as used in this passage.

Step 4: Eliminate incorrect answers. Eliminate (C) because "accumulate" does not mean "break down."

Step 5: Scan to find the answer. (D) is the correct answer. If you accumulate something you gather it. You can actually tell from the context that (A) is incorrect because disperse means the opposite of accumulate. Disperse is an antonym. (B) is incorrect because bits of rock do not renew themselves. Instead, they combine with other bits of rock.

12. According to the passage, most rocks at Earth's surface are formed from

     (A) oxygen, silicon, calcium, and potassium.
     (B) aluminum, iron, and magnesium.
     (C) one of eight elements.
     (D) elements combined in a number of ways.

Step 2: Read the question and answers.

Step 3: Determine what the question is really asking. Look in the details to find which elements are mentioned.

Step 4: Eliminate incorrect answers. Eliminate (A) and (B) because each of them is just a partial list of the elements that form most rocks. Correctly eliminating two choices means you would have a 50 percent chance of guessing correctly instead of a 25 percent chance. That is a big difference if you had to guess.

Step 5: Scan to find the answer. The correct answer is (D) because the passage states that elements are combined in a number of ways to form rocks. (C) is incorrect because the passage says that rocks are a combination of elements.

13. Why does the author mention that rocks are continually changing?

     (A) To make the reading more technical
     (B) To provide a visual description
     (C) To provide the reader with a physical description of rocks
     (D) To provide information to the reader as to why all rocks look different

Step 2: Read the question and answers.

Step 3: Determine what the question is really asking. The correct answer will be the one that identifies why the author wrote that rocks are continually changing.

Step 4: Eliminate incorrect answers. Eliminate (A) because the author did not mention that rocks continually change in order to make the reading more technical. Eliminate (B) and (C) because the passage gives neither a visual nor a physical description of rocks.

Step 5: Scan to find the answer. (D) is the correct answer. First, all other choices were eliminated. Second, the author mentions that rocks are continually changing to explain why rocks look different.

14. Which of the following is the best description of the organization of this passage?

     (A) An overall description is followed by some specific examples.
     (B) A discussion of one topic ends with a discussion of an entirely different topic.
     (C) Specific examples are given, followed by an explanation of those examples.
     (D) A significant question is raised, followed by possible answers to that question.

Step 2: Read the question and answers.

Step 3: Determine what the question is really asking. The answer correctly summarizes the overall organization of the passage.

Step 4: Eliminate incorrect answers. Eliminate choice (D) because no significant question is raised in the passage.

Step 5: Scan to find the answer. Choice (A) is correct. The author writes about how rocks are formed and then discusses rocks formed deep in the planet or from a coral reef. (B) is incorrect because the last sentence mentions Earth's history, but the passage does not discuss Earth's history. (C) is incorrect because this is more or less the opposite of the actual structure of the passage.

15. What can be reasonably inferred from the passage? That the author

    (A) believes only what he or she can personally observe.
    (B) is open to accepting theories presented by others.
    (C) believes science is a mixture of fact and fiction.
    (D) knows how Earth itself was created.

Step 2: Read the question and answers.

Step 3: Determine what the question is really asking. The correct answer draws an inference from the passage.

Step 4: Eliminate incorrect answers. Eliminate (C) because nothing in passage suggests that science is a mixture of fact and fiction.

Step 5: Scan to find the answer. (B) is correct. In the second paragraph, the author presents a theory from other scientists about the age of rocks found on Earth. (A) is incorrect because most of what the author presents cannot be personally observed. (D) is incorrect because the author presents information about the age of rocks and the age of Earth but nothing about how the planet was formed.

16. Which of the following statements from the paragraph is *most* convincingly an opinion as opposed to a fact?

    (A) A simple rock collection captures the enormous sweep of the history of our planet.
    (B) Thousands of different types of rocks and minerals have been found on Earth.
    (C) Today in the Guadalupe Mountains of western Texas, you can find limestone, a sedimentary rock, that was a coral reef in a tropical sea about 250 million years ago.
    (D) Wind and water wear them down and carry bits of rock away. The tiny particles accumulate in a lake or ocean and harden into rock again.

Step 2: Read the question and answers.

Step 3: Determine what the question is really asking. The correct answer will be the choice that is an opinion.

Step 4: Eliminate incorrect answers. Eliminate the choices that are facts. Choices (B), (C), and (D) are all facts.

Step 5: Scan to find the answer. Choice (A) is the correct answer. It is clearly the author's opinion about a simple rock collection. (A) could never be proven either true or false.

Passage for item 17 is on page 99.

17. Which of the following conclusions can be reasonably drawn from this passage?

    (A) The potential for television in the classroom is more important than the opposition against it.
    (B) A lack of understanding of appropriate strategies is the reason cable in the classroom has not been fully implemented.
    (C) The reason cable in the classroom has not been accepted goes beyond being informed about this instructional tool.
    (D) Cable in the classroom ensures that teachers' views will receive the appropriate attention.

Step 2: Read the question and answers.

Step 3: Determine what the question is really asking. The correct answer is a conclusion that can be drawn from the passage.

Step 4: Eliminate incorrect answers. Eliminate (D) because the passage says learners will be exposed to "perspectives beyond their teachers' own views."

Step 5: Scan to find the answer. (C) is the correct answer. The first five lines in the passage mention both technical ability and familiarity as the reasons cable in the classroom has not been accepted. Use those two bits of information to draw the conclusion. (A) is incorrect because the beginning of the passage says the opposite—that acceptance of cable in the classroom is eclipsed by the number of practitioners who do not use it. (B) is incorrect because the passage mentions other reasons beyond strategies as why cable in the classroom has not been accepted.

Graph for item 18 is on page 100.

18. This graph *best* demonstrates which of the following?

    (A) NOP has more employees.
    (B) From August to September, the differences in sales grew by about $450,000.
    (C) In October, NOP had over $600,000 more in sales than HIJ.
    (D) In total, HIJ had more sales this year than NOP.

Step 2: Read the question and answers.

Step 3: Determine what the question is really asking. The correct answer best describes the graph. You have to use a little commonsense math to answer this question.

Step 4: Eliminate incorrect answers. Choice (A) is incorrect because the graph does not indicate the number of employees. Choice (C) is false because the graph shows that NOP had gross sales of about $700,000 and HIJ had gross sales of about $150,000 in October. $700,000 − $150,000 = $550,000. Choice (D) is false. The graph shows that NOP had higher sales every month except May. Since the difference in sales was so great during several months, such as September, October, and November, NOP clearly had higher sales during this year. No math is needed to eliminate (D).

Step 5: Scan to find the answer. Choice (B) must be right because all others were eliminated. In August, the difference in sales was about $750,000 – $600,000 = $150,000. The difference in September was about $800,000 – $200,000 = $600,000. To find the sales difference, subtract $600,000 – $150,000 = $450,000.

Picture for item 19 is on page 100.

19. Which of the following best describes the picture?

    (A) A brick plaza sweeping by open latticed rectangles
    (B) A surreal world visited by real people
    (C) A visitors center at a spaceport
    (D) A central spire framed by sphere, semicircle, and sky

Step 2: Read the question and answers.

Step 3: Determine what the question is really asking. The correct answer best describes the picture.

Step 4: Eliminate incorrect answers. Eliminate choices (A) and (B) right away. No bricks are evident anywhere, and nothing about the picture is surreal.

Step 5: (D) is the correct answer because it realistically describes the picture. There is some outside chance that this could be the visitors center at some futuristic spaceport (C). However, answer (D) is certainly the best answer.

Answers 20–21. Map is on page 101.

20. Which cattle trail passes through the fewest states or territories?

    (A) Chisholm
    (B) Sedalia
    (C) Goodnight-Loving
    (D) Western Trail

Step 2: Read the question and answers.

Step 3: Determine what the question is really asking. The correct answer is the trail that passes through the fewest states or territories.

Step 4: Eliminate incorrect answers.

Step 5: Scan to find the answer. List the trails and count the number of states or territories through which they pass. The Chisholm Trail, choice (A), passes through three states, Kansas, Oklahoma, and Texas. The Sedalia Trail, choice (B), passes through four states, Missouri, Arkansas, Oklahoma, and Texas. The Goodnight-Loving Trail, choice (C), passes through four states and territories, Wyoming, Colorado, New Mexico Territory, and Texas. The Western Trail, choice (D), passes through four states, Nebraska, Kansas, Oklahoma, and Texas. Since the question asks which trail passes through the fewest states or territories, the correct answer is (A), the Chisholm Trail.

21. If drovers move a herd of cattle about 25 kilometers per day, about how many days would it take to move a herd from Fort Smith to Sedalia on the Sedalia Trail?

(A) 8
(B) 16
(C) 24
(D) 32

Step 2: Read the question and answers.

Step 3: Determine what the question is really asking. The answer shows the number of days needed to drive the cattle from Fort Smith to Sedalia on the Sedalia Trail.

Step 4: Eliminate incorrect answers. No answer immediately seems either right or wrong.

Step 5: Scan to find the answer. Find Sedalia, Missouri and Fort Smith, Arkansas on the map. Estimate the distance in kilometers between those two places. On the bottom left of the map is a scale. Use the edge of a pencil measure the length between Sedalia and Fort Smith. Compare that length to the map scale. The two towns are about 400 kilometers apart. The question states that a herd of cattle can be driven about 25 kilometers per day. To find the number of days needed to drive the herd 400 kilometers, divide 400 by 25. The answer is 16 days. Choice (B) is correct.

22. At the shipping center, the coordinator is planning to send 87 cartons containing electronics equipment to Rochester, New York. The shipments will go in trucks specifically designed to carry the cartons containing these parts. Exactly 16 cartons will fit in each truck. What is the fewest number of trucks the coordinator can use to ship the cartons?

(A) 5
(B) 6
(C) 7
(D) 8

Step 2: Read the question and answers.

Step 3: Determine what the question is really asking. The correct answer is the minimum number of trucks required to ship the packages.

Step 4: Eliminate incorrect answers. Divide 87 by 16. Since the answer is between 5 and 6, eliminate choices (C) and (D).

Step 5: Scan to find the answer. Choice (B) is the correct answer because 87 divided by 16 is 5 with a remainder of 7. If 5 trucks are filled with 16 cartons each, another truck is needed to carry the other 7 cartons. That means the smallest number of trucks needed to ship 87 cartons is 6.

Writing

Nouns and Verbs

The better you write, the higher your essays will score. Know the different types of nouns and verbs. Learn how to use them properly.

Use Nouns Correctly

Nouns name a person, place, thing, characteristic, or concept. Nouns give a name to everything that is, has been, or will be. Here are some simple examples.

Person	Place	Thing	Characteristic	Concept (Idea)
Abe Lincoln	Lincoln Memorial	beard	mystery	freedom
judge	courthouse	gavel	fairness	justice
professor	college	chalkboard	intelligence	number

SINGULAR AND PLURAL NOUNS

Singular nouns refer to only one thing. Plural forms refer to more than one thing. Plurals are usually formed by adding an *s* or dropping a *y* and adding *ies*. Here are some examples.

Singular	Plural
college	colleges
professor	professors
Lincoln Memorial	Lincoln Memorials
mystery	mysteries

Possessive Nouns

Possessive nouns show that the noun possesses a thing or a characteristic. Make a singular noun possessive by adding *'s*. Here are some examples.

> The *child's* sled was in the garage ready for use.
> The *school's* mascot was loose again.
> The rain interfered with *Jane's* vacation.
> *Ron's* and *Doug's* fathers were born in the same year.
> Ron and *Doug's* teacher kept them after school.

Make a singular noun ending in *s* possessive by adding *'s* unless the pronunciation is too difficult.

> The teacher read *James's* paper several times.
> The angler grabbed the *bass'* fin.

Make a plural noun possessive by adding an apostrophe (') only.

> The *principals'* meeting was delayed.
> The report indicated that *students'* scores had declined.

Use Verbs Correctly

Some verbs are action verbs. Other verbs are linking verbs that link the subject to words that describe it. Here are some examples.

Action Verbs	Linking Verbs
Blaire *runs* down the street.	Blaire *is* tired.
Blaire *told* her story.	The class *was* bored.
The crowd *roared*.	The players *were* inspired.
The old ship *rusted*.	It *had been* a proud ship.

TENSE

A verb has three principal tenses: present tense, past tense, and future tense. The present tense shows that the action is happening now. The past tense shows that the action happened in the past. The future tense shows that something will happen. Here are some examples.

Present:	I *enjoy* my time off.
Past:	I *enjoyed* my time off.
Future:	I *will enjoy* my time off.

Present:	I *hate* working late.
Past:	I *hated* working late.
Future:	I *will hate* working late.

Agreement

Each pronoun must agree in number (singular or plural) and gender (male or female) with the noun it refers to. Here are some examples.

1. *Nonagreement in Number*

    The children played all day, and *she* came in exhausted.
    [*Children* is plural, but *she* is singular.]

    The child picked up the hat and brought *them* into the house.
    [*Child* is singular, but *them* is plural.]

2. *Agreement*

    The children played all day, and *they* came in exhausted.

    The child picked up the hat and brought *it* into the house.

3. *Nonagreement in Gender*

    The lioness picked up *his* cub. [*Lioness* is female, and *his* is male.]

    A child must bring in a doctor's note before *she* comes to school.
    [The child may be a male or female but *she* is female.]

4. *Agreement*

    The lioness picked up *her* cub.

    A child must bring in a doctor's note before *he* or *she* comes to school.

Be Sure Subjects and Verbs Agree

Singular and Plural

Singular nouns take singular verbs. Plural nouns take plural verbs. Singular verbs usually end in *s*, and plural verbs usually do not. Here are some examples.

Singular:	My father wants me home early.
Plural:	My parents want me home early.

Singular:	Ryan runs a mile each day.
Plural:	Ryan and Chad run a mile each day.

Singular:	She tries her best to do a good job.
Plural:	Liz and Ann try their best to do a good job.

Correctly Identify Subject and Verb

The subject may not be in front of the verb. In fact, the subject may not be anywhere near the verb. Say the subject and the verb to yourself. If it makes sense, you probably have it right.

1. Words may come between the subject and the verb.

    Chad's final exam score, which he showed to his mother, improved his final grade.

    - The verb is *improved.* The word *mother* appears just before improved.
    - Is this the subject? Say it to yourself. [Mother improved the grade.]
    - That can't be right. Score must be the subject. Say it to yourself. [Score improved the grade.] That's right. *Score* is the subject, and *improved* is the verb.

        The racer running with a sore arm finished first.

    - Say it to yourself. [Racer finished first.] *Racer* is the noun, and *finished* is the verb.
    - It wouldn't make any sense to say the arm finished first.

2. The verb may come before the subject.

    Over the river and through the woods romps the merry leprechaun.

    - *Leprechaun* is the subject, and *romps* is the verb.
      [Think: Leprechaun romps.]

        Where are the car keys?

    - *Keys* is the subject, and *are* is the verb. [Think: The car keys are where?]

Examples of Subject-Verb Agreement

Words such as *each, neither, everyone, nobody, someone,* and *anyone* are singular pronouns. They always take a singular verb.

Everyone *needs* a good laugh now and then.

Nobody *knows* more about computers than Bob.

Words that refer to number such as *one-half, any, most,* and *some* can be singular or plural.

One-fifth of the students *were* absent. [*Students* is plural.]

One-fifth of the cake *was* eaten. [There is only one cake.]

Sentences

Complete sentences contain both a subject and a verb. If either is missing, you have written a sentence fragment. Additionally, the ideas within each sentence must be in parallel form.

Avoid Sentence Fragments

English sentences require a subject and a verb. Fragments are parts of sentences written as though they were sentences. Fragments are writing mistakes that lack a subject, a predicate, or both subject and predicate. Here are some examples.

Since when.

To enjoy the summer months.

Because he isn't working hard.

If you can fix old cars.

What the principal wanted to hear.

Include a subject and/or a verb to rewrite a fragment as a sentence.

Fragment	Sentence
Should be coming up the driveway now.	The *car* should be coming up the driveway now.
Both the lawyer and her client.	Both the lawyer and her client *waited* in court.
Which is my favorite subject.	I *took math*, which is my favorite subject.
If you can play.	If you can play, *you'll improve with practice.*

Verbs such as *to be, to go, winning, starring,* etc., need a main verb.

Fragment	Sentence
The new rules to go into effect in April.	The new rules *will* go into effect in April.
The team winning every game.	The team *was* winning every game.

Often, a fragment is related to a complete sentence. Combine the two to make a single sentence.

Fragment:	Reni loved vegetables. *Particularly corn, celery, lettuce, squash, and eggplant.*
Revised:	Reni loved vegetables, particularly corn, celery, lettuce, squash, and eggplant.

Fragment:	*To see people standing on Mars.* This could happen in the 21st century.
Revised:	To see people standing on Mars is one of the things that could happen in the 21st century.

Sometimes short fragments can be used for emphasis. However, you should not use fragments in your essay. Here are some examples.

Stop! Don't take one more step toward that apple pie.
I need some time to myself. *That's why.*

Use Parallel Form

When two or more ideas are connected, use a parallel structure. Parallelism helps the reader follow the passage more clearly. Here are some examples.

Not Parallel:	Toni stayed in shape by eating right and exercising daily.
Parallel:	Toni stayed in shape by eating right and *by* exercising daily.

Not Parallel:	Lisa is a student who works hard and has genuine insight.
Parallel:	Lisa is a student who works hard and *who* has genuine insight.

Not Parallel:	Art had a choice either to clean his room or take out the garbage.
Parallel:	Art had a choice either to clean his room or *to* take out the garbage.

Not Parallel:	Derek wanted a success rather than failing.
Parallel:	Derek wanted a success rather than a failure.
Parallel:	Derek wanted success rather than failure.

Steps for Writing Passing Essays

Follow these steps to write a passing essay. You should allow about an hour to complete all the steps. The time estimates below are approximate.

1. **Understand the assignment. (2 minutes)**
   Each topic provides a subject and then describes the subject in more detail. Read the topic carefully to ensure that you understand each of these parts.

2. **Choose thesis statement. Write it down. (3 minutes)**
   Readers expect you to have one clear main point of view about the topic. Choose yours; make sure it addresses the entire topic, and stick to it.

3. **Write an outline. (10 minutes)**

Write a brief outline summarizing the following essay elements.

- Thesis statement
- Introduction
- Topic sentence and details for each paragraph
- Conclusion

Use this time to plan your essay.

4. **Write the assignment. (40 minutes)**
Essays scoring 2 or 3 typically have five, six, or seven paragraphs totaling 300–600 words. Writing an essay this long does not guarantee a passing score, but most passing essays are about this long.
Use this time to write well.

5. **Proofread and edit your writing. (5 minutes)**
Read your essay over and correct any errors in usage, spelling, or punctuation. The readers understand that your essay is a first draft and they expect to see corrections.

Constructed-Response Assignment

Here's how to apply these steps for a particular constructed response. Follow along and write in your own ideas when called for. Remember, for any written assignment, there are many different thesis statements and essays that would receive a passing score.

SAMPLE CONSTRUCTED RESPONSE

Overall, do machines help people or do machines cause difficulty for people, and what type of machine fits the category you choose? The information below presents both sides of this question.

Overall, machines help people. Machines have lessened the workload for mankind and have enabled workers to be more productive. Other machines help keep people healthier and sustain life. Still other machines make life easier at home and help people travel easily from one place to the other to visit loved ones. Does anyone really want to do away with machines and return to earlier times when humans were consumed with manual labor? There can be no doubt that, overall, machines help people and there are many examples of helpful machines.

Overall, machines cause difficulty for people. Just look at one of our favorite machines, the automobile. More than 40,000 people are killed in automobile accidents each year and hundreds of thousands more are seriously injured or completely disabled. Other machines fill the atmosphere with poisonous fumes and may well lead to the ultimate destruction of mankind when there is no oxygen left to breathe. Sure there are *some* helpful machines. But, there can be no doubt overall that machines cause difficulty for people, and there are very many examples of machines that cause difficulty for people.

Overall, do machines help people or do machines cause difficulty for people?

Review and evaluate the opposing positions presented above.

Choose one of these positions. Support your position with a specific example of a machine that helps people or a machine that causes difficulty.

Write an essay that supports your position following the guidelines presented above.

1. **Understand the assignment. (2 minutes)**

   The assignment is about machines. I have to decide whether to write about machines that cause difficulty for people OR about machines that help people. I have to give a specific example of a machine that is a difficulty or a machine that helps. It does not make any difference which one I pick.

   I've got to stick to this topic.

   I'm going to choose machines that help people.

   A complete response to the topic is an essay about a machine that helps people. There are many machines to choose from. An incomplete response will significantly lower the score.

2. **Choose thesis statement. Write it down. (3 minutes)**

   This important step sets the stage for your entire essay. Work through this section actively. Write down the names of several machines that help people. There is no one correct answer, so it does not have to be an exhaustive list.

   > Computers
   >
   > Escalator
   >
   > Car
   >
   > Heart-lung machine
   >
   > Fax machine

Suppose you choose the heart-lung machine.

Now write how, what, and why heart-lung machines help people.

How: Circulate blood in place of the heart?
What: Replaces the heart during heart surgery.
Why: The heart is unable to pump blood when it is being operated on.

Now write the choice from your list of machines. _____

Thesis statement

My thesis statement is "Overall, machines help people." A heart-lung machine is an example of a helpful machine. Heart-lung machines are machines that help people by taking the place of the heart during heart surgery.

The thesis statement establishes I have chosen the position that machines are helpful and the heart-lung machine is my example of a machine that helps people and explains the basis for my choice of the heart-lung machine. Both parts are needed for an effective thesis statement.

Write your thesis statement.

_____

3. **Write an outline. (10 minutes)**

   - Introduction, including the thesis statement

     _____

   - A heart-lung machine saves lives.
     People would die if the machines were not available.

   - The machine circulates and filters blood during operations.
     Special membranes filter the blood, removing impurities.

     _____

   - The heart can literally stop while the heart-lung machine is in use.
     Doctors have to restart the heart.

     _____

   - Conclusion

     Write an outline to plan your essay. Your outline consists of an introduction, topic sentences and supporting details for three paragraphs, and a conclusion. That's five paragraphs in all.

Write an outline for your constructed response.

_____

_____

_____

_____

_____

_____

_____

_____

_____

_____

_____

4. **Write the essay. (40 minutes)**

   I spent the time writing an outline to plan my essay. I am going to rely on that plan as I write my essay.

   Use a separate piece of paper.

   Write your own essay about the heart-lung machine—a machine that helps people.

5. **Proofread and edit your essay. (5 minutes)**

   Edit your essay. Remember that readers expect to see changes.

Check

You will find four rated sample essays on this topic on the following pages. Compare your essays to these sample essays. Rate your essay 1–4 using these samples and the scoring guide on page 17.

Practice

Write, proofread, and edit an essay on your topic. Rate your essay 1–4. Try to show your essays to an English professor or an experienced essay evaluator. Ask that person to evaluate your essays and make recommendations for improving your writing.

SAMPLE ESSAYS

ESSAY 1

This essay would likely receive a total score of 1–2 out of 8.

I think that machines are mostly helpful to people.

Look at the heart-lung machine which are a medical miracle. Heart lung machines are use in hospitals all over the country. Doctors use this machine while doing surgery. Heart lung machines keep people alive during surgery and they use them to do open heart surgery. Lots of people can than the heart lung machine for keeping them alive.

Some people say that their are too many bypass surgerys done every year and this may cause more problems than it fixes. However, lots of people would die without the machine. Its a good thing that the heart lung machine was invented.

ESSAY 2

This essay would likely receive a total score of 3 or 4 out of 8.

Overall, machines are mostly helpful to people. A heart lung machine is an example of a machine that helps.

Heart lung machines are use in hospitals all over the world. They get use every day. People are hook up to them when they are having surgery like if they are having open heart surgery.

I will now present one way heart lung machines are in use. Once we didn't have heart lung machines to help a doctor. When the machine was invent we see lots of changes in surgry that a doctor can do. The doctor can operate during the person heart not work. My grandmother went to the hospital for have surgry and they use the machine. Where she would been without the machine.

And the machine keep blood move through the body. The doctor can take their time to fix a person heart while they are laying their on the operating room. I know someone who work in a hospital and they say didn't know how it was possible before machine.

Last, that machine clean a bodies blood as it goes through. The blood won't poison the person wh blood it is. But it wood be better if body clean its own blood. A body better machine. I did tell you how the machine work and what it did. The machine can save a lifes.

ESSAY 3

This essay would likely receive a total score of 4–6 out of 8.

    This is what this essay looked like after editing. Note the editorial changes the student made during the editing process. This is the essay raters would actually see. The raters expect to see these changes and marks.

Machines and People

Overall, machines are helpful to people. I have cho-sen the heart lung machine as an example of a machine that helps people. Heart lung machines are a ~~medicine~~ medical miracle. They are used in hospitals all over the world. Heart lung machines are used during open heart surgery to circulate a patient's blood and clean the blood.

These machines can save lots of ~~lifes~~ lives.

Heart-lung machines have made open heart surgery possible. Before they were invented, many people died of disease or during surgery. Surgery would not have been ~~impossible~~ before then. And many peo-ple are alive today because of them. Besides sur-gery can now go ~~on for~~ hours. Sometimes the surgery can last as long as 12 hours. The heart lung machine makes things ~~very~~ possible and saves lives. Heart lung machines circulate blood ~~thru~~ through the body. It pumps like a heart. The heart can stop and the heart lung machine will pump instead. Then the blood moves through the body just like the heart pumping. So the blood gets to all the veins. It is ~~how~~ unbelievable ~~why~~ how the heart lung machine can work and keep people from dying.

The heart lung machine can clean a person's blood. All the bad stuff gets taken out of the blood before it goes back into the body. That way the body won't get ~~poison~~. I know of someone who had their blood cleaned by the machine while they were operated on. The person was ~~unconscience~~ unconscious. The doctor fixed his heart. ~~Since~~ Because the machine was going the person's heart was stopped. The doctor had to start it up again. It was pretty scary to think about that happening to a person. But the machine took the bad stuff out of the blood and the person lived.

To conclude, I believe that the heart lung machine is great for people who need open heart surgery. It pumps and cleans their blood too. They are a medical miracle.

ESSAY 4

This essay would likely receive a total score of 6 or 7 out of 8.

The Heart Lung Machine--Proof That Overall, Machines Help People

In my opinion, machines are likely to help people than to cause difficulty. I have chosen the heart lung machine as an example of a helpful machine. In this essay I will explain what the heart-lung machine does and how it is helpful.

Every day the heart-lung machine saves someone's life. The heart-lung machine is a wonderful machine that makes open-heart surgery possible by pumping and cleaning a person's blood. Surgeons use the machine during open-heart surgery. Each day we walk by someone who is alive because of the heart-lung machine. Each day throughout the world skilled surgeons perform difficult surgery with the aid of a heart-lung machine.

The heart-lung machine makes open-heart surgery possible. Open-heart surgery means the doctor is operating inside of the heart. In order to operate on the inside of the heart, the flow of blood must be stopped. But without blood flow the patient would die. Researchers worked for decades to find a way to keep a patient alive while the hearty was stopped. They were eventually successful and they named the machine a heart-lung machine. The first heart-lung machines were probably very primitive, but today's machines are very sophisticated.

The heart-lung machine circulates blood while the heart is not pumping. The blood is taken from the body into one side of the machine and pumped back into the body though the other side. The blood pumped back into the body travels through the circulatory system.

However, just pumping blood is not enough. As blood passes through a person's body, the body uses oxygen stored in the blood. Blood starts from the heart full of oxygen and returns to the heart without much oxygen. The lungs take in oxygen and pass that oxygen on to the blood. But during surgery the heart-lung machine does the lung's work and puts oxygen in the blood as the blood passes through the machine.

The heart-lung machine makes open-heart surgery possible. The machine circulates and oxygenates a person's blood while the heart is stopped. Without the machine, many people would die from heart disease or would die during surgery. The heart-lung machine is a machine that helps people by keeping them alive and holds the promise of even more amazing machines to come.

CHAPTER 7

Practice LAST

TEST INFO BOX

This practice test contains the types of items you will encounter on the real test. The distribution of items varies from one test administration to another.

Take this test in a realistic, timed setting.

The setting will be most realistic if another person times the test and ensures that the test rules are followed exactly. But remember that many people do better on a practice test than on the real test. If another person is acting as test supervisor, he or she should review these instructions with you and say "Start" when you should begin and "Stop" when time has expired.

You have 4 hours to complete the 80 selected-response questions and the constructed response. Keep the time limit in mind as you work.

Each selected-response question or statement in the test has four answer choices. Exactly one of these choices is correct. Mark your choice on the answer sheet provided for this test.

Use a pencil to mark the answer sheet. The actual test will be machine scored so completely darken in the answer space.

Once the test is complete, review the answers and explanations for each item.

When you are ready, turn the page and begin.

Answer Sheet

PRACTICE LAST

1 Ⓐ Ⓑ Ⓒ Ⓓ	21 Ⓐ Ⓑ Ⓒ Ⓓ	41 Ⓐ Ⓑ Ⓒ Ⓓ	61 Ⓐ Ⓑ Ⓒ Ⓓ
2 Ⓐ Ⓑ Ⓒ Ⓓ	22 Ⓐ Ⓑ Ⓒ Ⓓ	42 Ⓐ Ⓑ Ⓒ Ⓓ	62 Ⓐ Ⓑ Ⓒ Ⓓ
3 Ⓐ Ⓑ Ⓒ Ⓓ	23 Ⓐ Ⓑ Ⓒ Ⓓ	43 Ⓐ Ⓑ Ⓒ Ⓓ	63 Ⓐ Ⓑ Ⓒ Ⓓ
4 Ⓐ Ⓑ Ⓒ Ⓓ	24 Ⓐ Ⓑ Ⓒ Ⓓ	44 Ⓐ Ⓑ Ⓒ Ⓓ	64 Ⓐ Ⓑ Ⓒ Ⓓ
5 Ⓐ Ⓑ Ⓒ Ⓓ	25 Ⓐ Ⓑ Ⓒ Ⓓ	45 Ⓐ Ⓑ Ⓒ Ⓓ	65 Ⓐ Ⓑ Ⓒ Ⓓ
6 Ⓐ Ⓑ Ⓒ Ⓓ	26 Ⓐ Ⓑ Ⓒ Ⓓ	46 Ⓐ Ⓑ Ⓒ Ⓓ	66 Ⓐ Ⓑ Ⓒ Ⓓ
7 Ⓐ Ⓑ Ⓒ Ⓓ	27 Ⓐ Ⓑ Ⓒ Ⓓ	47 Ⓐ Ⓑ Ⓒ Ⓓ	67 Ⓐ Ⓑ Ⓒ Ⓓ
8 Ⓐ Ⓑ Ⓒ Ⓓ	28 Ⓐ Ⓑ Ⓒ Ⓓ	48 Ⓐ Ⓑ Ⓒ Ⓓ	68 Ⓐ Ⓑ Ⓒ Ⓓ
9 Ⓐ Ⓑ Ⓒ Ⓓ	29 Ⓐ Ⓑ Ⓒ Ⓓ	49 Ⓐ Ⓑ Ⓒ Ⓓ	69 Ⓐ Ⓑ Ⓒ Ⓓ
10 Ⓐ Ⓑ Ⓒ Ⓓ	30 Ⓐ Ⓑ Ⓒ Ⓓ	50 Ⓐ Ⓑ Ⓒ Ⓓ	70 Ⓐ Ⓑ Ⓒ Ⓓ
11 Ⓐ Ⓑ Ⓒ Ⓓ	31 Ⓐ Ⓑ Ⓒ Ⓓ	51 Ⓐ Ⓑ Ⓒ Ⓓ	71 Ⓐ Ⓑ Ⓒ Ⓓ
12 Ⓐ Ⓑ Ⓒ Ⓓ	32 Ⓐ Ⓑ Ⓒ Ⓓ	52 Ⓐ Ⓑ Ⓒ Ⓓ	72 Ⓐ Ⓑ Ⓒ Ⓓ
13 Ⓐ Ⓑ Ⓒ Ⓓ	33 Ⓐ Ⓑ Ⓒ Ⓓ	53 Ⓐ Ⓑ Ⓒ Ⓓ	73 Ⓐ Ⓑ Ⓒ Ⓓ
14 Ⓐ Ⓑ Ⓒ Ⓓ	34 Ⓐ Ⓑ Ⓒ Ⓓ	54 Ⓐ Ⓑ Ⓒ Ⓓ	74 Ⓐ Ⓑ Ⓒ Ⓓ
15 Ⓐ Ⓑ Ⓒ Ⓓ	35 Ⓐ Ⓑ Ⓒ Ⓓ	55 Ⓐ Ⓑ Ⓒ Ⓓ	75 Ⓐ Ⓑ Ⓒ Ⓓ
16 Ⓐ Ⓑ Ⓒ Ⓓ	36 Ⓐ Ⓑ Ⓒ Ⓓ	56 Ⓐ Ⓑ Ⓒ Ⓓ	76 Ⓐ Ⓑ Ⓒ Ⓓ
17 Ⓐ Ⓑ Ⓒ Ⓓ	37 Ⓐ Ⓑ Ⓒ Ⓓ	57 Ⓐ Ⓑ Ⓒ Ⓓ	77 Ⓐ Ⓑ Ⓒ Ⓓ
18 Ⓐ Ⓑ Ⓒ Ⓓ	38 Ⓐ Ⓑ Ⓒ Ⓓ	58 Ⓐ Ⓑ Ⓒ Ⓓ	78 Ⓐ Ⓑ Ⓒ Ⓓ
19 Ⓐ Ⓑ Ⓒ Ⓓ	39 Ⓐ Ⓑ Ⓒ Ⓓ	59 Ⓐ Ⓑ Ⓒ Ⓓ	79 Ⓐ Ⓑ Ⓒ Ⓓ
20 Ⓐ Ⓑ Ⓒ Ⓓ	40 Ⓐ Ⓑ Ⓒ Ⓓ	60 Ⓐ Ⓑ Ⓒ Ⓓ	80 Ⓐ Ⓑ Ⓒ Ⓓ

Practice LAST

Directions: Each item on this test includes four answer choices. Select the best choice for each item and mark that letter on the answer sheet.

Native Americans came to this continent about 30,000 years ago. They passed over a land bridge near what is now the Bering Strait between Siberia and Alaska. The Aleuts established a culture on the Aleutian Islands off southern Alaska by 5000 B.C. Primitive northern woodland cultures developed in the northeastern United States about 3000 B.C. These cultures included the Algonquin tribes, such as the Shawnee and the Iroquois Federation. Once glaciers withdrew from the area, Eskimos and Intuits established a culture in northern Alaska about 1800 B.C.

1. Which Native-American group established a culture in Alaska about 7,000 years ago?

   (A) Aleuts
   (B) Algonquians
   (C) Eskimos
   (D) Intuits

2. Astronomers are studying a star about 5 light-years from Earth. One light-year is the distance light travels in a year. That distance is about 6 trillion miles. During one observation, that star exploded. The astronomers concluded that the star had exploded about

   (A) 30 trillion years ago, the approximate distance light travels in 6 years.
   (B) 10 trillion years ago, the time for light to travel to the star from Earth and back.
   (C) 5 years ago, the time for light from the star to reach Earth.
   (D) right then because time travel is not possible.

0115857   ANCIENT EGYPT: AFRICAN.
Credit: The Granger Collection, New York

3. The pendant pictured above shows

   (A) evidence of pain.
   (B) evidence of ancient alien visitors.
   (C) a warrior armed with a rifle.
   (D) a musician playing an instrument.

Items 4–6 refer to this passage.

AIDS has already claimed more than ten million lives, and AIDS in Africa is at the same pandemic levels as the Black Plague was in the Middle Ages. In some African nations more than 10 percent of the population, already infected with AIDS, will die from the disease.

The AIDS rate may be highest in Zimbabwe where a culture of promiscuity fosters spread of the disease. In the United States and other countries, both men and women make unwise decisions about sexual partners. Freedom from pressure to engage in sex may be one of the most important tools for helping eradicate the AIDS epidemic.

Researchers were not sure at first what caused AIDS or how it was transmitted. They did know early on that those who developed AIDS usually died. Then researchers began to understand that the disease is caused by the HIV virus, which could be transmitted through blood and blood products. Even after knowing this, some blood companies resisted testing blood for the HIV virus. Today we know that the HIV virus is transmitted through blood and other bodily fluids. Women may be more susceptible than men, and the prognosis hasn't changed.

4. The main intent of this passage is to

   (A) show that blood companies can't be trusted.
   (B) detail the history of AIDS research.
   (C) detail the causes and consequences of AIDS.
   D) raise awareness about AIDS.

5. Which of the following questions could be answered from this passage?

   (A) How do intravenous drug users acquire AIDS?
   (B) Is AIDS caused by blood transfusions?
   (C) Through what mediums is AIDS transmitted?
   (D) How do blood companies test for AIDS?

6. Which of the following would be the best concluding summary sentence for this passage?

   (A) AIDS research continues to be under-funded in the United States.
   (B) Sexual activity and intravenous drug use continue to be the two primary ways that AIDS is transmitted.
   (C) People develop AIDS after being HIV positive.
   (D) Our understanding of AIDS has increased significantly over the past several years, but we are no closer to a cure.

Items 7–9 refer to this map.

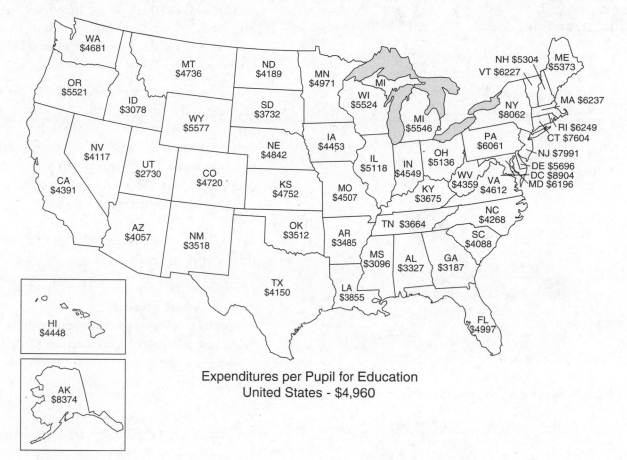

Expenditures per Pupil for Education
United States - $4,960

7. Among the states listed below, you can deduce from the map that teachers' salaries are probably lowest in

(A) Georgia, Alabama, and Idaho.
(B) South Dakota, Tennessee, and Oklahoma.
(C) Kentucky, Louisiana, and New Mexico.
(D) Florida, Hawaii, and Iowa.

8. You can deduce from the map that school taxes are probably highest in

(A) the southeastern states.
(B) the northeastern states.
(C) the northwestern states.
(D) the southwestern states.

9. Based on the information on this map, which of these states would be in the second quartile of per pupil expenditures?

(A) Alaska
(B) Alabama
(C) Idaho
(D) Arizona

An iron curtain has fallen across the continent.
Winston Churchill

10. What does this quote from Churchill refer to?

(A) The establishment of the French Maginot Line
(B) Germany's occupation of Western Europe
(C) Postwar Eastern Europe secretiveness and isolation
(D) The establishment of flying bomb launching ramps across Europe

11. Study the above shapes, and select A, B, C, or D, according to the rule:
    (small or striped) and large.
    Which pieces are selected?

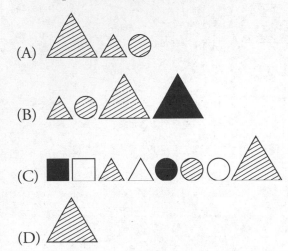

(A)

(B)

(C)

(D)

Items 12–14 refer to this passage.

Archaeological techniques can be relatively simple, or very complex. One method of archaeology uses magnetic
Line imaging to locate sites that may yield
(5) useful archaeological artifacts. Topsoil magnetic mapping is used to identify patterns in the landscape and to identify these resonance patterns that indicate where archaeological site work is indicated.
(10) The movement of topsoil into ditches and other features often leads to the development of pockets of material that may later be transformed into the topsoil by agricultural activity. It may be that the resulting
(15) patterns from agricultural activity will lead to the discovery of even smaller prehistoric ditches and other features. Magnetically, the presence of prehistoric features is reflected in the lower magnetic readings,

(20) particularly when compared to the higher background readings. These magnetic surveys can be combined with the results from other surveys to determine the efficacy of further archaeological investigations.

(25) Other techniques may just rely on the examination of existing relics for sustained patterns or relationships. Frequently, advanced numeric methods are useful for a full analysis of these patterns. In other
(30) cases, informed observation alone may reveal striking cultural information.

12. According to the passage, as a general rule, prehistoric features

   (A) have to be compared with higher background readings.
   (B) require advanced numerical analysis.
   (C) must rely on the examination of existing relics.
   (D) have lower magnetic readings.

13. Which of the following words could be used in place of the word "efficacy" in the last two lines of the first paragraph?

   (A) placement
   (B) usefulness
   (C) results
   (D) relationship

14. According to this passage, the resulting patterns from agricultural activity

   (A) may later be transformed into topsoil.
   (B) offer a great deal of assistance to archaeologists.
   (C) require a knowledge of mathematics or physics.
   (D) may lead to the discovery of prehistoric ditches.

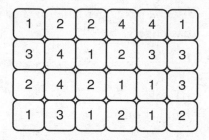

15. A ball is dropped randomly into the container shown above. What is the probability that the ball will land in a hole labeled "1"?

(A) 8/12
(B) 1/2
(C) 1/3
(D) 1/4

Items 16–17 refer to this passage.

County highway officials have to submit all road construction plans to the state highway department for approval. The state highway department must approve all plans, but officials are most attentive to plans for new construction, and less concerned about plans for work on existing roads. A state highway inspector visits every site for a limited access highway. The department also uses a computer-simulation analysis to determine the traffic-flow impact of these roads. The state highway department may require a county to identify a similar road configuration elsewhere in the state to fully determine traffic-flow characteristics. The department is also very cautious about roads that may be used by school buses. The state highway department has found that there are more accidents on narrow, rural roads and they have taken planning steps to ensure that roads of this type are not built.

The state highway department has sets of regulations for the number of lanes a highway can have and how these lanes are to be used. A summary of these regulations follows.

• All highways must be five lanes wide and either three or four of these lanes must be set aside for passenger cars only.

• If four lanes are set aside for passenger cars, then one of these lanes must be set aside for cars with three or more passengers, with a second lane of the four passenger lanes also usable by school vehicles such as buses, vans, and cars.

• If three lanes are set aside for passenger cars, then one of these lanes must be set aside for cars with two or more passengers, except that school buses, vans, and cars may also use this lane.

16. Officials in one county submit a plan for a five-lane highway, with three lanes set aside for passenger cars and school buses able to use the lane set aside for cars with two or more passengers. Based on their regulations, which of the following is most likely to be the state highway department's response to this plan?

(A) Your plan is approved because you have five lanes with three set aside for passenger cars and one set aside for passenger cars with two or more passengers.
(B) Your plan is approved because you permitted school buses to use the passenger lanes.
(C) Your plan is disapproved because you don't include school vans and school cars among the vehicles that can use the lane for cars with two or more passengers.
(D) Your plan is disapproved because you include school buses in the lane for passenger cars with two or more passengers.

17. County officials send a list of three possible highway plans to the state highway department. Using their regulations, which of the following plans would the state highway department approve?

I. 5 lanes—3 for passenger cars, 1 passenger lane for cars with 3 or more passengers, school buses and vans can also use the passenger lane for 3 or more people

II. 5 lanes—4 for passenger cars, 1 passenger lane for cars with 3 or more passengers, 1 of the 4 passenger lanes can be used by school buses, vans, and cars

III. 5 lanes—3 for passenger cars, 1 passenger lane for cars with 2 or more passengers, school vehicles can also

use the passenger lane for 2 or more passengers

(A) I only
(B) II only
(C) III only
(D) I and II only

Items 18–20 refer to these pictures.

(A)

(C)

(B)

(D)

18. Which of these pictures most likely involves dissent?

19. Which picture has the least realistic depictions of people?

20. Which picture features Presidents' names?

The Board of Adjustment can exempt a person from the requirements of a particular land use ordinance. Several cases have come before the board concerning three

ordinances. It is interesting to note how a person can be in favor of an exemption in one case but opposed to exemption in another. For example, one homeowner applied to build a garage 45 percent of the size of her house but was opposed to a neighbor converting his house from a one-family to a two-family house. This second homeowner was opposed to a church being built in his neighborhood. The woman opposed to his proposal was all for the church construction project. The pressure on Board of Adjustment members who also live in the community is tremendous. It must sometimes seem to them that any decision is the wrong one. But that is what Boards of Adjustment are for, and we can only hope that this example of America in action will best serve the community and those who live there.

21. Which of the following sentences is the author of the passage most likely to DISAGREE with?

    (A) These boards serve a useful purpose.
    (B) No exemptions should be granted to any zoning ordinance.
    (C) People can be very fickle when it comes to the exemptions they favor.
    (D) Some people may try to influence Board of Adjustment members.

22. Which of the following songs begins with the four bars shown above?

    (A) "My Country 'Tis of Thee"
    (B) "Appalachian Spring"
    (C) "I Fall to Pieces"
    (D) "Star-Spangled Banner"

23. Which diagram shows object • to have the most potential energy?

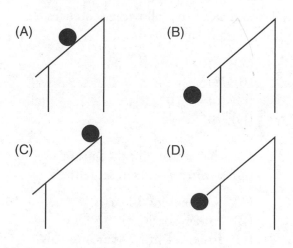

An archaeologist was investigating the books of an old civilization. She found the following table, which showed the number of hunters on top and the number of people they could feed on the bottom. For example, 3 hunters could feed 12 people. The archaeologist found a pattern in the table.

Hunters	1	2	3	4	5	6	7
Eaters	2	6	12	20	30		

24. Look for the pattern. How many eaters can 6 hunters feed?

    (A) 42
    (B) 40
    (C) 30
    (D) 36

25. What is the formula for the pattern:

    *H stands for hunters and
    E stands for eaters?*

    (A) $E = 3 \times H$
    (B) $E = 4 \times H$
    (C) $E = H^2 + H$
    (D) $E = 3 \times (H + 1)$

    Following a concert, a fan asked a popular singer why the songs sounded so different in person than on the recording. The singer responded, "I didn't record my emotions!"

26. Which of the following statements is suggested by this passage?

    (A) The singer was probably not in a good mood during that performance.
    (B) The fan was being intrusive, and the performer was "brushing them off."
    (C) The performance was outdoors where sound quality is different.
    (D) The performance may vary depending on the mood of the performer.

27. Which of the following diagrams represents a situation that could result in a solar eclipse?

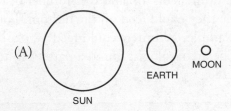

(A)

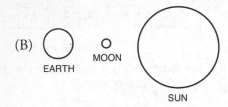

(B)

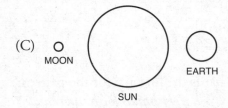

(C)

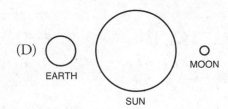

(D)

Items 28–29 refer to this passage.

In response to my opponent's question about my record on environmental issues, I want to say that the real problem in this election is not my record. Rather the problem is the influence of my opponent's rich friends in the record industry. I hope you will turn your back on his rich supporters and vote for me.

28. What type of rhetorical argument does this passage reflect?

(A) narration
(B) reflection
(C) argumentation
(D) exposition

29. What type of fallacious reasoning is found in the passage?

(A) ad hominem
(B) non sequitur
(C) false analogy
(D) bandwagon

Items 30–33 refer to this passage.

(1) The choice of educational practices sometimes seems like choosing fashions. (2) Fashion is driven by the whims, tastes, and zeitgeist of the current day. (3) The education system should not be driven by these same forces. (4) But consider, for example, the way mathematics is taught. (5) Three decades ago, teachers were told to use manipulative materials to teach mathematics. (6) In the intervening years, the emphasis was on drill and practice. (7) Now teachers are being told again to use manipulative materials. (8) This cycle is more akin to _____ than to sound professional practice.

30. Which of these sentences contains a simile?

(A) (1)
(B) (2)
(C) (5)
(D) (6)

31. Which of the following sentences contains an opinion?

(A) (4)
(B) (5)
(C) (6)
(D) (8)

32. For what reason did the author use the phrase *three decades* in sentence 5?

(A) To represent 30 years
(B) For emphasis
(C) To represent 10-year intervals
(D) To represent the passage of years

33. Which of the following choices best fits in the blank in sentence 8?

    (A) unsound practice
    (B) a fashion designer's dream
    (C) the movement of hemlines
    (D) a fashion show

Items 34–37 refer to this passage.

Computer graphing programs are capable of graphing almost any equations, including advanced equations from calculus. The student just types in the equation and the graph appears on the computer screen. The graphing program can also show the numerical solution for any entered equation. I like having a computer program that performs the mechanical aspects of these difficult calculations. However, these programs do not teach about graphing or mathematics because the computer does not "explain" what is going on. A person could type in an equation, get an answer, and have not the slightest idea what either meant.

Relying on this mindless kind of graphing and calculation, students will be completely unfamiliar with the meaning of the equations they write or the results they get. They will not be able to understand how to create a graph from an equation or to understand the basis for the more complicated calculations.

It may be true that a strictly mechanical approach is used by some teachers. There certainly is a place for students who already understand equations and graphing to have a computer program that relieves the drudgery. But these computer programs should never and can never replace the teacher. Mathematical competence assumes that understanding precedes rote calculation.

34. What is the main idea of this passage?

    (A) Mechanical calculation is one part of learning about mathematics.
    (B) Teachers should use graphing programs as one part of instruction.
    (C) Graphing programs are not effective for initially teaching mathematics.
    (D) Students who use these programs won't learn mathematics.

35. Which of the following questions could be answered from the information in the passage?

    (A) How does the program do integration and differentiation?
    (B) What type of mathematics learning experiences should students have?
    (C) When is it appropriate to use graphing programs?
    (D) Why do schools buy these graphing programs?

36. Which of the following information can be found in the passage?

    I. The type of computer that graphs the equation
    II. The graphing program's two main outputs
    III. How to use the program to teach about mathematics

    (A) I only
    (B) II only
    (C) I and II only
    (D) II and III only

37. Which aspect of graphing programs does the author of the passage like?

    (A) That you just have to type in the equation
    (B) That the difficult mechanical operations are performed
    (C) That the calculations and graphing are done very quickly
    (D) That you don't have to know math to use them

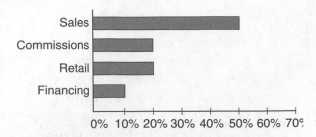

38. The sales department staff draws its salary from four areas of the company's income. Based on the graph above, what percentage is drawn from retail income?

   (A) 10%
   (B) 20%
   (C) 30%
   (D) 40%

   Writers of standardized tests have noticed a phenomenon about students who take and then retake tests. In general, scores increase among students who originally scored less than the mean and decrease among students who originally scored higher than the mean. Test makers noticed that the losses, or gains, were greatest for those students whose original scores were furthest from the mean. This phenomenon is called regression to the mean.

39. In trying to provide a commonsense explanation for the phenomenon, what might one say?

   (A) Students who scored well above the mean were more likely to have guessed better on the first test administration.
   (B) Students who scored well below the mean on the first administration were likely less intelligent.
   (C) The mean for the tests was actually inaccurate and should have been a different number.
   (D) That much change in the scores indicates that test scores are pretty meaningless.

   High-pressure systems are usually associated with good weather. In the Northern Hemisphere, wind circulates to the right (clockwise) around a high-pressure system and to the left (counterclockwise) around a low-pressure system.

40. You are standing on the eastern end of Long Island in New York State. A strong high-pressure system is directly opposite you to the east, some miles offshore. Where you are standing, from which direction is the wind is most likely coming?

   (A) northwest
   (B) northeast
   (C) southwest
   (D) southeast

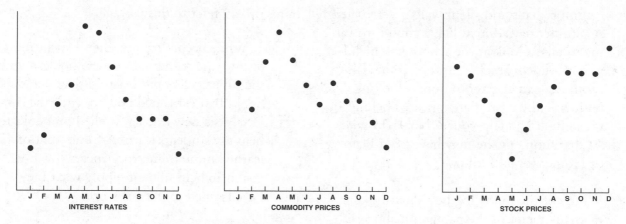

Graphs of Three Economic Indicators for the Same 12-month Period

41. Which of the following conclusions can be drawn from the information on the three graphs shown above?

    (A) Higher interest rates cause lower stock prices.
    (B) Interest rates and stock prices are inversely related.
    (C) Commodity prices and interest rates are not related to one another.
    (D) Commodity prices and stock prices are directly related.

Items 42–44 refer to this passage.

As a child he read the *Hardy Boys* series of books and was in awe of the author Franklin Dixon. As an adult, he read a book entitled the *Ghost of the Hardy Boys,* which revealed that there was no Franklin Dixon and that ghost writers had authored the books. The authors were apparently working for a large publishing syndicate.

42. Which of the following is the likely intent of the author of this passage?

    (A) To describe a book-publishing practice
    (B) To contrast fiction and fact
    (C) To contrast childhood and adulthood
    (D) To correct the record

43. Which of the following does the word *syndicate* in the last sentence most likely refer to?

    (A) A business group
    (B) An illegal enterprise
    (C) An illegal activity
    (D) A large building

44. What does the word *Ghost* in the title of the second mentioned book refer to?

    (A) A person who has died or was dead at the time the book was published
    (B) A person who writes books without credit
    (C) A person who influences the way a book is written
    (D) The mystical images of the mind that affect the way any author writes

"The cause of liberty becomes a mockery if the price to be paid is the wholesale destruction of those who are to enjoy it."

45. The quote above from Mohandas Gandhi is best reflected in which of the following statements about the American civil rights movement?

    (A) Bus boycotts are not effective because boycotters are punished.
    (B) Nonviolence and civil disobedience are the best approach to protest.
    (C) Desegregation laws were a direct result of freedom marches.
    (D) America will never be free as long as minorities are oppressed.

Empty halls and silent walls greeted me. A summer day seemed like a good time for me to take a look at the school in which I would student teach. I tiptoed from classroom door to classroom door—looking. Suddenly the custodian appeared behind me and said, "Help you?" "No sir," I said. At that moment she may have been Plato or Homer for all I knew.

46. Which of the following best describes the main character in the paragraph above?

(A) timid and afraid
(B) confident and optimistic
(C) pessimistic and unsure
(D) curious and respectful

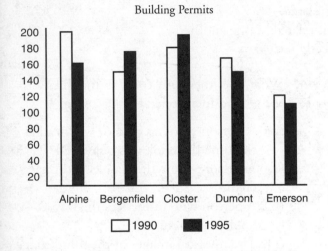

Building Permits

47. This graph best demonstrates which of the following?

(A) The town with the most building permits every year is Closter.
(B) Alpine has the biggest difference in permits between 1990 and 1995.
(C) The town with the fewest permits every year is Emerson.
(D) Bergenfield had more building permits in 1990 than Dumont had in 1995.

Items 48–49 refer to this passage.

While becoming a teacher, I spent most of my time with books. I read books about the subjects I would teach in school and books that explained how to teach the subjects. As a new teacher, I relied on books to help my students learn. As time went on, I learned more from experience. Now my goal is to help students apply what they have learned to the real world.

48. Which of the following would most likely be the next line of this passage?

(A) The world is a dangerous and intimidating place; be wary of it.
(B) Children should be taught to seek whatever the world has to offer.
(C) A teacher has to be in the world, not just study about the world.
(D) You cannot forget about books.

49. Which of the following is the underlying moral of this passage?

(A) Teaching art is very rewarding.
(B) Children learn a lot from field trips.
(C) There is much to be said of teachers who think of their students' experiences first.
(D) Firsthand experiences are most important for a teacher's development.

Items 50–51 refer to this passage.

The American alligator is found primarily in Florida and Georgia. It has also been reported in other states, including North and South Carolina. In the United States, the crocodile is found mainly in Southernmost Florida. It has also been reported in South Carolina. An adult alligator weighs more than 400 pounds (180 kg). American crocodiles can grow larger. Adult alligators eat fish and small mammals, while crocodiles consume similar prey.

An untrained person may mistake a crocodile for an alligator. Crocodiles are found in the same areas as alligators, and both have prominent snouts with many teeth. The crocodile has a long, thin snout with teeth in both jaws. The alligator's snout is wider with teeth only in the upper jaw.

50. Which of the following would be a good title for this passage?

    (A) "Large Reptiles"
    (B) "Eating Habits of Alligators"
    (C) "The American Alligator"
    (D) "How Alligators and Crocodiles Differ"

51. Which of the following would be a way to distinguish an alligator from a crocodile?

    (A) number of teeth
    (B) hape of snout
    (C) habitat
    (D) diet

Items 52–55 refer to this passage.

The Iroquois were present in upstate New York about 500 years before the Europeans arrived. According to Iroquois oral history, this Indian nation was once a single tribe, subject to the rule of the Adirondack Indians. This tribe was located in the valley of the St. Lawrence River, but they left and moved south to be free from Adirondack control. According to reports from French explorers, there were still Iroquoian villages around the St. Lawrence between Quebec and Montreal in the early 1500s. But when explorers returned around 1600, these villages had disappeared. It was about this time that the Iroquois launched a fifty-year war against the Adirondacks. When the French reached Montreal around 1609, they found a vast deserted area along the St. Lawrence because Adirondack, and other Indian tribes avoided the river for fear of attacks from Iroquois raiding parties. The French sided with the local tribes and fought against the Iroquois, using firearms, which caused the Iroquois to give up mass formations and to replace wooden body armor with the tactic of falling to the ground just before the mus-

kets were discharged. The Iroquois were engaged in many conflicts until the Revolutionary war, when the Iroquois sided with the British. The Iroquois were defeated and their lands were taken.

The Iroquois nation consisted of five main tribes—Cayuga, Mohawk, Oneida, Onondaga, and Seneca. Called the Five Nations or the League of Five Nations, these tribes occupied much of New York State. Since the tribes were arranged from east to west, the region they occupied was called the long house of the Iroquois.

The Iroquois economy was based mainly on agriculture. The main crop was corn, but they also grew pumpkins, beans, and fruit. The Iroquois used wampum (hollow beads) for money, and records were woven into wampum belts.

The Iroquois nation had a remarkable democratic structure, spoke a common Algonquin language, and were adept at fighting. These factors had made the Iroquois a dominant power by the early American Colonial period. In the period just before the Revolutionary War, Iroquoian conquest had overcome most other Indian tribes in the northeastern United States as far west as the Mississippi River.

During the Revolutionary War, most Iroquoian tribes sided with the British. At the end of the Revolutionary War the tribes scattered, with some migrating to Canada. Only remnants of the Seneca and Onondaga tribes remained in their tribal lands.

52. Which of these statements best explains why the Iroquois were so successful at conquest?

    (A) The Iroquois had the support of the British.
    (B) The Iroquois had a cohesive society and were good fighters.
    (C) All the other tribes in the area were too weak.
    (D) There were five tribes, more than the other Indian nations.

53. Which of the following best describes the geographic location of the five Iroquoian tribes?

   (A) the northeastern United States as far west as the Mississippi River
   (B) southern Canada
   (C) Cayuga
   (D) New York State

54. Which of the following best describes why the area occupied by the Iroquois was called the long house of the Iroquois?

   (A) The tribes were arranged as though they occupied different sections of a long house.
   (B) The Iroquois lived in structures called long houses.
   (C) The close political ties among tribes made it seem that they were all living in one house.
   (D) The Iroquois had expanded their original tribal lands through conquest.

55. According to the passage, which of the following best describes the economic basis for the Iroquoian economy?

   (A) wampum
   (B) corn
   (C) agriculture
   (D) conquest

Items 56–57 refer to this passage.

   I believe that there is extraterrestrial life—probably in some other galaxy. It is particularly human to believe that our solar system is the only one that can support intelligent life. But our solar system is only an infinitesimal dot in the infinity of the cosmos and it is just not believable that there is not life out there—somewhere.

56. What is the author of this passage proposing?

   (A) There is other life in the universe.
   (B) That there is no life on earth.

   (C) That humans live on other planets.
   (D) That the sun is a very small star.

57. The words *infinitesimal* and *infinite* are best characterized by which pair of words below?

   (A) small and large
   (B) very small and very large
   (C) very small and limitless
   (D) large and limitless

Items 58–60 refer to this passage.

   It is striking how uninformed today's youth are about Acquired Immune Deficiency Syndrome. Because of their youth and ignorance, many young adults engage in high-risk behavior. Many of these young people do not realize that the disease can be contracted through almost any contact with an infected person's blood and bodily fluids. Some do not realize that symptoms of the disease may not appear for ten years or more. Others do not realize that the danger in sharing needles to inject intravenous drugs comes from the small amounts of other's blood injected during this process. A massive education campaign is needed to fully inform today's youth about AIDS.

58. The main idea of this passage is

   (A) previous education campaigns have failed.
   (B) AIDS develops from the HIV virus.
   (C) the general public is not fully informed about AIDS.
   (D) young people are not adequately informed about AIDS.

59. Which of the following is the best summary of the statement about what young people don't realize about how AIDS can be contracted?

   (A) The symptoms may not appear for ten years or more.
   (B) AIDS is contracted because of ignorance.

(C) AIDS is contracted from intravenous needles.

(D) AIDS is contracted through contact with infected blood or bodily fluids.

60. Which of the following best describes how the author views young people and their knowledge of AIDS?

(A) Stupid
(B) Unaware
(C) Dumb
(D) Unintelligible

Use this passage to answer items 61–63.

In humans, a DNA molecule consists of two strands that wrap around one another. Each strand of these linear arrangements of *Line* repeating similar units called nucleotides, is
(5) composed of one sugar, one phosphate, and a nitrogen base. The two DNA strands are held together by weak bonds between the bases forming base pairing rules. Base pairing rules are adhered to meaning that each
(10) daughter cell receives one old and one new DNA strand. This ensures that the new strand is an exact copy of the old one. Each DNA molecule includes many genes. The human genome consists of approximately
(15) 80,000–100,000 genes. Only about 10 percent of the genome is known to carry the protein coding (exons) of genes. The rest of the genome is thought to consist of other non-coding genomes.

61. What is the guaranteed outcome of base pairing rules?

(A) They will wrap around one another.
(B) New strands replicate old strands.
(C) DNA strands are held together by weak bonds.
(D) Daughter cells receive old strands.

62. When it comes to coding:

(A) DNA consists of two strands.
(B) the function of many regions on the genome are obscure.
(C) DBA strands are held together by weak bonds.
(D) Each DNA module contains many genes.

63. According to the passage, what does a nucleotide consist of?

(A) phosphate, sugar, nitrogenous base
(B) the ability to create daughter cells
(C) DNA consists of nucleotides
(D) the human genome

64. This poster depicts

(A) the horrors of animal cruelty in early U.S. history.
(B) the break up of the United States leading to the Civil War.
(C) the need for the colonies to ratify the Constitution.
(D) the need for the colonies to unite against England.

Items 65–66 refer to this passage.

Alice in Wonderland, written by Charles Dodgson under the pen name Lewis Carroll, is full of symbolism, so much so that a book titled *Understanding Alice* was written containing the original text with marginal notes explaining the symbolic meanings.

65. By symbolism, the author of the passage above meant that much of Alice in Wonderland

  (A) was written in a foreign language.
  (B) contained many mathematical symbols.
  (C) contained no pictures.
  (D) had a figurative meaning.

66. What does the author mean by the phrase "marginal notes" found in the last sentence?

  (A) Explanations of the musical meaning of the text
  (B) Notes that may not have been completely correct
  (C) Notes written next to the main text
  (D) Notes written by Carroll but not included in the original book

67. This picture best expresses

  (A) action and warmth.
  (B) isolation and cold.
  (C) fluctuation and flatness.
  (D) concern and denseness.

68. It is Monday at 6 P.M. near the coast of California when you call your friend who lives near the coast of New Jersey. It takes you 5½ hours to get through. What time is it in New Jersey when you get through?

  (A) 8:30 P.M. Monday
  (B) 9:30 P.M. Monday
  (C) 2:30 A.M. Tuesday
  (D) 3:30 P.M. Tuesday

During a Stage 4 alert, workers in an energy plant must wear protective pants, a protective shirt, and a helmet except that protective coveralls can be worn in place of protective pants and shirt. When there is a Stage 5 alert, workers must also wear filter masks in addition to the requirements for the Stage 4 alert.

69. During a Stage 5 alert, which of the following could be worn?

  I. masks, pants, shirt
  II. coveralls, helmet, mask
  III. coveralls, mask

  (A) I only
  (B) II only
  (C) III only
  (D) I and II only

Time	8 A.M.	9 A.M.	10 A.M.	11 A.M.	12 NOON
Temp	45°	55°	60°	60°	70°
Time	1 P.M.	2 P.M.	3 P.M.	4 P.M.	
Temp	75°	75°	70°	65°	
Time	5 P.M.	6 P.M.	7 P.M.	8 P.M.	
Temp	55°	50°	50°	45°	

70. The accompanying table shows the temperature tracked for a 12-hour period of time. Which graph best illustrates this information?

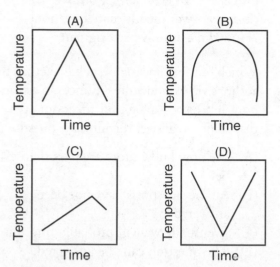

71. This sequence of images of a galloping horse is most likely

(A) part of a motion picture
(B) taken with a digital camera
(C) a photo finish at a horse race
(D) a study of the horse's movement

72. *C* is 5 more than half of *B*. Which of the following expressions states this relationship?

(A) $C + 5 = B/2$
(B) $C = \frac{1}{2} B + 5$
(C) $C + 5 = 2B$
(D) $C + 5 > B/2$

Base your answers to 73–76 on this passage from *Uncle Tom's Cabin* by Harriett Beecher Stowe.

    Eliza, a runaway slave, made her desperate retreat across the river just in the dusk of twilight. The gray mist of evening,
Line rising slowly from the river, enveloped
(5) her as she disappeared up the bank, and the swollen current and floundering masses of ice presented a hopeless barrier between her and her pursuer. Haley the pursuer, therefore slowly and discontentedly returned
(10) to the little tavern, to ponder further what was to be done. He was startled by the loud and dissonant voice of a man who was apparently dismounting at the door. He hurried to the window.
(15) "By the land! if this yer an't the nearest, now, to what I've heard folks call Providence," said Haley, "I do b'lieve that ar's Tom Loker." Haley hastened out. Standing by the bar, in the corner of the room,
(20) was a brawny; muscular man, full six feet in height and broad in proportion. In the head and face every organ and lineament expressive of brutal and unhesitating violence was in a state of the highest possible
(25) development. Indeed, could our readers fancy a bull-dog come into man's estate, and walking about in a hat and coat, they would have no unapt idea of the general style and effect of his physique. He was
(30) accompanied by a traveling companion, in many respects an exact contrast to himself.
    The large man poured out a big tumbler half full of raw spirits, and gulped it down without a word. The little man stood
(35) tiptoe, and putting his head first to one side and then to the other, and snuffing considerately in the directions of the various bottles, ordered at last a mint julep, in a thin and quivering voice, and with an air
(40) of great circumspection.

73. Which of the following events occurs between the time when the brawny man is standing at the bar and when the last mint julep was ordered?

    (A) Haley hastens out.
    (B) The little man stood tiptoe.
    (C) Gray mist rises.
    (D) Tom Loker is recognized.

74. Based on the passage, which of the following is true about Haley?

    (A) He looked like a bulldog.
    (B) He was startled by a dissonant voice.
    (C) He was himself a little man.
    (D) He drank mint juleps in the Southern tradition.

75. Which of the following statements is true, according to the passage?

    (A) The runaway slave crossed the river just before sunrise.
    (B) The runaway slave was brought back to the tavern.
    (C) The runaway slave disappeared into the river.
    (D) The runaway slave was not captured.

76. Which of the following statements is the most accurate about Tom Loker?

    (A) Tom Loker stood by the bar in the corner of the room.
    (B) Haley saw him through the tavern window.
    (C) Haley met Tom Loker outside the tavern.
    (D) Tom Loker's real name was not Loker; it was Marks.

77. A person throws a black cloth over a pile of snow to make the snow melt faster. Why is that?

    (A) Cloth will make snow melt faster.
    (B) The black material absorbs more sunlight and more heat.
    (C) The black material holds the heat in.
    (D) The black cloth reflects light better and so absorbs more heat.

Advances in astronomy and space exploration during the past twenty-five years have been significant, and we now know more answers to questions about the universe than ever before, but we still cannot answer the ultimate question, "How did our universe originate?"

78. Which of the following best characterizes the author's view of how the advances in astronomy and space exploration affect our eventual ability to answer the ultimate question?

    (A) We now know more answers than ever before.
    (B) All the questions have not been answered.
    (C) Eventually we will probably find out.
    (D) The question can't be answered.

The sunrise in the desert sky was accompanied by a strange and eerie glow. Normally the sun shone big and bright and yellow. Now all eyes squinted to see the cause. Suddenly, as if out of the sun itself, horsemen thundered into our midst. They spared no one the wrath of the guns which they held in their hands. I hid as I could among some baskets and then, as fast as they had come, the horsemen galloped away. I looked out and saw that almost none were moving and listened as the sound of horses faded in the distance.

79. The glow in the sky was probably caused by

    (A) an especially hot day.
    (B) the sun shining through dust from the horses.
    (C) the glint from the rider's guns.
    (D) an emotional reaction on the part of the observers.

80. You flip a fair coin three times and it comes up heads each time. What is the probability that the fourth flip will be a head?

    (A) 1/16
    (B) 1/4
    (C) 1/2
    (D) 1/3

Written Assignment

Directions: Write an essay on the topic below. Use the lined pages that follow. Write your essay on this topic only. An essay on another topic will be rated Unscorable (U).

Is it better to group students homogeneously or heterogeneously?

It is better to group students homogeneously. Homogeneous grouping means that students with similar ability or similar achievement are grouped together. This is the correct way to group because students work more comfortably when they are around other similar students. The teacher can concentrate on a narrower range of objectives and does not have to worry about students who are surging ahead or lagging behind. This homogeneous approach offers the best opportunity for student learning.

It is better to group students heterogeneously. Heterogeneous grouping means that students with varying ability and achievement are grouped together. The first point to note is that homogeneous grouping for, say, reading does not produce heterogeneous grouping for mathematics. So no matter how you group, students will be heterogeneously grouped in most classes. But heterogeneous grouping is the best choice anyhow. There is no research to show that homogeneously grouped students do better, but there are studies that indicate that students who act as peer tutors do better, and this peer tutoring is most likely to occur in heterogeneous groupings.

Is it better to group students homogeneously or heterogeneously?

Review and evaluate the opposing positions presented above.

Choose one of these two positions.

Write an essay that supports your position following the guidelines presented above.

Answer Key
PRACTICE LAST

1. A	21. B	41. B	61. B
2. C	22. A	42. D	62. B
3. D	23. C	43. A	63. A
4. D	24. A	44. B	64. D
5. C	25. C	45. B	65. D
6. D	26. D	46. D	66. C
7. A	27. B	47. B	67. B
8. B	28. C	48. C	68. C
9. D	29. A	49. C	69. B
10. C	30. A	50. D	70. A
11. D	31. D	51. B	71. D
12. D	32. B	52. B	72. B
13. B	33. C	53. D	73. B
14. D	34. C	54. A	74. B
15. C	35. C	55. C	75. D
16. C	36. B	56. A	76. A
17. B	37. B	57. C	77. B
18. D	38. B	58. D	78. B
19. B	39. A	59. D	79. B
20. C	40. B	60. B	80. C

Answer Explanations

1. **(A)** According to the passage, the Aleuts established a culture around 5000 B.C., which stands for "before the Common Era." The Common Era began about 2,000 years ago, so 5000 B.C. is about 7,000 years ago. The Eskimos and Intuits established cultures about 3,000 years ago.

2. **(C)** If an event happens five light-years from Earth, the light occurring at that event will take five years to reach Earth. (A) is incorrect because this answer approximates the distance light traveled in five years, not how long the light took to travel that distance. (B) is incorrect because the light just has to travel from the star to Earth, not both ways. (D) is incorrect because this question is not about time travel but about how long the light took to reach Earth.

3. **(D)** This primitive pendant shows a musician playing an instrument. (A) is incorrect because there is no evidence of pain. (B) is incorrect because choice (D) is a much more likely answer. (C) is incorrect because the rifle was not found in primitive times.

4. **(D)** The author is trying to raise AIDS awareness by presenting a wide range of information about AIDS. The remaining choices are incorrect for the following reasons: (A) There are statements in the passage that might lead a person to believe that drug companies can't be trusted, but that is not the main idea of the passage. (B) The passage does not focus on the history of AIDS research. (C) There is information about the causes and consequences of AIDS, but that is not the main idea.

5. **(C)** The passage explains that AIDS is transmitted through blood and other bodily fluids. (A) is incorrect because the passage does not explain how IV drug users acquire AIDS. (B) is incorrect because AIDS is not caused by blood transfusions. (D) is incorrect because the passage does not describe how blood companies tests for AIDS.

6. **(D)** The combination of increased awareness, but no cure, sums up this passage. (A) This statement may be true, but this is not discussed in the passage and it is not a reasonable conclusion. (B) is incorrect because the passage does not mention intravenous drug use. (C) is incorrect because the paragraph does not mention that people develop AIDS after they become HIV positive.

7. **(A)** These states have the lowest per pupil expenditures ($3,187, $3,327, $3,078) among the states listed. The states in (B), (C), and (D) all have higher per pupil expenditures than the states in choice (A).

8. **(B)** Just a quick scan shows that all northeastern states have per pupil expenditures above $5,000, with many above $6,000. Only a few states in the

remaining choices have per pupil expenditures above $5,000, and only Alaska in these other regions has per pupil expenditures above $6,000.

9. **(D)** The second quartile is the second one-fourth of per pupil expenditures ranked from highest to lowest. That's the 14th through the 26th highest expenditures. Arizona is the 14th score at the top of the second quartile. You can answer this question best by eliminating answers. (A) is incorrect because Alaska's expenditures are near the very top in the first quartile. (B) and (C) are incorrect because Alabama's and Idaho's expenditures are at the very bottom in the fourth quartile. That leaves (D), Arizona, as the only possible answer.

10. **(C)** This famous quote from Churchill referred to the isolation of Communist Bloc countries. You would have to be familiar with a little history to know what this Churchill quote refers to, and that (A), (B), and (D) are incorrect. Questions like this do pop up on the LAST from time to time.

11. **(D)** First find all the pieces that are either small or striped and cross out the pieces that don't meet one of these rules. Then find all the pieces not crossed out that are "and large," and circle these pieces. The circled piece below shows the correct answer.

12. **(D)** Lines 18 and 19 state that as a general rule "the presence of prehistoric features is reflected in the lower magnetic readings." The remaining choices are found in the passage but do not answer the question. (A) This is how to tell that the magnetic readings are lower. (B) The passage indicates that advanced numerical readings may be useful for a full analysis of prehistoric patterns. (C) The passage notes that some techniques rely on the examination of existing relics.

13. **(B)** Usefulness is a synonym for efficacy. The placements (A) and the relationships (D) of features are the results (C) used to determine the efficacy of further investigations.

14. **(D)** Lines 14–17 explain that "the resulting patterns from agricultural activity will lead to the discovery of even smaller prehistoric ditches and other features." (A) is incorrect because the passage says "pockets of material [not patterns of agricultural activity] may later be transformed into the topsoil by agricultural activity." (B) is incorrect because the passage does not mention offering assistance to archaeologists. (C) is incorrect because the passage indicates that advanced numerical methods may presuppose a knowledge of mathematics or physics.

15. **(C)** There are 24 holes altogether, and 8 of them are labeled "1." So the probability of landing on a "1" is 8/24 or 1/3. (A) and (B) are incorrect because less than half the holes are labeled "1." (D) is incorrect because more than one in four holes are labeled "1."

16. **(C)** The plan must be disapproved because the third regulation states that if three lanes are set aside for passenger cars, then school buses, school vans, and school cars can all use the lane for cars with two or more passengers. (A) is incorrect because the extra provisions of the third regulation apply to this situation. (B) is incorrect because both the first and third regulation apply also to the situation described in this item. (D) is incorrect because the reason given conflicts with the third regulation.

17. **(B)** Consider each Roman numeral in turn and then choose your answer.

   I. Disapproved. It sets aside lanes for passenger cars with three passengers, not the two or more passengers required by the third regulation.
   II. Approved. It meets the requirements in the second regulation for when four lanes are set aside for passenger cars.
   III. Disapproved. It does not meet the requirements of the third regulation for when three lanes are set aside for passenger cars.
   Only Plan II would be approved—(B).

18. **(D)** Dissent involves people, and only pictures (A), (C), and (D) involve people. A closer look at (D) reveals a crowd burning something in protest. Picture (A) shows people gathering after the San Francisco earthquake. (B) does not show dissent because there are no people.

19. **(B)** This 225 year old painting has a stiffer, less realistic depiction of people than choices (A) and (D).

20. **(C)** The tomb of Ulysses Grant in the foreground and the George Washington bridge in the background both feature President's names.

21. **(B)** This statement puts the author at odds with the Board of Adjustment, but the author never questions or attacks the board or its responsibilities. The remaining choices paraphrase the author's statements in the passage.

22. **(A)** These notes show the distinctive beginning of "My Country 'Tis of Thee," to the exception of choices (B), (C), and (D).

23. **(C)** The ball at the top of the ramp has the furthest to roll and that means it has the most potential to create energy. Diagrams (A), (B), and (D) show that some of that potential energy has been used. Diagram (D) shows the least potential energy.

24. **(A)** The correct answer is 42. The number of "eaters" increases by 4, 6, 8, 10, and then 12. 30 + 12 = 42. Choices (B), (C), and (D) do not continue that pattern.

25. **(C)** To get the number of "eaters," multiply the number of hunters and one more than the number of hunters. This gives the formula: $H \times (H + 1) = H^2 + H$. This is the formula shown in (C). You can also find the answer to this question by just trying out "1" for the number of hunters. (A) is incorrect because 3 (1) = 3, but the number of eaters for one hunter is 2. (B) is incorrect because 4 (1) = 4, but the number of eaters for one hunter is 2. (D) is incorrect because 3 (1 + 1) = 6, but the number of eaters for one hunter is 2.

26. **(D)** Music is more than just notes and varies with the mood of the performer. (A) is incorrect because there is nothing to indicate that the songs sounded worse in person. (B) is incorrect because there is nothing dismissive about what the performer has to say. (C) is incorrect because there is nothing to indicate that the concert was outdoors.

27. **(B)** In a solar eclipse, the moon blocks the sun's light from reaching earth. The moon must be between the sun and the earth for a solar eclipse to occur. (A) is incorrect because this situation could result in a lunar eclipse, in which the earth casts a shadow on the moon. (C) and (D) are incorrect because these diagrams show the sun between the earth and the moon, which is not possible.

28. **(C)** The speaker is making an argument to convince the audience of his or her position. An argument is an attempt to be persuasive, and is not the same as being argumentative. (A) is incorrect because a narration presents a fictional or factual story. (B) is incorrect because reflective passages describe a scene, person, or emotion. (D) is incorrect because expository passages simply explain.

29. **(A)** The speaker is making an "ad hominem" argument because he or she seeks to discredit the person rather than respond to the position in the question. (B) is incorrect because a "non sequitur" means presenting a conclusion that does not flow logically from the facts. (C) is incorrect because "false analogy" means using an analogy that does not match the situation under discussion. (D) is incorrect because "bandwagon" means arguing for a position because of its popularity.

30. **(A)** The first sentence contains the simile "choice of educational practices . . . like choosing fashions." A simile is a figure of speech that compares two things and usually uses the words "like" or "as." (B), (C), and (D) are incorrect because none of these sentences contains a comparison.

31. **(D)** Only sentence (8) contains an opinion among the sentences listed. (A) is incorrect because sentence (4) contains a statement that seems to be leading up to an opinion, but it is not an opinion itself. (B) and (C) are incorrect because sentences (5) and (6) contain statements of fact.

32. **(B)** The author is being a little dramatic to emphasize the length of time. The other choices do not capture the reason the author chose the phrase.

33. **(C)** Hemlines move without apparent reason, which is the author's point about educational practices. (A) is incorrect because nothing in the passage suggests this is unsound practice. (B) and (D) are incorrect because nothing about the passage is about fashion.

34. **(C)** The main point is that the author objects to using these programs with students who don't know mathematics. (A) and (B) are incorrect because they include information found in the passage, but it is not the author's main point. (D) is incorrect because the author never makes the claim that students who use these programs won't learn mathematics.

35. **(C)** This is the only question that can be answered from information in the passage. The answer is found in the third paragraph, "There certainly is a place for students who already understand equations and graphing to have a computer program that relieves drudgery." (A) is incorrect because the passage never mentions how the program does anything. (B) is incorrect because the passage does not detail the kinds of mathematics learning experiences students should have. (D) is incorrect because the passage never mentions schools' purchasing practices.

36. **(B)** Consider each Roman numeral in turn.

    I. Incorrect. The passage never mentions the type of computer that graphs the equations.
    II. Correct. The first paragraph mentions graphs and numerical solutions as the two main outputs.
    III. Incorrect. The passage never mentions how to use the program to teach mathematics.

    Only II is correct—(B).

37. **(B)** The middle of the first paragraph mentions that the author likes the fact that the difficult mechanical operations are performed. (A), (C), and (D) are incorrect because the author never says that he or she likes the things given in these choices.

38. **(B)** Simply read down from the end of the bar next to retail and see that it matches 20% on the horizontal scale.

39. **(A)** Scores above the mean are more likely to contain positive errors of measurement. A simple way to explain this is that those who scored above the mean may have made better guesses. (B) is incorrect because nothing in the passage says scores below the mean to indicate lower intelligence. (C) is incorrect because the mean for the test is based on the actual scores and the number of test takers. It is an artifact of the test that cannot be wrong. (D) is incorrect

because the pattern does not indicate the scores are meaningless. However, the pattern might indicate that scores should be reported as a range of scores rather than as a single score.

40. **(B)** Draw a diagram.

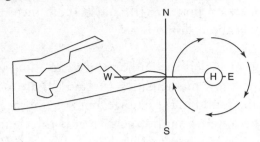

The high pressure is to your east some miles offshore. The wind circulates clockwise around the high-pressure system. The diagram shows that the winds could come from only the southeast or the south. The best answer is (B) southeast.

41. **(B)** These charts show that stock prices in the third graph and interest rates in the first graph generally went in opposite directions. (A) is incorrect because correlation charts do not show a cause-and-effect relationship. (C) is false because the charts do show some relationship. (D) is incorrect because the commodity price chart does not match the stock price chart.

42. **(D)** The author wants to share what he or she learned about the Hardy Boys books. (A) is incorrect because the author does not describe the practice. (B) and (C) are incorrect because the author does not contrast fact and fiction, nor childhood and adulthood.

43. **(A)** The word *syndicate* can have many meanings. The context reveals that the word *syndicate* means a publishing business group. (B) and (C) are incorrect because there is no indication of illegal activity. (D) is incorrect because *syndicate* does not mean "large building."

44. **(B)** The term ghost writer has a specific meaning—it is someone who writes books but does not receive credit. (A) is incorrect here because "ghost" in this context does not refer to a dead person. (C) is incorrect because a ghost writer has a more significant role than influence. (D) is incorrect because a ghost writer has nothing to do with mystical images.

45. **(B)** The quote supports the nonviolent, nondestructive approach to protest supported by Gandhi. The other choices are incorrect because none of them coincides with Ghandi's quote.

46. **(D)** The person visited the school and is certainly curious. The person's response to the custodian shows respect. (A) is incorrect because there may be some evidence of timidity as the student tiptoes in the hallway, but there is no

evidence of fear. (B) is incorrect because there is no particular evidence of either confidence or optimism. (C) is incorrect because there is no evidence of pessimism, although the tiptoeing may show that the student is unsure.

47. **(B)** Alpine has a difference of about 40 permits between 1990 and 1995. There are smaller differences in other towns between 1990 and 1995. (A) and (C) are incorrect because these statements include the words "every year" and the chart shows information for only 1990 and 1995. You can't tell from the chart whether or not these statements are true. (D) is incorrect because Bergenfield had the same number of permits in 1990 as Dumont had in 1995.

48. **(C)** The author spends a lot of time in the passage discussing the time he or she spent with books while learning to be a teacher. After focusing on the real world in the classroom, the author emphasizes teaching from a real world perspective. (A) is incorrect because nothing is intimidating in the passage. (B) is incorrect because this theme never comes up in the passage. (D) is incorrect because this author has clearly had enough of books.

49. **(C)** The author makes the point that he or she has moved beyond books and that a teacher's firsthand experiences now come first. (A) and (B) are incorrect because nothing in the passage discusses teaching art or field trips. (D) is incorrect because the passage never says that firsthand experiences are the most important factor in a teacher's development.

50. **(D)** The title "How Alligators and Crocodiles Differ." is the clear choice. Half of this passage discusses both the alligator and the crocodile. The other choices unnecessarily limit the scope of the title.

51. **(B)** The shape of the shout differentiates an alligator from a crocodile. (A) is incorrect because the placement of teeth is different in an alligator and a crocodile, not by the number of teeth. (C) is incorrect because the article indicates that both reptiles have the same habitat. (D) is incorrect because the passage discusses the diet of alligators but not of crocodiles.

52. **(B)** The first sentence in the fourth paragraph explains that the Iroquois had a cohesive society and were adept at fighting. (A) is incorrect because the Iroquois did side with the British, but they lost. (C) is incorrect because the passage never mentions the weakness of other tribes. (D) is incorrect because the number of tribes was not a significant factor compared to choice (B).

53. **(D)** The second paragraph clearly states that the tribes occupied much of what is now New York State. (A) is incorrect because this choice describes the area conquered by the Iroquois before the Revolutionary War. (B) is incorrect because this choice shows where some Iroquois migrated after the Revolutionary War. (C) is incorrect because this is the name of an Iroquois tribe.

54. **(A)** The last sentence in the second paragraph explains that the region was called the long house of the Iroquois. (B) is incorrect because the region looked like the long house. (C) and (D) are incorrect because the arrangement of the tribes was not directly related to political ties or to conquest.

55. **(C)** The first sentence in the third paragraph says the Iroquois economy was based mainly on agriculture. (A) and (B) are incorrect because wampum and corn are mentioned in the paragraph about the economy, but not as the basis for the economy. (D) is incorrect because conquest is not mentioned as a basis for the economy.

56. **(A)** The first sentence in the passage proposes that there is other life in the universe. (B) is incorrect because the author never suggests the absence of life on earth. (C) is incorrect because the author never suggests that there are humans on other planets. (D) is incorrect because the author compares the entire solar system, not the sun, to the entire cosmos.

57. **(C)** *Infinitesimal* means very small and *infinite* means without limit or limitless. (A) and (B) are incorrect at least because "large" and "very large" are not synonyms for limitless. (D) is incorrect because "large" is the opposite of *infinitesimal*.

58. **(D)** The passage is about youth and constantly refers to what youths do and do not know about AIDS. (A), (B), and (C) are either true or can reasonably be implied from the passage, but none of them are the main idea of the passage.

59. **(D)** This choice paraphrases the third sentence in the paragraph. (A) and (B) are incorrect because they do not describe *how* AIDS can be contracted. (C) is incorrect because it incorrectly describes how AIDS can be contracted.

60. **(B)** The passage uses many synonyms of the word "unaware" to describe young people's knowledge of AIDS. (A) and (C) are incorrect because someone may characterize another person as "stupid" or "dumb," but a person can't be stupid or dumb about AIDS. (D) is incorrect because "unintelligible" describes a person who can't be understood.

61. **(B)** Choice (B) paraphrases lines 11 and 12 in the passage about the outcome of base pairing rules. Choice (A) is incorrect because it describes the appearance of DNA strands, and includes no information about base pairing rules. Choice (C) is incorrect because, while it is taken directly from lines 6 and 7, it does not answer the question about base pairing rules. Choice (D) is incorrect because it misrepresents the information about daugther cells in lines 9 and 10.

62. **(B)** Choice (B) is correct because the last lines of the passage indicate that genes are not involved in coding, implying that the function of many regions

of the genome are obscure, or unknown. Choices (A), (C), and (D) are all correct, based on the passage, but each choice is the incorrect answer to this question because none of the answers directly address coding.

63. **(A)** Choice (A) is correct because it states what a nucleotide consists of from lines 4 and 5 in the passage, but in a different order than in the passage. Choice (B) is incorrect because it talks about daughter cells and not about nucleotides. Choice (C) is incorrect because it describes what DNA consists of, not what nucleotides consist of. Choice (D) is incorrect beacuse a nucleotide does not consist of the human genome.

64. **(D)** This famous poster with the words "JOIN or DIE" reflects the sentiment "United We Stand, Divided We Fall," current before the Revolutionary War. The poster suggests the pieces need to be brought together. (A) does not reflect the words "JOIN or DIE." (B) does correspond with bringing pieces together. (C) is incorrect because ratifying a constitution does not have the urgency found in the words "join or die."

65. **(D)** *Alice in Wonderland,* a fanciful story about a young girl's adventures underground, has underlying figurative meanings and is not to be taken literally. (A) is incorrect because symbolism does not mean in a foreign language. (B) is incorrect because symbolism in this context does not literally mean symbols. (C) is incorrect because nothing in the passage suggests there were no pictures.

66. **(C)** The context reveals that marginal means explanatory notes written next to the main text. (A) is incorrect because "notes" in this context does not mean musical notes. (B) is incorrect because "marginal" in this context does not mean suspect. (D) is incorrect because the passage indicates that the notes were not written in the book authored by Carroll.

67. **(B)** The barren landscape and muddled bison in this print show isolation and cold. (A) is incorrect because the picture does not show action and it is not warm. (C) is incorrect because the picture does not show fluctuation—change. (D) is incorrect because nothing in the picture suggests danger.

68. **(C)** There is a three-hour time difference between coasts, and the time is later on the East Coast. It was 11:30 P.M. on Monday in California when you got through. That means it was three hours later, or 2:30 A.M. Tuesday in New Jersey. (A) indicates that the time was three hours earlier on the East Coast, not three hours later. (B) indicates two hours earlier, and (D) four hours later in New Jersey.

69. **(B)** Consider each Roman numeral in turn.

   I. Incorrect. It does not include a helmet.
  II. Correct. Coveralls can be worn in place of pants and a shirt.
 III. Incorrect. A helmet is missing.

Only Roman numeral II is correct—(B).

70. **(A)** This graph is not a perfect reflection of the chart, but it best represents the steady movement up and then down of the temperatures. Graph (B) incorrectly shows that the temperature went straight up, not up gradually. Graph (C) incorrectly shows that the temperature did not go down until late afternoon, and then only partly. Graph (D) incorrectly shows that the temperature went down in the morning and up in the afternoon.

71. **(D)** The lines in the background indicate the images are a study of the horse's movement. (A) There is nothing to suggest these images are part of a motion picture or (B) the images were taken with a digital camera. (C) A photo finish would show more than one horse.

72. **(B)** Rewrite the words as symbols: $C = 5 + \frac{1}{2}B$. That formula is the same as $C = \frac{1}{2}B + 5$. None of the other equations or inequalities matches the words in this item.

73. **(B)** The brawny man standing at the bar appears in lines 18–21. "[A]t last a mint julep" is ordered in line 38. The correct answer, "The little man stood tiptoe," appears between them on lines 34–35. (A) Haley hastened out in line 18. (C) The gray mist rises in lines 3–4. (D) Tom Loker is recognized in lines 17–18.

74. **(B)** Haley was startled by a dissonant voice in lines 11–12. (A) It was Tom Loker who looked like a bulldog, lines 25–26. (C) Haley is never described as a little man. (D) It was the "little man" who was drinking mint juleps, line 38.

75. **(D)** On line 5 we read that "she (Eliza) disappeared up the bank." (A) The first few lines indicate that this was happening at dusk. (B) Nothing in the passage indicates the slave was brought back to the tavern. (C) Lines 6–8 indicate that the river placed a barrier between the slave and her pursuer.

76. **(A)** Lines 18–22 indicate that it was Tom Loker standing by the door in the corner of the room. (B) on lines 14–18 indicates someone saw Tom Loker, but the statement is not about Tom Loker. (C) Line 17 indicates that Haley met Loker inside the tavern. The name Marks does not appear in the passage.

77. **(B)** It is the dark color. Dark material absorbs more heat than light material. (A) is incorrect because snow melts more quickly under a black cloth than under a white cloth. (C) is incorrect because white material actually reflects more heat in, as well as away from, the snow. (D) White cloth absorbs less heat because it reflects light better.

78. **(B)** The author writes that the question still cannot be answered. (A) is true but does not describe our eventual ability to answer the ultimate question. (C) The author does not say that the question will eventually be answered. (D) The author does not say the question cannot be answered.

79. **(B)** The dust from the horses is the most likely cause of the eerie glow that was seen that morning. (A) A hot day does not produce a glow in the sky. (C) There could not be enough guns to create a strange and eerie glow. (D) An emotional reaction cannot produce an actual glow in the sky.

80. **(C)** The probability is always ½ regardless of what happens on previous flips. (A) is the probability of flipping four heads in a row. (B) is the probability of flipping two heads in a row. (D) is not related to the probability of flipping coins.

Constructed Response

Show your essay to an English professor or a high school English teacher. Ask them to rate your essay 1–4 using this scale.

4 A well developed, complete written assignment.
Shows a thorough response to all parts of the topic.
Clear explanations that are well supported.
An assignment that is free of significant grammatical, punctuation, or spelling errors.

3 A fairly well developed, complete written assignment.
It may not thoroughly respond to all parts of the topic.
Fairly clear explanations that may not be well supported.
It may contain some significant grammatical, punctuation, or spelling errors.

2 A poorly developed, incomplete written assignment.
It does not thoroughly respond to most parts of the topic.
Contains many poor explanations that are not well supported.
It may contain some significant grammatical, punctuation, or spelling errors.

1 A very poorly developed, incomplete written assignment.
It does not thoroughly respond to the topic.
Contains only poor, unsupported explanations.
Contains numerous significant grammatical, punctuation, or spelling errors.

LAST Essay Scoring

Your goal is to write an essay that scores in the upper half. Score your essay using the scale above and the sample essay that follows. Scoring your own essay can be difficult. Showing your essay to English expert will probably help you evaluate your performance.

Sample Essay

This essay would likely receive a score in the upper half. The essay takes a clear position. It discusses the points raised in the assignment description and is largely free of errors in grammar or punctuation. Nothing about the writing style interferes with the reader's ability to understand the author's position.

The length of this essay also indicates that it is worthy of a score in the upper half. The number of words itself is not enough to earn a high score. However, an essay of about this length or longer will likely be required for a high score.

Let's Treat Everyone Equally

This topic raises an important issue for today's schools. Should students be grouped because the students are alike, or because the students are different? This question, which is often referred to as ability grouping, has been with us for over a century. There are good arguments on both sides of this issue, and it can be hard to find just right or just wrong in this debate. It is also worth noting that there are other grouping choices between these polar opposites. Many schools employ one of those other options.

However, given a choice between heterogeneous grouping and homogeneous grouping, I favor heterogeneous grouping. I am going to find much of the support for my position in the weakness of the argument for homogeneous grouping. Then I'll point out some of the strengths of heterogeneous grouping. Finally I will summarize my conclusion in favor of heterogeneous grouping.

What constitutes a homogeneous group of students? Are they all reading at the same level? If so, are they also all capable of doing the same level math? Or history? Or art? Or . . . ? A class containing a homogeneous group of students across all subjects would be extremely small, consisting of maybe two or three students. It is not a practical option in public schools. Each school district would need to hire at least three times the number of teachers they currently have. In these cash-strapped times, no school district can afford that luxury of employing more teachers. Studies do not prove that homogeneous grouping increases students' abilities to learn. This holds true particularly in the elementary and middle school grades.

There are many good arguments for heterogeneous grouping. Heterogeneous classes are inclusive by nature. There is a natural mixing of students. Another advantage is students in heterogeneous grouped classes develop an increased sense of teamwork and collaboration. Students tutor each other. This collaboration helps students improve reading scores, as the students help each other learn. Reports indicate that heterogeneous classrooms offer more learning opportunities for low-ability students. What is more, there is no evidence that high-ability students in heterogeneous classes achieve lower test scores. Emotional development seems to improve when students are in mixed ability classrooms.

In response to the concerns about ability grouping, many schools have begun a process of "de-tracking". Early results indicate that this process can have a positive impact on students morale and student performance. This process may hold the most hope for heterogeneous classrooms.

The topic for this essay forces me to choose between homogeneous grouping and heterogeneous grouping. In the schools, the choice is seldom that definite. Given that forced choice, I come down squarely on the side of heterogeneous grouping, because of the inherent weakness of the argument in favor of homogeneous grouping and the inclusive strengths of heterogeneous grouping.

See pages 58–70 at *http://www.nystce.nesinc.com/PDFs/NY_fld001_prepguide.pdf* for a scoring guide and additional samples of weak and strong essays.

Answer Explanations

PART 3

ATS-W PREPARATION

CHAPTER 8

ATS-W Objectives

TEST INFO BOX

There are two versions of the ATS-W—Elementary and Secondary. The following pages contain the official list of ATS-W Objectives for each version. Review the objectives for the version of the ATS-W you will take.

Elementary ATS-W, page 171

Secondary ATS-W, page 182

Following your review of these objectives, complete the ATS-W Diagnostic Review Quiz in Chapter 9 on page 195 to further prepare for the test. Then take the Practice Elementary ATS-W in Chapter 10 on page 245 or the Secondary ATS-W in Chapter 11 on page 289.

SUBAREAS

SELECTED RESPONSE

I.   Student Development and Learning
II. Instruction and Assessment
III. The Professional Environment

CONSTRUCTED RESPONSE

IV. Instruction and Assessment

Objectives for the ATS-W—Elementary

SUBAREA I—STUDENT DEVELOPMENT AND LEARNING

1. Understand human development, including developmental processes and variations, and use this understanding to promote student development and learning.

EXAMPLES

• Demonstrate knowledge of the major concepts, principles, and theories of human development (physical, cognitive, linguistic, social, emotional, and moral) as related to children from birth to grade six.

• Identify sequences (milestones) and variations of physical, cognitive, linguistic, social, emotional, and moral development in children from birth to grade six.

- Recognize the range of individual developmental differences in children within any given age group from birth to grade six and the implications of this developmental variation for instructional decision making.

- Identify ways in which a child's development in one domain (physical, cognitive, linguistic, social, emotional, moral) may affect learning and development in other domains.

- Apply knowledge of developmental characteristics of learners from birth to grade six to evaluate alternative instructional goals and plans.

- Select appropriate instructional strategies, approaches, and delivery systems to promote development in given learners from birth to grade six.

   2. Understand learning processes, and use this understanding to promote student development and learning.

EXAMPLES

- Analyze ways in which development and learning processes interact.

- Analyze processes by which students construct meaning and develop skills, and apply strategies to facilitate learning in given situations (e.g., by building connections between new information and prior knowledge; by relating learning to world issues and community concerns; by engaging students in purposeful practice and application of knowledge and skills; by using tools, materials, and resources).

- Demonstrate knowledge of different types of learning strategies (e.g., rehearsal, elaboration, organization, metacognition) and how learners use each type of strategy.

- Analyze factors that affect students' learning (e.g., learning styles, contextually supported learning versus decontextualized learning), and adapt instructional practices to promote learning in given situations.

- Recognize how various teacher roles (e.g., direct instructor, facilitator) and student roles (e.g., self-directed learner, group participant, passive observer) may affect learning processes and outcomes.

- Recognize effective strategies for promoting independent thinking and learning (e.g., by helping students develop critical-thinking, decision-making, and problem-solving skills; by enabling students to pursue topics of personal interest) and for promoting students' sense of ownership and responsibility in relation to their own learning.

   3. Understand how factors in the home, school, and community may affect students' development and readiness to learn; and use this understanding to create a classroom environment within which all students can develop and learn.

EXAMPLES

- Recognize the impact of sociocultural factors (e.g., culture, heritage, language, socioeconomic profile) in the home, school, and community on students' development and learning.

- Analyze ways in which students' personal health, safety, nutrition, and past or present exposure to abusive or dangerous environments may affect their development and learning in various domains (e.g., physical, cognitive, linguistic, social, emotional, moral) and their readiness to learn.

- Recognize the significance of family life and the home environment for student development and learning (e.g., nature of the expectations of parents, guardians, and caregivers; degree of their involvement in the student's education).

- Analyze how schoolwide structures (e.g., tracking) and classroom factors (e.g., homogeneous versus heterogeneous grouping, student-teacher interactions) may affect students' self-concept and learning.

- Identify effective strategies for creating a classroom environment that promotes student development and learning by taking advantage of positive factors (e.g., culture, heritage, language) in the home, school, and community and minimize the effects of negative factors (e.g., minimal family support).

- Analyze ways in which peer interactions (e.g., acceptance versus isolation, bullying) may promote or hinder a student's development and success in school, and determine effective strategies for dealing with peer-related issues in given classroom situations.

- Demonstrate knowledge of health, sexuality, and peer-related issues for students (e.g., self-image, physical appearance and fitness, peer-group conformity) and the interrelated nature of these issues, and recognize how specific behaviors related to health, sexuality, and peer-issues (e.g., eating disorders, drug and alcohol use, gang involvement) can affect development and learning.

4. Understand language and literacy development, and use this knowledge in all content areas to develop the listening, speaking, reading, and writing skills of students, including students for whom English is not their primary language.

EXAMPLES

- Identify factors that influence language acquisition, and analyze ways students' language skills affect their overall development and learning.

- Identify expected stages and patterns of second-language acquisitions, including analyzing factors that affect second-language acquisition.

- Identify approaches that are effective in promoting English Language Learners' development of English language proficiency, including adapting teaching strategies and consulting and collaborating with teachers in the ESL program.

- Recognize the role of oral language development, including vocabulary development, and the role of the alphabetic principle, including phonemic awareness and other phonological skills, in the development of English literacy, and identify expected stages and patterns in English literacy development.

- Identify factors that influence students' literacy development, and demonstrate knowledge of research-validated instructional strategies for addressing the literacy needs of students at all stages of literacy development, including applying strategies for facilitating students' comprehension of texts before, during, and after reading, and using modeling and explicit instruction to teach students how to use comprehension strategies effectively.

- Recognize similarities and differences between the English literacy development of native English speakers and English Language Learners, including how literacy development in the primary language influences literacy development in English, and apply strategies for helping English Language Learners to transfer literacy skills in the primary language to English.

- Use knowledge of literacy development to select instructional strategies that help students use literacy skills as tools for learning; that teach students how to use, access, and evaluate information from various resources; and that support students' development of content-area reading skills.

5. Understand diverse student populations, and use knowledge of diversity within the school and community to address the needs of all learners, to create a sense of community among students, and to promote students' appreciation of and respect for individuals and groups.

EXAMPLES

- Recognize appropriate strategies for teachers to use to enhance their own understanding of students (e.g., learning about students' family situations, cultural backgrounds, individual needs) and to promote a sense of community among diverse groups in the classroom.

- Apply strategies for working effectively with students from all cultures, students of both genders, students from various socioeconomic circumstances, students from homes where English is not the primary language, and students whose home situations involve various family arrangements and lifestyles.

- Apply strategies for promoting students' understanding and appreciation of diversity and for using diversity that exists within the classroom and the community to enhance all students' learning.

- Analyze how classroom environments that respect diversity promote positive student experiences.

6. Understand the characteristics and needs of students with disabilities, developmental delays, and exceptional abilities (including gifted and talented students), and use this knowledge to help students reach their highest levels of achievement and independence.

EXAMPLES

- Demonstrate awareness of types of disabilities, developmental delays, and exceptional abilities and of the implications for learning associated with these differences.

- Apply criteria and procedures for evaluating, selecting, creating, and modifying materials and equipment to address individual special needs, and recognize the importance of consulting with specialists to identify appropriate materials and equipment, including assistive technology, when working with students with disabilities, developmental delays, or exceptional abilities.

- Identify teacher responsibilities and requirements associated with referring students who may have special needs and with developing and implementing Individualized Education Plans (IEPs), and recognizing appropriate ways to integrate goals from IEPs into instructional activities and daily routines.

- Demonstrate knowledge of basic service delivery models (e.g., inclusion models) for students with special needs, and identify strategies and resources (e.g., special education staff) that help support instruction in inclusive settings.

- Demonstrate knowledge of strategies to ensure that students with special needs and exceptional abilities are an integral part of the class and participate to the greatest extent possible in all classroom activities.

SUBAREA II—INSTRUCTION AND ASSESSMENT

7. Understand how to structure and manage a classroom to create a safe, healthy, and secure learning environment.

EXAMPLES

- Analyze relationships between classroom management strategies (e.g., in relation to discipline, student decision making, establishing and maintaining standards of behavior) and student learning, attitudes, and behaviors.

- Recognize issues related to the creation of a classroom climate (e.g., with regard to shared values and goals, shared experiences, patterns of communication).

- Demonstrate knowledge of basic socialization strategies, including how to support social interaction and facilitate conflict resolution among learners, and apply strategies for instructing students on the principles of honesty, personal responsibility, respect for others, observance of laws and rules, courtesy, dignity, and other traits that will enhance the quality of their experiences in, and contributions to, the class and the greater community.

- Organize a daily schedule that takes into consideration and capitalizes on the developmental characteristics of learners.

- Evaluate, select, and use various methods for managing transitions (e.g., between lessons, when students enter and leave the classroom), and handle routine classroom tasks and unanticipated situations.

- Analyze the effects of the physical environment, including different special arrangements, on students' learning and behavior.

8. Understand curriculum development, and apply knowledge of factors and processes in curricular decision making.

EXAMPLES

- Apply procedures used in classroom curricular decision making (e.g., evaluating the current curriculum, defining scope and sequence).

- Evaluate curriculum materials and resources for their effectiveness in addressing the development and learning needs of given students.

- Apply strategies for modifying curriculum based on learner characteristics.

- Apply strategies for integrating curricula (e.g., incorporating interdisciplinary themes).

9. Understand the interrelationship between assessment and instruction and how to use formal and informal assessment to learn about students, plan instruction, monitor student understanding in the context of instruction, and make effective instructional modifications.

EXAMPLES

- Demonstrate understanding that assessment and instruction must be closely integrated.

- Demonstrate familiarity with basic assessment approaches, including the instructional advantages and limitations of various assessment instruments and techniques (e.g., portfolio, teacher-designed classroom test, performance assessment, peer assessment, student self-assessment, teacher observation, criterion-referenced test, norm-referenced test).

- Use knowledge of the different purposes (e.g., screening, diagnosing, comparing, monitoring) of various assessments and knowledge of assessment concepts (e.g., validity, reliability, bias) to select the most appropriate assessment instrument or technique for a given situation.

- Use rubrics, and interpret and use information derived from a given assessment.

- Recognize strategies for planning, adjusting, or modifying lessons and activities based on assessment results.

10. Understand instructional planning and apply knowledge of planning processes to design effective instruction that promotes the learning of all students.

EXAMPLES

- Recognize key factors to consider in planning instruction (e.g., New York State Learning Standards for students, instructional goals and strategies, the nature of the content and/or skills to be taught, students' characteristics and prior experiences, students' current knowledge and skills as determined by assessment results, available time and other resources).

- Analyze and apply given information about specific planning factors (see above statement) to define lesson and unit objectives, select appropriate instructional approach(es) to use in a given lesson (e.g., discovery learning, explicit instruction), determine the appropriate sequence of instruction/learning for given content or learners within a lesson and unit, and develop specific lesson and unit plans.

- Identify the background knowledge and prerequisite skills required by a given lesson, and apply strategies for determining students' readiness for learning (e.g., through teacher observations, student self-assessment, pretesting) and for ensuring students' success in learning (e.g., by planning sufficient time to preteach key concepts or vocabulary, by planning differentiated instruction).

- Use assessment information before, during, and after instruction to modify plans and to adapt instruction for individual learners.

- Analyze a given lesson or unit plan in terms of organization, completeness, feasibility, etc.

- Apply strategies for collaborating with others to plan and implement instruction.

11. Understand various instructional approaches, and use this knowledge to facilitate student learning.

EXAMPLES

- Analyze the uses and benefits, or limitations of a specific instructional approach (e.g., direct instruction, cooperative learning, interdisciplinary instruction, exploration, discovery learning, independent study, lectures, hands-on activities, peer tutoring, technology-based approach, various discussion methods such as guided discussion, various questioning methods) in relation to given purposes and learners.

- Recognize appropriate strategies for varying the role of the teacher (e.g., working with students as instructor, facilitator, observer; working with other adults in the classroom) in relation to the situation and the instructional learning situations.

- Apply procedures for promoting positive and productive small-group interactions (e.g., establishing rules for working with other students in cooperative learning situations).

- Compare instructional approaches in terms of teacher student responsibilities, expected student outcomes, usefulness for achieving instructional purposes, etc.

   12. Understand principles and procedures for organizing and implementing lessons, and use this knowledge to promote student learning and achievement.

EXAMPLES

- Evaluate strengths and weaknesses of various strategies for organizing and implementing a given lesson (e.g., in relation to introducing and closing a lesson, using inductive and deductive instruction, building on students' prior knowledge and experiences).

- Recognize the importance of organizing instruction to include multiple strategies for teaching the same content so as to provide the kind and amount of instruction/practice needed by each student in the class.

- Evaluate various instructional resources (e.g., textbooks and other print resources, primary documents or artifacts, guest speakers, films and other audiovisual materials, computers and other technological resources) in relation to given content, learners (including those with special needs), and goals.

- Demonstrate understanding of the developmental characteristics of students (e.g., with regard to attention and focus, writing or reading for extended periods of time) when organizing and implementing lessons.

- Apply strategies for adjusting lessons in response to student performance and student feedback (e.g., responding to student comments regarding relevant personal experiences, changing the pace of a lesson as appropriate).

   13. Understand the relationship between student motivation and achievement and how motivational principles and practices can be used to promote and sustain student cooperation in learning.

EXAMPLES

- Distinguish between motivational strategies that use intrinsic and extrinsic rewards, and identify the likely benefits and limitations of each approach.

- Analyze the effects of using various intrinsic and extrinsic motivational strategies in given situations.

- Recognize factors (e.g., expectations, methods of providing specific feedback) and situations that tend to promote or diminish student motivation.

- Recognize the relationship between direct engagement in learning and students' interest in lessons/activities.

- Apply procedures for enhancing student interest and helping students find their own motivation (e.g., relating concepts presented in the classroom to students' everyday experiences; encouraging students to ask questions, initiate activities, and pursue problems that are meaningful to them; highlighting connections between academic learning and the workplace).

- Recognize the importance of utilizing play to benefit young children's learning.

- Recognize the importance of encouragement in sustaining students' interest and cooperation in learning.

- Recognize the importance of utilizing peers (e.g., as peer mentors, in group activities) to benefit students' learning and to sustain their interest and cooperation.

   14. Understand communication practices that are effective in promoting student learning and creating a climate of trust and support in the classroom, and how to use a variety of communication modes to support instruction.

EXAMPLES

- Analyze how cultural, gender, and age differences affect communication in the classroom (e.g., eye contact, use of colloquialisms, interpretation of body language), and recognize effective methods for enhancing communication with all students, including being a thoughtful and responsive listener.

- Apply strategies to promote effective classroom interactions that support learning, including teacher-student and student-student interactions.

- Analyze teacher-student interactions with regard to communication issues (e.g., those related to communicating expectations, providing feedback, building student self-esteem, modeling appropriate communication techniques for specific situations).

- Recognize purposes for questioning (e.g., encouraging risk taking and problem solving, maintaining student engagement, facilitating factual recall, assessing student understanding), and select appropriate questioning techniques.

- Apply strategies for adjusting communication to enhance student understanding (e.g., by providing examples, simplifying a complex problem, using verbal and nonverbal modes of communication, using audiovisual and technological tools of communication).

- Demonstrate knowledge of the limits of verbal understanding of students at various ages with different linguistic backgrounds and strategies for ensuring that these limitations do not become barriers to learning (e.g., by linking to known language; by saying things in more than one way; by supporting verbalization with gestures, physical demonstrations, dramatizations, and/or media and manipulatives).

15. Understand uses of technology, including instructional and assistive technology, in teaching and learning, and applying this knowledge to use technology effectively and to teach students how to use technology to enhance their learning.

EXAMPLES

- Demonstrate knowledge of educational uses of various technology tools, such as calculators, software applications, input devices (e.g., keyboard, mouse, scanner, modem, CD-ROM), and the Internet.

- Recognize purposes and uses of common types of assistive technology (e.g., amplification devices, communication boards).

- Recognize issues related to the appropriate use of technology (e.g., privacy issues, security issues, copyright laws and issues, ethical issues regarding the acquisition and use of information from technology resources), and identify procedures that ensure the legal and ethical use of technology resources.

- Identify and address equity issues related to the use of technology is the classroom (e.g., equal access to technology for all students).

- Identify effective instructional uses of current technology in relation to communication (e.g., audio and visual recording and display devices).

- Apply strategies for helping students acquire, analyze, and evaluate electronic information (e.g., locating specific information on the Internet and verifying its accuracy and validity).

- Evaluating students' technologically produced products using established criteria related to content, delivery, and the objective(s) of the assignment.

SUBAREA III—THE PROFESSIONAL ENVIRONMENT

16. Understand the history, philosophy, and role of education in New York State and the broader society.

EXAMPLES

- Analyze relationships between education and society (e.g., schools reflecting and affecting social values, historical dimensions of the school-society relationship, the role of education in a democratic society, the role of education in promoting equity in society).

- Demonstrate knowledge of the historical foundations of education in the United States and of past and current philosophical issues in education (e.g., teacher-directed versus child-centered instruction).

- Apply procedures for working collaboratively and cooperatively with various members of the New York State educational system to accomplish a variety of educational goals.

- Analyze differences between school-based and centralized models of decision making.

- Apply knowledge of the roles and responsibilities of different components of the education system in New York (e.g., local school boards, Board of Regents, district superintendents, school principals, Board of Cooperative Educational Services [BOCES], higher education, unions, professional organizations, parent organizations).

17. Understand how to reflect productively on one's own teaching practice and how to update one's professional knowledge, skills, and effectiveness.

EXAMPLES

- Assess one's own teaching strengths and weaknesses.

- Use different types of resources and opportunities (e.g., journals, inservice programs, continuing education, higher education, professional organizations, other educators) to enhance one's teaching effectiveness.

- Apply strategies for working effectively with members of the immediate school community (e.g., colleagues, mentor, supervisor, special needs professionals, principal, building staff) to increase one's knowledge or skills in a given situation.

- Analyze ways of evaluating and responding to feedback (e.g., from supervisors, students, parents, colleagues).

18. Understand the importance of and apply strategies for promoting productive relationships and interactions among the school, home, and community to enhance student learning.

EXAMPLES

- Identify strategies for initiating and maintaining effective communication between the teacher and parents or other caregivers, and recognize factors that may facilitate or impede communication in given situations (including parent-teacher conferences).

- Identify a variety of strategies for working with parents, caregivers, and others to help students from diverse backgrounds reinforce in-school learning outside the school environment.

- Apply strategies for using community resources to enrich learning experiences.

- Recognize various ways in which school personnel, local citizens, and community institutions (e.g., businesses, cultural institutions, colleges and universities, social agencies) can work together to promote a sense of neighborhood and community.

19. Understand reciprocal rights and responsibilities in situations involving interactions between teachers and students, parents/guardians, community members, colleagues, school administrators, and other school personnel.

EXAMPLES

- Apply knowledge of laws related to students' rights in various situations (e.g., in relation to due process, discrimination, harassment, confidentiality, discipline, privacy).

- Apply knowledge of a teacher's rights and responsibilities in various situations (e.g., in relation to students with disabilities, potential abuse, safety issues).

- Apply knowledge of parents' rights and responsibilities in various situations (e.g., in relation to student records, school attendance).

- Analyze the appropriateness of a teacher's response to a parent, a community member, another educator, or a student in various situations (e.g., when dealing with differences of opinion in regard to current or emerging policy).

SUBAREA IV—INSTRUCTION AND ASSESSMENT: CONSTRUCTED-RESPONSE ITEM

The content to be addressed by the constructed-response assignment is described in Subarea II, Objectives 7–15.

Objectives for the ATS-W—Secondary

SUBAREA I—STUDENT DEVELOPMENT AND LEARNING

1. Understand human development, including developmental processes and variations, and use this understanding to promote student development and learning.

EXAMPLES

- Demonstrate knowledge of the major concepts, principles, and theories of human development (physical, cognitive, linguistic, social, emotional, and moral) as related to young adolescents and adolescents (i.e., as related to students in grades five to twelve).

- Identify sequences (milestones) and variations of physical, cognitive, linguistic, social, emotional, and moral development of young adolescents and adolescents.

- Recognize the range of individual developmental differences in children within any given age group in grades five to twelve and the implications of this developmental variation for instructional decision making.

- Identify ways in which a young adolescent's or an adolescent's development in one domain (physical, cognitive, linguistic, social, emotional, moral) may affect learning and development in other domains.

- Apply knowledge of developmental characteristics of young adolescents and adolescents to evaluate alternative instructional goals and plans.

- Select appropriate instructional strategies, approaches, and delivery systems to promote young adolescents' and adolescents' development and learning.

2. Understand learning processes, and use this understanding to promote student development and learning.

EXAMPLES

- Analyze ways in which development and learning processes interact.

- Analyze processes by which students construct meaning and develop skills, and apply strategies to facilitate learning in given situations (e.g., by building connections between new information and prior knowledge; by relating learning to world issues and community concerns; by engaging students in purposeful practice and application of knowledge and skills; by using tools, materials, and resources).

- Demonstrate knowledge of different types of learning strategies (e.g., rehearsal, elaboration, organization, metacognition) and how learners use each type of strategy.

- Analyze factors that affect students' learning (e.g., learning styles, contextually supported learning versus decontextualized learning), and adapt instructional practices to promote learning in given situations.

- Recognize how various teacher roles (e.g., direct instructor, facilitator) and student roles (e.g., self-directed learner, group participant, passive observer) may affect learning processes and outcomes.

- Recognize effective strategies for promoting independent thinking and learning (e.g., by helping students develop critical-thinking, decision-making, and problem-solving skills; by enabling students to pursue topics of personal interest) and for promoting students' sense of ownership and responsibility in relation to their own learning.

3. Understand how factors in the home, school, and community may affect students' development and readiness to learn, and use this understanding to create a classroom environment within which all students can develop and learn.

EXAMPLES

- Recognize the impact of sociocultural factors (e.g., culture, heritage, language, socioeconomic profile) in the home, school, and community on students' development and learning.

- Analyze ways in which students' personal health, safety, nutrition, and past or present exposure to abusive or dangerous environments may affect their development and learning in various domains (e.g., physical, cognitive, linguistic, social, emotional, moral) and their readiness to learn.

- Recognize the significance of family life and the home environment for student development and learning (e.g., nature of the expectations of parents, guardians, and caregivers; degree of their involvement in the student's education).

- Analyze how schoolwide structures (e.g., tracking) and classroom factors (e.g., homogeneous versus heterogeneous grouping, student-teacher interactions) may affect students' self-concept and learning.

- Identify effective strategies for creating a classroom environment that promotes student development and learning by taking advantage of positive factors (e.g., culture, heritage, language) in the home, school, and community and minimize the effects of negative factors (e.g., minimal family support).

- Analyze ways in which peer interactions (e.g., acceptance versus isolation, bullying) may promote or hinder a student's development and success in school, and determine effective strategies for dealing with peer-related issues in given classroom situations.

- Demonstrate knowledge of health, sexuality, and peer-related issues for students (e.g., self-image, physical appearance and fitness, peer-group conformity) and the interrelated nature of these issues, and recognize how specific behaviors related to health, sexuality, and peer issues (e.g., eating disorders, drug and alcohol use, gang involvement) can affect development and learning.

4. Understand language and literacy development, and use this knowledge in all content areas to develop the listening, speaking, reading, and writing skills of students, including students for whom English is not their primary language.

EXAMPLES

- Identify factors that influence language acquisition, and analyze ways students' language skills affect their overall development and learning.

- Identify expected stages and patterns of second-language acquisitions, including analyzing factors that affect second-language acquisition.

- Identify approaches that are effective in promoting English Language Learners' development of English language proficiency, including adapting teaching strategies and consulting and collaborating with teachers in the ESL program.

- Recognize the role of oral language development, including vocabulary development, and the role of the alphabetic principle, including phonemic awareness and other phonological skills, in the development of English literacy, and identify expected stages and patterns in English literacy development.

- Identify factors that influence students' literacy development, and demonstrate knowledge of research-validated instructional strategies for addressing the literacy needs of students at all stages of literacy development, including applying strategies for facilitating students' comprehension of texts before, during, and after reading, and using modeling and explicit instruction to teach students how to use comprehension strategies effectively.

- Recognize similarities and differences between the English literacy development of native English speakers and English Language Learners, including how literacy development in the primary language influences literacy development in English, and apply strategies for helping English Language Learners transfer literacy skills in the primary language to English.

- Use knowledge of literacy development to select instructional strategies that help students use literacy skills as tools for learning; that teach students how to use, access, and evaluate information from various resources; and that support students' development of content-area reading skills.

5. Understand diverse student populations, and use knowledge of diversity within the school and community to address the needs of all learners, to create a sense of community among students, and to promote students' appreciation of and respect for individuals and groups.

EXAMPLES

- Recognize appropriate strategies for teachers to use to enhance their own understanding of students (e.g., learning about students' family situations, cultural backgrounds, individual needs) and to promote a sense of community among diverse groups in the classroom.

- Apply strategies for working effectively with students from all cultures, students of both genders, students from various socioeconomic circumstances, students from homes where English is not the primary language, and students whose home situations involve various family arrangements and lifestyles.

- Apply strategies for promoting students' understanding and appreciation of diversity and for using diversity that exists within the classroom and the community to enhance all students' learning.

- Analyze how classroom environments that respect diversity promote positive student experiences.

6. Understand the characteristics and needs of students with disabilities, developmental delays, and exceptional abilities (including gifted and talented students), and use this knowledge to help students reach their highest levels of achievement and independence.

EXAMPLES

- Demonstrate awareness of types of disabilities, developmental delays, and exceptional abilities, and of the implications for learning associated with these differences.

- Apply criteria and procedures for evaluating, selecting, creating, and modifying materials and equipment to address individual special needs, and recognize the importance of consulting with specialists to identify appropriate materials and equipment, including assistive technology, when working with students with disabilities, developmental delays, or exceptional abilities.

- Identify teacher responsibilities and requirements associated with referring students who may have special needs and with developing and implementing Individualized Education Plans (IEPs), and recognizing appropriate ways to integrate goals from IEPs into instructional activities and daily routines.

- Demonstrate knowledge of basic service delivery models (e.g., inclusion models) for students with special needs, and identify strategies and resources (e.g., special education staff) that help support instruction in inclusive settings.

- Demonstrate knowledge of strategies to ensure that students with special needs and exceptional abilities are an integral part of the class and participate to the greatest extent possible in all classroom activities.

SUBAREA II—INSTRUCTION AND ASSESSMENT

7. Understand how to structure and manage a classroom to create a safe, healthy, and secure learning environment.

EXAMPLES

- Analyze relationships between classroom management strategies (e.g., in relation to discipline, student decision making, establishing and maintaining standards of behavior) and student learning, attitudes, and behaviors.

- Recognize issues related to the creation of a classroom climate (e.g., with regard to shared values and goals, shared experiences, patterns of communication).

- Demonstrate knowledge of basic socialization strategies, including how to support social interaction and facilitate conflict resolution among learners, and apply strategies for instructing students on the principles of honesty, personal responsibility, respect for others, observance of laws and rules, courtesy, dignity, and other traits that will enhance the quality of their experiences in, and contributions to, the class and the greater community.

- Organize a daily schedule that takes into consideration and capitalizes on the developmental characteristics of learners.

- Evaluate, select, and use various methods for managing transitions (e.g., between lessons, when students enter and leave the classroom), and handle routine classroom tasks and unanticipated situations.

- Analyze the effects of the physical environment, including different special arrangements, on students learning and behavior.

8. Understand curriculum development, and apply knowledge of factors and processes in curricular decision making.

EXAMPLES

- Apply procedures used in classroom curricular decision making (e.g., evaluating the current curriculum, defining scope and sequence).

- Evaluate curriculum materials and resources for their effectiveness in addressing the developmental and learning needs of given students.

- Apply strategies for modifying curriculum based on learner characteristics.

- Apply strategies for integrating curricula (e.g., incorporating interdisciplinary themes).

9. Understand the interrelationship between assessment and instruction and how to use formal and informal assessment to learn about students, plan instruction, monitor student understanding in the context of instruction, and make effective instructional modifications.

EXAMPLES

- Demonstrate understanding that assessment and instruction must be closely integrated.

- Demonstrate familiarity with basic assessment approaches, including the instructional advantages and limitations of various assessment instruments and techniques (e.g., portfolio, teacher-designed classroom test, performance assessment, peer assessment, student self-assessment, teacher observation, criterion-referenced test, norm-referenced test).

- Use knowledge of the different purposes (e.g., screening, diagnosing, comparing, monitoring) of various assessments and knowledge of assessment concepts (e.g., validity, reliability, bias) to select the most appropriate assessment instrument or technique for a given situation.

- Use rubrics, and interpret and use information derived from a given assessment.

- Recognize strategies for planning, adjusting, or modifying lessons and activities based on assessment results.

10. Understand instructional planning and apply knowledge of planning processes to design effective instruction that promotes the learning of all students.

EXAMPLES

- Recognize key factors to consider in planning instruction (e.g., New York State Learning Standards for students, instructional goals and strategies, the nature of the content and/or skills to be taught, students' characteristics and prior experiences, students' current knowledge and skills as determined by assessment results, available time, and other resources).

- Analyze and apply given information about specific planning factors (see above statement) to define lesson and unit objectives, select appropriate instructional approach(es) to use in a given lesson (e.g., discovery learning, explicit instruction), determine the appropriate sequence of instruction/learning for given content or learners within a lesson and unit, and develop specific lesson and unit plans.

- Identify the background knowledge and prerequisite skills required by a given lesson, and apply strategies for determining students' readiness for learning (e.g., through teacher observation, student self-assessment, pretesting) and for ensuring students' success in learning (e.g., by planning sufficient time to preteach key concepts or vocabulary, by planning differentiated instruction).

- Use assessment information before, during, and after instruction to modify plans and to adapt instruction for individual learners.

- Analyze a given lesson or unit plan in terms of organization, completeness, feasibility, etc.

- Apply strategies for collaborating with others to plan and implement instruction.

11. Understand various instructional approaches, and use this knowledge to facilitate student learning.

EXAMPLES

- Analyze the uses and benefits, or limitations of a specific instructional approach (e.g., direct instruction, cooperative learning, interdisciplinary instruction, exploration, discovery learning, independent study, lectures, hands-on activities, peer tutoring, technology-based approach, various discussion methods such as guided discussion, various questioning methods) in relation to given purposes and learners.

- Recognize appropriate strategies for varying the role of the teacher (e.g., working with students as instructor, facilitator, observer; working with other adults in the classroom) in relation to the situation and the instructional learning situations.

- Apply procedures for promoting positive and productive small-group interactions (e.g., establishing rules for working with other students in cooperative learning situations).

- Compare instructional approaches in terms of teacher/student responsibilities, expected student outcomes, usefulness for achieving instructional purposes, etc.

12. Understand principles and procedures for organizing and implementing lessons, and use this knowledge to promote students' learning and achievement.

EXAMPLES

- Evaluate strengths and weaknesses of various strategies for organizing and implementing a given lesson (e.g., in relation to introducing and closing a lesson, using inductive and deductive instruction, building on students' prior knowledge and experiences).

- Recognize the importance of organizing instruction to include multiple strategies for teaching the same content so as to provide the kinds and amount of instruction/practice needed by each student in the class.

- Evaluate various instructional resources (e.g., textbooks and other print resources, primary documents or artifacts, guest speakers, films and other audiovisual materials, computers and other technological resources) in relation to given content, learners (including those with special needs), and goals.

- Demonstrate understanding of the developmental characteristics of students (e.g., with regard to attention and focus, writing or reading for extended periods of time) when organizing and implementing lessons.

- Apply strategies for adjusting lessons in response to student performance and student feedback (e.g., responding to student comments regarding relevant personal experiences, changing the pace of a lesson as appropriate).

13. Understand the relationship between student motivation and achievement and how motivational principles and practices can be used to promote and sustain student cooperation in learning.

EXAMPLES

- Distinguish between motivational strategies that use intrinsic and extrinsic rewards, and identify the likely benefits and limitations of each approach.

- Analyze the effects of using various intrinsic and extrinsic motivational strategies in given situations.

- Recognize factors (e.g., expectations, methods of providing specific feedback) and situations that tend to promote or diminish student motivation.

- Recognize the relationship between direct engagement in learning and students' interest in lessons/activities.

- Apply procedures for enhancing student interest and helping students find their own motivation (e.g., relating concepts presented in the classroom to students' everyday experiences; encouraging students to ask questions, initiate activities, and pursue problems that are meaningful to them; highlighting connections between academic learning and the workplace).

- Recognize the importance of encouragement in sustaining students' interest and cooperation in learning.

- Recognize the importance of utilizing peers (e.g., as peer mentors, in group activities) to benefit students' learning and to sustain their interest and cooperation.

14. Understand communication practices that are effective in promoting student learning and creating a climate of trust and support in the classroom, and how to use a variety of communication modes to support instruction.

EXAMPLES

- Analyze how cultural, gender, and age differences affect communication in the classroom (e.g., eye contact, use of colloquialisms, interpretation of body language), and recognize effective methods for enhancing communication with all students, including being a thoughtful and responsive listener.

- Apply strategies to promote effective classroom interactions that support learning, including teacher-student and student-student interactions.

- Analyze teacher-student interactions with regard to communication issues (e.g., those related to communicating expectations, providing feedback, building student self-esteem, modeling appropriate communication techniques for specific situations).

- Recognize purposes for questioning (e.g., encouraging risk taking and problem solving, maintaining student engagement, facilitating factual recall, assessing student understanding), and select appropriate questioning techniques.

- Apply strategies for adjusting communication to enhance student understanding (e.g., by providing examples, simplifying a complex problem, using verbal and nonverbal modes of communication, using audiovisual and technological tools of communication).

- Demonstrate knowledge of the limits of verbal understanding of students at various ages with different linguistic backgrounds and strategies for ensuring that these limitations do not become barriers to learning (e.g., by linking to known language; by saying things in more than one way; by supporting verbalization with gestures, physical demonstrations, dramatizations, and/or media and manipulatives).

15. Understand uses of technology, including instructional and assistive technology, in teaching and learning; and apply this to knowledge to use technology effectively and to teach students how to use technology to enhance their learning.

EXAMPLES

- Demonstrate knowledge of educational uses of various technology tools, such as calculators, software applications, input devices (e.g., keyboard, mouse, scanner, modem, CD-ROM), and the Internet.

- Recognize purposes and uses of common types of assistive technology (e.g., amplification devices, communication boards).

- Recognize issues related to the appropriate use of technology (e.g., privacy issues, security issues, copyright laws and issues, ethical issues regarding the acquisition and use of information from technology resources), and identify procedures that ensure the legal and ethical use of technology resources.

- Identify and address equity issues related to the use of technology in the class-room (e.g., equal access to technology for all students).

- Identify effective instructional uses of current technology in relation to com-munication (e.g., audio and visual recording and display devices).

- Apply strategies for helping students acquire, analyze, and evaluate electronic information (e.g., locating specific information on the Internet and verifying its accuracy and validity).

- Evaluating students' technologically produced products using established crite-ria related to content, delivery, and the objective(s) of the assignment.

SUBAREA III—THE PROFESSIONAL ENVIRONMENT

16. Understand the history, philosophy, and role of education in New York State and the broader society.

EXAMPLES

- Analyze relationships between education and society (e.g., schools reflecting and affecting social values, historical dimensions of the school-society relation-ship, the role of education in a democratic society, the role of education in promoting equity in society).

- Demonstrate knowledge of the historical foundations of education in the United States and of past and current philosophical issues in education (e.g., teacher-directed versus child-centered instruction).

- Apply procedures for working collaboratively and cooperatively with various members of the New York State educational system to accomplish a variety of educational goals.

- Analyze differences between school-based and centralized models of decision making.

- Apply knowledge of the roles and responsibilities of different components of the education system in New York (e.g., local school boards, Board of Regents, district superintendents, school principals, Boards of Cooperative Educational Services [BOCES], higher education, unions, professional organizations, par-ent organizations).

17. Understand how to reflect productively on one's own teaching practice and how to update one's professional knowledge, skills, and effectiveness.

EXAMPLES

- Assess one's own teaching strengths and weaknesses.

- Use different types of resources and opportunities (e.g., journals, inservice programs, continuing education, higher education, professional organizations, other educators) to enhance one's teaching effectiveness.

- Apply strategies for working effectively with members of the immediate school community (e.g., colleagues, mentor, supervisor, special needs professionals, principal, building staff) to increase one's knowledge or skills in a given situation.

- Analyze ways of evaluating and responding to feedback (e.g., from supervisors, students, parents, colleagues).

18. Understand the importance of and apply strategies for promoting productive relationships and interactions among the school, home, and community to enhance student learning.

EXAMPLES

- Identify strategies for initiating and maintaining effective communication between the teacher and parents or other caregivers, and recognize factors that may facilitate or impede communication in given situations (including parent-teacher conferences).

- Identify a variety of strategies for working with parents, caregivers, and others to help students from diverse backgrounds reinforce in-school learning outside the school environment.

- Apply strategies for using community resources to enrich learning experiences.

- Recognize various ways in which school personnel, local citizens, and community institutions (e.g., businesses, cultural institutions, colleges and universities, social agencies) can work together to promote a sense of neighborhood and community.

19. Understand reciprocal rights and responsibilities in situations involving interactions between teachers and students, parents/guardians, community members, colleagues, school administrators, and other school personnel.

EXAMPLES

- Apply knowledge of laws related to students' rights in various situations (e.g., in relation to due process, discrimination, harassment, confidentiality, discipline, privacy).

- Apply knowledge of a teacher's rights and responsibilities in various situations (e.g., in relation to students with disabilities, potential abuse, safety issues).

- Apply knowledge of parents' rights and responsibilities in various situations (e.g., in relation to student records, school attendance).

- Analyze the appropriateness of a teacher's response to a parent, a community member, another educator, or a student in various situations (e.g., when dealing with differences of opinion in regard to current or emerging policy).

SUBAREA IV—INSTRUCTION AND ASSESSMENT: CONSTRUCTED-RESPONSE ITEM

The content to be addressed by the constructed-response assignment is described in Subarea II, Objectives 7–15.

ATS-W Diagnostic Quiz and Review

Using This Chapter

I want a quick ATS-W diagnostic review. (BEST FOR MOST PEOPLE)

❑ Take and correct the ATS-W Diagnostic Review Quiz on page 196.

I want a thorough ATS-W diagnostic review.

❑ Take the ATS-W Diagnostic Review Quiz on page 196.
❑ Correct the Diagnostic Review Quiz and read the indicated parts of the review.

ATS-W Diagnostic Review Quiz

This Diagnostic Quiz tests your knowledge of topics included on the ATS-W. The quiz will help you refresh your memory about these topics.

This diagnostic quiz is not like the ATS-W. It does not use a selected-response format. The idea here is to find out what you know and what you don't know. So don't guess answers on this diagnostic review quiz.

The answers are found immediately after the diagnostic quiz. It is to your advantage not to look at them until you complete the quiz. Once you complete and correct the diagnostic quiz, you can use the diagnostic information on the answer checklist to decide which sections to study.

Directions: Write the answers in the space provided.

1. At about what age do boys and girls enter adolescence?
   Boys _____ Girls _____

2. Who provided an experimental basis for behaviorism?
   _____
   _____

3. Give Piaget's four stages of cognitive development along with the approximate ages and one characteristic of each stage.
   _____
   _____
   _____
   _____

4. According to Eriksen, what is the primary emotional crisis experienced by children in grades 6–9?
   _____
   _____
   _____

5. Generally speaking, what moral behavior do children exhibit in Kohlberg's stage of Preconventional Morality?
   _____
   _____
   _____

6. What do social learning theorists mean when they talk about modeling?
   _____
   _____

7. Which has the most significant impact on human development, nature or nurture?
   _____
   _____

8. About what percent of American families have children, a mother at home, and a father at work?
   _____
   _____

9. About when would we expect the school population in America to be evenly divided between Caucasian and minority students?
   _____
   _____

10. To what country do most Hispanic Americans trace their origin?
    _____
    _____

11. Which ethnic group in America has the highest suicide rate and alcoholism rate?

_____

_____

12. About what percent of those who commit serious crimes are caught?

_____

_____

13. What is the most used and abused drug?

_____

_____

14. How is the HIV virus transmitted?

_____

_____

15. The New York Learning Standards are presented in which six categories?

_____

_____

16. Planning for instruction begins with what first step?

_____

_____

17. What is the highest order of thinking in cognitive domain?

_____

_____

18. What types of diversity might require modification of objectives?

_____

_____

19. What should an objective describe?

_____

_____

20. What are prerequisite competencies?

_____

_____

21. According to Madeline Hunter, what is an anticipatory set?

_____

_____

22. Describe formative evaluation.

_____

_____

23. What is the most common error made when reading standardized test reports?

_____

_____

24. What is content validity?

_____

_____

25. What is authentic assessment?

_____

_____

26. What factor correlates most highly with normed scores?

_____

_____

27. What is extrinsic motivation?

_____

_____

28. Do students learn more when they are being taught or when they are working independently?

_____

_____

29. Lectures and explanations are most effective when they begin with what first step?

_____

_____

30. Using Bloom's Taxonomy, what level of questions should be asked in classrooms?

_____

_____

31. About how long should a teacher wait for a student to respond to a question?

_____

_____

32. What types of questions do teachers ask in a student-centered classroom?

_____

_____

33. What important aspects characterize active learning?

_____

_____

34. What is the last step in inquiry learning?

_____

_____

35. How would you adapt instruction for learning disabled students?

_____

_____

36. Overall, what factor correlates most highly with school achievement?

_____

_____

37. Where do most seventh and eighth graders typically turn for leadership?

_____

_____

38. List three characteristics of successful teachers.

_____

_____

39. Initially, how should the teacher arrange classroom seating?

_____

_____

40. Kounin's approach of with-it-ness has been shown to be an effective disciplinary technique. What is with-it-ness?

_____

_____

41. Under the approach recommended by Canter and Canter, how should a teacher respond when students break rules during class?

_____

_____

42. What are nonverbal cues?

_____

_____

43. How can modeling change student behavior?

_____

_____

44. How can negative reinforcement change student behavior?

_____

_____

45. Which groups or entities in the United States are legally responsible for education?

_____

_____

46. What New York regional organization provides services to local school districts?

_____

_____

47. How has the acculturation of ethnic groups changed during the last 40 years?

_____

_____

48. What federal document establishes responsibility for education?

_____

_____

49. When in the process of hiring and dismissing teachers may "reverse discrimination" be legal?

_____

_____

50. What limits have the courts placed on the free speech rights of teachers?

_____

_____

51. How may students publish a paper not subject to review and editing by school officials?

_____

_____

52. About when and where did formal education begin?

_____

_____

53. What educator is credited with establishing the kindergarten?

_____

_____

54. Where did dame schools offer classes?

_____

_____

55. What was the primary teaching device during the American colonial period?

_____

_____

56. What was the main feature of Dewey's progressive schools?

_____

_____

57. How did PL 94-142 impact American education?

_____

_____

Practice Written Assignment

Directions: Use the following lined pages to write a brief essay based on this topic. Use one hour.

Teachers may base their own classroom practices on the way they were taught as children. Teachers may embrace practices or approaches they liked as a child or avoid practices or approaches they found distasteful.

Assume that this is true and choose an elementary school teacher who had a style or approach that you would either use or avoid.

Write an essay appropriate for a group of teachers in New York State that

- identifies the teacher and grade level and describes the approach you would use or avoid
- explains why the approach was appropriate or inappropriate
- explains what made the approach appropriate or inappropriate

DIAGNOSTIC CHECKLIST

The answers are organized by review section. Check your answers. If you miss any question in a section, check the box and review that section.

Knowledge of the Learner

☐ *Human Development, page 206*

1. Boys about 12, girls about 10
2. Pavlov with his experiments on dogs
3. *Sensorimotor* (Birth–18 months) Children develop the idea of object permanence, out of sight not out of mind, during this stage. *Preoperational* (18 months–7 years) Children develop language and are able to solve some problems. Students' thinking is egocentric and they have difficulty developing concepts such as the conservation of number task. *Concrete Operational* (7 years to 12 years) During this period, students' thinking becomes operational. This means that concepts become organized and logical, as long as they are working with or around concrete materials or images. Students master the conservation tasks. *Formal Operational* (12 years–) Children develop and demonstrate concepts without concrete materials or images. Students think fully in symbolic terms about concepts. Children become able to reason effectively, abstractly, and theoretically.

4. Identity vs. Identity confusion
5. No conscience, no clear morality
6. Acting in a way you want others to act
7. The issue remains unresolved.

☐ *Diversity, page 211*

8. About 10 percent
9. By about 2020 (Count your answer correct if you were within 10 years.)
10. Mexico
11. Native Americans
12. About 30 percent
13. Alcohol
14. Exchange of blood and bodily fluids (Intravenous drug users can acquire AIDS when they share needles and inject small quantities of infected blood.)

Instructional Planning and Assessment

☐ *New York Learning Standards, page 216*

15. – The Arts
    – Mathematics, Science and Technology
    – English/Language Arts

– Social Studies
– Languages Other than English
– Health, Physical Education/Home Economics

❑ *Objectives, page 220*
16. Write an objective

❑ *Taxonomy of Objectives, page 220*
17. Evaluation

❑ *Choosing and Modifying Objectives, page 221*
18. Academic, Cultural, Linguistic

❑ *Writing Objectives, page 221*
19. What a student should know or be able to do *after* instruction

❑ *Planning to Teach the Lesson, page 222*
20. What a student should know or be able to do *before* instruction
21. Anticipatory set— something that is said or done to focus students on the lesson.

❑ *Evaluating Instruction, page 229*
22. Formative is used to plan instruction.
23. Looking at a single score instead of a range of scores.
24. Content validity describes the extent to which a test measures the material being taught.

25. Students are evaluated as they demonstrate knowledge or a skill in a real life setting.
26. Socioeconomic status (SES)

❑ *Motivation, page 232*
27. External rewards to improve student performance

❑ *Successful Learning, page 233*
28. Students learn more when they are being taught.

❑ *Classroom Approaches, page 234*
29. Motivation
30. Questions should be asked at all levels.
31. 4 to 5 seconds
32. More open-ended questions
33. Group work, active learning, full participation, democratic structure
34. Metacognition—that is, students analyze their thought processes.

❑ *Adapting Instruction, page 237*
35. Provide structured brief assignments, manipulative activities, and auditory learning

❑ *Cultural and Linguistic Diversity, page 238*
36. Socioeconomic status (SES)

Instructional Delivery

❑ *Managing the Instructional Environment, page 240*

37. They turn to their peer group

38. Any three of the following:
    - Accept children within a teacher-student relationship.
    - Set firm and clear but flexible limits.
    - Enforce rules clearly and consistently.
    - Have positive, realistic expectations about student's achievement.
    - Have clear reasons for expectations about students.
    - Practice what they preach (model acceptable behavior).
    - Don't take it personally. Students usually misbehave or act out because of who they are, not because of who you are.

39. So that they can see the faces of all the students

❑ *Specific Management Techniques, page 242*

40. With-it-ness means that the teacher is constantly monitoring and aware of what is happening in the classroom.

41. Write the names of the students on the board.
    One violation—no action
    Two violations—conference
    Three violations—parental conference

42. A silent gesture or signal to alert students to a transition or to gain attention

❑ *Changing Behavior, page 243*

43. Students who observe a person behaving a particular way often emulate that person.

44. Negative reinforcement means showing students how to avoid undesirable consequences by doing acceptable work.

The Professional Environment

❑ *The Schools in Society, page 227*

45. The states

46. Boards of Cooperative Educational Services (BOCES)

47. Recent immigrants have been less acculturated and have maintained more of their cultural identity and language.

❑ *Legal, Legislative, and Political Influences, page 227*

48. Constitution of the United States

49. May be legal for hiring, but not for dismissal

50. Teachers cannot disrupt the curriculum or the schools.

51. Publish it with private funds off school property.

❑ *Historical and Philosophical Foundations, page 227*

52. About 2000 B.C. in Northern Africa and China. Formal education that led to our system began about 500 B.C. in Athens, Greece

53. Herbart

54. In the houses of the female teachers

55. The Horn Book

56. Student-centered education

57. It mandated an appropriate education in the least restrictive environment for handicapped Americans aged 3–21.

Essay

This essay would likely receive a total score in the upper half.

> *Miss Stendel – The Teacher I Want to be Like*
>
> It has been a long time since I have been in elementary school, and the school I went to is not even there anymore. I would choose Miss Dorothea T. Stendel as the teacher I want to be like. She was my fifth grade teacher In Emerson School and she liked to visit Native American reservations. She used to spend a lot of time in the western states.
>
> The main appropriate technique she used was to be very nice to me. She seemed to understand boys, which a lot of teachers do not. I worked hard because she was nice to me and I would try to use that same approach in my classroom. It may not be scientific but it certainly was a very appropriate approach for me.
>
> The approach was appropriate because it motivated me. I guess you would call it intrinsic motivation. I did not want to work hard for grades. I wanted to work hard just for the work itself.

Miss Stendel used an approach that I thought was not appropriate. I will avoid this approach when I am a teacher. She had piles of mathematics worksheets all around the window sill. You had to work your way around the window sill to do the math program. When you reached the last window you were done.

The approach was inappropriate because the sheets were boring and you really got nothing out of them. There was just a lot of exercises and skill problems on the sheets. You could do the entire windowsill and not learn anything.

The reason the approach was inappropriate is because it did not teach anything, and because it did not show real world applications of mathematics or how mathematical ideas were connected. In my classroom I would make sure students mastered mathematics concepts and be sure to show how to transfer the learning to real world situations. I would emphasize the meaning of mathematics and show students how mathematics ideas were connected.

I do not know where Miss Stendel is today, but I would like to be able to than her for helping me so much. I guess motivating someone to learn can be more important than teaching them mathematics. The more I think about it, I realize now that she certainly understood more and was more strategic than I ever understood. I want to be like that.

ATS-W Review

Physical Development of the Learner

Adequate nutrition in mothers is essential for proper fetal development. Adequate nutrition and exercise are essential for a child's physical growth. Inadequate nutrition can hamper growth and lead to inattentiveness and other problems that interfere with learning.

Alcohol and drug abuse by mothers can cause irreparable brain damage to unborn children. Children of drug-and-alcohol-abusing mothers tend to have lower birth weights. Low birth weight is associated with health, emotional, and learning problems. Alcohol and drug addiction, smoking, stress, and adverse environmental factors are among the other causes of abnormal physical and emotional development.

During the first 12 months after birth, the body weight of infants triples and the brain size doubles. Infants crawl by about 7 months, eat with their hands at about 8 months, sit up by about 9 months, stand up by about 11 months, and walk by about 1 year.

From 12–15 months to 2.5 years, children are called toddlers. During this period, children become expert walkers, learn to feed themselves, show evidence of self control, and spend a great deal of their time playing. This period is characterized by the word *no* and is also when children begin bowel training.

The preschool years span the time from the end of toddlerhood to the entry into kindergarten. Children start to look more like adults with longer legs and shorter torsos. Play continues but becomes more sophisticated.

The elementary school years refer to ages 6–10 in girls and 6–12 in boys. During this period children enter a period of steady growth. Most children double their body weight and increase their height by one-half. Play continues but it involves more sophisticated games and physical activities, often involving groups or teams of other children.

Adolescence begins at about age 10 for girls and at about age 12 for boys. The growth rate spurt begins during this time. Because this period begins earlier for girls than for boys, girls are more mature than boys for a number of years. Sexual and secondary sex characteristics appear during this time. Most adolescents rely heavily on peer-group approval and respond to peer pressure.

Behavioral Development of the Learner

Behaviorism was the first significant theory of development. Behaviorism is concerned with observable, measurable behavior and with those events that stimulate or reinforce the behavior.

WATSON

John Watson originated the behaviorist movement during the early 1900s. His theoretical ideas centered around conditioned responses in children. Conditioned response means that a child was "taught" to respond in a particular way to a stimulus that would not naturally elicit that response. Watson's experiment to condition a child to fear a white rat that the child initially liked is most quoted in texts. Many claim that the success of the experiment was overstated.

PAVLOV

Many trace the experimental basis for behaviorism to the Russian psychologist Pavlov who, in the 1920s, conducted classical conditioning experiments with dogs. Dogs naturally salivate in an unconditioned response to the unconditioned stimulus of food. Pavlov showed that dogs would salivate in response to any neutral stimulus.

The neutral stimulus is called a conditioned stimulus, and the salivation that occurs is called a conditioned response.

THORNDIKE

Also in the early 1900s Edward Thorndike developed his own form of behaviorism called instrumental conditioning. Thorndike's work with animals led him to two significant conclusions:

- The law of exercise—a conditioned response can be strengthened by repeating the response (practice).
- The law of effect—rewarded responses are strengthened while punished responses are weakened.

SKINNER

Skinner was the most influential behaviorist. Skinner referred to his approach as operant conditioning, which studied how voluntary behavior could be shaped. Operant conditioning relies on these basic mechanisms.

- Reward or positive reinforcement—Students are rewarded for repeating desired responses.

- Negative reinforcement—Students escape punishment by repeating desired responses.

- Extinction—Undesired responses are not reinforced.

- Punishment—Undesired responses are punished.

Skinner showed that he could condition very complex behaviors in animals. He believed that students learned when teachers gave immediate positive feedback for a desired behavior and used extinction or punishment for undesirable behaviors.

Cognitive Development of the Learner

JEAN PIAGET

Jean Piaget is the most prominent of cognitive psychologists who believe that students develop concepts through a series of stages. Stage theory is currently the most popular form of child development.

According to Piaget, children proceed through a fixed but uneven series of stages of cognitive development. His stages help us understand the general way in which students learn and develop concepts.

Action and logic versus perception are at the center of Piaget's theory. He believed that children learn through an active involvement with their environment. He also believed that students have developed a concept when their logical understanding overcomes their perceptual misunderstanding of the concept.

His conservation experiments explain this last point. In conservation of number, students are shown two matched rows of checkers. The child confirms that there are the same number of checkers in each row. Then one row of checkers is spread out and the child is asked if there are still the same number of checkers.

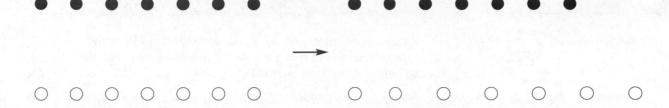

Children who believe there are more checkers in one of the rows do not understand the concept of number because their perception holds sway over their logic. Piaget presents these four stages of cognitive development.

- Sensorimotor (birth to 18 months)—Children exhibit poor verbal and cognitive development. Children develop the idea of object permanence (out of sight not out of mind) during this stage.

- Preoperational (18 months to 7 years)—Children develop language and are able to solve some problems. Students' thinking is egocentric, and they have difficulty developing concepts. For example, students in this stage may not be able to complete the conservation of number task shown above.

- Concrete operational (7–12 years)—Students' thinking becomes operational. This means that concepts become organized and logical, as long as they are working with or around concrete materials or images. During this stage, students master the number conservation and other conservation tasks, but most students do not understand symbolic concepts.

- Formal operational (12+ years)—Children develop and demonstrate concepts without concrete materials or images. In this stage, students think fully in symbolic terms about concepts. Children become able to reason effectively, abstractly, and theoretically. Full development of this stage may depend on the extent to which children have had a full range of active manipulative experiences in the concrete operational stage.

Personality Development

Freud's psychoanalytic theories have profoundly affected modern thought about psychological and personality development. He believed that humans pass through four stages of psychosexual development: oral, anal, phallic, and genital. The personality itself consists of the id, ego, and superego. According to Freud, an integrated personality develops from the gratification experienced at each of these stages.

Psychosocial Development

Eriksen built on Freud's work and partitioned the life span into eight psychosocial stages. An emotional crisis at each stage can lead to a positive or negative result. The result achieved at each stage determines the development pattern for the next stage. Four of these stages fall within the school years.

Stage	Characteristic	Description
Kindergarten	Initiative vs. Guilt	Children accepted and treated warmly tend to feel more comfortable about trying out new ideas. Rejected children tend to become inhibited and guilty.
Elementary grades	Industry vs. Inferiority	Students who are accepted by their peer group and do well in school, and those who believe they are accepted and do well, are more successful than those who do not feel good about themselves.
Grades 6–9	Identity vs. Identity Confusion	Students who establish an identity and a sense of direction and who develop gender, social, and occupational roles experience an easier transition into adulthood than those students who do not establish these roles.
Grades 10–12	Intimacy vs. Isolation	Students who have passed successfully through the other stages will find it easier to establish a relationship with a member of the opposite sex. Those students who are unsuccessful at this stage may face an extremely difficult transition into adult life.

Moral Development

Kohlberg built on Piaget's original work to develop stages of moral development. Kohlberg proposed three levels of moral development with two stages at each level. His stages provide a reasonable approach to understanding moral development. Not everyone moves through all stages.

PRECONVENTIONAL MORALITY (PRESCHOOL AND PRIMARY GRADES)

Stage 1   Children do not demonstrate a conscience but do react to fear of punishment. Children are very egocentric.

Stage 2   Children still have no clear morality. Children concentrate on their own egocentric needs and let others do the same. Children may not be willing to help others meet their needs even though it would help them meet their own needs.

[Some children and antisocial adults may not pass this stage.]

CONVENTIONAL MORALITY (MIDDLE GRADES THROUGH HIGH SCHOOL)

Stage 3   These children want to be good. They associate themselves with parents and other adult authority figures. They show concern for others and evidence a number of virtues and try to live up to expectations.

Stage 4   These children shift from wanting to please authority figures to a more generalized sense of respect for rules and expectations. These children see their responsibility to maintain society through a strict enforcement of society's laws.

[Many adults do not progress beyond this stage of development.]

POSTCONVENTIONAL MORALITY (HIGH SCHOOL AND BEYOND)

Stage 5   People at this stage differentiate between legality and morality. They have a more flexible view of right and wrong and realize that societal needs often take precedence over individual needs.

Stage 6   Very few people reach this stage. Those at stage six have pure, cosmic understanding of justice and dignity. These principles always take precedence when they conflict with what is considered legal or socially acceptable.

Social Learning Theory

Social learning theory is a fairly new field. Social learning theorists seek to combine behavioral and cognitive learning theories along with other types of learning.

Albert Bandura is the leading social learning theorist. He believes that a great deal of learning can take place through modeling. That is, students often act the way they see others act, or they learn vicariously by observing others. Bandura believes that verbal explanations and reinforcement are also important and that students become socialized through systematic modeling of appropriate behavior. Students can also develop cognitive skills by observing a problem-solving process and learn procedures by observing these procedures in action.

Nature Versus Nurture

The relative effects of nature (heredity and genes) and nurture (environment and experience) on growth and development is still not resolved. Certain traits, sex, eye color, some forms of mental retardation, and susceptibility to some mental illnesses such as schizophrenia are linked to genes and heredity. However, other developmental questions are not clear, and even studies of twins separated at birth have not yielded the kind of conclusive results needed to draw conclusions.

Diversity—Society and Culture

America is a multiethnic and multicultural society. Consequently, the culture of the community and the culture of the school varies widely depending on the school's geographic location, socioeconomic setting, and local norms. To understand schools, we must understand society and culture.

Anthropology and sociology provide a scientific basis for studying society and culture. Anthropology is the formal study of culture and the development of society. Much of the early anthropological work dealt with primitive cultures. However, in recent years anthropologists have turned their attention to communities and schools. Sociology is the study of how people behave in a group. Sociology can help us understand how students behave in school, how teachers function on a faculty, and how citizens interact in the community.

Culture is directly affected by the ethnicity of the community. Each ethnic group brings its own culture, its own language, and its own customs to this country.

Until recently, most immigrant groups have been acculturated. That is, they have largely adopted the dominant language and culture of the United States. Lately there has been a shift toward cultural pluralism in which immigrants maintain their cultural, and occasionally linguistic, identity.

Under cultural pluralism, the challenge is to provide equal educational opportunity while also providing for these cultural differences among students. There is little prospect, however, that non-English speakers will realize their full potential in the United States.

Socioeconomic status has a direct affect on culture and on the schools. As noted earlier, there is a strong correlation between SES and academic achievement. In the United States, groups, communities, and schools are stratified by social class. Social stratification often occurs within schools. Unlike many other countries, individuals are able to move among social classes, usually in an upward direction.

The Family

The family remains the predominant influence in the early lives of children. However, the nature of the American family has changed, and for the worse.

Divorce rates are very high and some say that a majority of Americans under 40 will be divorced. American families are fragmented with about 30 percent of children living with a stepparent. About one-quarter of children are raised in one-parent families, and about two-thirds of these children live below the poverty level.

An increasing number of children, called latchkey children, return from school with no parents at home. School programs developed for these students cannot replace effective parenting.

In many respects, the school, social or religious institutions, peer groups, and gangs have replaced parents. This means that parents and families have less influence on children's values and beliefs.

The pressures of economic needs have drastically changed the American family. Less than 10 percent of American families have children, a mother at home, and a father at work. Over 30 percent of married couples have no children, and over 70 percent of mothers with children are working mothers.

Ethnicity

In 2000 the population of the United States was about 72 percent Caucasian, 13 percent African American, 11 percent Hispanic, 4 percent Asian, and 1 percent Indian or Eskimo. Hispanics are the fastest growing ethnic group. By the year 2025 we expect about 62 percent of the population to be white, 17 percent Hispanic, 14 percent African American, 8 percent Asian, and 1 percent Native American. By the year 2050 America's school population will be about evenly divided between white and minority students.

About 15 percent of the families in the United States live below the poverty level. Some 30 percent of African American and Hispanic families do so, and an astonishing 65 percent of Native American families also live below the poverty level.

HISPANICS

Hispanics come predominantly from Mexico and from other countries in Central and South America and the Caribbean. Many Mexican American families have been in this country for more than 100 years. Puerto Ricans form another large Hispanic group.

Language is the primary difficulty faced by this ethnic group. About half of the Hispanics in this country speak Spanish as their first language.

The nature of the Hispanic population varies by region. Most Hispanics living in California or their forbearers are from Mexico. Many Hispanics living in and around New York City are from Puerto Rico or the Dominican Republic, while many Hispanics in Florida trace their ancestry to Cuba.

Hispanic students have more school problems than white students. Hispanics are disproportionately poor and low achieving.

AFRICAN AMERICANS

African Americans have been in this country for centuries, but they began their lives here as slaves. There is not a recent history of large-scale African immigration to the United States.

Their status as slaves and second-class citizens denied African Americans the education, experience, and self-sufficiency needed for upward social mobility. Even when African Americans developed these qualities, they were frequently discriminated against just because of their race. It took almost 200 years from the founding of this country for the Supreme Court to rule that overt school segregation was unconstitutional. Of course, de facto segregation continues to exist.

Many African Americans have achieved middle class status. However, the overwhelming proportion of poor in urban areas are African Americans. The unemployment rate of young African Americans can be near 50 percent in some areas.

NATIVE AMERICANS

Groups of Eskimos and other Native Americans have lived on the North American continent for over 25,000 years. Most Native Americans living today are descendents of tribes conquered and put on reservations about 100 years ago.

During this time of conquest, treaties made with tribes were frequently broken. Native Americans lost their lands and their way of life. They were made dependent on the federal government for subsidies and were not able to develop the education, experience, or self-sufficiency needed for upward mobility.

Native Americans have the largest family size and fastest growth rate of any ethnic group. They also have among the highest suicide and alcoholism rates of any ethnic group.

Native Americans are disproportionally poor and disenfranchised. They live in poverty on reservations and are often alienated when they move off reservations to metropolitan areas.

ASIAN AMERICANS

Asian Americans are predominately Chinese and Japanese together with recent immigrants from Korea and Southeast Asia. Asian Americans represent a countertrend among American minorities. Their achievement and success tend to be above the national average.

Many recent immigrants do not have the educational background of other Asian Americans. They tend to be more ghettoized and to attain a lower SES than other Asian Americans.

However, overall, Asian students perform better on American standardized tests than non-Asian students. This finding holds also for those Asian Americans who immigrated to this country unable to speak, read, or understand English.

Some researchers have said that a particular work ethic currently found in Asian countries together with a strong family structure are responsible for these trends.

Societal Problems

This decade finds our society beset with unprecedented problems of crime and violence, alcohol and drug abuse, sex, AIDS, high dropout rates, and child abuse. Many of these problems can be traced directly to poverty. Schools are a part of society so that they too are affected by these problems.

CRIME AND VIOLENCE

The number of serious crimes in the United States is at the highest level in memory. Students bring guns to school, and large urban areas report dozens of deaths each year from violent acts in school. Murder is the leading cause of death among African American teens. More than 70 percent of those who commit serious crimes are never caught. We live in a society where crime is rampant and crime pays.

Crime in school presents a particular problem for teachers. Some estimate that 3 to 7 percent of all students bring a gun with them to school. Students attack teachers every day in America. While this behavior is not defensible, attention to the principles of classroom management mentioned earlier can help in averting some of these incidents.

ALCOHOL AND DRUG ABUSE

Alcohol is the most used and abused drug. Even though it is legal, there are serious short- and long-term consequences of alcohol use. Alcoholism is the most widespread drug addiction and untreated alcoholism can lead to death.

Tobacco is the next most widely used and abused substance. Some efforts are being made to declare tobacco a drug. Irrefutable evidence shows that tobacco use is a causative factor in hundreds of thousands of deaths each year.

Other drugs including marijuana, cocaine, heroin, and various drugs in pill form carry with them serious health, addiction, and emotional problems. The widespread illicit availability of these drugs creates additional problems. Many students engage in crimes to get money to pay for drugs. Others may commit crimes while under the influence of drugs. Still others may commit crimes by selling drugs to make money.

More than 90 percent of students have used alcohol by the time they leave high school. About 70 percent of high school graduates have used other illegal drugs. Awareness programs that focus on drug use can have some positive effects. However, most drug and alcohol abuse and addiction have other underlying causes. These causes must be addressed for any program to be effective.

SEX

Many teens, and preteens, are sexually active. While many of these children profess to know about sex, they do not. It is in this environment that we find increases in teenage pregnancies, abortions, dropouts, and ruined lives. Sex spreads disease. So we also note increases in syphilis, gonorrhea, and other sexually transmitted diseases.

About 10 percent of teenage girls will become pregnant. Teenage pregnancy is the primary reason why girls drop out of high school. These girls seldom receive appropriate help from the child's father and are often destined for a life of poverty and dependence.

AIDS

AIDS stands for Acquired Immune Deficiency Syndrome. AIDS is a breakdown in the body's immune system caused by a virus called HIV. This virus can be detected with blood tests. People with the HIV virus may take 10 years or longer to develop AIDS. Those who develop AIDS die.

The HIV virus is transmitted by infected blood and other bodily fluids. Sexual relations and contact with infected blood, including blood injected with shared hypodermic needles, are all examples of ways that AIDS can be transmitted. Some 2 to 5 percent of the teens in some urban areas may be HIV positive.

Students can try to avoid becoming HIV positive by reducing their risk factors. Abstinence from sex and never injecting drugs will virtually eliminate the likelihood that a teenager will become HIV positive. Less effective measures can be taken to help sexually active students reduce the likelihood of becoming HIV positive. Girls run a higher risk than boys of becoming HIV positive through sexual activity.

Acquiring the HIV virus is associated with drug and alcohol use. Even when students know the risks, and how to avoid them, alcohol and drug use can lower inhibitions and lead to unsafe practices.

DROPOUTS

About 10 percent of white students, 15 percent of African American students, and 30 percent of Hispanic students drop out of school. Dropout rates are worst in urban areas, with over half the students dropping out of some schools. High school dropouts are usually headed for a life of lower wages and poorer living conditions.

Many of these students feel alienated from society or school and need support or alternative learning environments. Intervention, counseling, and alternative programs such as therapeutic high schools, vocational high schools, and other special learning arrangements can help prevent a student from dropping out.

CHILD ABUSE

Child abuse is the secret destroyer of children's lives. Some estimate that between two and three million children are abused each year. Child abuse is a primary cause of violent youth, runaways, and drug abusers.

Physical and sexual abuse are the most destructive of the abuses heaped upon children. Contrary to popular belief, most child abuse is perpetrated by family members, relatives, and friends. Younger children are often incapable of talking about their abuse and may not reveal it even when asked.

In many states, teachers are required to report suspected child abuse. When child abuse is suspected, a teacher should follow the guidelines given by the school, the district, or the state.

New York Learning Standards

Those at the New York State Education Department recently developed 28 preliminary Learning Standards in broad curricular areas. These final standards will form the basis for instruction in New York State schools. Elementary school, middle school, and high school assessments will be based on these broad standards. The standards are summarized below.

THE ARTS—DANCE, MUSIC, THEATER, AND VISUAL ARTS

1. **Creating, Performing, and Participating in the Arts**
   Students will actively engage in the processes that constitute creation and performance in the arts (dance, music, theater, and visual arts) and participate in various roles in the arts.

2. **Knowing and Using Arts Materials and Resources**
   Students will be knowledgeable about and make use of the materials and resources available for participating in the arts in various roles.

3. **Responding to and Analyzing Works of Art**
   Students will respond critically to a variety of works in the arts, connecting the individual work to many other works and to other aspects of human endeavor and thought.

4. **Understanding the Cultural Dimensions and Contributions of the Arts**
   Students will develop an understanding of the personal and cultural forces that shape artistic communication and how the arts in turn shape the diverse cultures of past and present society.

MATHEMATICS, SCIENCE, AND TECHNOLOGY

1. **Analysis, Inquiry, and Design**
   Students will use mathematical analysis, scientific inquiry, and engineering design, as appropriate, to pose questions, seek answers, and develop solutions.

2. **Information Systems**
   Students will access, generate, process, and transfer information using appropriate technologies.

3. Mathematics

Students will understand mathematics and become mathematically confident by communicating and reasoning mathematically, by applying mathematics in real-world settings, and by solving problems through the integrated study of number systems, geometry, algebra, data analysis, probability, and trigonometry.

4. Science

Students will understand and apply scientific concepts, principles, and theories pertaining to the physical setting and living environment and recognize the historical development of ideas in science.

5. Technology

Students will apply technological knowledge and skills to design, construct, use, and evaluate products and systems to satisfy human and environmental needs.

6. Interconnectedness: Common Themes

Students will understand the relationships and common themes that connect mathematics, science, and technology and apply the themes to these and other areas of learning.

7. Interdisciplinary Problem Solving

Students will apply the knowledge and thinking skills of mathematics, science, and technology to address real-life problems and make informed decisions.

ENGLISH LANGUAGE ARTS

1. Language for Information and Understanding

Students will listen, speak, read, and write for information and understanding. As listeners and readers, students will collect data, facts, and ideas, discover relationships, concepts, and generalizations, and use knowledge generated from oral, written, and electronically produced texts. As speakers and writers they will use oral and written language to acquire, interpret, apply, and transmit information.

2. Language for Literary Response and Expression

Students will listen, speak, read, and write for literary response and expression. Students will listen to oral, written, and electronically produced texts and performances, relate texts and performances to their own lives, and develop an understanding of the diverse social, historical, and cultural dimensions the texts and performances represent. As speakers and writers, students will use oral and written language for self-expression and artistic creation.

3. Language for Critical Analysis and Evaluation

Students will listen, speak, read, and write for critical analysis and evaluation. As listeners and readers, students will collect and analyze experiences, ideas, information, and issues presented by others using a variety of established criteria. As speakers and writers, they will present, in oral and written language and form, a variety of perspectives and opinions.

4. **Language for Social Interaction**
   Students will use oral and written language for effective social communication with a wide variety of people. As readers and listeners, they will use the social communications of others to enrich their understanding of people and their views.

SOCIAL STUDIES

1. **History of the United States and New York**
   Students will use a variety of intellectual skills to demonstrate their understanding of major ideas, eras, themes, developments, and turning points in the history of the United States and New York.

2. **World History**
   Students will use a variety of intellectual skills to demonstrate their understanding of major ideas, eras, themes, developments, and turning points in world history and examine the broad sweep of history from a variety of perspectives.

3. **Geography**
   Students will use a variety of intellectual skills to demonstrate their understanding of the geography of the independent worlds in which we live—local, national, and global—including the distribution of people, places, and environments over the earth's surface.

4. **Economic Systems**
   Students will use a variety of intellectual skills to demonstrate their understanding of how the United States and other societies develop economic systems and associated institutions to allocate scarce resources. Students will also use these skills to understand how major decision-making units function in the United States and other national economies, and how an economy solves the scarcity problem through market and nonmarket mechanisms.

5. **Civics, Citizenship, and Government**
   Students will use a variety of intellectual skills to demonstrate their understanding of the necessity for establishing governments; the governmental system of the United States and other nations; the United States Constitution; the basic civil values of American constitutional democracy; and the roles, rights, and responsibilities of citizenship, including avenues of participation.

LANGUAGES OTHER THAN ENGLISH

1. **Communication Skills**
   Students will be able to use a language other than English for communication.

2. **Cultural Understanding**
   Students will develop cross-cultural skills and understandings.

HEALTH, PHYSICAL EDUCATION, AND HOME ECONOMICS

1. **Personal Health and Fitness**
   Students will have the necessary knowledge and skills to establish and maintain physical fitness, participate in physical activity, and maintain personal health.

2. **A Safe and Healthy Environment**
   Students will acquire the knowledge and ability necessary to create and maintain a healthy environment.

3. **Resource Management**
   Students will understand and be able to manage their personal and community resources.

CAREER DEVELOPMENT AND OCCUPATIONAL STUDIES

1. **Career Development**
   Students will be knowledgeable about the world of work, explore career options, and relate personal skills, aptitudes, and abilities to future career decisions.

2. **Integrated Learning**
   Students will demonstrate how academic knowledge and skills are applied in the workplace and other settings.

3a. **Universal Foundation Skills**
   Students will demonstrate mastery of the foundation skills and competencies essential for success in the workplace.

3b. **Career Options**
   Students who choose a career major will acquire the career-specific technical knowledge/skills necessary to progress toward gainful employment, career advancement, and success in post-secondary programs.

Thematic Unit Plans and Interdisciplinary, Integrated Approaches to Instruction

Contemporary instructional units are built around themes. Within these themes many different subject areas are taught in an integrated way. For example:

Consider a thematic unit about weather. Weather seems to be a unit about science and yet this unit can be used to teach almost every subject area in an integrated way. Look at the following examples.

Art — Students draw or paint clouds and create weather maps.

Reading — Students read books and articles about weather.

Technology — Students gather information about weather, including weather forecasts on the Internet.

Writing/Language Arts — Students write reports about their research on weather. Students write original short stories or poems about weather.

Social Studies — Students learn about the effects of local climates on the lives of people and about the impact of climates worldwide.

Science — Students learn about the mechanics of cloud building, such as the forces that create cumulonimbus storm clouds.

Thematic units such as the one outlined here provide a basis for teaching needed skills and concepts in all subject areas while emphasizing the interrelatedness of these topics.

Objectives

All useful instruction has some purpose. Planning for instruction begins with choosing an objective that expresses this purpose. Objectives usually refer to outcomes, while goals usually refer to more general purposes of instruction. The terms *aim, competency, outcome*, and *behavioral objective* are also used to refer to an objective. Each New York Learning Standard is accompanied by an extensive set of objectives.

Objectives are also established by national or state organizations. The national or state English, mathematics, and science professional organizations may recommend objectives for their subject. The national or state organizations for speech, primary education, elementary education, preschool education, and special education may recommend objectives for specific grades or specialties.

Most school texts contain objectives, usually given for each text unit or lesson. These objectives are also reflected in national, state, and local achievement tests.

School districts usually have their own written objectives. There may be a scope and sequence chart that outlines the objectives for each subject and grade. The district may also have a comprehensive set of objectives for each subject and grade level.

TAXONOMY OF OBJECTIVES AND CRITICAL THINKING

Benjamin Bloom and others described three domains of learning: cognitive, affective, and psychomotor. The cognitive domain refers to knowledge, intellectual ability, and the other things we associate with school learning. The affective domain refers to values, interests, attitudes, and the other things we associate with feelings. The psychomotor domain refers to motor skills and other things we associate with movement.

Each domain describes various levels of objectives. The six levels on the cognitive domain, noted below, are most useful in classifying objectives. Students should be exposed to objectives at all levels of the taxonomy, particularly analysis, synthesis, and evaluation, which foster critical thinking.

1. Knowledge—Remembering specifics, recalling terms and theories.

2. Comprehension—Understanding or using an idea but not relating it to other ideas.

3. Application—Using concepts or abstractions in actual situations.

4. Analysis—Breaking down a statement to relate ideas in the statement.

5. Synthesis—Bringing or putting together parts to make a whole or find a pattern.

6. Evaluation—Judging value, comparing work or product to a criteria.

CHOOSING AND MODIFYING OBJECTIVES

Initially, you will identify an objective from the Learning Standards or one of the sources noted previously. Consider these criteria when choosing and sequencing objectives.

- The objective should meet the intent of the New York Learning Standards and overall goals of the school district.

- The objective should be appropriate for the achievement and maturation level of students in the class.

- The objective should be generally accepted by appropriate national, regional, or state professional organizations.

TIP

The objective you select may not exactly describe the lesson or unit you are going to teach. Modify the objective to meet your needs. You also may need to select or modify objectives and other plans to meet the needs of diverse student populations.

Your class may be academically diverse. You may teach special-needs students or you may have special-needs students in your class under the inclusion model. When you select and modify objectives for academically diverse students, consider the different achievement levels or learning styles of these students.

Your class may be culturally diverse. When you select and modify objectives for a culturally diverse class, consider the range of experiences and backgrounds found among the class. Do not reduce the difficulty of the objective.

Your class may be linguistically diverse. You may have limited English proficiency (LEP) students in your class. For a linguistically diverse class, take into account the limits that language places on learning. You may have to select or modify objectives to help these students learn English.

WRITING OBJECTIVES

An objective should answer the question: "What are students expected to do once instruction is complete?" Objectives should not describe what the teacher does during the lesson. Objectives should not be overly specific, involved, or complicated.

Whenever possible, objectives should begin with a verb. Here are some examples.

Not an objective:	I will teach students how to pronounce words with a silent *e*. [This is a statement of what the teacher will do.]
Not an objective:	While in the reading group, looking at the reading book, students will pronounce words with a silent *e*. [This statement is overly specific.]
Objective:	Sound out words with a silent *e*. [This is an objective. It tells what the student is expected to do.]
Objective:	State what he or she liked about the trip to the zoo.
Objective:	Read a book from the story shelf.
Objective:	Serve a tennis ball successfully twice in a row.

Do not limit objectives to skills or tiny bits of strictly observable behavior. Specific objectives are not limited objectives. Objectives can include statements that students will appreciate or participate in some activity. Objectives should include integrating subject matter, applying concepts, problem solving, decision making, writing essays, researching projects, preparing reports, exploring, observing, appreciating, experimenting, and constructing and making art work and other projects.

Special Education Classification and IEPs

Students are generally classified as special education students by the district Committee on Special Education (CSE) with the approval of the student's parents. The classification process includes thorough testing along with observations and reports by the social worker, the psychologist, the teacher, the occupational therapist, and other education evaluators.

Once students are classified, each receives an Individualized Education Plan (IEP). The IEP is a complete education plan for that student. The plan includes test scores and reports prepared as a part of the classification process.

The IEP prominently contains the goals and objectives for the student in all applicable academic and nonacademic areas and their placement in classes. This listing is extensive. Also included are the modifications to be made for this student. Some typical modifications are listed here.

- ✔ extra test time
- ✔ hearing aid
- ✔ preferential class seating
- ✔ extra homework help
- ✔ writing aid
- ✔ test exemptions
- ✔ sessions with a psychologist or a social worker

The final version of the IEP is discussed and agreed to at a CSE meeting with the teacher, psychologist, social worker, parent advocate, and child's parent(s) in attendance. Once enacted the district must provide the services and arrange for the modifications described in the IEP.

Planning to Teach the Lesson

Once you have decided what to teach, you must plan how to teach it. Consider these factors as you plan the lesson or unit.

- Determine the prerequisite competencies. This is the knowledge and skills students must possess before they can learn the objective. Draw up a plan that ensures students will demonstrate prerequisite competencies before you teach the lesson.

- Determine the resources you need to help students reach the objective. The resources could include books, manipulatives, overhead transparencies, and other materials for you or the students to use. The resources could also include technological resources including computers or computer software and human resources including teacher aides, students, or outside presenters.

- Devise a plan to help students reach the objective. In addition to the factors discussed previously, the plan will usually include motivation and procedures.

Madeline Hunter posited the following important stages for effective lessons.

- Anticipatory set—Something that is said or done to prepare students and focus the students on the lesson.
- Objective and purpose—The teacher should state the objective of the lesson, and the students should be aware of the objective.
- Input—New information is presented during this stage.
- Modeling—The skills or procedures being taught or demonstrated.
- Checking for understanding—Following the instructional components in the previous two stages, the teacher should ensure that students understand the concept before moving to the next phases of the lesson.
- Guided practice—Students are given the opportunity to practice or use the concept or skill with the teacher's guidance.
- Independent practice—Students practice or use the concept on their own.

A sample lesson plan format follows.

SAMPLE LESSON PLAN FORMAT

Name _____   Date _____
Class _____

Objective: The objective answers the question "What do I expect students to be able to do once instruction is complete?"

Integration: Indicate which, if any, topics are "integrated" in this lesson.

Resources: The materials and the technological and human resources needed to teach the lesson.

Motivation: An introduction that interests the students and focuses their attention on the lesson.

Procedures

Review (Warm-up)

Review the prerequisite competencies. Reteach these competencies if students have forgotten them.

Preview

Fully inform students about the lesson objective and the way they will learn the objective.

Teach

The actual procedures, approaches, and methods for teaching the lesson.

Assessment

Use interaction, observation of students, tests, or other means to determine if the objective has been reached.

Practice

Students practice the skill or concept embodied in the objective.

Independent Work (Seatwork-Homework)

Assign up to fifteen minutes of work for students to do on their own.

The School in Society

The school is a part of society. It reflects the society and socializes students. To that end, the schools prepare students to function in society. Students are taught, directly and indirectly, acceptable social values and behavior.

The academic curriculum reflects society's expectations. Students are taught a generally accepted body of knowledge. Students are also prepared for society by being exposed to potential careers as a part of the school curriculum.

Every society has a culture. The culture combines the history of the society and the society's current norms. The culture includes customs, values, ethical and moral structures, religions and beliefs, laws, and a hierarchy of most valued contributions by members of society.

The School as a Society

The school is a society in itself. The school society consists of a complex interrelationship of teachers, students, administrators, parents, and others. Each school has its own character, practices, and informal hierarchy. Generally speaking, new teachers must find a niche in the school's society to be successful. The school has a formal decision-making hierarchy of teachers, supervisors, principals, superintendents, and school boards. The new teacher must usually gain acceptance at each level of this hierarchy to experience success.

Each state in the United States has its own system of education. States are legally responsible for education. Locally elected or appointed school boards usually have the most direct legal impact on the schools. Within state and federal laws, school boards pay for the schools from tax receipts and other funds, hire teachers and administrators, approve curricula, and set school policy.

Many of the decisions made by school boards are affected by the amount of money available to the schools. Generally speaking, wealthier districts have more money to spend on schools. The difference in the funds available may create a difference in the quality of schooling.

Structure and Organization of the New York Education System

The Constitution of the United States does not assign the responsibility for education to the federal government, leaving this responsibility to each state. The state government, including the governor, the legislature, and the courts have the ultimate responsibility for public education. The Board of Regents of the State University of New York (SUNY) has overall responsibility for all educational activities in New York State. The Board of Regents was established on May 1, 1784. The State University of New York includes all elementary, secondary, and postsecondary institutions, both public and private, offering education in New York. The board acts primarily as a policy-making body.

The Board of Regents appoints the New York State Commissioner of Education who is also president of the State University of New York, chief executive officer for the board, and head of the New York State Education Department.

The New York State Education Department supervises all educational institutions in New York State. Among these responsibilities, the Education Department charters all schools in the state, develops and approves school curricula and assessments, and supervises teacher certification.

There are 38 Boards of Cooperative Educational Services (BOCES) located throughout New York State. Each BOCES superintendent reports directly to the New York State Commissioner of Education and serves as the commissioner's local representative. Every public school system in New York is affiliated in some way with a BOCES that offers vocational and special education programs as well as administrative services to member districts.

Local or regional boards of education are directly responsible for operating schools in their district or town. In most cases, these boards are elected. A local or regional superintendent of schools reports to the board and, along with other administrators and support staff, has the daily responsibility for operating the schools.

Building principals report to the superintendent and are responsible for the daily operations of their school building. Teachers have the responsibility for teaching their students and carrying out district and state education policies.

It's the Law

A complex set of federal, state, and local laws govern education. Court cases are changing the interpretation of these laws each day. Here is a brief summary of legal rights they may apply to schools, teachers, and students. This summary should not be used to make any decisions related to school law. Any specific interest in legal issues should be referred to a competent attorney.

SCHOOLS

- Schools may not discriminate against students, teachers, or others because of their race, sex, ethnicity, or religion. "Reverse discrimination" *may* be legal when hiring teachers, but it is not legal when dismissing teachers.

- Prayer is not permitted in schools. In all other ways, schools may not embrace or support religion.

- Schools must make children's school records available to parents and legal guardians.

- Schools may remove books from the school library. However, a book may not be removed from the library just because a school board member or other school official does not agree with its content.

TEACHERS

- Teachers do not have to provide information unrelated to employment on an employment form or to an interviewer. You do not have to give your age, your marital status, sexual orientation, or any other unrelated information.

- Nontenured teachers usually have very limited rights to reappointment. Generally speaking, schools may not rehire a nontenured teacher for any reason. For example, the schools may simply say that they want to find someone better, that the teacher doesn't fit in, or that they just don't want to renew the contract.

- Teachers cannot be fired for behavior that does not disrupt or interfere with their effectiveness as teachers. However, even personal behavior away from school, which significantly reduces teaching effectiveness, might be grounds for dismissal.

- Pregnant teachers may not be forced to take a maternity leave. Decades ago, pregnant teachers were often forced to resign.

- Teachers may be dismissed or suspended for not doing their job. Any such action must follow a due process procedure.

- Teachers may be sued and be liable for negligence. Successful suits and actions against teachers have occurred when the evidence showed that the teacher could have reasonably foreseen what was going to happen or that the teacher acted differently than a reasonable teacher would have acted in that same situation.

- Teachers have the right to associate freely during off-school hours with whomever they wish. They may belong to any political party, religious group, or other group even if the group is not supported in the community or is disapproved of by board members, administrators, or others.

- Teachers have freedom of speech. Teachers have the same free speech rights as other citizens. They may comment publicly on all issues, including decisions of the school administrators or the school board. However, a teacher may not disclose confidential information or be malicious, and the statements can't interfere with teaching performance. Teachers do not have unlimited academic freedom or freedom of speech in the classroom or elsewhere in the school. Teachers are not permitted to disrupt the school or the school curriculum.

- Corporal punishment is not unconstitutional. However, corporal punishment is generally not permitted in New York. Teachers should never strike children in anger and should administer corporal punishment if permitted only as a part of a due process procedure.

STUDENTS

- Handicapped students from ages 3 to 21 are entitled to a free and appropriate public education as a matter of federal law. This education should take place in the least restrictive environment available.

- Students have limited freedom of the press. Student newspapers supported by school funds may be reviewed and edited by school officials. However, papers paid for and produced by students off school property may not be censored by school officials.

- Students are entitled to due process. In particular, students have a right to a hearing and an opportunity to present a defense before being suspended. Students who pose a threat to others in the school are not entitled to this due process.

- Students have freedom of speech unless it causes a significant disruption in the school. They may display messages or symbols on their persons, and refuse to participate in the pledge of allegiance. However, they may not use speech considered vulgar or offensive.

Development of Formal Education

Education is a fairly recent development. Formal education has existed for only a fraction of the time that humans have been on earth. Many events in the history of education led to the structure of our education system today.

The first formal education probably began about 2000 B.C. in northern Africa and China. It was about 500 B.C. when the formal education that led to our system was instituted in Athens, Greece. Boys were educated in schools, and girls were educated at home.

Three philosopher-intellects of this time—Socrates, Plato, and Aristotle—left an indelible mark on education. Socrates developed the Socratic or inquiry method of teaching. Plato believed that an education should help a person fully develop body and soul. Aristotle introduced a scientific and practical approach to education. Plato and Aristotle both believed in the superiority of the ruling classes and the inferiority of women and slaves.

Formal Roman education began about 50 B.C., after Rome had conquered Greece. The grammiacticus schools, developed in Rome, taught such subjects as Latin, history, mathematics, and music and were like our high schools.

Around 70 A.D. Quintilian wrote a series of twelve books that described current and preferred Roman educational practices. These books may have been the first educational methods and psychology texts.

Education continued to develop and began to bring a unified language and thought throughout the known world. Then the Dark Ages (400 to 1000 A.D.) began. Enormous amounts of learning were lost during this period, and schooling was set back. The revival of learning following the Dark Ages was led by religious leaders such as St. Thomas Aquinas, who devised scholasticism (the formal study of knowledge).

During the Renaissance and the Reformation (1300–1700 A.D.), schooling was freed from control by the church. Church groups, particularly the Jesuits and the Christian Brothers, established religious schools.

Beginning around 1700, thought and schooling focused more on reason and logic. During this time, the "common man" in Europe sought a better life and better education. Great educators emerged from this period. Jean Jacques Rousseau, who wrote *Emile* in 1762, held a positive view of children and believed that education should be a natural process. Pestalozzi established schools that incorporated Rousseau's ideas. The schools featured understanding and patience for children and methods that enabled students to develop concepts through manipulative materials.

Herbart was Pestalozzi's student. In the early 1800s, Herbart formalized the approach to education. He presented some steps for teaching including presentation, generalization, and application. These steps bear a remarkable similarity to the stages from the taxonomy of educational objectives presented earlier.

Froebel was another educator influenced by Rousseau and Pestalozzi. Froebel established the first kindergarten with emphasis on social development and learning through experience. Kindergarten means child's garden.

American Education

In the 1600s American children were educated at home by their parents. Later that century, Dame schools began in the East. Classes were offered in a woman's home and often amounted to no more than child care. Secondary education consisted of Latin grammar schools, which provided a classical education.

In the mid-1600s laws were introduced in Massachusetts requiring education. Some localities provided schooling, and this form of local school lasted into the 1800s. Private schools also offered an education during this period. Admission to these schools was limited to those who could afford to pay.

In rural America there were not enough students in one locality to form a school. In these areas schooling was provided by tutors through the 1700s and by itinerant teachers through the 1900s.

English grammar schools and academies began operation as secondary schools during the 1700s. English grammar schools prepared students for careers while academies combined the features of Latin and English grammar schools.

Common schools provided free, public education for all students beginning in the 1800s. About that same time high schools were established to provide free, public secondary education. Junior high schools were introduced in the early 1900s, and middle schools were introduced in the 1950s.

Horn books, the alphabet covered by a transparent horn, were the predominant teaching device of the colonial period. The New England primer was the first substantial text and was used as a reading text until the late 1700s. The American spelling book, written by Noah Webster, contained stories and the alphabet along with lists of spelling words and was the most popular school book in the early 1800s. McGuffey's readers were reading books geared for different grade levels and were the main education materials for Americans from around 1840 to 1920.

American schools from the early 1800s through the early 1900s were based on the teachings of Pestalozzi and Herbart. These schools showed both the compassion suggested by Pestalozzi and the severe formalism based on Herbart's ideas.

Maria Montessori established her school, Casa Bambini, in 1908. She believed that students thrive in an environment that naturally holds their interest and that offers specially prepared materials. Schools following a modified version of her approach are found throughout the United States today.

Around 1900 John Dewey established the first "progressive" school. Progressive schools sought to build a curriculum around the child rather than around the subject matter. Progressive schools were very popular through the 1930s, and the progressive education movement continued into the 1950s.

The essentialist movement has a view opposite to progressivism. Educators associated with this movement favor a teacher-centered classroom. They believe in a more challenging, subject-oriented curriculum, and have a heavy reliance on achievement test results. Most school practices today primarily reflect the essentialist approach.

With the Depression of the 1930s, the federal government took a more active role in the schools. This active role increased through 1960 with programs designed to improve mathematics and science programs to bolster the national defense. In the 1960s and 1970s federal government focused on social issues as they relate to the schools, such as desegregation and equal educational opportunity.

Public Law 94-142 marked the federal government's first direct intervention in school instruction. This law and Public Law 99-457 mandate an appropriate public education in the least restrictive environment for handicapped Americans aged 3–21. Public Law 98-199 mandates transitional services for high school students. The federal government remains a vital force in American education today.

Jerome Bruner, B. F. Skinner, and Jean Piaget had an impact on American schools in the last half of this century.

In the *Process of Education,* Bruner urged the student's active involvement in the learning process. He called for more problem solving and believed that any topic could be taught in some significant way to children of any age.

B. F. Skinner took a different view than Bruner. He thought that material to be learned should be broken down into small manageable steps. Then students should be taught step by step and rewarded for success. Skinner's approach, behaviorism, built on the work of the Russian scientist Pavlov. Token reinforcement is an example of the behaviorist approach. Behaviorism is characterized by many as too limiting and controlling for regular classrooms.

Jean Piaget posited that students go though a series of stages—sensorimotor, pre-operational, concrete operational, and formal operational—as they develop concepts. He believed that students need to work individually, based on their stage of development, and that movement through the stages for a concept could not be accelerated. Piaget's work indicates that more concrete and pictorial materials should be used in the schools and that students should be actively involved in the learning process.

Assessment Program

Every teacher evaluates instruction. The assessment program and the assessment instruments should measure mastery and understanding of important topics. The assessment program should also be used as a teaching tool. That is, the program should be used to help students learn and to improve instruction. The program should include authentic assessment of students' work as well as teacher-made and standardized tests.

Formative assessment information is usually gathered before or during teaching. Formative information is used to help you prepare appropriate lessons and assist students. Formative evaluations help teachers decide which objectives to teach, which instructional techniques to use, and which special help or services to provide to individual students.

Summative assessment information is usually gathered once instruction is complete. Summative evaluation is used to make judgments about student achievement and the effectiveness of the instructional programs. Summative evaluations lead to grades, to reports about a student's relative level of accomplishment, and to alterations of instructional programs.

Assessment information may be used for both purposes. For example, you may give a test to determine grades for a marking period or unit. You may then use the information from this test to plan further instruction and arrange individual help for students.

You may informally gather formative and summative information. Just walking around the room observing students' work can yield a lot of useful information. You can frequently discern the additional work that students need and identify different levels of student achievement.

Assessment Instruments

Tests have long been used to determine what students have learned and to compare students. Every test is imperfect. Many tests are so imperfect that they are useless. It is important to realize how this imperfection affects test results.

Some students are poor test takers. Every test assumes that the test taker has the opportunity to demonstrate what they know. A student may know something but be unable to demonstrate it on a particular test. We must also consider alternative assessment strategies for these students.

Familiarize yourself with these basic assessment concepts.

- Errors of Measurement—Every test contains errors of measurement. In other words, no one test accurately measures a student's achievement or ability. Carefully designed standardized tests may have measurement errors of 5 percent or 10 percent. Teacher-designed tests typically have large errors of measurement.

A test result shows that a student falls into a range of scores and not just the single reported score. Focusing on a single score and ignoring the score range is among the most serious of score-reporting errors.

- Reliability—A reliable test is consistent. That is, a reliable test will give similar results when given to the same person in a short time span. You can't count on unreliable tests to give you useful scores. Use only very reliable standardized tests and be very aware of how important reliability is when you make up your own tests.

- Validity—Valid tests measure what they are supposed to measure. There are two important types of validity: content validity and criterion validity.

  — A test with high content validity measures the material covered in the curriculum or unit being tested. Tests that lack high content validity are unfair. When you make up a test it should have complete content validity. This does not mean that the test has to be unchallenging. It does mean that the questions should refer to the subject matter covered.

  — A test with high criterion validity successfully predicts the ability to do other work. For example a test to be an automobile mechanic with high criterion validity will successfully predict who will be a good mechanic.

NORM-REFERENCED AND CRITERION-REFERENCED TESTS

Norm-referenced tests are designed to compare students. Intelligence tests are probably the best-known norm-referenced tests. These tests yield a number that purports to show how one person's intelligence compares to everyone else's. The average IQ score is 100.

Standardized achievement tests yield grade-level equivalent scores. These tests purport to show how student achievement compares to the achievement of all other students of the same grade level.

A fifth grader who earns a grade level equivalent of 5.5 might be thought of as average. A second-grade student with the same grade equivalent score would be thought of as above average. About half of all the students taking these tests will be below average.

Standardized tests also yield percentile scores. Percentile scores are reported as a number from 0 through 100. A percentile of 50 indicates that the student did as well as or better than 50 percent of the students at that grade level who took the test. The higher the percentile, the better the relative performance.

Criterion-referenced tests are designed to determine the degree to which an objective has been reached. Teacher-made tests and tests found in teachers' editions of texts are usually criterion-referenced tests. Criterion-referenced tests have very high content validity.

AUTHENTIC ASSESSMENT

Standardized and teacher-made tests have significant drawbacks. These types of tests do not evaluate a student's ability to perform a task or demonstrate a skill in a real-life situation. These tests do not evaluate a student's ability to work cooperatively or consistently.

In authentic assessment, students are asked to demonstrate the skill or knowledge in a real-life setting. The teacher and students collaborate in the learning assessment process and discuss how learning is progressing and how to facilitate that learning. The idea is to get an authentic picture of the student's work and progress.

Students have an opportunity to demonstrate what they know or can do in a variety of settings. Students can also demonstrate their ability to work independently or as part of a group.

Authentic assessment might include the following approaches.

- The student might be observed by the teacher, or occasionally by other students. The observer takes notes and discusses the observation later with the students.

TIP

Portfolio assessment is another name for authentic assessment. Students evaluated through a system of authentic assessment frequently keep a portfolio of their work.

- Students establish portfolios that contain samples of their work. Students are told which work samples they must include in their portfolios. The students place their best work for each requirement in the portfolio. Portfolios are evaluated periodically during a conference between the teacher and the student.

- Students maintain journals and logs containing written descriptions, sketches, and other notes that chronicle their work and the process they went through while learning. The journals and logs are reviewed periodically during a conference between the teacher and the student.

Grading and Interpreting Test Scores

The grade level at which you are teaching determines the approach you will take to grading. In the primary grades, you are often asked to check off a list of criteria to show how a student is progressing. Starting in intermediate grades, you will usually issue letter grades.

You should develop a consistent, fair, and varied approach to grading. Students should understand the basis for their grades. You should give students an opportunity to demonstrate what they have learned in a variety of ways.

It is not necessary to adopt a rigid grading system in the elementary grades. Remember, the purpose of a grading system should be to help students learn better, not just to compare them to other students.

Beginning about sixth or seventh grade, the grade should reflect how students are doing relative to other students in the class. By this age, students need to be exposed to the grading system they will experience through high school and college. The grading system should always be fair, consistent, and offer students a variety of ways to demonstrate their mastery.

You will need to interpret normed scores. These scores may be reported as grade equivalents or as percentiles. You may receive these results normed for different groups. For example, one normed score may show performance relative to all students who took the test. Another normed score may show performance relative to students from school districts that have the same socioeconomic status (SES) as your school district.

When interpreting normed scores for parents, point out that the student's performance falls into a range of scores. A student's score that varies significantly from the average score from schools with a similar SES requires attention followed by remediation or enriched instruction.

TIP

When interpreting district-wide normed scores, remember that these scores correlate highly with SES

Instructional Delivery

Planning instruction and implementing instruction are intertwined. Many of the points discussed here will have been considered during the planning process.

Classrooms are dynamic places. Students and teachers interact to further a student's learning and development. Follow these guidelines to establish a successful classroom and teach successful lessons.

Motivation

Most good lessons begin with a motivation. The motivation interests the learner and focuses their attention on the lesson. It is also important to maintain students' motivation for the duration of the lesson.

The motivation for a lesson may be intrinsic or extrinsic. Intrinsic motivation refers to topics that students like or enjoy. Effective intrinsic motivations are based on a knowledge of what is popular or interesting to students of a particular age.

For example, you might introduce a lesson about the French and Indian War to older students by discussing the book and movie *Last of the Mohicans*. You might introduce a lesson on patterns to young children by picking out patterns in children's clothes. You might introduce a lesson on fractions to middle school students with a discussion about the stock market.

Extrinsic motivation focuses on external rewards for good work or goal attainment. Extrinsic rewards are most successful when used in conjunction with more routine work. Extrinsic motivations may offer an appropriate reward for completing an assignment or for other acceptable performance. Establish rewards for activities that most students can achieve and take care to eliminate unnecessary competition.

For example, you might grant a period of free time to students who successfully complete a routine but necessary assignment. You might offer the whole class a trip or a party when a class project is successfully completed. Special education programs feature token reinforcement in which students receive or lose points or small plastic tokens for appropriate or inappropriate activity.

Motivation needs to be maintained during the lesson itself. Follow these guidelines for teaching lessons in which the students remain motivated. Lessons will be more motivating if you have clear and unambiguous objectives, give the students stimulating tasks at an appropriate level, get and hold the students' attention, and allow students some choices. Students will be most motivated if they like the topic or activities, believe that the lesson has to do with them, believe that they will succeed, and have a positive reaction to your efforts to motivate them.

Individual work gives a further opportunity to use intrinsic motivation. Use the interests and likes of individual students to spark and maintain their motivation.

The extrinsic motivation of praise can be used effectively during a lesson. For praise to be successful, it must be given for a specific accomplishment, including effort, and focus on the student's own behavior. It does not compare behavior with other students nor establish competitive situations.

Successful Learning

Research indicates that the following factors are likely to lead to successful learning.

- Students who are engaged in the learning process tend to be more successful learners, particularly when they are engaged in activities at the appropriate level of difficulty.

- Students learn most successfully when they are being taught or supervised as opposed to working independently.

- Students who are exposed to more material at the appropriate level of difficulty are more successful learners.

- Students are successful learners when their teachers expect them to master the curriculum and use available instructional time for learning activities.

- Students who are in a positive, uncritical classroom environment are more successful learners than students who are in a negative, critical classroom environment. This does not mean that students cannot be corrected or criticized but that students learn best when the corrections are done positively and when the criticisms are constructive.

- Students generally develop positive attitudes to teachers who appear warm, have a student orientation, praise students, listen to students, accept student ideas, and interact with them.

Classroom Interaction

Flander's interaction analysis gives a way to understand how teachers teach. His scheme focuses on the kind of teacher talk and student talk in a classroom. In Flander's work, one of the codes on page 234 was assigned to every three seconds of classroom instruction. This kind of frequent coding and the numbers or precise names of the categories are not important. However, the coding system can help you understand how to structure successful learning experiences.

> ### INDIRECT TEACHER TALK
>
> 1. Accepts feelings—Teacher acknowledges and accepts students' feelings.
> 2. Praises and encourages—Teacher praises students' contributions and encourages students to continue their contributions.
> 3. Accepts or uses students' ideas—Teacher helps students develop their own ideas and uses students' own ideas in the lesson.
> 4. Asks questions—Teacher asks questions about lesson content or solicits students' opinions. Rhetorical questions and questions not related to the lesson content are not included in this category.
>
> ### DIRECT TEACHER TALK
>
> 5. Lectures, explains, or demonstrates—Teacher presents facts, opinions, or demonstrations related to the lesson topic.
> 6. Gives directions—Teacher gives directions to which students are expected to comply.
> 7. Criticizes or justifies authority—Teacher responds negatively to students, criticizes, or justifies authority.
>
> ### STUDENT TALK
>
> 8. Student talk (response)—Student responds to a teacher's question. The correct answer is predictable and anticipated by the teacher.
> 9. Student talk (initiation)—Student initiates response that is not predictable. The response may follow an open-ended or indirect question from the teacher.
> 10. Silence or confusion—The classroom is silent or you can't make out what is being said.

Classroom Approaches

Effective classrooms are characterized by a variety of teaching approaches. The approaches should be tailored to the ability of the learner and the lesson objectives.

TEACHER-CENTERED APPROACHES

Teacher-centered approaches are characterized by teacher presentation, a factual question, and a knowledge-based response from the student.

LECTURE OR EXPLANATION

You can present material through a lecture or an explanation. A lecture is a fairly long verbal presentation of material. Explanation refers to a shorter presentation. Lecture and explanation are efficient ways to present information that must be arranged and structured in a particular way. However, lecture and explanation may place learners in too passive a role.

Lecture and explanation work best under the following circumstances: (1) the lesson begins with a motivation, (2) the teacher maintains eye contact, (3) the teacher supplies accentuating gestures but without extraneous movements, (4) the presentation is limited to about 5–40 minutes depending on the age of the student, and (5) the objective is clear and the presentation is easy to follow and at an appropriate level.

DEMONSTRATIONS

Demonstrations are lectures or explanations in which you model what you want students to learn. That is, you exhibit a behavior, show a technique, or demonstrate a skill to help students reach the objective. Demonstrations should follow the same general rules as lectures and the actual demonstration should be clear and easy to follow.

TEACHER QUESTIONS

Teachers frequently ask questions during class. The following guidelines describe successful questions.

- Formulate questions so that they are clear, purposeful, brief, and at an appropriate level for the class.

- Address the vast majority of questions to the entire class. Individually addressed questions are appropriate to prepare "shy" students to answer the question.

- Avoid rhetorical questions.

- Use both higher and lower level questions on Bloom's taxonomy (knowledge, comprehension, application, analysis, synthesis, evaluation). All types of questions have their place.

- Avoid question-and-answer drills. A consistent pattern of teacher questions that call for responses at the first level of Bloom's taxonomy is too limiting for most classrooms.

- Pause before you call on a student to answer the question, giving students an opportunity to formulate their responses.

- Call on a wide range of students to answer. Do not pick students just because they are either likely or unlikely to respond correctly.

- Wait 4 or 5 seconds for an answer. Don't cut off students who are struggling with an answer.

- Rephrase a question if it seems unclear or vague.

- Set a target for about 70 percent or so of questions to be answered correctly.

Student-Centered Approaches—Active Learning

In a student-centered or active learning environment, the teacher ceases to be the prime presenter of information. The teacher's questions are more open-ended and indirect. Students will be encouraged to be more active participants in the class. This type of instruction is characterized by student-initiated comments, praise from the teacher, and the teacher's use of students' ideas.

TIP

Just because there is student involvement does not mean that the teacher is using a student-centered or active approach. For example, the pattern of questions and answers referred to as drill is not a student-centered approach.

COOPERATIVE LEARNING

Students involved in cooperative learning work together in groups to learn a concept or skill or to complete a project. Students, in groups of two to six, are assigned or choose a specific learning task or project presented by the teacher. The group consults with the teacher and devises a plan for working together.

Students use many resources, including the teacher, to help and teach one another and to accept responsibilities for tasks as they complete their work. The students summarize their efforts and, typically, make a presentation to the entire class or the teacher.

Cooperative learning is characterized by active learning, full participation, and democracy within a clearly established structure. Cooperative learning also engages students in learning how to establish personal relationships and a cooperative working style.

INQUIRY LEARNING

Inquiry learning uses students' own thought processes to help them learn a concept, solve a problem, or discover a relationship. This kind of instruction has also been referred to as Socratic. Inquiry learning often requires the most structure and preparation by the teacher. The teacher must know that the situation under study will yield useful results.

The teacher begins by explaining inquiry procedures to students, usually through examples. Next the teacher presents the problem to be solved or the situation that will lead to the concept or relationship. Students gather information and ask questions of the teacher to gain additional information. The teacher supports students as they make predictions and provide tentative solutions or results. Once the process is complete, the teacher asks students to think over and describe the process they used to arrive at the solution. This last step is referred to as a metacognition.

Resources for Instruction

You may have to assemble a number of resources for instruction. It often helps to jot down the resources you will need to teach a lesson or a unit. The materials you select should help the students meet the lesson objectives and match the teaching-learning approach you will use. The resources may include textual, manipulative, technological, and human resources.

Be sure to assemble in advance the materials you need to teach a lesson. The materials may include texts, workbooks, teacher-made handouts, or other printed materials. Check the materials to ensure that they are intact and in appropriate condition.

You may use manipulative materials to teach a lesson. Be sure that the materials are assembled and complete. Any laboratory materials should be tested and safe. Be sure that the materials are at an appropriate level for the students.

You may use technological resources, such as a computer, during your lesson. Be sure that the computer will be available during your lesson. Try the computer out and be sure that it is working. Be sure that any software you will use is at an appropriate grade and interest level and matches the objectives of the lesson.

You will frequently use human resources in your lesson. You may decide to cooperatively teach a lesson or unit with another teacher. This approach requires advanced planning and regular communication. You may need to arrange for a guest speaker to speak to the class about a particular topic.

Special education teachers frequently teach in consultative or collaborative roles. That is, they work in classrooms with regular education teachers. In this arrangement, teachers must coordinate their activities and agree on how they will interact during the lesson.

Inclusion

Inclusion means that special-needs students are included in a regular school setting and placed in more restrictive environments only when needed. This does not mean that every special education student will be in a regular classroom all day. It does mean that students will be given every opportunity to function in a regular environment.

For some students, inclusion means attending a local special education school instead of a residential school. For other students it may mean attending a neighborhood school instead of a special education school. For still other students it means spending the maximum amount of time in regular classrooms.

Inclusion may mean placing students in regular education class and then switching them to special education settings as needed during the day. Inclusion may mean that a special education teacher goes into a regular education classroom to work with special education students in the class during the regular class periods. Teams of regular education and special education teachers frequently work together with students moving easily from regular education to special education settings.

It is impossible to include all students. Some students with severe physical disabilities require a special setting. Other students with severe mental handicaps will not be able to function effectively in a regular setting. Other students with severe emotional disorders or who are extremely disruptive will have to be educated in a self-contained special education class.

Parental Involvement

The key to a successful special education program is parental involvement. Parents are naturally concerned about their child's special education classification. They need to be constructively involved in their child's program. Keep parents abreast of the child's progress on a regular basis. If there are issues or concerns about the child, notify the parents immediately. Help parents understand the academic gains their child is making.

Adapting Instruction

Adapt instruction for the following factors, types of learners, and students.

> Age—Primary students should have more structure, short lessons, less explanation, more public praise, more small group and individual instruction, and more experiences with manipulatives and pictures. Older students should have less structure, increasingly longer lessons, more explanation, less public praise, more whole-class instruction, more independent work, and less work with manipulatives.

ACADEMICALLY DIVERSE

> Aptitude—Students exhibit different abilities to learn. You can provide differentiated assignments to enable students at different aptitude levels to maximize their potential.

Reading Level—Ensure that a student is capable of understanding the reading material. Do not ask students to learn from material that is too difficult. Identify materials at an appropriate reading level or with an alternative learning mode (tapes, material read to student). Remember that a low reading level does not mean that a student cannot learn a difficult concept.

Learning Disabled—Learning-disabled students evidence at least a 2-year discrepancy between measures of ability and performance. Learning-disabled students should be given structured, brief assignments, manipulative experiences, and many opportunities for auditory learning.

Visually Impaired—Place the visually impaired student where he or she can most easily see the instruction. Use large learning aids and large print books. Use a multisensory approach.

Hearing Impaired—Ensure that students are wearing an appropriate hearing aid. Students with less than 50 percent hearing loss will probably be able to hear you if you stand about 3 to 5 feet away.

Mildly Handicapped—Focus on a few, highly relevant skills, more learning time, and lots of practice. Provide students with concrete experiences. Do not do for students what they can do for themselves, even if it takes these students an extended time.

Gifted—Gifted students have above average ability, creativity, and a high degree of task commitment. Provide these students with enriched or differentiated units. Permit them to test out of required units. Do not isolate these students from the rest of the class.

CULTURAL AND LINGUISTIC DIVERSITY

SES (Socioeconomic Status)—Socioeconomic status and school achievement are highly correlated. Overall, students with higher SES will have higher achievement scores. In America, SES differences are typically associated with differences in race and ethnicity. However, the achievement differences are not caused by and are not a function of these differences in race or ethnicity. Rather, achievement differences are typically caused by differences in home environment, opportunity for enriched experiences, and parental expectations.

Teachers frequently have a higher SES than their students. These students often behave differently than teachers expect. The crushing problems of poor and homeless children may produce an overlay of acting out and attention problems. All this frequently leads the teacher to erroneously conclude that these students are less capable of learning. In turn, the teacher may erroneously lower learning expectations. This leads to lower school performance and a compounding of students' difficulty.

A teacher must consciously and forcibly remind herself or himself that lower SES students are capable learners. These teachers must also actively guard against reducing learning expectations for lower SES students.

There are appropriate ways of adapting instruction for students with different SES levels. For high SES students, minimize competitiveness, provide less structure, and present more material. For low SES students, be more encouraging, guard against feelings of failure or low self-esteem, and provide more structure. Do not lower learning expectations, but do present less material and emphasize mastery of the material.

Culturally Diverse—Almost every class will have students from diverse cultural backgrounds. Use the values embedded in these cultures to motivate individual learners.

Language Diverse—The first language for many students is not English. In addition, a number of American students speak local variants of the English language. Teachers frequently, and erroneously, lower their learning expectations for these students. There are a number of useful strategies for adapting instruction for these students.

A number of students are referred to as Limited English Proficiency (LEP) who need English as a second language (ESL) instruction. Teaching English as a second language can be accomplished in the classroom, but often requires a specialist who works with students in "pull-out programs." When teaching these students, use simpler words and expressions, use context clues to help students identify word meaning, clearly draw students' attention to your speech, and actively involve students in the learning process.

Multiple Intelligences and Learning Styles

Multiple intelligences means there are many different ways students can demonstrate their ability. It follows that students have different learning styles. This approach is in sharp contrast to the current approach of measuring ability on a single scale, usually with an IQ test.

Howard Gardner of Harvard is credited with originating this approach to understanding intelligence. According to Gardner, there are seven ways to be smart. These seven intelligences are listed below.

1. verbal/linguistic
2. logical/mathematical
3. visual/spatial
4. bodily/kinesthetic
5. musical/rhythmic
6. interpersonal
7. the naturalist

Gardner also says that if students are smart in different ways then they learn in different ways. Children will have a learning style that matches their particular intelligence or intelligences. The idea is to use instructional approaches that match the learner's style. For example, use art to teach visual learners and use music to reach musical learners.

Managing the Instructional Environment

Classroom management is a more encompassing idea than discipline or classroom control. Classroom management deals with all the things a classroom teacher can do to help students become productive learners. The best management system for any classroom will establish an effective learning environment with the least restrictions.

Teachers who are proactive and take charge stand the best chance of establishing an effective learning environment. Classroom management is designed to prevent problems, not react to them.

Classroom management begins with understanding the characteristics of students in your class.

TIP

Other factors, such as low self-esteem, anxiety, and tension, can also cause students to have difficulty in school.

Characteristics of Students

We can make some general statements about the students in a class. We know that 3–7 percent of girls and 12–18 percent of boys will have some substantial adjustment problems. Prepare yourself for these predictable sex differences.

Boys are more physically active and younger children have shorter attention spans. Respond to this situation by scheduling activities when students are most likely to be able to complete them.

A teacher's management role is different at different grade levels. Prepare for these predictable differences in student reaction to teacher authority.

In the primary grades, students see teachers as authority figures and respond well to instruction and directions about how they should act in school. In the middle grades, students have learned how to act in school and still react well to the teacher's instruction.

In seventh through tenth grade, students turn to their peer group for leadership and resist the teacher's authority. The teacher must spend more time fostering appropriate behavior among students. By the last two years of high school, students are somewhat less resistant and the teacher's role is more academic.

We know that many adolescents resent being touched and that teachers may anger adolescents by taking something from them. Avoid this problem by not confronting adolescent students.

We know that there will be cultural differences among students. Many minority students, and other students, may be accustomed to harsh, authoritarian treatment. Respond to these students with warmth, acceptance, and structure. Many minority students will feel completely out of place in school. These students also need to be treated warmly and also with the positive expectation that they will succeed in school.

Many other students may be too distracted to study effectively in school. These students may need quiet places to work and the opportunity to schedule some of their own work time.

Classroom Management Techniques

The following guidelines for effective classroom management include techniques for dealing with student misbehavior.

TEACHER'S ROLE

Teachers who are good classroom managers understand their dual role as an authority figure and as someone who helps children adapt to school and to life. Teachers are authority figures. Students expect the teacher to be an authority figure and expect teachers to establish a clear and consistent classroom structure.

Teachers must also help students learn how to fit into the classroom and how to get along with others. Teachers fare better in their role as authority figures than they do in this latter role. But teachers who have realistic expectations and know how to respond to problems can have some success.

CHARACTERISTICS OF SUCCESSFUL TEACHERS
In general effective teachers have these general characteristics.

- Accept children within a teacher-student relationship.
- Set firm and clear but flexible limits.
- Enforce rules clearly and consistently.
- Have positive, realistic expectations about students' achievements and adaptations.
- Have clear reasons for expectations about students.
- Practice what they preach (model acceptable behavior).
- Don't take students' actions personally. Students usually misbehave or act out because of who they are, not because of who the teacher is.

Establishing an Effective Climate for Management

CLASSROOM PHYSICAL LAYOUT

There are several general rules to follow for a successful classroom layout. Set up the initial layout of the room so that you can see the faces of all the students. Rearrange the desks for individual and group work. Ensure that heavily used areas are free of all obstacles. Arrange the room so students do not have to stand in line, by having books and supplies available at several locations.

CLASSROOM LEADERSHIP

Research indicates that the following factors are most important in establishing effective classroom leadership. Develop a cohesive class by promoting cooperative experiences and minimizing competition among class members. Identify and gain the confidence of peer leaders, particularly in grades 7–10. Establish an authoritative, but not authoritarian, leadership style.

Depending on the grade level, set three to six reasonable, adaptable rules that describe the overall nature of acceptable and unacceptable behavior. The expectations that accompany these rules should be stated clearly. The rules should be posted for students to see.

Much of the first two weeks of school should be spent establishing these rules, which may be stated by the teacher and/or developed through class discussion. Once the rules are established and the expectations are understood, the teacher should follow through. Student misbehavior should be handled immediately and appropriately but without causing a confrontation or alienating the student from the class.

Effective classroom managers take steps to ensure that the majority of class time is spent on instruction. They also take steps to ensure that students use their seat work and other in-class study time to complete assignments.

Specific Management Techniques

There are some specific management techniques that a teacher can apply to all classes. These techniques are summarized here.

KOUNIN

Kounin is a well-known expert on classroom management. Research results show that a number of Kounin's management techniques are effective. The following techniques have the most research support:

Kounin noted that teacher with-it-ness is an important aspect of classroom management. In other words, teachers who are constantly monitoring and aware of what is happening in the classroom are better managers.

Kounin also showed that effective managers' lessons have smoothness and momentum. By this he meant that these lessons are free of teacher behavior that interrupts the flow of activities or slows down lesson pacing.

Finally, Kounin showed that group alerting was an effective technique. In group alerting, the teacher keeps bringing uninvolved students back into the lesson by calling their attention to what is happening and forewarning them of future events.

CANTER AND CANTER

Canter and Canter developed an approach called assertive discipline. Their approach is popular but lacks the research support of the approach recommended by Kounin.

The Canters recommend a direct and assertive approach to problem children. They point out that passive and hostile reactions to student misbehavior are not effective. Among other approaches, they recommend that the teacher and students establish rules and post those rules in the classroom. During each class session, the teacher writes and then marks the names of students who have violated rules. One rule violation in a session requires no action. Two rule violations, and the student meets with the teacher after school. Three violations requires a parental visit to the school.

CUEING

Cues are words, gestures, or other signals that alert students to a coming transition or that gain their attention. A cue may be spoken, such as "We'll be leaving for art in about 5 minutes. Take this time to get ready." Another cue might be, "Your group has about 15 minutes to complete your project."

Other cues are nonverbal. You may glance at a student or make eye contact to re-engage them in the lesson. You may raise your arm or hold your hand in a particular way to gain attention. You may flick the classroom lights quickly to indicate that groups should stop working and return to whole-class instruction.

> **OTHER EFFECTIVE TECHNIQUES FOR MAINTAINING ATTENTION DURING A LESSON**
>
> The techniques listed below have proven effective in classrooms.
>
> - Stand where you can scan and see the entire class.
> - Ask questions of the whole class and then call on individuals for a response.
> - Involve all students in the question-and-answer sessions and don't call on students just to catch them in a wrong answer or because they will give the correct answer.
> - Gain attention through eye contact or a gesture.
> - If a comment is required, make it very brief.
> - Ensure that the material being taught is at an appropriate level.
> - Base seat work or group work on an established system that is monitored closely and positively.

Changing Behavior

Students may act so unacceptably that their behavior must be changed. Here are some suggestions for changing behavior.

MODELING

Students learn how to behave from observing others. In the classroom the teacher is the authority figure and the one whom students may model their behaviors after. The following teacher behaviors can have a positive impact on student behaviors. In general, teachers should act as they expect their students to act.

- Listen carefully to what students say.
- Act after thoughtful consideration, not in anger or on an impulse.
- Treat students with respect.
- Do not be sarcastic or hostile with students.
- Respond to difficulty or criticism carefully. Don't take it personally.

REINFORCEMENT

All teachers use positive reinforcement, whether through grades, praise, tokens, or other means. Teachers also use negative reinforcement by showing students how to avoid an undesirable consequence (poor grade) by doing acceptable work. Negative reinforcement is not punishment.

In the classroom you should increase the duration or quality of the desired behavior before reinforcing. Reach explicit agreements with students about the level of performance that will yield rewards (positive reinforcement). Praise is often an ineffective reinforcer.

CONTRACTS AND LOGS

You may be able to help children change behavior by using contracts or by asking students to maintain logs. These approaches cause students to think about their behavior and both have been proven effective.

When writing a contract, work with a student to establish desired learning goals or classroom behavior. The contract, signed by the teacher and the student, sets short-term goals for classroom conduct and academic achievement. A teacher may also ask students to maintain a log of their classroom behavior. A brief daily review of the log may improve behavior.

PUNISHMENT

Punishment is a temporary measure. It should be administered to improve student performance, not to make the teacher feel better. Limited punishment given for a specific reason when students are emotionally stable can be effective. Other punishments, such as extra work, punishment of the entire class, and corporal punishment, are usually not effective.

Effective punishment should be reasonable, deliberate, and unemotional. The punishment should also be short and somewhat unpleasant. The reason for the punishment should be clear, and the punishment should be accompanied by examples of appropriate behavior.

Practice ATS-W— Elementary

CHAPTER 10

TEST INFO BOX

This practice test contains the types of items you will encounter on the real test, but don't be surprised if the real test seems different. The distribution of items varies from one test administration to another.

Take this test in a realistic timed setting. You should not take this practice test until you have completed your subject matter review.

The setting will be most realistic if another person times the test and ensures that the test rules are followed. But remember that many people do better on a practice test than on the real test.

You have four hours to complete the selected-response items and the constructed response. Keep this time limit in mind as you work. Answer the easier questions first. Be sure you answer all the questions. There is no penalty for guessing. You may write in the test booklet and mark up the questions.

Each selected-response item has four answer choices. Exactly one of these choices is correct. Use a pencil to mark your choice on the answer sheet provided for this test.

The constructed response immediately follows the selected-response items. Once the test is complete, review the answers and explanations as you correct the answer sheet.

When you are ready, turn the page and begin.

Answer Sheet

PRACTICE ATS-W—ELEMENTARY

1 Ⓐ Ⓑ Ⓒ Ⓓ   21 Ⓐ Ⓑ Ⓒ Ⓓ   41 Ⓐ Ⓑ Ⓒ Ⓓ   61 Ⓐ Ⓑ Ⓒ Ⓓ
2 Ⓐ Ⓑ Ⓒ Ⓓ   22 Ⓐ Ⓑ Ⓒ Ⓓ   42 Ⓐ Ⓑ Ⓒ Ⓓ   62 Ⓐ Ⓑ Ⓒ Ⓓ
3 Ⓐ Ⓑ Ⓒ Ⓓ   23 Ⓐ Ⓑ Ⓒ Ⓓ   43 Ⓐ Ⓑ Ⓒ Ⓓ   63 Ⓐ Ⓑ Ⓒ Ⓓ
4 Ⓐ Ⓑ Ⓒ Ⓓ   24 Ⓐ Ⓑ Ⓒ Ⓓ   44 Ⓐ Ⓑ Ⓒ Ⓓ   64 Ⓐ Ⓑ Ⓒ Ⓓ
5 Ⓐ Ⓑ Ⓒ Ⓓ   25 Ⓐ Ⓑ Ⓒ Ⓓ   45 Ⓐ Ⓑ Ⓒ Ⓓ   65 Ⓐ Ⓑ Ⓒ Ⓓ

6 Ⓐ Ⓑ Ⓒ Ⓓ   26 Ⓐ Ⓑ Ⓒ Ⓓ   46 Ⓐ Ⓑ Ⓒ Ⓓ   66 Ⓐ Ⓑ Ⓒ Ⓓ
7 Ⓐ Ⓑ Ⓒ Ⓓ   27 Ⓐ Ⓑ Ⓒ Ⓓ   47 Ⓐ Ⓑ Ⓒ Ⓓ   67 Ⓐ Ⓑ Ⓒ Ⓓ
8 Ⓐ Ⓑ Ⓒ Ⓓ   28 Ⓐ Ⓑ Ⓒ Ⓓ   48 Ⓐ Ⓑ Ⓒ Ⓓ   68 Ⓐ Ⓑ Ⓒ Ⓓ
9 Ⓐ Ⓑ Ⓒ Ⓓ   29 Ⓐ Ⓑ Ⓒ Ⓓ   49 Ⓐ Ⓑ Ⓒ Ⓓ   69 Ⓐ Ⓑ Ⓒ Ⓓ
10 Ⓐ Ⓑ Ⓒ Ⓓ   30 Ⓐ Ⓑ Ⓒ Ⓓ   50 Ⓐ Ⓑ Ⓒ Ⓓ   70 Ⓐ Ⓑ Ⓒ Ⓓ

11 Ⓐ Ⓑ Ⓒ Ⓓ   31 Ⓐ Ⓑ Ⓒ Ⓓ   51 Ⓐ Ⓑ Ⓒ Ⓓ   71 Ⓐ Ⓑ Ⓒ Ⓓ
12 Ⓐ Ⓑ Ⓒ Ⓓ   32 Ⓐ Ⓑ Ⓒ Ⓓ   52 Ⓐ Ⓑ Ⓒ Ⓓ   72 Ⓐ Ⓑ Ⓒ Ⓓ
13 Ⓐ Ⓑ Ⓒ Ⓓ   33 Ⓐ Ⓑ Ⓒ Ⓓ   53 Ⓐ Ⓑ Ⓒ Ⓓ   73 Ⓐ Ⓑ Ⓒ Ⓓ
14 Ⓐ Ⓑ Ⓒ Ⓓ   34 Ⓐ Ⓑ Ⓒ Ⓓ   54 Ⓐ Ⓑ Ⓒ Ⓓ   74 Ⓐ Ⓑ Ⓒ Ⓓ
15 Ⓐ Ⓑ Ⓒ Ⓓ   35 Ⓐ Ⓑ Ⓒ Ⓓ   55 Ⓐ Ⓑ Ⓒ Ⓓ   75 Ⓐ Ⓑ Ⓒ Ⓓ

16 Ⓐ Ⓑ Ⓒ Ⓓ   36 Ⓐ Ⓑ Ⓒ Ⓓ   56 Ⓐ Ⓑ Ⓒ Ⓓ   76 Ⓐ Ⓑ Ⓒ Ⓓ
17 Ⓐ Ⓑ Ⓒ Ⓓ   37 Ⓐ Ⓑ Ⓒ Ⓓ   57 Ⓐ Ⓑ Ⓒ Ⓓ   77 Ⓐ Ⓑ Ⓒ Ⓓ
18 Ⓐ Ⓑ Ⓒ Ⓓ   38 Ⓐ Ⓑ Ⓒ Ⓓ   58 Ⓐ Ⓑ Ⓒ Ⓓ   78 Ⓐ Ⓑ Ⓒ Ⓓ
19 Ⓐ Ⓑ Ⓒ Ⓓ   39 Ⓐ Ⓑ Ⓒ Ⓓ   59 Ⓐ Ⓑ Ⓒ Ⓓ   79 Ⓐ Ⓑ Ⓒ Ⓓ
20 Ⓐ Ⓑ Ⓒ Ⓓ   40 Ⓐ Ⓑ Ⓒ Ⓓ   60 Ⓐ Ⓑ Ⓒ Ⓓ   80 Ⓐ Ⓑ Ⓒ Ⓓ

Answer Sheet

Practice ATS-W—Elementary

Directions: Each item on this test includes four answer choices. Select the best choice for each item and mark that letter on the answer sheet.

Items 1–4.

Ms. Elenora Brown has been teaching seventh grade for just one month. She is having difficulty with discipline and with classroom management. For example, when Ms. Brown checks homework assignments, the students act as though it is free time. They talk, take other's personal property, exchange notes, and just generally make a nuisance of themselves. Sometimes students wander in and out of the class. Many students deliberately do not copy down their homework assignment. Preparing good lessons that are unappreciated by students leaves her frustrated. Ms. Brown has begun to teach in a negative and critical fashion.

1. Ms. Brown's colleague says, "Don't take it personally" about the misbehavior of students in her class. This is good advice because

   (A) the teacher doesn't need to change.
   (B) most seventh graders are unmanageable.
   (C) student misbehavior results from students' needs.
   (D) the teacher must be more authoritative and not so concerned about students.

2. Which of the following is a good suggestion to Ms. Brown about becoming a more effective classroom leader?

   (A) Set up a series of firm precise rules that students should memorize.
   (B) Take steps to establish relationships with peer leaders.
   (C) Discourage cooperative learning experiences.
   (D) Promote competition among class members.

3. The critical approach Ms. Brown has begun to use, compared to a more positive uncritical approach, will generally result in which of the following?

   (A) More learning will take place.
   (B) Less learning will take place.
   (C) More homework assignments will be handed in.
   (D) More parental involvement will take place.

4. To become a more effective classroom manager, Ms. Brown should take steps to ensure that the majority of class time is devoted to

   (A) individual work.
   (B) on-task activities.
   (C) lecturing.
   (D) group work.

5. Students in Ms. Stendel's class are reading a science-fiction story. In the story, Nayr the alien tries to trick the astronauts away from their spaceship so Nayr can look inside. Ms. Stendel wants to ask questions that promote higher-level thinking. Which of the following questions would be most appropriate?

   (A) What are other ways Nayr could have gotten inside the ship?
   (B) How did Nayr trick the astronauts?
   (C) Why did Nayr say he wanted to go inside the ship?
   (D) How many times did Nayr succeed in getting the astronauts away from their ship?

6. Teachers on the Carteret elementary school technology committee are discussing computer use in classrooms. Lee Mombello raises the issue of equity. He says, "In a country where most homes have a computer and the Internet, many of our students have no access to computers outside the school." With this in mind, which of the following is the best policy for the committee to establish about the classroom use of computers?

(A) "Special after-school computer clubs should be set up for students who do not have a computer at home."

(B) "Teachers should integrate computers in their teaching whenever possible."

(C) "Each student should be given his or her own computer to use at school and at home."

(D) "The school should hire a technology specialist who will help teachers integrate computers in their classrooms."

7. Renita Lopez is teaching language arts in the upper elementary grades and she wants to evaluate students' writing techniques and plan for further writing experiences. Which of the following is the most appropriate choice?

(A) Administer a standardized grammar test and use the scores as a planning device.

(B) Use a writing checklist to assess a variety of creative writing samples that include writing summaries and examples.

(C) Have students prepare a composition on a subject of their choice and holistically evaluate the composition.

(D) Have students answer a series of higher-level, short-answer questions about a specific writing sample.

8. Sheneoi Goldman is a fifth-grade teacher who conducts science class using the inquiry approach. Which of the following would a person be most likely to observe during Sheneoi Goldman's science class?

(A) Sheneoi Goldman deliberately does not try out an experiment in advance of the class so everyone in the class is seeing the results together for the first time.

(B) Sheneoi Goldman tells the students to avoid analyzing thought processes and rather, to rely on what happens in the experiment.

(C) Sheneoi Goldman presents a problem for the students to solve or a situation for them to explore.

(D) Sheneoi Goldman asks students to present a problem for the class to solve or a situation for the class to explore.

9. Here is a brief part of a conversation between Alex Whitby, a third-grade teacher, and Marciella Atkins, the school district reading specialist.

Alex: "Thanks for coming by. I wanted to talk to you about one of my students."
Marciella: "Which one?"
Alex: "Savaro—he's still having trouble with reading."
Marciella: "I remember Savaro from last year in second grade."
Alex: "I was thinking about more phonics—what do you think?"
Marciella: "That's OK—just remember that phonics does not help much . . . "

Which of the following finishes the reading specialist's last sentence?

(A) to associate sounds with printed letters.

(B) with reading comprehension.

(C) to attack new words independently.

(D) to develop a sight vocabulary.

10. Morina Meridcu is planning to teach a fourth-grade geography lesson. When it comes to ability level, Ms. Meridcu should

    (A) present the lesson below students' ability level.
    (B) present the lesson above students' ability level.
    (C) present the lesson at students' ability level.
    (D) present the lesson in a way that does not take ability level into account.

11. Tara Kirk is concerned about the way she responds to students' questions in science and she wants to develop a more effective approach. The best advice for Ms. Kirk is to respond in which of the following ways?

    I. Encourage exploration of the answer with activities and materials that stimulate curiosity.
    II. Model good responding skills.
    III. Answer all items as quickly and concisely as possible.
    IV. Include children's questions in evaluation techniques.

    (A) I, II
    (B) III, IV
    (C) I, II, III
    (D) I, II, IV

12. Gerard Lancaster is a new teacher who wants to use cooperative learning groups to supplement a teacher-centered approach to social studies instruction. In order to accomplish that task, which of the following should Mr. Lancaster employ when compared to teacher-centered presentations?

    I. More student involvement
    II. More content coverage
    III. More varied outcomes
    IV. More brainstorming

    (A) I, II
    (B) I, III, IV
    (C) III, IV
    (D) II, III, IV

13. Jovina Crockett is planning a lesson to integrate art with haiku, a Japanese poetic form. Which of the following approaches is LEAST likely to meet Ms. Crockett's needs?

    (A) Use the computer as an artistic tool to illustrate the haiku.
    (B) Provide a display of classical Japanese paintings for children to color.
    (C) Provide clay as a means to illustrate their haiku.
    (D) Provide paints and brushes for illustrations to the haiku.

14. Jim Prendergast teaches in a school where most of the students are economically disadvantaged. Mr. Prendergast knows that economically disadvantaged students, as a whole, tend to have lower achievement than other students, leading Mr. Prendergast to which of the following understandings that will enable him to help his students?

(A) Economically disadvantaged students, as a whole, are usually less capable learners than other students.
(B) Minority teachers are more effective with minority students.
(C) Learning expectations should usually be lowered for minority students.
(D) Economically disadvantaged students usually have fewer enriched learning opportunities at home.

15. Gina Selberding is a beginning teacher in the Herneck School. Gina realizes that she has no criteria whatever for deciding which students to call on to answer a question. Which of the following is the best criteria for Ms. Selberding to use?

(A) Be sure students know who will answer a question before it is asked.
(B) Ask questions of the entire class, then call on a student.
(C) Ask questions of students who are not paying attention.
(D) Ask questions of students who usually have the correct answers.

16. John Cohen is a new sixth-grade teacher who seems to be having every problem that a new teacher can have. But his main problem this day is trying to maintain attention during a lesson. Which of the following actions on John's part is most likely to be effective?

(A) He stands where he can see the entire class.
(B) He limits the number of students who participate in question-and-answer sessions.
(C) He ensures that the material being taught is very difficult.
(D) He does not proceed with the lesson if even a single student is not paying attention.

17. Sam Meletto, a second-grade teacher, and the principal are discussing Sam's reasons for instituting a whole language program in his classroom. Which among the following is the best reason Sam Meletto could give?

(A) Whole language instruction is widely accepted.
(B) It is not necessary to teach word recognition.
(C) Children comprehend more after using a whole language approach.
(D) Children have a better attitude toward reading.

18. Jaedo Purmen, a second grade teacher, says he has found modeling to be an effective form of instruction, meaning that he is most likely to

(A) show students how to construct replicas of historic buildings.
(B) respond courteously to students' questions.
(C) tell students when they have mispronounced a word.
(D) demonstrate students' inappropriate behavior.

19. Lucien Cardot joined the child study team for a meeting because of a second-grade student in his class. Most of the team members favor a special education classification because of the child's very low test scores. Mr. Cardot says, "From what I've seen, the problem is with the testing and not with the child," most likely meaning

    (A) tests used by the school are inappropriate and should be discontinued.
    (B) some students' difficulty with tests masks their true capability.
    (C) the person administering the tests was not a qualified examiner.
    (D) the members of the child study team are too removed from the classroom and do not have an appropriate concern about the welfare of students.

20. Damaris Jones and one of his students are discussing the student's most recent report card. Mr. Jones chooses his words carefully to have the most impact, and finally decides on these. "Your grades would have been better if all homework assignments were handed in." Which of the following approaches has the teacher decided to use?

    (A) positive reinforcement
    (B) reverse psychology
    (C) threats
    (D) negative reinforcement

21. The school year has just begun and Mr. Lamum Ngu realizes that his class is culturally and linguistically diverse. Which of the following actions by Mr. Ngu would be the most appropriate modification of the objectives or plans to meet the needs of this class?

    (A) Modify the objectives to focus more on basic skills.
    (B) Modify the objectives to reduce their difficulty level.
    (C) Modify the plans to teach the class in the foreign language.
    (D) Modify the plans to focus on the cultural heritage of those in the class.

22. Lisa is a student in DeShala Washington's third-grade class. At a parent-teacher conference, Lisa's mother says she has heard about the school using a basal reading program and asks what basal reading programs are NOT good for. Which of the following would be Ms. Washington's best response?

    (A) Skills are taught and developed in a systematic sequential manner.
    (B) One should meet individual differences and needs of the child.
    (C) A basic vocabulary is established and reinforced.
    (D) Manuals provide a detailed outline for teaching.

Items 23–24.

Ms. Lorene Archibald, a third-grade teacher, prepared a chart for students in her class to complete. Ms. Archibald has small stickers of a child walking, a school bus, a car, a bike, and a rail car for students to put on the chart. Students come up to the chart and put a sticker over the word or phrase that describes how he or she gets to school.

```
┌─────────────────────────────────────────────────────┐
│                  HOW I GET TO SCHOOL                  │
│                                                       │
│                                                       │
│    Walk        Bus        Car       Bike    Rail/Train│
└─────────────────────────────────────────────────────┘
```

23. Ms. Archibald is most likely having students complete this activity in order to

    (A) gather information about how students get to school.
    (B) help students learn about different modes of transportation.
    (C) give students experience with graphing.
    (D) give students an important opportunity for tactile experiences.

24. A student who recently arrived in the United States does not speak English, and does not know the words "car," "bus," and so on. The most appropriate action that Ms. Archibald can take with this student is to

    (A) say the word in the child's native tongue so that the child can participate in the activity.
    (B) help the student pronounce the words in English.
    (C) not involve the child in the lesson so he or she will not be embarrassed.
    (D) refer the student for English-language help.

25. Elizabeth Del Corso is an experienced fifth-grade teacher. Ms. Del Corso notices that one student in her class has particular difficulty when he is reading the problems in the mathematics textbook. In an effort to help this student, it would be most appropriate for Ms. Del Corso to recognize that this difficulty is most likely to be the result of

(A) faulty word identification and recognition.
(B) inability to locate and retain specific facts.
(C) deficiencies in basic comprehension abilities.
(D) inability to adapt to reading needs in this content field.

26. Luraine Watson is arranging the desks for her fourth-grade class at the beginning of the school year. Which of the following arrangements is LEAST appropriate?

(A)
```
X     X     X
X     X     X
X     X     X
X     X     X
X     X     X
X     X     X
X     X     X
X  -  X     X
X     X     X
      T
```

(B)
```
X   X   X   X   X
X   X   X   X   X
X   X   X   X   X
X   X   X   X   X
          T
```

(C)
```
           X  X  X
        X           X
       X              X
      X                X
    X          T         X
      X                X
       X              X
        X            X
           X  X  X
```

(D)
```
  X   X   X   X   X
    X   X   X   X
      X   X   X   X
    X   X   X   X
      X   X   X   X
    X   X   X   X

              T
```

27. The Carson Hills school district is preparing a pamphlet about effective schools to distribute to teachers. Which of the following choices should be listed as characteristic of effective schools in the pamphlet?

   I. A climate of high expectations
  II. Accountability for student performance
 III. Eliminating standardized tests

(A) I only
(B) I and II
(C) III only
(D) II and III

28. Cindy Weiss is concerned about how she uses her class time in her departmentalized fifth-grade English class. She realizes after a year of teaching that she must learn to be an effective classroom manager, which means that she will take steps to ensure that the majority of class time is devoted to

(A) individual work.
(B) on-task activities.
(C) cooperative learning.
(D) lecturing.

29. Terry Koolfian is a teacher with decades of experience. Recently, Terry has grasped the importance of a multicultural approach and wants to use this approach to teach social studies, which means Terry's approach will most appropriately include

(A) a comparison of how different cultures respond to similar issues.
(B) how people from different cultures contribute to world events.
(C) how people around the world have common characteristics.
(D) how events in one part of the globe influence the rest of the world.

30. There is frequently a lot of movement and activity when students in Francois le Bente's class are getting ready to go outside for recess, and it can be difficult to maintain discipline. At these times Mr. le Bente needs to recall that, above all, students usually expect the teacher to be

(A) very assertive.
(B) extremely understanding.
(C) a tough taskmaster.
(D) an authority figure.

31. Tom Karel has a number of students in his class who are significantly below grade level in reading. Mr. Karel realizes that he needs to adapt social studies instruction for these students. Mr. Karel's choice among the following options would be appropriate EXCEPT to

(A) use instructional materials that have a lower reading level.
(B) use instructional materials with less difficult concepts.
(C) read information about social studies to the students.
(D) use recorded tapes that contain social studies information.

32. Frank Rios is a primary teacher who is incorporating authentic assessment in his evaluation techniques. That means that Mr. Rios will

(A) collect and evaluate students' work.
(B) use only tests provided by the publisher of the books he uses.
(C) evaluate only students in real situations outside of school.
(D) collect evaluative information from other teachers.

Items 33–34.

Mr. Adolphus Batsawani is a fifth-grade teacher with high standards. This has created a few run-ins with parents. Mrs. Sivar is one of those parents. "My Tim doesn't finish his tests in Mr. Batsawani's class because the tests are too long," Mrs. Sivar tells the principal. "It is certainly not because he's fooling around," she adds. Mrs. Price, another parent, thinks it is unfair for her daughter Estelle to get a "B" in Mr. Batsawani's class when all her test grades are "A." "So what if she misses a few assignments?" snaps Mrs. Price. Mr. Allen says it is unfair for his son Sam to have to take a test when Sam was absent the previous day. He says, "I don't care if Sam knew about the test at the beginning of the week. And I certainly don't care that Mr. Batsawani sent home a test guide. Sam wasn't in class the day before and he shouldn't have to take the test."

33. It would NOT be appropriate for Mr. Batsawani to respond to which of the following requests from a parent?

(A) Please show me a folder of my child's work and point out areas of needed remediation.

(B) Please show me a folder of my child's work and point out areas of possible acceleration.

(C) Please show me a report of individual students' test scores so that I can tell how my child is doing.

(D) Please show me how my child is doing compared to the average class performance.

34. Which of the following is LEAST likely to enable Mr. Batsawani to promote good communication with parents?

(A) Make phone calls to parents.

(B) Write personal notes on report cards.

(C) Initiate a series of home/school letters.

(D) Meet with groups of parents to discuss individual student achievement.

Items 35–36.

There is a school board meeting tonight. Items on the agenda include a budget discussion and a discussion of a tracking system for a fifth-grade mathematics program based on standardized test results. The meeting is open to the public. Harvey Rios, a teacher in the district but not a town resident, is in the audience to support pro-school board members who want the school budget passed. Registered voters in the community vote on the budget at the same time that they vote for school board candidates. A large group of parents will be at the Board of Education meeting.

35. Which of the following describes the most appropriate action for Mr. Rios?

(A) Tell parents that the school needs their support and ask them to get out and vote.

(B) Tell parents to vote yes on the school budget.

(C) Tell the parents that the voting records are clear and to vote for the pro-school candidates.

(D) Tell parents that a vote for antibudget candidates is a vote against school programs.

36. An opponent of the tracking system could most effectively argue against this approach before the board by saying

(A) "The standardized tests used to place students in the program are deliberately designed to trick minority students."

(B) "Tracking programs have been shown to consistently discriminate against minority students."

(C) "The best teachers are always assigned to the highest and lowest classes."

(D) "The school administration cannot be counted on to accurately report test scores."

37. Betty Ann Hotop is helping her first-grade students learn about counting. She uses shapes as counters and makes sure students point to a shape each time they say the next counting word. What is the most likely reason why she is using this approach?

    (A) Ms. Hotop wants to be sure the students are paying attention to what they are doing.
    (B) Ms. Hotop wants to be sure students are developing eye-hand coordination.
    (C) Ms. Hotop is going to ask the students questions about the shapes once they have finished counting.
    (D) Ms. Hotop wants to be sure the students are not just saying counting words.

38. A fourth-grade student in Geovanna Savorsi's class hands in an assignment, containing the writing sample shown below.

    > It is a nice day today. I are going swimming. I go to the lake by the park with my friends.

    Based on this sample, Ms. Savorsi should concentrate on which of the following with that student?

    I. Subject-verb agreement
    II. Pronouns
    III. Sentence fragments

    (A) I only
    (B) I and II
    (C) II and III
    (D) I and III

39. Lucy Small is a fifth-grade teacher who has heard that a student in her class has AIDS, but she is not sure which student it is. When Ms. Small inadvertently sees his health record she correctly concludes that Louis is the one. Once she has reasonably reached this conclusion, she

    (A) has the right to refuse to have Louis in her class because of concerns about her own personal safety.
    (B) should keep this information to herself, even though it may be considered important by others in the school who have families.
    (C) has a responsibility to inform parents of other students in the class so that these parents may safeguard their children's safety.
    (D) has a legal responsibility under New York law to confidentially inform other teachers so that they may protect students in their classes.

40. A voucher program is one in which students use public funds to attend nonpublic schools. In New York, as a general rule, vouchers are legal when

    (A) the student's family incomes are below the poverty level.
    (B) the student is not attending a religious school or a school owned or controlled by a religious group.
    (C) parents make the choice between religious and nonreligious schools.
    (D) the school district test scores fall below an established level for three continuous years.

Items 41–42.

Frank Damico, a special education teacher, is working with Kathy McCoy in Kathy's fifth-grade class that includes mainstreamed students. Mr. Damico and Ms. McCoy have regular meetings with the parents of mainstreamed students in the class.

41. Which of the following best describes Frank Damico's role in the classroom?

    (A) Observe the mainstreamed students to identify the out-of-class support they need.
    (B) Teach the entire class cooperatively with the teacher.
    (C) Help the mainstreamed students during the teacher's lesson.
    (D) Observe the nonmainstreamed students to get tips on their successful learning styles to pass on to the special education student.

42. During one meeting, a parent expresses extreme concern about how her child James is doing in school. The parent is concerned that continued academic problems will make it impossible for her son to attend college or to be a success in life. Which of the following choices is the best response for these teachers to give?

    (A) "Don't be concerned; we are confident that James will do fine and be successful."
    (B) "We enjoy working with James and we have the highest hopes for him."
    (C) "That James is still in a special education setting at this age indicates that there are likely some real problems that may or may not be resolved over time."
    (D) "We are sorry you feel that way but we just cannot discuss these things with parents."

43. Lucie Montelone's class is reading a science fiction story about space travel. Which of the following approaches by Ms. Montelone is most likely to help students differentiate between science fact and science fiction?

    (A) She should guide students to understand that science fiction stories are creative writing and not based on science fact.
    (B) She should guide students as they identify examples of science fact and science fiction based on the story they just completed.
    (C) She should ask students to work independently to make their own list of science fact and science fiction.
    (D) She should ask students to work independently as they identify examples of science fact and science fiction in the story they just completed.

44. Dr. Samson, the school principal, was explaining to a group of beginning teachers that children can learn vicariously, meaning children can

    (A) learn by doing.
    (B) learn through a wide variety of activities.
    (C) learn if there is a clear structure.
    (D) learn from others' experiences.

45. At a "Back-to-School-Night" Frances Zimolo, a second-grade teacher, displays student work and explains to parents in her brief presentation that it is not a conference time. But one parent corners Ms. Zimolo and asks about her child's progress. Which of the following is the most professional response Ms. Zimolo can make?

    (A) "I'm sorry. I am not prepared to discuss your child's progress with others here."
    (B) "When would you like to meet to discuss your concerns?"
    (C) "Would you please call the office to arrange a conference time?"
    (D) Answer the parent's questions as quickly and quietly as possible.

46. Punishment can be an effective way to change a student's behavior when

    (A) the whole class is involved.
    (B) it involves pertinent extra work.
    (C) it is used for limited and specific reasons.
    (D) it makes the teacher feel better.

47. Les Levy is preparing for "back-to-school" night. He plans to explain cooperative learning groups and he is typing a list of the practices consistent with this instructional approach. Which of the following is LEAST likely to appear on Mr. Levy's list?

    (A) Group members themselves devise a working plan.
    (B) Group members are actively involved in learning.
    (C) Groups include ten to twelve members.
    (D) The teacher presents the project or topic to be worked on.

48. Each Friday a group of teachers from the Roosevelt Elementary School get together after school at Jim Stanley's restaurant. It seems that they talk about every administrator and about every problem they have had during the week. In fact, this after-school get-together

    (A) may be common practice in many schools but its actually illegal under New York law.
    (B) gives any administrator mentioned at the meeting the right to suspend the teacher.
    (C) gives school administrators the right to take disciplinary action against teachers in the group.
    (D) is fine as long as they do not discuss confidential information.

49. Entu Geranhi reads a story to her primary class about a sailor on an old-time sailing boat. She asks each student to write one sentence about the story. One student's writing contains this sentence.

    > He had enuf rope.

    Which of the actions listed below best addresses the problem in the sentence?

    (A) instruction on phonics-based word attack skills
    (B) instruction on context-based word attack skills
    (C) instruction on the use of homonyms
    (D) instruction on variable spelling phonemes

50. Sylvia Negbutu is a new teacher who seeks to use a constructivist approach to teaching. Which of the following is most consistent with that approach?

    (A) Ms. Negbutu encourages students to respond quickly and alertly to questions.
    (B) Ms. Negbutu encourages students to construct complex models of their thought processes.
    (C) Ms. Negbutu encourages students to elaborate on their initial responses.
    (D) Ms. Negbutu discourages students from creating metaphors.

51. A teacher using Gardner's Multiple Intelligences as the basis for instruction is most likely to do which of the following?

    (A) Implement interdisciplinary units.
    (B) Help students learn about each of the intelligences.
    (C) Eliminate assessments.
    (D) Allow students to determine criteria for quality.

52. Elma Topper is discussing one of her second-grade students with the school principal. The student has difficulty pronouncing some printed words. The problem may reflect all of the following EXCEPT

    (A) phonetic analysis.
    (B) sight vocabulary.
    (C) language comprehension.
    (D) context analysis.

53. Iraidia Lonia is a member of a committee to formulate a policy for calculator use in the school district. There are a wide variety of opinions, but which of the choices below would be most appropriate for Ms. Lonia to recommend?

    (A) Calculators should be banned from classrooms until high school.
    (B) Calculators should not be used when the reason for the lesson is to teach computation.
    (C) Calculators should not be used to add, subtract, multiply, or divide. These operations should be completed only with "paper and pencil."
    (D) Calculators should be used only to check "paper and pencil" computations.

54. Priscilla Mitchell constructs her own content-valid multiple-choice test to assess performance on a social studies unit. One student correctly answers 91 percent of the questions, while another student gets 89 percent correct. How confident should Ms. Mitchell be about assigning grades according to the school grading rules shown below?

SCHOOL GRADING RULES	
A	91–100
B	81–90
C	71–80

    (A) Very confident—the teacher should just follow the grading rules.
    (B) Very confident—the difference between the grades is clear.
    (C) Somewhat confident—the test is content-valid and probably measures important concepts.
    (D) Not confident—the errors of measurement in the test could eliminate the meaning of the difference between the scores.

55. Gina Telione just finished teaching a three-day unit on nouns. She wants to determine whether or not the students learned the material in the unit before going on. Which of the following assessment techniques would be best for Ms. Telione to use?

    (A) Obtain and have the students complete standardized assessment.
    (B) Prepare and have the students complete a teacher-made assessment.
    (C) Observe students' writing over the next week.
    (D) Review writing that students have previously completed.

56. Stan Powell makes extensive use of portfolio assessment in his anthropology class, so he knows the most significant difficulty with portfolio assessment reliability is that

    (A) students put samples of widely different types of work in their portfolio.
    (B) scoring machines don't work reliably with materials in the portfolio.
    (C) different teachers place different emphasis on the portfolios when giving grades.
    (D) different teachers assign widely different grades to the same portfolio.

57. A soccer game over the weekend led to a reaction among some students from the Del Rios Elementary School. The students did not like many of the referee's decisions. On Monday, all students wore replica team jerseys to school and decided on their own to leave the school grounds during lunch to show how they felt. In all likelihood, these students

    (A) were just expressing their free speech rights and should not be interfered with.
    (B) were a model of democracy and truly represent American values.
    (C) were not doing anything wrong because they were not on the school grounds.
    (D) were violating school rules and might be disciplined.

58. Repeated testing of a fourth-grade student in Ray Maw's class reveals an IQ in the 110 to 115 range, but standardized test scores that are two or more years below grade level. Which of the following is the most appropriate interpretation of these test scores?

    (A) The student is a poor test taker.
    (B) The student's achievement and potential match.
    (C) The student is gifted.
    (D) The student has a learning disability.

Items 59–60.

Lucille Davenport is meeting with parents of a student in her fifth-grade class to interpret their child's test scores. These scores include the results of a standardized achievement test that show the student at the 34th percentile in mathematics. The reading test shows a grade equivalent of 6.3. The average reading score reported for the school district is 6.8. The English test shows a grade equivalent of 6.6. A criterion-referenced test shows that a student has mastered 75 percent of the science objectives for that grade level. Ms. Davenport also has a folder with representative samples of the student's writing. In Ms. Davenport's opinion, these writing samples are well above average for the school.

59. How would Ms. Davenport explain the mathematics test score?

    (A) "This means that your child did better than all but 34 students on this test."
    (B) "This means that your child did better than all but about 34 percent of the students who took this test."
    (C) "This means that your child did better than about 34 percent of the students who took this test."
    (D) "This means that your child has better mathematics ability than about 34 percent of the students who took this test."

60. The parents ask for your overall assessment of their child based on these results. Which of the following is the most appropriate response?

    (A) "We can't really draw any meaningful conclusions from these results."
    (B) "The results indicate that your child may do better when evaluated in real-world settings."
    (C) "The results indicate that your child does markedly better in English than in mathematics."
    (D) "The results indicate that your child performs better in science than in reading."

61. Ezequiel Sanchez administers an end of chapter test from the teacher's edition of a language arts text to students in his fourth-grade class. In all likelihood, this is a

    (A) portfolio evaluation.
    (B) standardized test.
    (C) norm-referenced test.
    (D) summative evaluation.

Items 62–63.

Suzanna Lilanni teaches English and writing to the upper elementary grades. Ms. Lilanni is currently teaching a unit that includes creative writing, writing journals, and following directions.

62. Which of the following would be most appropriate for Ms. Lilanni to use to evaluate students' writing techniques and plan for further writing experiences?

    (A) Administer a standardized grammar test and use the scores as a planning device.
    (B) Use a writing checklist to assess a variety of students' writing samples.
    (C) Have the students hand in a composition of their choice.
    (D) Have the students answer a series of short-answer questions from a specific reading selection.

63. Ramona is a student in this class who writes well, understands verbal directions, but often has trouble understanding written directions. Her difficulty might be related to all of the following EXCEPT

    (A) auditory discrimination.
    (B) visual discrimination.
    (C) sight vocabulary.
    (D) context clues.

64. The personal journals that students write in class should NOT be used

    (A) as a record of feelings.
    (B) to share their thoughts with others.
    (C) as a means of expressing thoughts.
    (D) as a means for writing ideas.

65. Lucinda Crawford uses holistic scoring to evaluate her fifth-grade students' writing. She will make a brief presentation to the Board of Education about this method. This is best described as a scoring technique in which

    (A) essays are scored using advanced imaging technology.
    (B) essays are scored by several readers who do not discuss the essay.
    (C) readers rank essays relative to the "whole" of essays written for that testing cycle.
    (D) readers rank essays based on the overall impression, not on a detailed analysis.

66. Pam is a fifth-grade student who is extremely anxious about tests. Which of the following is NOT an effective way for her teacher, Ms. Rosa, to respond?

    (A) Give extra time, when practical for students to finish the test.
    (B) Don't draw attention to the student by providing emotional support.
    (C) Reduce tension before a test with humor.
    (D) Use alternative assessment.

Items 67–68.

A fifth-grade student has been classified as a special education student. The child study team, which includes Jeremy Jones, the student's fifth-grade teacher, classified the student as learning disabled. The child study team is deciding the appropriate placement for this student, discussing the basis for the placement and discussing the different strategies to help this student learn.

67. Which of the following describes an appropriate placement strategy for this student?

(A) Place the student in a self-contained class with other learning-disabled students and send the student out for music and art specials.

(B) Place the student in a fifth-grade class with support from a special education teacher.

(C) Place the student in a self-contained class with other learning-disabled students and send the student to a fifth-grade class for some subjects.

(D) Place the student in a fifth-grade class and meet with the parents to arrange extra tutoring.

68. Which of the following best describes an effective approach for Mr. Jones to use with this learning-disabled student?

(A) Use large-print books.

(B) Apply highly relevant skills with a minimum of practice.

(C) Provide brief assignments and auditory learning.

(D) Permit the student to test out of requirements.

69. Kisa Amman is called to an emergency meeting along with other teachers in the school. School administrators are concerned that just released tests results have again fallen below the school's goal level. The administrators are primarily concerned because

(A) they think teacher effort needs to be improved.

(B) they think the test scores may have been falsified.

(C) parents may have the legal right to remove students.

(D) the Commissioner of Education in New York does not have the power to invalidate the scores.

70. An aid has been assigned to Ms. Stanair's first-grade class because there are more students than the district usually allows. Which of the following represents the LEAST appropriate instructional duties for Ms. Stanair to assign to the aid?

(A) Help preschool children dress themselves.

(B) Duplicate instructional worksheets.

(C) Read to small groups of students.

(D) Help manage difficult children.

71. The assignment of a special education child to an appropriate learning environment is most likely based on which of these education laws?

(A) PL 99-457

(B) PL 98-199

(C) The Emancipation Proclamation

(D) PL 94-142

Items 72–74.

It is Holly Ritzkovik's first month in school. She is concerned about maintaining discipline, keeping the students interested and on task, having an effective management style, and just surviving. The principal comes by to observe the class and notices that the teacher calls on only about 40 percent of the students and that too much teacher-centered instruction is taking place. The principal also notices that classroom management needs to be improved and that students are often confused about transitions during the lesson. The principal has a conference with the teacher following the observation.

72. Which of the following is the most constructive professional advice Ms. Ritzkovik could expect the principal to give during the conference?

    (A) "Try to call on about 65 percent of the students during any lesson."
    (B) "Make a check on a list of names, a seating chart, or something like that, and try to get to everyone."
    (C) "Research shows that student participation is important, so try to call on all the students."
    (D) "I can see why you don't call on some of these students—they're very difficult—but do your best."

73. The principal notices that several of Ms. Ritzkovik's students are discipline problems just to gain her attention. Which of the following is the best advice the principal could give for dealing with the attention-seeking students?

    (A) "Point out misbehavior each time it occurs."
    (B) "Deliberately ignore appropriate behavior when it occurs."
    (C) "Send students to the office after several misbehaviors."
    (D) "Ignore the misbehavior whenever possible."

74. Which of the following is the most appropriate way for Ms. Ritzkovik to alert students to a transition from group work to a whole-class activity?

    (A) Say, "Time's up—put away your work."
    (B) Use a recognized signal, such as putting the lights on and off.
    (C) Stand silently in front of the room and wait for students to realize that you want their attention.
    (D) Begin making the presentation and then wait for students' attention.

75. Ellen Archibald is about to engage her third-grade class in a lesson on the value of coins. Which of the following should Ms. Archibald say at the beginning of the lesson to have the best chance to motivate students?

    (A) "Hi, class—I have some make-believe coins that look like real coins. I'll hold them up and tell you what each coin is worth."
    (B) "Here are some make-believe coins. Pretend I am a bank. We'll say the value of the coin as you put the coins in."
    (C) "Does anyone know when coins were first used? It is interesting because coins were used a long time ago."
    (D) "Before we begin, let me review with you the value of each one of these coins. Knowing the value of the coins is the secret to our lesson today."

76. Marcie Sola-Vega is a first-year teacher and she carefully planned a lesson and wrote an excellent lesson plan. Once the lesson was underway, Ms. Sola-Vega's observation of students indicates the plan is very clearly not working. In light of this, Ms. Sola-Vega should

    (A) stay with the plan and analyze later why the plan was not successful.
    (B) stay with the plan and discipline any students disrupting the lesson.
    (C) stay with the plan and give other work to those students who can't keep up.
    (D) abandon the plan and try another approach.

77. Samantha Smithson is a third-grade teacher who has just finished reviewing the mathematics assignments her students completed in the last few weeks. Based on her assessment, Ms. Smithson decides to reschedule subjects so that mathematics is first thing in the morning and reading is after a recess but before lunch. Which of the following is the most appropriate response to her plan?

    (A) This is poor planning because the students will be late from recess.
    (B) This is good planning, because if her math lesson runs over, she can always cut out recess.
    (C) It doesn't make any difference when she schedules these subjects, as long as she gets them in somewhere.
    (D) This is good planning because the students have a break before reading.

78. When it comes to the general characteristics of elementary school students,

    (A) all ethnic groups adapt equally well to school.
    (B) boys have more adjustment problems than girls do.
    (C) girls are more physically active than boys of the same age.
    (D) primary students rebel against the teacher's authority.

79. Students come from varying types of families, but overall, which of the following does NOT accurately characterize the American family?

    (A) A majority of families have mothers who work.
    (B) An increasing number of children are "latchkey" children.
    (C) Less than 10 percent of American families have a mother (as a homemaker), a father (as the breadwinner), and children.
    (D) Families are groups of people living together who are related to one another.

80. The gifted and talented (G&T) program in the Almay School has always been self-contained. That is, May Riverbark, the G&T teacher, had always taught students in her own classroom. Then the Almay School implemented a collaborative teaching program that includes the G&T teacher. This most likely means that Ms. Riverbark will

    (A) meet with students' parents to discuss the G&T curriculum.
    (B) work on an interdisciplinary team to plan the G&T curriculum.
    (C) teach both G&T and learning disabled students.
    (D) teach with classroom teachers in their classrooms.

CONSTRUCTED RESPONSE

Teachers are asked to suggest goals and objectives for different grades and subject matter areas. A goal is a more general statement about what should be accomplished at the end of a school year or at the completion of a teaching unit. An objective is a more specific statement of expected learning outcomes. Here is one example of a goal drawn up by a joint committee of teachers, parents, and administrators.

> Students should read at or above grade level by the end of third grade.

Write an essay for New York State educators that accomplishes the following.

- Explains the importance of providing reading instruction in the primary grades and comments on the appropriateness of the goal for students in elementary school.
- Describes two teaching techniques designed to help students reach the goal.
- Explains why the strategies you describe would help students reach this goal.

Answer Key

PRACTICE ATS-W—ELEMENTARY

1. C	21. D	41. C	61. D
2. B	22. B	42. B	62. B
3. B	23. C	43. B	63. A
4. B	24. B	44. D	64. B
5. A	25. D	45. B	65. D
6. B	26. C	46. C	66. B
7. B	27. B	47. C	67. B
8. C	28. B	48. D	68. C
9. B	29. A	49. D	69. C
10. C	30. D	50. C	70. B
11. D	31. B	51. A	71. D
12. B	32. A	52. C	72. A
13. B	33. C	53. B	73. D
14. D	34. D	54. D	74. B
15. B	35. A	55. B	75. B
16. A	36. B	56. D	76. D
17. D	37. D	57. D	77. D
18. B	38. A	58. D	78. B
19. B	39. B	59. C	79. D
20. D	40. C	60. B	80. D

Answer Explanations

1. **(C)** This is good advice because teachers are authority figures and a student's misbehavior toward an authority figure usually reflects who the student is. (A) is incorrect. The teacher may need to change, but it's still not personal. (B) is incorrect because most seventh graders are not unmanageable. (D) is incorrect because "don't take it personally" has nothing to do with not being concerned about students' misbehavior.

2. **(B)** Peer leaders and peer pressures have the most impact on students this age. (A) is incorrect because students will not necessarily follow rules just because they are firm or just because the teacher asks that the rules be memorized. (C) is incorrect simply because Ms. Brown will not become more effective because she uses cooperative learning experiences. (D) is incorrect because promoting competition among students may turn the students against one another, but that will not make Ms. Brown a more effective leader.

3. **(B)** Students learn less when teachers are negative and critical; being negative and critical is very different from having high expectations. (A) is incorrect because less learning actually takes place. (C) and (D) are incorrect because a negative and critical approach will not increase homework participation and parent involvement. However, as the scenario shows, there will likely be an increase in parent complaints.

4. **(B)** Good classroom managers create on-task learning opportunities, and research clearly shows that students learn more when they spend more time on task. Each of the remaining choices could be an effective management technique, but none carries the proven assurance of more time on task.

5. **(A)** The question in this choice fits the Analysis category, which is at the upper end of Bloom's scale. The remaining choices contain questions that ask from information and knowledge about the story. These questions fit Knowledge and Comprehension categories at the lower end of Bloom's Taxonomy.

6. **(B)** This policy statement gives the best guidance to ensure that students have the most opportunities to use computers. (A) and (C) are incorrect because the committee's work is focused on the computer use in classrooms and these policies do not address that area. (D) is incorrect because this policy is not within the committee's control, and it holds little promise of helping since it would require additional approval to implement.

7. **(B)** This choice describes the best way to consistently determine a student's writing ability, and to prepare for the future. The teacher gathers specific information that can be used for future plans. (A) is incorrect because standardized grammar tests do not reveal detailed information about a student's writing. (C) is incorrect because holistic evaluations reflect the evaluator's view of the overall quality of the writing. A holistic evaluation does not yield a specific

analysis that can lead to instructional plans. (D) is incorrect because it evaluates reading, not writing.

8. **(C)** This choice describes the essence of the inquiry approach, to solve problems as a way to understand scientific principles. (A) is incorrect because a teacher must have prior experience with an experiment so he or she can guide students. (B) is incorrect because students analyze their thought processes when using the inquiry approach. (D) is incorrect because the inquiry approach is student centered not student directed.

9. **(B)** The reading specialist was most likely going to say phonics does not address word meaning or reading comprehension. Phonics primarily addresses word recognition and word pronunciation. Each of the remaining choices describes a benefit that can be derived directly from the phonics approach.

10. **(C)** Students learn best when the lesson is at their level of ability. Students become too frustrated when asked to do something they cannot do. Naturally, there is a difference between ability level and achievement level. Students frequently learn successfully when reasonably challenged beyond their achievement level, but not beyond their ability level. Lessons at advanced achievement levels can be adapted to a student's ability level. (A) is incorrect because teaching below an ability level may not cause a problem, but it is not what Ms. Meridcu should do. (B) is incorrect because a lesson above a student's ability level may prove too frustrating for the student. (D) is incorrect because Ms. Meridcu should take ability level into account.

11. **(D)** Consider each Roman numeral in turn, and then choose your answer.

   I. Correct. It is a good technique to handle a question with encouragement for more explanation.
   II. Correct. It is effective to demonstrate how to respond to questions.
   III. Incorrect. It is generally not a good idea to answer quickly. Ms. Kirk may be able to help the student find the answer for himself or herself.
   IV. Correct. Students' questions often reveal what is most difficult for them to understand and it is a good technique to include their questions in evaluations.

   I, II, and IV are correct—(D).

12. **(B)** Consider each Roman numeral in turn, and then choose your answer.

   I. Correct. Group learning means more student involvement.
   II. Incorrect. Cooperative learning groups do not lead to more content coverage. In fact, teacher centered lessons would most likely lead to more content coverage.
   III. Correct. The more people involved, the more varied the outcomes.
   IV. Correct. A cooperative learning group means more brainstorming.

   I, III, and IV are correct—(B).

13. **(B)** This is the least effective method because this choice, alone, does NOT integrate haiku with fine arts because only art is displayed. Each of the remaining choices describes an effective way of integrating haiku and art.

14. **(D)** Economically disadvantaged students are not less capable, but as a group economically disadvantaged students do have fewer home learning opportunities. This leads to lower achievement scores. (A) and (C) are factually incorrect stereotypes about minority students. (B) is incorrect because there is no evidence that minority teachers are more effective with minority students. Effective teaching is related to factors other than ethnicity.

15. **(B)** It is generally most appropriate to address questions to the entire class. This maximizes the number of students who are thinking about the answer. (A) is incorrect because calling on a student before you ask the question may mean others in the class will not try to formulate an answer. (C) is incorrect because this approach may bring a student back into the lesson, but it is not the best criteria for Ms. Selberding to use. (D) is incorrect because this approach severely limits the number of students who will actively participate in a class.

16. **(A)** The best advice, and the only good advice, among the four choices is to stand where you can see all the students. (B) is incorrect because Mr. Cohen should not limit the number of students who participate, even though he will probably not be able to involve everyone. (C) is incorrect because Mr. Cohen will likely frustrate these sixth graders if the material is consistently very difficult. (D) is incorrect because this rigid approach may actually create discipline problems.

17. **(D)** Students develop a better attitude toward reading when they use the real literature found in a whole language approach. (A) is incorrect because it may be reassuring that an approach is widely accepted, but that is never the best reason to use it. (B) is incorrect because word recognition must always be taught. Students can't read if they can't recognize words. (C) is incorrect because research does not uniformly support the conclusion that students comprehend better after using a whole language approach. Rather, it seems a combination of approaches, including aspects of the whole language approach, best develops reading comprehension.

18. **(B)** Modeling means the teacher demonstrates the behavior students should replicate. (A) is incorrect because classroom modeling does not refer to this hobby. (C) is incorrect because just telling a student to do something is not modeling. (D) is incorrect because a teacher would not model incorrect behavior for students to copy.

19. **(B)** Mr. Cardot means that some students are not able to show their true achievement on a test. It seems he has observed something to make him believe that's the case for this child. (A) Mr. Cardot never says the tests are inappropriate. (C) and (D) Mr. Cardot never implies that the test administrator was

not competent, or that the child study team did not want to act in the best interests of this child.

20. **(D)** One example of negative reinforcement means explaining how to improve positive outcomes. (A) Positive reinforcement is praise or rewards for good work. (B) Reverse psychology is suggesting the opposite of what you want a student to do. (C) Threats, or bullying, are not appropriate classroom techniques.

21. **(D)** It is most appropriate to alter the objectives or plans to focus on the cultural heritage of those in the class. It is not appropriate to adopt the other practices in a culturally and linguistically diverse class. A teacher should not assume that students need (A) basic skills instruction, (B) reduced difficulty, or (C) to have the class taught in a foreign language.

22. **(B)** This choice is correct because a basal reading program is not designed to meet the individual needs of students. Note the word NOT in the item. A basal program is typically designed to be used with all the students in a class. A basal program must be supplemented to meet the individual needs of students. The remaining choices describe some of the characteristics of a basal reading program.

23. **(C)** Putting stickers on this chart creates a pictograph, which is one way to graph information. (A) is incorrect because Ms. Archibald has more direct ways to gather this information. (B) is incorrect because students may learn something about different modes of transportation but this is not the most likely reason Ms. Archibald is conducting this activity. (D) is incorrect because placing stickers on a chart does not give these young students useful tactile experiences.

24. **(B)** Using the ESL (English as a Second Language) approach is the most appropriate step because the child will be best served if he or she can communicate with others in his or her class. (A) is incorrect because using the child's native language does not further the child's mastery of English. (C) is incorrect because it is best if the child participates in the lesson with the teacher's help and support. (D) is incorrect because this may help, but it does not respond to the immediate situation in the classroom and is not the teacher's most appropriate action.

25. **(D)** Ms. Del Corso notices the reading difficulty when the student is reading mathematics problems. This indicates that the difficulty is reading in the context of mathematics and there is no mention that the reading problem occurs elsewhere. The remaining choices are all potential causes of reading difficulties, but not this reading difficulty, even though they may contribute to the problem in some way.

26. **(C)** This arrangement makes it too difficult for the teacher to see all the students, and Ms. Watson must always have her back to at least some of them. Having students out of sight, particularly on the first day of class, is not a good idea. The other chair arrangements are acceptable, particularly when compared to (C).

27. **(B)** Consider each Roman numeral in turn. Then choose your answer.

    I. Correct. High expectations are a hallmark of effective schools.
    II. Correct. Students do better when teachers and administrators are held accountable for their performance.
    III. Incorrect. Standardized tests are used in effective schools.

    I and II are correct—(B).

28. **(B)** More time on task is among a relatively few classroom practices shown to enhance learning. It has a proven and more powerful impact than all the other choices listed. There is room in the classroom for all of the other choices. However, if Ms. Weiss had to choose, as you do, she would choose (B).

29. **(A)** It is the comparison of cultures that creates a multicultural approach to teaching social studies. This approach emphasizes the varying responses across cultures. The intent of multicultural social studies education is to help students recognize differences and yet develop a unified bond among the students. The emphasis is on cultures in this country. The remaining choices may be interesting in a classroom, but they do not best characterize a multicultural approach.

30. **(D)** Students expect the teacher to be an authority figure. Students may complain, but an authority figure is what students expect and what it is usually best to give them. (A), (B), and (C) are incorrect because some authority figures may be very assertive, or extremely understanding, or tough taskmasters. None of these specific strategies serve Mr. le Bente as well as having students associate him with an authority figure.

31. **(B)** Just because a student is reading below grade level does *not* mean they cannot understand social studies topics that are on or above grade level. Do not adapt instruction to include less difficult topics on the basis of a low reading level. Each of the remaining choices represents an acceptable way to adapt social studies instruction for students reading significantly below grade level.

32. **(A)** Authentic assessment means Mr. Rios will observe students as they work or review students' actual work as described in this choice. (B) is incorrect because Mr. Rios would not use tests as a part of authentic assessment, although he may use them for other purposes in his class. (C) is incorrect because authentic assessment does not have to be conducted in real-life settings. (D) is incorrect because Mr. Rios would not rely on evaluative information from other teachers as a part of authentic assessment.

33. **(C)** A teacher should never show a parent individual test scores from a child other than their own. (A) and (B) are incorrect because a parent could reasonably be interested in this information and Mr. Batsawani should share it with the parents. (D) is incorrect because reports about average performance are usually available in schools and if it is available for his class, Mr. Batsawani should share it with the parent.

34. **(D)** Note that the question asks for the choice LEAST likely to help Mr. Batsawani promote communication. The communication generated by this choice is likely to lead to parents talking among themselves or with school administrators. The teacher should never discuss individual test scores with groups of parents. The remaining choices are examples of effective techniques for promoting good communication with parents.

35. **(A)** This action furthers the teacher's aims and does not run the risk of alienating parents. (B) is too self-serving; it does not give parents a reason to vote yes, and may not further the teacher's goal. (C) and (D) are incorrect because they inject Mr. Rios into town politics, in which he has an interest but no standing, and would likely not further his goal.

36. **(B)** Minority students' standardized test scores tend to fall below their actual ability and that is one of the reasons minority students are disproportionately represented in the lower tracks of a tracking system. (A) is incorrect because the flaws in standardized tests are not deliberately designed for that purpose, but that is often the outcome. (C) is incorrect because this statement is not necessarily true, and is more properly a suggestion for how teachers are assigned to classes. (D) is incorrect because as a general rule, administrators do accurately report scores.

37. **(D)** Just because a student can say counting words in order does not mean the student can count. You may have seen a child correctly count to five as the child counts seven objects. It is the correspondence between the counting words and the objects being counted that indicates a child is actually counting. (A) and (B) are incorrect because the activity is not designed to focus attention or to develop eye-hand coordination, but it may help. (C) Ms. Hotop may ask students about the shapes, but that is not the primary reason for the activity.

38. **(A)** Analyze the writing sample. The second sentence contains the grammatical error. The singular subject "I" does not agree with the plural verb "are." Consider each Roman numeral in turn.

   I. Correct. Ms. Savorsi should concentrate on subject-verb agreement because of the agreement error in the second sentence.
   II. Incorrect. The sample contains no pronoun errors.
   III. Incorrect. The sample contains no sentence fragments.

   Only I is correct—(A).

39. **(B)** Health information about students, and particularly about students with AIDS, is confidential and should not be shared. (A) is incorrect because a teacher has no right to have a child with AIDS removed from his or her class. (C) is incorrect because teachers are not permitted to inform anyone that a student has AIDS. (D) is incorrect because Ms. Small should not inform other teachers that Louis has AIDS.

40. **(C)** The Supreme Court ruled in 2002 that vouchers were constitutional if there was a choice between religious and nonreligious schools, and if parents, not the government, decided which school their child would attend. Voucher programs in New York State are legal for that reason, but the state is not required to offer a voucher program. (A) is incorrect because voucher programs do not have to take income into account. (B) is incorrect because students are permitted to use vouchers to attend religious schools. (D) is incorrect because a voucher program does not have to require that schools fall below established criteria for three years.

41. **(C)** This choice accurately describes why the special education teacher is in the classroom, to help special education students while the teacher conducts the lesson. (A) is incorrect because Frank Damico's job is to be the support, not to arrange for support. (B) and (D) are incorrect because Mr. Damico's responsibility is not with nonmainstreamed students, although he may spend some time working with nonmainstreamed students.

42. **(B)** This is the best response to give a parent. It is positive and truthful, but it neither holds out too much hope nor is too negative. (A) is incorrect because this choice is too positive and unrealistically raises a parent's expectations. (C) is incorrect because this response is likely the most candid of the four responses, but it is too stark and it is not the kind of response that should be given at a parent-teacher conference. (D) is incorrect because this response unnecessarily puts the parent off.

43. **(B)** Guiding students as they work is a very effective strategy for teaching reading. Picking out science fact and science fiction in a space exploration story is certainly the best kind of guidance among the choices given. (A) is incorrect because most science fiction stories contain some science fact. (C) and (D) are incorrect because working independently is one of the least effective ways to learn to pick out science fact and science fiction because it lacks interaction with Ms. Montelone and with other students.

44. **(D)** It's a definition; vicarious learning means to learn from the others' experiences rather than from direct experience. None of the other choices reflects the definition of vicarious learning.

45. **(B)** This nonconfrontational response is professional and it furthers the teacher's goals. (A) and (C) are not technically incorrect, but they are not the most professional response and they do not further the teacher's goals. (D) A teacher should never discuss an individual child's work with the child's parent(s) when others are around.

46. **(C)** Punishment means denial of privileges such as being kept after school. It does not mean corporal punishment. Punishment is an ineffective way to change a student's behavior except when used for very limited and specific reasons. (A) is incorrect because punishing the entire class is not required to

change one student's behavior. (B) is incorrect because extra work is not required for punishment to be effective. (D) is incorrect because there is no known correlation between a teacher feeling better and effective punishment.

47. **(C)** Groups with ten or twelve members are too large for effective interaction. Cooperative learning groups are typically limited to six group members. The remaining choices describe essential elements of cooperative learning groups.

48. **(D)** This kind of after-school, off-campus meeting is fine, as long as teachers don't discuss students' confidential information. There is no indication that they do. (A) This meeting is not illegal. (B) and (C) are incorrect because teachers have the right to criticize school administrators.

49. **(D)** This student is a phonetic speller. "Enuf" is misspelled, but the student followed phonetic rules. This student needs instruction in the alternative spelling used for phonemes (sounds associated with letters and groups of letters). For example, English spelling uses the letters "gh" to represent the "f" sound as in eno<u>ugh</u>. Using many spellings for the same sound can make English a difficult language to learn. (A) and (B) are incorrect because word attack skills lead to the correct pronunciation of "enuf." (C) is incorrect because "enough" and "enuf" sound the same, so they are homonyms. However, confusing homonyms is not the problem here.

50. **(C)** A constructivist approach encourages students to build their own understanding of concepts. One important way to do this is for students to build on their initial responses. (A) is incorrect because a more reflective approach to questions is in keeping with the constructivist approach. (B) is incorrect because this is not the kind of construction that constructivists have in mind. (D) is incorrect because the constructivist approach encourages students to create metaphors.

51. **(A)** Gardner's theory supports the use of interdisciplinary units. It holds that students have many intelligences, not just a cognitive intelligence. Interdisciplinary units promote utilization of these multiple intelligences. (B) is incorrect because students don't need to know about the intelligences. (C) and (D) are incorrect because there is nothing in Gardner's theory that supports the elimination of assessments nor having students establish the criteria for quality.

52. **(C)** You do not have to understand the meaning of a word to properly pronounce it. Note the word EXCEPT in the item. Both word recognition and comprehension are important parts of reading instruction. (A) and (B) are incorrect because a child might not be able to sound out the word phonetically, or the word might not be a part of the child's sight vocabulary. (D) is incorrect because the context of the word reveals the correct pronunciation, so a problem with context analysis could lead to difficulty pronouncing a word.

Answer Explanations

53. **(B)** This is the most common way to limit the use of calculators. If students are learning a computation method, calculators should not be used. (A) is incorrect because calculators are now required on many tests and in many real-life situations as well. It would not be in the student's best interest to ban them. (C) is incorrect because calculators can be very useful for completing complex computations involving these operations. (D) is incorrect because this sort of checking might happen, but calculators should not be limited "only" to this use.

54. **(D)** The teacher should not be confident. Errors of measurement that occur on all teacher-made tests quite likely eliminate any meaning in the small difference between these scores. (A) is incorrect because the teacher should not be confident, whether or not she follows the grading rules. (B) is incorrect because a difference of 2 or 4 percent between scores on a teacher-made test may be clear, but it means very little. (C) is incorrect because content validity means the test actually measures the content in the social studies unit. Content validity does not mean the difference noted in the scores is meaningful.

55. **(B)** In a brief unit such as this one, a teacher-made assessment is almost always best. There may also be an appropriate assessment available from a text publisher or other source, but this is clearly the best among the choices given. (A) is incorrect because standardized tests are used to establish an achievement level, or to compare results between students or groups of students. Standardized tests are not particularly useful for finding out whether or not a student has learned something. (C) is incorrect because the item states that the teacher wants to know whether the students have learned about nouns before going on. While observing students' written work is an excellent assessment technique, there is not enough time to employ that technique and gather the information needed here. (D) is incorrect because reviewing students' previous work, alone, will not help the teacher determine what they learned since that time.

56. **(D)** Reliability means the same work consistently receives the same evaluation. Many schools that implemented portfolio assessment had to alter their policies because different teachers assigned widely different grades to the same portfolio. Clear rubrics or standards have to be established for portfolio assessment to be effective. (A) is incorrect because it is not the diverse group of work students put in portfolios that causes the problem. Rather, it is the way teachers assess these samples. (B) is incorrect because machines do not typically score the materials in a portfolio. (C) is incorrect because this may be an issue in some circumstances; however, it is not an issue of reliability.

57. **(D)** These students couldn't just decide themselves to leave school grounds during school hours; school hours include lunch. (A) and (B) are incorrect because it's one thing to express your free speech rights, or to represent democracy, and another thing to leave school grounds without permission. (C) is incorrect because the fact that the students left the school grounds without permission is the problem.

Answer Explanations

58. **(D)** This is the classic test-based definition of a learning disability—at or above average ability but achievement two or more years below grade level. (A) is incorrect because there is nothing in this record to indicate that the student is a poor test taker, and the IQ score of 110 to 115 may indicate the child is not a poor test taker. (B) is incorrect because the student's achievement is well below the student's potential. (C) is incorrect because these IQ test results are not high enough for a gifted classification.

59. **(C)** This choice is the correct interpretation of percentile. The percentile is the percentage of students who took the test and received a lower score. That means that Ms. Davenport's child scored better than 34 percent of those who took the test. (A) is incorrect because the percentile does not refer to students in the class. (B) is incorrect because this is a description of a student who scored better than about 66 percent of the students who took the test. (D) is incorrect because a standardized achievement test does not measure ability.

60. **(B)** The writing sample that Ms. Davenport believes is above average for the class *may* indicate that this student does better on authentic assessments. (A) is incorrect because there is a meaningful conclusion shown in choice (B). (C) is incorrect because there is no basis for this conclusion. Both the writing sample and the mathematics test score show good performance. (D) is incorrect because there is no basis to compare these results. The reading results are from a standardized test. The science results are from a criterion-referenced test, which shows the objectives a student has mastered.

61. **(D)** A summative evaluation assesses what a student learned about a specific objective or objectives. (A) is incorrect because a portfolio evaluation relies on samples of students' actual work. (B) and (C) are incorrect because a standardized test and a norm-referenced test are essentially the same type of test. These tests have been standardized on a large population of students. End of chapter tests are not standardized.

62. **(B)** Evaluation of students' writing is distinct from mastery of specific English skills. Ms. Lilanni's evaluation of a student's writing must be based on actual writing samples. Using a checklist helps ensure that the writing will be evaluated consistently. (A) is incorrect because this choice does not use actual writing samples. (C) is incorrect because this choice does not include an assessment and would rely on only one sample. (D) is incorrect because this choice evaluates reading, not writing.

63. **(A)** Auditory discrimination refers to hearing and a hearing problem would not be a cause of difficulty understanding written instructions. Difficulty with written instructions has to do with reading or some other visual problem such as those reflected in choices (B), (C), and (D).

64. **(B)** Personal journals are just that—personal—and they are not meant to be shared with others. There are other types of journals that can be used to achieve the ends noted in the other answer choices.

65. **(D)** Holistic grading is based on the evaluator's informed impression of the writing sample, not a detailed analysis. (A) This choice may remind you of a hologram, but it has nothing to do with holistic scoring. (B) is incorrect because tests scored holistically are often evaluated by several readers, but this does not happen in Ms. Crawford's class. (C) is incorrect because holistic scoring is not about this kind of whole.

66. **(B)** This is what Ms. Rosa should *not* do; she should give Pam extra support. Ms. Rosa does not want a fifth-grade student to do poorly on a test because of test anxiety. Choices (A), (C), and (D) represent appropriate ways to respond to a test-anxious child.

67. **(B)** This choice represents the least restrictive environment that meets the student's needs for additional support. (A) and (C) are incorrect because they represent learning environments that are more restrictive for the student. (D) This choice will not provide the additional support the child needs.

68. **(C)** Learning-disabled students benefit most from brief, structured assignments and auditory opportunities for learning. (A) is incorrect because large-print books are most appropriate for visually impaired students. (B) is incorrect because it is good to provide highly relevant skills, but learning-disabled students need practice. (D) is incorrect because learning-disabled students can do well on a test one day and not know the skills and concepts on that test the next day.

69. **(C)** Under the federal No Child Left Behind Act, parents have the right to remove their children from "failing schools." (A) is incorrect because administrators might see teacher effort as a reason for the low scores, but this is not their primary concern. (B) is incorrect because there is no evidence that this is a concern. (D) is incorrect because the Commissioner of Education in New York State *can* invalidate test scores if he or she believes there is just cause.

70. **(B)** Duplicating instructional worksheets is the least useful endeavor for an aid working in an instructional capacity. Choices (A), (C), and (D) all describe activities that are more useful than the activity described in (B).

71. **(D)** Public Law 94-142 was originally called the "Education of All Handicapped Children Act" and is now codified under the name "Individuals with Disabilities Education Act" (IDEA). This special education act was the first significant intervention in public schooling, and it is the only federal act listed that could be the basis for the decision.

72. **(A)** This choice is best because it gives the teacher a specific recommendation to follow. Choice (B) is incorrect because the advice to "try to get to everyone" is too vague." Ms. Ritzkovik could believe she was trying to reach everyone and only got to 30 percent of the students. (C) is incorrect because this advice is similar to Choice (B) but now the teacher is told to "try to call on all the students." It is often impossible to call on all the students and there is no

minimum standard to meet. (D) is incorrect because the advice to "do your best" is almost permission not to call on a higher percent of students in the class.

73. **(D)** It is best to ignore the behavior whenever possible because when a student is misbehaving to get attention, reprimanding the student just increases the behavior. Choices (A) and (C) are incorrect because they give students the attention they want. (B) is incorrect because Ms. Ritzkovik should make an extra effort to reward positive behavior exhibited by attention-seeking students. This approach may reduce the number of times students misbehave just to get attention.

74. **(B)** This approach is cueing, which is designed to let students know that a transition will occur soon, but not immediately. Using a recognized signal alerts students and gives them time to put away their work. (A) and (D) are incorrect because they represent too rapid a transition and do not give students an opportunity to adjust. (C) is incorrect because this approach will likely take too long and you may never achieve your goal, unless "standing there" is a recognized signal.

75. **(B)** This choice draws attention to the coins and actively involves students in the lesson. (A) is incorrect because this choice might sound interesting, but it does not involve students in the lesson. (C) is incorrect because the question of where coins came from may be interesting to some, but usually not to a class of primary students. (D) is incorrect because it is not a motivation, it is an anticipatory set designed to focus students on the lesson.

76. **(D)** Plans often fail, and for many reasons. It is a reality of teaching, particularly for beginning teachers. If a plan is clearly failing, Ms. Sola-Vega should try to find alternative ways to teach the lesson. The remaining choices recommend that Ms. Sola-Vega "stick with" her plan and give varying reasons why this is the correct approach. But she should not stick with a failed plan. That's not to say she should abandon a plan at the first sign of trouble. However, Ms. Sola-Vega should let the plan go if it is "very clearly not working."

77. **(D)** It is a good plan because it provides students with a break before reading. Reading does not have to be the first subject taught. (A) is incorrect because the students might not be late from recess. This is not a basis for criticizing the plan. There are always things that can happen during a day to create a problem for any plan. (B) is incorrect because the recess is a regular part of the school day and cannot be "cut out" by the teacher. (C) is incorrect because it does make a difference. For example, Ms. Smithson should not schedule reading as the last thing in the day.

78. **(B)** It is a research fact that about twice as many boys as girls have problems adjusting to school. (A) is incorrect because minority students adapt more poorly to school than majority students. (C) is incorrect because girls are not

more physically active than boys the same age. (D) is incorrect because primary students typically do not rebel against the teacher's authority.

79. **(D)** This choice does *not* reflect the modern American family. The other choices do accurately describe aspects of the American family, including (A) a majority of families have mothers who work. (B) When the responsible adult or adults at home both work, students let themselves into an empty house after school. That's what "latchkey child" means. (C) It may be because there is only one parent, or it may be because both parents work, but a very small number of American families have one parent who stays home.

80. **(D)** Collaborative teaching generally means that special education teachers work in regular classrooms along with the classroom teacher. This situation will most likely apply to Ms. Riverbark. Choices (A) and (B) may still be a significant part of Ms. Riverbark's job, but the main impact of collaborative teaching will most likely move her into classrooms. (C) is incorrect because she may come into contact with learning disabled students in classrooms, but this is not the main impact of the shift to collaborative teaching.

Constructed Response

Show your essay to a professor of education. Ask that a person to rate your essay from 1–4 using this scale.

4　A well developed, complete lesson plan.
　Shows a thorough response to all parts of the plan.
　Clear objective and lesson plan parts.
　A lesson that is free of significant planning errors.

3　A fairly well developed, complete lesson plan.
　It may not thoroughly include all parts of an effective plan.
　Fairly clear objective and lesson plan parts.
　It may contain some significant planning errors.

2　A poorly developed, incomplete lesson plan.
　It does not contain most parts of an effective plan.
　Contains an unclear objective, poor planning.
　It contains some significant planning errors.

1　A very poorly developed, incomplete plan.
　It does not contain any elements of an effective plan.
　Contains only poor planning.
　Contains numerous significant planning errors.

ATS-W—Elementary Essay Scoring

Your goal is to write an essay with a score in the upper half. Score your essay using the scale on the previous page and the sample essay that follows. Scoring your own essay can be difficult. Showing your essay to a scoring expert will probably help you evaluate your performance.

Sample Essay

This essay would likely receive a score in the upper half. There are three main points to address, and this essay addresses them all. Most importantly, it responds appropriately to each of these points. It is easier for students to learn to read during their early years. The goal of all students reading on or above grade level is unrealistic. The two strategies listed in the essay are appropriate strategies, and the 1992 National Reading Study is the recognized authority on reading instruction.

The length of this essay also indicates that it is worthy of a score of 3 or 4. The number of words itself is not enough to earn a high score. However, an essay of about this length will likely be required for a high score.

READING IS TRULY FUNDAMENTAL

Children learn to read most effectively during the early years of their lives. That is why so much of instructional time in school is devoted to reading instruction. The goal of any reading program should be to help every child read to his or her maximum potential. That is going to be different for every child. When educators write about reading at grade level, they are writing about the average tested reading level for all children in a large sample. So reading at the third-grade reading level means that half the students in third grade are reading above that level. At the same time, half the students are reading below that level. It would be extremely difficult for every student in any school district to be reading above grade level. I commend the committee for paying attention to reading when they set the goal. However, the goal as currently stated will never be fully achieved.

I would concentrate on phonemes. Phonemes are the basic sounds that make up a language. I believe there are around 40 English phonemes. Slashes / / are usually placed on either side to show that it is a phoneme. Phonemes are matched up with different letters or groups of letters.

When teaching reading, I would concentrate on phoneme identity and phoneme deletion. Phoneme identity means that children recognize the same sounds in different words. Think of the phoneme for /m/ like in mouse. Children would be able to identify that sound in words like my, me, mile, and many. Recognizing the same sound in different words helps students understand that a sound can appear it lots of different words.

I would also teach phoneme deletion. Phoneme deletion shows students that a word can be left after a phoneme is removed. My favorite example is the word smile. If you remove the /s/ from smile, you end up with the word mile. Phoneme deletion helps children see that smaller words can be found within larger words.

The strategies I mentioned above would help students because a large national reading student found that teaching phonics is the most effective way to help students learn to read. Teaching phonics would help students focus on the letters and words they read and on the sounds of those letters and words. Reading means to be able to identify phonemes and the letter or letters that form phonemes. Reading is not about knowing what the words mean. The study did show that phonics also helped students understand word meanings better. Phonics is so important that this national study found that phonics became less useful when it was combined with other approaches.

See pages 58–66 at *http://www.nystce.nesinc.com/PDFs/NY_fld090_prepguide.pdf* for a scoring guide and additional samples of weak and strong Elementary ATS-W essays.

Practice ATS-W— Secondary

TEST INFO BOX

This practice test contains the types of items you will encounter on the real test but don't be surprised if the real test seems different. The distribution of items varies from one test administration to another.

Take this test in a realistic timed setting. You should not take this practice test until you have completed your subject matter review.

The setting will be most realistic if another person times the test and ensures that the test rules are followed. But remember that many people do better on a practice test than on the real test.

You have four hours to complete the selected-response items and the constructed response. Keep this time limit in mind as you work. Answer the easier questions first. Be sure you answer all the questions. There is no penalty for guessing. You may write in the test booklet and mark up the questions.

Each selected-response item has four answer choices. Exactly one of these choices is correct. Use a pencil to mark your choice on the answer sheet provided for this test.

The constructed response immediately follows the selected-response items. Once the test is complete, review the answers and explanations as you correct the answer sheet.

When you are ready, turn the page and begin.

Answer Sheet

PRACTICE ATS-W–SECONDARY

1 Ⓐ Ⓑ Ⓒ Ⓓ	21 Ⓐ Ⓑ Ⓒ Ⓓ	41 Ⓐ Ⓑ Ⓒ Ⓓ	61 Ⓐ Ⓑ Ⓒ Ⓓ
2 Ⓐ Ⓑ Ⓒ Ⓓ	22 Ⓐ Ⓑ Ⓒ Ⓓ	42 Ⓐ Ⓑ Ⓒ Ⓓ	62 Ⓐ Ⓑ Ⓒ Ⓓ
3 Ⓐ Ⓑ Ⓒ Ⓓ	23 Ⓐ Ⓑ Ⓒ Ⓓ	43 Ⓐ Ⓑ Ⓒ Ⓓ	63 Ⓐ Ⓑ Ⓒ Ⓓ
4 Ⓐ Ⓑ Ⓒ Ⓓ	24 Ⓐ Ⓑ Ⓒ Ⓓ	44 Ⓐ Ⓑ Ⓒ Ⓓ	64 Ⓐ Ⓑ Ⓒ Ⓓ
5 Ⓐ Ⓑ Ⓒ Ⓓ	25 Ⓐ Ⓑ Ⓒ Ⓓ	45 Ⓐ Ⓑ Ⓒ Ⓓ	65 Ⓐ Ⓑ Ⓒ Ⓓ
6 Ⓐ Ⓑ Ⓒ Ⓓ	26 Ⓐ Ⓑ Ⓒ Ⓓ	46 Ⓐ Ⓑ Ⓒ Ⓓ	66 Ⓐ Ⓑ Ⓒ Ⓓ
7 Ⓐ Ⓑ Ⓒ Ⓓ	27 Ⓐ Ⓑ Ⓒ Ⓓ	47 Ⓐ Ⓑ Ⓒ Ⓓ	67 Ⓐ Ⓑ Ⓒ Ⓓ
8 Ⓐ Ⓑ Ⓒ Ⓓ	28 Ⓐ Ⓑ Ⓒ Ⓓ	48 Ⓐ Ⓑ Ⓒ Ⓓ	68 Ⓐ Ⓑ Ⓒ Ⓓ
9 Ⓐ Ⓑ Ⓒ Ⓓ	29 Ⓐ Ⓑ Ⓒ Ⓓ	49 Ⓐ Ⓑ Ⓒ Ⓓ	69 Ⓐ Ⓑ Ⓒ Ⓓ
10 Ⓐ Ⓑ Ⓒ Ⓓ	30 Ⓐ Ⓑ Ⓒ Ⓓ	50 Ⓐ Ⓑ Ⓒ Ⓓ	70 Ⓐ Ⓑ Ⓒ Ⓓ
11 Ⓐ Ⓑ Ⓒ Ⓓ	31 Ⓐ Ⓑ Ⓒ Ⓓ	51 Ⓐ Ⓑ Ⓒ Ⓓ	71 Ⓐ Ⓑ Ⓒ Ⓓ
12 Ⓐ Ⓑ Ⓒ Ⓓ	32 Ⓐ Ⓑ Ⓒ Ⓓ	52 Ⓐ Ⓑ Ⓒ Ⓓ	72 Ⓐ Ⓑ Ⓒ Ⓓ
13 Ⓐ Ⓑ Ⓒ Ⓓ	33 Ⓐ Ⓑ Ⓒ Ⓓ	53 Ⓐ Ⓑ Ⓒ Ⓓ	73 Ⓐ Ⓑ Ⓒ Ⓓ
14 Ⓐ Ⓑ Ⓒ Ⓓ	34 Ⓐ Ⓑ Ⓒ Ⓓ	54 Ⓐ Ⓑ Ⓒ Ⓓ	74 Ⓐ Ⓑ Ⓒ Ⓓ
15 Ⓐ Ⓑ Ⓒ Ⓓ	35 Ⓐ Ⓑ Ⓒ Ⓓ	55 Ⓐ Ⓑ Ⓒ Ⓓ	75 Ⓐ Ⓑ Ⓒ Ⓓ
16 Ⓐ Ⓑ Ⓒ Ⓓ	36 Ⓐ Ⓑ Ⓒ Ⓓ	56 Ⓐ Ⓑ Ⓒ Ⓓ	76 Ⓐ Ⓑ Ⓒ Ⓓ
17 Ⓐ Ⓑ Ⓒ Ⓓ	37 Ⓐ Ⓑ Ⓒ Ⓓ	57 Ⓐ Ⓑ Ⓒ Ⓓ	77 Ⓐ Ⓑ Ⓒ Ⓓ
18 Ⓐ Ⓑ Ⓒ Ⓓ	38 Ⓐ Ⓑ Ⓒ Ⓓ	58 Ⓐ Ⓑ Ⓒ Ⓓ	78 Ⓐ Ⓑ Ⓒ Ⓓ
19 Ⓐ Ⓑ Ⓒ Ⓓ	39 Ⓐ Ⓑ Ⓒ Ⓓ	59 Ⓐ Ⓑ Ⓒ Ⓓ	79 Ⓐ Ⓑ Ⓒ Ⓓ
20 Ⓐ Ⓑ Ⓒ Ⓓ	40 Ⓐ Ⓑ Ⓒ Ⓓ	60 Ⓐ Ⓑ Ⓒ Ⓓ	80 Ⓐ Ⓑ Ⓒ Ⓓ

Practice ATS-W—Secondary

Directions: Each item on this test includes four answer choices. Select the best choice for each item and mark that letter on the answer sheet.

Items 1–4.

Wayne Yarborough is in his fourth year as a social studies teacher in Roosevelt High School. He is giving some thought to the way he teaches. While teaching a social studies lesson, Mr. Yarborough can get the student's interest but he is not so good at maintaining that interest. Wayne uses a wide variety of questions as he teaches and is very interested in changing and reinforcing appropriate student behavior.

1. Mr. Yarborough has the best chance of maintaining student interest in the lesson if:

    (A) he is animated.
    (B) his objectives are clear and unambiguous.
    (C) the students understand that what they are learning will help them learn other material later.
    (D) there are no choices available to students.

2. When questioning students, which of the following techniques should Mr. Yarborough generally follow?

    (A) Make sure students know who will answer a question before it is asked
    (B) Ask questions of the whole class
    (C) Ask questions of students who are not paying attention.
    (D) Ask questions of students who usually have the correct answers.

3. Mr. Yarborough knows that modeling is one appropriate way to modify behavior. Which of the following is an example of a good modeling technique?

    (A) Respond courteously to students' questions.
    (B) Show students how to construct replicas of historic buildings.
    (C) Demonstrate students' inappropriate behavior.
    (D) Stress the importance of appearance and show students how to dress.

4. Which of the following would be an appropriate way for Mr. Yarborough to reinforce student behavior?

    I. Grading on the basis of performance
    II. Praising appropriate behavior
    III. Ignoring inappropriate behavior

    (A) I, II
    (B) I, III
    (C) II, III
    (D) II

5. During a chemistry lesson, Samantha Lione notices that Emetria, a student in her class, is very anxious about remembering the symbols for elements. Which of the following is NOT an effective way for Ms. Lione to respond to Emetria's needs?

    (A) Don't draw attention to Emetria by providing emotional support.
    (B) Give extra time when practical for Emetria to learn the notation.
    (C) Reduce the tension with a little humor.
    (D) Don't criticize Emetria for lack of progress.

Items 6–9.

Ungu Zmbui is a new ninth-grade teacher in her first month of teaching. She is having difficulty with discipline and with classroom management. Particular problems seem to arise when she is distributing books and other materials. While usually quite effective, Ms. Zmbui can teach in a negative fashion. She is unsure of how to deal with parents and has had some difficulties with a few of them.

6. Which of the following would educators generally agree is the best strategy for Ms. Zmbui to follow when placing or distributing books and supplies in a classroom?

   (A) Use group monitors to pass them out.
   (B) Have students line up alphabetically at the teacher's desk.
   (C) Have books and supplies available at several locations around the room.
   (D) Place needed books and materials in each student's desk before school.

7. In order to be an effective classroom leader, Ms. Zmbui should

   (A) establish and post a series of firm, precise rules that students should memorize and follow.
   (B) establish lines of communication with peer leaders.
   (C) prevent students from engaging in cooperative learning experiences.
   (D) establish competitive situations among class members.

8. Which of the following is LEAST likely to promote good communication with parents?

   (A) Make phone calls to parents.
   (B) Write personal notes on report cards.
   (C) Initiate a series of home/school letters.
   (D) Meet with groups of parents to discuss individual student achievement.

9. As an effective classroom manager, Ms. Zmbui should be most careful to take steps that ensure the majority of class time is devoted to

   (A) individual work.
   (B) on-task activities.
   (C) lecturing.
   (D) group work.

10. Chuck Galesky has been teaching a few years but like most newer teachers he still has some problems with discipline. He overhears the assistant principal say "Chuck should try a more 'with-it' teaching approach to handle his discipline problems," most probably meaning Mr. Galesky should

    (A) always be aware of new disciplinary techniques.
    (B) always be aware of current popular trends among students.
    (C) always be aware of what is happening in the classroom.
    (D) be well respected by other teachers.

Just before the beginning of the school year Maritza Gonzalez finds out that she has a problem student, Lucretia, in her class. Many teachers complain about Lucretia, and about her unwillingness to do work or to be cooperative. Ms. Gonzalez leaves school saying, "Just what I need—I better rest up so I'm ready for this problem child." Using the same scenario, another teacher calls Lucretia's parents to open up a line of communication.

11. Which of the following best summarizes the description above about the two different reactions to words that a problem child is in the class?

    (A) This is an example of proactive vs. reactive teachers. Ms. Gonzalez is proactive; the other teacher is reactive.
    (B) This is an example of reactive vs. proactive teachers. Ms. Gonzalez is reactive, the other teacher is proactive.

(C) This is an example of one teacher knowing the parents and Ms. Gonzalez not knowing the parents.

(D) This is an example of two proactive teachers with different styles.

12. Frank Carmody usually uses a lecture approach to present his history lessons. Which of the following approaches is most likely to help Mr. Carmody enhance instruction?

(A) Begin the lesson with a motivation.

(B) Focus his instruction on the entire class and avoid making eye contact with individual students.

(C) Walk around the room while he delivers his lecture.

(D) Choose a topic above the student's ability level.

13. Lisa Germanio has significant discipline problems with her ninth-grade students. However, if Ms. Germanio were teaching high school seniors, she would find that discipline is less difficult because

(A) it is left to the administration.

(B) it is the parent's concern.

(C) students are less resistant.

(D) teachers are less authoritative.

14. When it comes to getting along in the school, Aaron Ruben's colleagues say that a school is a society in itself, meaning

(A) all races, creeds, and ethnic backgrounds will be represented in a school.

(B) the school reflects the larger community.

(C) students in the school reflect the society in particular and the country as a whole.

(D) a school has its own structure of formal and informal relationships, character, and practices.

Items 15–19.

A group of teachers meet with a school psychologist and a social worker to discuss some of their students' problems. One common problem is drug and alcohol abuse, and Harold Ramirez reports that a number of students discuss this problem with him. Cindy Gareki reports that a senior discussed her sexual abuse as a child. The student did not identify who the abuser was.

A number of teachers, including Beth Alugu and Fred Maarzan, reported that a large number of their students have dropped out of school or are thinking about dropping out of school. During the meeting, the group also discussed whether a particular student in Lee Bouce's class would benefit from an alternative learning environment.

15. Health professionals know that the abuser discussed by the student with Cindy Gareki is most likely a

(A) teacher or coach.

(B) relative or family member.

(C) convicted sexual abuser.

(D) stranger.

16. Which of the following would NOT be an appropriate intervention for Mr. Ramirez to suggest when the alcohol abuse, drug use, or child abuse discussed at the meeting is suspected?

(A) Go through a student's locker because the student smelled of alcohol.

(B) Pay particular attention to principles of classroom management.

(C) Provide awareness programs that focus on drug and alcohol use.

(D) Report suspected child abuse to proper authorities.

17. The counselor who is familiar with research on drug use would most likely say that which of the following choices represents the percent of students who have used illegal drugs, other than alcohol, before they graduate from this high school?

(A) 90 percent
(B) 70 percent
(C) 45 percent
(D) 25 percent

18. Which of the following problems of the student in Lee Bouce's class would probably NOT be helped by the alternative learning environment discussed at the meeting?

(A) drug abuse
(B) alcohol abuse
(C) child abuse
(D) dropping out

19. The most effective plan this group can devise to prevent students from dropping out of school is to

(A) have students who have dropped out describe what happens when a student drops out of school, and arrange other presentations and discussions.
(B) provide students with a list of national statistics on dropouts.
(C) provide positive support and alternative learning environments.
(D) provide for parent conferences to discuss keeping students in school.

Items 20–24.

Frank Zaranga is the principal of Archer High School. He holds regular faculty meetings, and the agenda for one recent meeting is shown below.

> **AGENDA**
> 1. Teachers' rights and responsibilities
> 2. Quality schools—effective schools
> 3. Board of Education role and responsibility

During the meeting, Mr. Zaranga distributes handouts, raises issues, and discusses situations about these agenda items.

20. Which of the following on the list below describes free speech that teachers are entitled to exercise without risk?

(A) Criticize the decisions of the school board and superintendent in a letter published by a local newspaper.
(B) Disclose a student's confidential school records to help the student get educational services.
(C) Organize rallies during school hours that disrupt the school but improve student learning.
(D) Make statements *away* from school that interfere with the teaching performance.

21. All of the teachers attending this meeting enjoy a number of employment related rights, including which of the ones shown on this list?

I. Immunity from civil suits for job-related activities
II. Academic freedom to teach what they wish
III. The freedom to associate out of school with any group
IV. Immunity from dismissal once tenured

(A) II
(B) III
(C) I, III
(D) IV

22. Responsibilities primarily attributed to local school boards include:

    I. Employ and supervise a superintendent.
    II. Assign teachers and staff to schools and designate their responsibilities.
    III. Assign individual pupils to schools.
    IV. Evaluate district goals.

    (A) I, II, IV
    (B) II, III
    (C) I, IV
    (D) I, III, and IV

23. In general, the characteristics of effective schools include all the following EXCEPT

    (A) a climate of high expectations
    (B) a high proportion of instructional time spent on task
    (C) strong and effective leadership
    (D) eliminating standardized tests

24. Mary Inoua is a school librarian who is discussing legitimate actions concerning books in school libraries, and she mentions that

    (A) school officials may remove books from school libraries.
    (B) parents can prevent school boards from removing books from school libraries.
    (C) individual teachers may prevent their students from reading books in school libraries.
    (D) books may not be removed from school libraries solely because a school official disagrees with its content.

Items 25–29.

Ingrid Johanssen is a science teacher who plans to begin the lesson by saying, "OK class, today we're going to learn about photosynthesis." The teacher wants to model photosynthesis for the students. She plans to write prerequisite competencies for the lesson on the board. Ms. Johanssen plans to use an inquiry approach and wants to motivate the students as much as possible.

25. Which of the following is the most powerful overall motivation Ms. Johanssen could use in the class?

    (A) praise
    (B) grades
    (C) privileges
    (D) learning

26. Which of the following best describes a prerequisite competency Ms. Johanssen plans to write on the board?

    (A) the knowledge and skills a teacher must possess to teach an objective
    (B) a subobjective to the main objective of the lesson
    (C) the basis for admitting students when they transfer from another school district
    (D) the knowledge and skills students must possess to learn an objective

27. Which is the best strategy for Ms. Johanssen to follow after she has asked a question?

    (A) Call on a student immediately and expect a quick answer.
    (B) Wait for a student to call out the answer.
    (C) Pause before calling on a student and expect a quick answer.
    (D) Pause before calling on a student and give four or five seconds to answer.

28. Approximately what percent of questions should Ms. Johanssen expect to be answered correctly?

    (A) 100 percent
    (B) 75 percent
    (C) 50 percent
    (D) 25 percent

29. Ms. Johanssen arranges her students in cooperative learning groups to work on photosynthesis, usually meaning

    (A) Ms. Johanssen will cooperate fully with the students.
    (B) Ms. Johanssen will give each group specific instructions on how to proceed.
    (C) a person from each group will report the group's findings.
    (D) each group of students will gather information about photosynthesis from the local Agriculture Department Cooperative Extension.

Items 30–31.

Ellen Echevira plans to teach a unit to her advanced history class that will lead them to discover concepts. To that end, Ms. Echevira will ask a number of questions during the lesson. At the end of the unit she will administer a test from the teacher's edition of the text.

30. Which of the following words best describes the discovery approach to teaching?

    (A) deductive
    (B) skill
    (C) concrete
    (D) inductive

31. In all likelihood, the test Ms. Echevira will give is a:

    (A) formative evaluation.
    (B) standardized test.
    (C) norm-referenced test.
    (D) summative evaluation.

Items 32–37.

Mike Rosspaph is the high school mathematics teacher and the department chairperson. He is reviewing the testing and assessment results for classes in the department. Mike uses a standardized mathematics test with high reliability to measure achievement in department classes. Students' average normed scores are significantly lower in his department than the average normed scores from districts with the same socioeconomic status. Mr. Rosspaph also knows that scores on the PSAT (Preliminary Scholastic Achievement Test) are used to decide which high school students receive Merit Scholarships. He is concerned about the impact that low PSAT scores will have on students in the school.

32. What do we know about the standardized test from the description given above?

    (A) The test is shipped on time.
    (B) The test is consistent.
    (C) The test predicts success in college.
    (D) The test can be used repeatedly without fear of cheating.

33. What action, if any, is indicated by the average normed scores reported above?

    (A) No action; the average normed scores are about where they should be.
    (B) The mathematics curriculum and teaching methods should be evaluated.
    (C) The national standards for mathematics should be reviewed.
    (D) The test company should be contacted and told not to use average scores.

34. Overall, Mr. Rosspaph knows that

    (A) college success correlates more significantly with PSAT scores than with high school grades.
    (B) the PSAT score is just like an IQ score.
    (C) the PSAT is a projective test.
    (D) girls score lower on the PSAT and boys get more Merit Scholarships.

35. Which factor below will correlate most significantly with overall student achievement of all high schools including this high school?

    (A) socioeconomic status
    (B) intelligence
    (C) cooperativeness
    (D) motivation

36. Mr. Rosspaph receives results of a norm-referenced test that indicate that a student has an IQ of 97, leading to the conclusion that the

    (A) student has below average intelligence.
    (B) student's intelligence is in the normal range.
    (C) student is mildly retarded.
    (D) standard deviation of the test is 3.

37. Which of the following could Mr. Rosspaph recommend to teachers as a way to implement authentic assessment in their classrooms?

    (A) Collect and evaluate student work.
    (B) Use a standardized test.
    (C) Use only tests that have been authenticated.
    (D) Ask students to evaluate each other.

Items 38–42.

Faith Bisone is teaching a United States history class that is culturally and linguistically diverse. Many of the students in her class have a first language other than English, and many come from homes where English is not spoken. Ms. Bisone knows that the minority students in her class, as a whole, tend to have lower achievement scores than other students. She wants to familiarize herself with the difficulties these students have and with the teaching approaches that will be effective in her classroom.

38. The data about the achievement of minority students leads Ms. Bisone to the valid conclusion that:

    (A) minority students are less capable learners than other students.
    (B) the parents of minority students care less about their children's education.
    (C) learning expectations should be lowered for minority students.
    (D) minority students have fewer enriched learning experiences at home.

39. Which of the following describes an acceptable approach to modifying the objectives or plans for this class?

    (A) Modify the plans to teach history topics about the parents' home countries.
    (B) Modify the objective to adjust its difficulty level.
    (C) Modify the plans to include direct instruction in English.
    (D) Modify the plans to account for the cultural heritage of those in the class.

40. Which of the following is consistent with Ms. Bisone using an ESL approach with a group of LEP students from the class?

    (A) Use context clues to help students identify English words.
    (B) Teach mathematics in the student's first language.
    (C) Help students learn their native language.
    (D) Encourage regional and local dialects.

41. Ms. Bisone could help the students in her class who are having difficulty in school by providing all of the following EXCEPT

    (A) a quiet place to work.
    (B) exceptions to classroom rules.
    (C) a flexible schedule.
    (D) a warm, supportive atmosphere.

42. Which of the following is an appropriate curriculum alteration for Ms. Bisone to make to accommodate the needs of students who are recent immigrants in her class?

    (A) Lower the expectations for the group.
    (B) Limit the amount of homework.
    (C) Teach in the native language.
    (D) Require English proficiency to make progress in school.

43. Throughout American history, schools have received waves of immigrant children. Which of the following best depicts the way in which schools have reacted to the most recent wave of immigration?

    (A) The academic atmosphere of our schools is not affected by the ethnic and cultural backgrounds of the students.
    (B) Recent immigrant groups are accustomed to the academic atmosphere of American schools.
    (C) There is no longer a need for schools to deal with the cultural differences of students.
    (D) The schools have noted a shift toward cultural pluralism.

44. If you were preparing to conduct a workshop on the changing American family, which of the following would be most helpful to keep in mind?

    (A) Families are no longer the predominant influence in the early lives of children.
    (B) The nature of the American family has changed for the better.
    (C) Schools have no influence on children's values.
    (D) School programs developed for those students of the changing American family cannot replace effective parenting.

Items 45–47.

Carolee Horlieb is an English teacher who wants to assess a student's understanding of a lesson while students are writing. Ms. Horlieb is trying to decide whether to teach a moderate amount or a lot of information and whether to teach below, at, or above grade level. The students in her English classes are able students with a lower socioeconomic status. That is, these students are poor children, largely from single-parent families where no one in the family has graduated from high school.

45. Which of the following is an effective instructional strategy for Ms. Horlieb to use in this class?

    (A) Do not be too encouraging.
    (B) Lower learning expectations.
    (C) De-emphasize mastery of the material.
    (D) Provide a structured learning environment.

46. Which of the following most accurately characterizes how Ms. Horlieb could conduct the desired assessment?

    (A) She should use a standardized test.
    (B) She should observe students during the lesson.
    (C) She should devise and write a quiz for students to complete.
    (D) She should use a test from a textbook publisher.

47. Which of the following activities indicates that Ms. Horlieb is using extrinsic motivation?

    (A) She discusses the book *20,000 Leagues Under the Sea.*
    (B) She identifies similarities in students' clothing.
    (C) She discusses the Federal Reserve Bank.
    (D) She identifies the points students can earn for class participation.

48. When completing an assignment, most successful learning takes place when students work

    (A) independently in school.
    (B) supervised by a parent at home.
    (C) supervised by the teacher.
    (D) on a computer.

49. Stan Joacmen is concerned about the level at which he should teach his foreign language classes. The best advice a colleague could give Mr. Joacmen from the following choices is to teach students

    (A) at their achievement level but above their ability level.
    (B) below their achievement level and below their ability level.
    (C) below their achievement level and above their ability level.
    (D) above their achievement level but at their ability level.

50. Stan Heligo is writing objectives based on the Taxonomy of Educational Objectives: Cognitive Domain, which means that he would teach which of these topics to be at the highest level of this taxonomy?

    (A) Evaluate a book.
    (B) Understand a reading passage.
    (C) Analyze a written paragraph.
    (D) Apply a mathematics formula to a real situation.

51. Inu Hgadu is a language teacher who is considering four different approaches to mastery and instructional time. Which of the following approaches that Ms. Hgadu is considering is most likely to result in successful learning?

    (A) Expect mastery and use all class time for learning activities.
    (B) Expect mastery and use some class time for discussing other issues.

    (C) Don't expect mastery and use all class time for learning activities.
    (D) Don't expect mastery and use some class time for discussion of other issues.

52. Ecchumati Mirandi is a new teacher who is reviewing the way she asks questions in her history class. Which of the several guidelines below should Ms. Mirandi most consistently follow when asking questions?

    (A) Ask complete questions.
    (B) Address questions to individual students.
    (C) Ask difficult questions to challenge students.
    (D) Address questions to the entire class.

53. Akando Shkaaboy is an English teacher who begins each lesson with a general overview of an English topic before teaching the topic to the class. Mr. Shkaaboy is using an approach called

    (A) anticipatory set.
    (B) metacognition.
    (C) inquiry learning.
    (D) advanced organizer.

Items 54–56.

Elaine Davies is a science teacher who has several special education students in her classes. Ms. Davies must be aware of the privacy requirements, particularly the privacy requirements of students' confidential records. At the same time she must plan lessons based on the student's IEP. Chad Keredo is a special education teacher who joins Ms. Davies in her room for three classes.

54. Which of the following could Ms. Davies do and still be in compliance with federal privacy requirements for confidential records of minor children?

    (A) Allow the natural father, who does not have child custody, to see his child's confidential school records.

(B) Refuse to let an unrelated legal guardian see the child's confidential records.

(C) Refuse a parent's request to show the child his or her own confidential records.

(D) Inform parents they have no right to see their child's records without the minor child's permission.

55. Students are completing a brief writing assignment at their seats. Alma, the only special education student mainstreamed in one class tells Ms. Davies that she wants her help with the assignment. Which of the following is Ms. Davies most appropriate response?

(A) Without explaining why, Ms. Davies asks Mr. Keredo to come over and help Alma with her work.

(B) Ms. Davies says, "Oh, I'm not supposed to do this, but let me see if I can help."

(C) Ms. Davies comes over, says, "OK," and helps Alma.

(D) Ms. Davies explains gently and carefully so that Alma will understand that Mr. Keredo is there just to help her, and that she, Ms. Davies, will get Mr. Keredo so that he can provide very special help for her.

56. Ms. Davies and Mr. Keredo work together to adapt instruction to meet the student's IEP guidelines. Which of the following choices best describes their responsibility for preparing lessons according to the IEP guidelines?

(A) They should follow the IEP guidelines as closely as possible but they should also use their common sense and experience if some provisions are impractical.

(B) They should set aside their own experience with the special education students and implement the guidelines exactly as described in the IEP.

(C) They should implement the spirit of the IEP guidelines, but not when the implementation interferes with overall instruction in the class.

(D) They should modify plans to come as close to the IEP guidelines as possible so that the classroom teacher does not have to work with the special education students.

57. Students are upset about a school board decision to cancel the senior prom. Students can show their displeasure with this decision without the possibility of legal interference from school officials by

(A) publishing editorials in the school newspaper.

(B) wearing large buttons that say "PROM POWER" while in school.

(C) refusing to attend classes.

(D) placing advertisements in the school newspaper.

Items 58–59.

The district's secondary curriculum committee is meeting for the first time this year to formulate a set of instructional goals. A teacher from each department is at this first meeting. The committee will try to agree on a basic definition of an instructional objective and to agree on what resources these objectives should come from.

58. As the committee does their work, which of the following is the LEAST appropriate source of instructional objectives?

(A) national professional organizations

(B) commercial textbooks

(C) parents

(D) current school district's objectives

59. Which of the following best characterizes an instructional objective?

(A) It describes how the teacher will teach the class.

(B) It describes the average achievement for all students at a grade level.

(C) It describes the books and materials to be used to teach a lesson.

(D) It describes what a student should know or be able to do.

60. In a seminar to help teachers understand their legal rights, an attorney could mention that which of the following would generally be the most valid grounds for a teacher's suit against a school district?

(A) not granting tenure to a teacher who is pregnant

(B) firing a nontenured black female without providing a specific reason concerning her performance

(C) firing a tenured white male with more experience than a black male teacher who was not fired

(D) actively recruiting black and Hispanic faculty to the exclusion of white faculty members

Items 61–62.

Lisa Pismenny is a student in Ms. Anderson's English class who writes well, understands verbal directions, but often has trouble understanding written directions. Lisa is trying very hard to become the best writer she can be.

61. Lisa's difficulty might be related to all of the following EXCEPT

(A) auditory discrimination.

(B) visual discrimination.

(C) sight vocabulary.

(D) context clues.

62. Ms. Anderson gave Lisa this advice: "The best thing students can do just before they start to write is

(A) decide on the best order for presenting ideas."

(B) have a clear beginning."

(C) decide on the audience and purpose."

(D) support the main idea."

63. Ezequiel Sanchez uses a computer-based multimedia encyclopedia in his social studies class. The multimedia encyclopedia includes hypertext links in most of its articles. To help understand how to use the hypertext links, Mr. Sanchez would best explain that

(A) the links tie together very (hyper) important ideas in the passage.

(B) clicking on a link gives additional information.

(C) the links move or vibrate to draw attention to important ideas.

(D) clicking on a link with a mouse cursor changes the link's color.

64. Felipe Victorino uses a token economy system to motivate students during a unit in his business class. Which of the following actions is most consistent with Mr. Victorino's approach?

(A) Mr. Victorino provides token (symbolic) reinforcement for work completed by students as opposed to real or meaningful reinforcement.

(B) Mr. Victorino distributes subway and bus tokens for reinforcement since this approach was pioneered in urban areas where many students took buses and subways to school.

(C) Mr. Victorino posts a description of how students can earn points and how students may exchange a certain number of points for a more tangible reward.

(D) Mr. Victorino posts a "token of my appreciation list" on the bulletin board and lists the names of students who perform outstanding work.

65. Rolanda Alvarez wants to conduct an ongoing assessment of her ninth-grade English class. Which one of the following actions on the part of the teacher would NOT indicate that the assessment was underway?

(A) Ms. Alvarez walks around the room regularly observing students' writing.

(B) Ms. Alvarez reviews students' written work at the end of the day.

(C) Ms. Alvarez assigns students an in-class composition about the environment.

(D) Ms. Alvarez collects and reviews daily performance samples of students' work.

Items 66–67.

Fran Ragovan keeps a portfolio of written work for students in her ninth-grade English class. In Ms. Ragovan's opinion, Rodney's writing sample is well above average for ninth grade at her school. A standardized language arts test administered last month shows Rodney has a writing grade equivalent of 7.9, which is above average for his class.

66. Which of the following is the best description of Rodney's language arts achievement?

(A) Rodney's writing test scores are above grade level.

(B) Rodney is writing below average for his class.

(C) Rodney needs intensive help in writing.

(D) Rodney seems to do better when evaluated with an authentic assessment.

67. Which of the following is the most reasonable explanation of why Rodney's standardized test score is below grade level, but above average for that class?

(A) The student answered fewer questions correctly for the ninth-grade level.

(B) The class did worse on average than the entire group who took the test.

(C) Half of those who take the test are below average.

(D) The averages are different because the number of students in each group is different.

68. Jim Brehm is a mathematics teacher who is going to introduce students to the number pi (3.14159…). Mr. Brehm plans to use the Internet to research the number. Which of the following could Mr. Brehm tell students would be LEAST helpful?

(A) "Use a search engine to look up pi."

(B) "Send e-mails to others to find out about pi."

(C) "Type in a Web address that seems related to pi."

(D) "Go to a chat room to discuss pi with others."

69. At the start of each technology class John Siegrist writes a "problem" on the board for his technology students to analyze and solve. Which of the following describes the most effective technique Mr. Siegrist can use to assess students' work?

(A) observation

(B) standardized test

(C) cooperative learning

(D) written work

70. Zulma Tolonio is a science teacher and some of her students have difficulty understanding the resistance (R)—fulcrum (F)—effort (E) characteristics of levers. Which of the following activities could Ms. Tolonio do to best help her students understand these concepts?

(A) Arrange a variety of levers RFE, FRE, and FER order so the students can demonstrate where to place a lever on a fulcrum to reduce or increase effort.

(B) Have students classify a group of pictorial representations of levers into RFE, FRE, and FER groups.

(C) Read a textbook description of each type of lever and listing examples under each type.

(D) Chart the resistance and effort levels of different types of levers.

71. Juan Herndido works hard to provide positive reinforcement for student behavior, which means that he would likely NOT

(A) grade on the basis of performance.
(B) praise appropriate behavior.
(C) explain to students that they will gain privileges for good behavior.
(D) stop giving corrective comments when inappropriate behavior stops.

72. In New York State, which of the groups listed below has overall legal responsibility for education?

(A) the federal government
(B) the State of New York
(C) local school boards
(D) local town and county governments

73. Joacim Jumundu has gathered a number of long newspaper articles about whales. He uses these articles to help students read science effectively. Which of the following approaches on his part will most likely help students identify the main idea(s) of each article?

(A) Mr. Jumundu has students work independently and summarize for themselves the main point(s) of each article.

(B) Mr. Jumundu has students work in cooperative learning groups to summarize and present the main point(s) of each article.

(C) Mr. Jumundu presents a brief summary of the main point(s) of each article.

(D) Mr. Jumundu prepares a brief summary of the main point(s) of each article and distributes them to his students.

74. Mr. Louis Derma is a first-year teacher. In his first evaluation, the supervisor recommends that Mr. Derma employ formative evaluation of students' writing in his class. Louis mentions the recommendation to some friends and colleagues. He receives advice summarized in the choices below. Which of the following advice should Mr. Derma take?

(A) You should engage in discussions with all of your students.

(B) You should keep a portfolio of students' writing samples.

(C) You should use the Iowa Test of Basic Skills.

(D) You should have an end of unit test.

Yi Ti is a music teacher who receives a composition from a student that includes this selection. Every teacher is a writing teacher, and Ms. Ti reviews the writing and considers how to best help this student.

> I sat in the audience while my sister play the clarinet. I saw her play while I sit there. I guess I will never be a profesional musician.

75. Ms. Ti is most likely to help improve this student's writing by providing instruction in which of the following areas?

(A) nouns
(B) pronouns
(C) spelling
(D) verbs

76. A school-wide goal is to integrate mathematics across the curriculum and to use estimation first to be sure an answer is reasonable. Dan Kelleher wants to incorporate this goal in his geography class. The best example of what he would ask his students is to estimate

    (A) the sum of the height of three mountains 6,294 feet, 3,094 feet, and 7,892 feet, before the students find the answer with a calculator.
    (B) the distance between two towns.
    (C) the number of rocks in a rockslide.
    (D) the volume of a lake.

77. Wayne Esposito teaches a unique computer repair class where he uses a cooperative learning approach. All of the following might occur in Mr. Esposito's class EXCEPT

    (A) students get help from other students.
    (B) groups of two to six students work together.
    (C) group members consult with the teacher.
    (D) the teacher summarizes students' work.

78. Norman Chestnut is a tenth-grade teacher who decides to use Gardner's multiple intelligences as the basis for instruction in his class. That means that Mr. Chestnut will most likely

    (A) implement interdisciplinary units.
    (B) help students learn about each of the intelligences.
    (C) eliminate assessments.
    (D) allow students to determine criteria for quality.

79. In her ten years as a superintendent of schools Dr. Kim Morgan has learned that, generally speaking, class discipline problems are most difficult during:

    (A) grades 2–3.
    (B) grades 5–6.
    (C) grades 8–9.
    (D) grades 11–12.

80. Weekly planning differs from individual lesson plans in that

    (A) weekly plans fit lessons and other activities into available time periods during the week, while lesson plans detail the lessons.
    (B) weekly plans detail the lessons, while lesson plans fit into available time periods during the week.
    (C) weekly plans should be prepared each week, while lesson plans should be prepared at the beginning of the year.
    (D) weekly plans are usually kept by the teacher, while lesson plans are usually submitted written in a plan book.

CONSTRUCTED RESPONSE

Computers are an indispensable part of everyday life. There was a time when computers in schools were limited to technology classes and business classes. Today, computers, computer software, and the Internet are integrated throughout the curriculum, and there are appropriate ways to use a computer as part of instruction in almost every subject or discipline. Here is a goal drawn up by an advisory committee.

Students will develop technology awareness and be able to integrate technology effectively with school subjects.

Write an essay for New York State educators that accomplishes the following.

- Explains why integrating technology with school subjects is important.
- Describes two strategies that you might use to integrate technology successfully with school subjects.
- Describes why the strategies you describe would be effective.

Answer Key

PRACTICE ATS-W—SECONDARY

1. B	21. B	41. B	61. A
2. B	22. C	42. B	62. C
3. A	23. D	43. D	63. B
4. A	24. D	44. D	64. C
5. A	25. B	45. D	65. C
6. C	26. D	46. B	66. D
7. B	27. D	47. D	67. B
8. D	28. B	48. C	68. C
9. B	29. C	49. D	69. D
10. C	30. D	50. A	70. A
11. B	31. D	51. A	71. D
12. A	32. B	52. D	72. B
13. C	33. B	53. D	73. B
14. D	34. D	54. A	74. B
15. B	35. A	55. C	75. D
16. A	36. B	56. B	76. A
17. B	37. A	57. B	77. D
18. C	38. D	58. C	78. A
19. C	39. D	59. D	79. C
20. A	40. A	60. C	80. A

Answer Explanations

1. **(B)** Clear and unambiguous objectives are fundamental and crucial to maintaining interest. There is a difference between students being responsive and students being interested in a lesson. (A) is incorrect because an animated presentation may maintain students' interest in the teacher, but not in the lesson at hand unless the teacher has clear objectives in mind. (C) is incorrect because students are typically not interested in a lesson because it holds the promise of subsequent understanding. (D) is incorrect because leaving students with no choice does not maintain their interest.

2. **(B)** Mr. Yarborough should address questions to the entire class. This increases the likelihood that students will be paying attention and actively thinking about an answer. (A) is incorrect because this technique focuses on just one student and only that student will be thinking about an answer to the question. (C) is incorrect because this is a poor questioning technique, although some teachers use it to bring students back into the discussion. (D) is incorrect because this is a poor questioning technique that keeps the majority of students from full participation.

3. **(A)** Modeling means Mr. Yarborough does things in the way he wants his students to copy or emulate. This choice shows that he is engaging in exactly that kind of behavior. (B) is incorrect because this is a different kind of model than the one Mr. Yarborough has in mind. (C) is incorrect because Mr. Yarborough would not model inappropriate behavior to be copied. (D) is incorrect because talking about the ways things should be or showing people how things should be is not modeling how things should be.

4. **(A)** Consider each Roman numeral in turn. Then choose your answer.

    I. Correct. This is an example of reinforcing behavior.
    II. Correct. This is also a way to reinforce student behavior.
    III. Incorrect. This is not a way to reinforce behavior, but rather a negative reinforcement.

    I and II are correct—(A)

5. **(A)** Note the word NOT in the question. This choice describes the inappropriate course of action for Ms. Lione to follow. It is fine for Ms. Lione to provide emotional support even if other students notice. Choices (B), (C), and (D) are all appropriate ways to respond to a student who is anxious about memorizing facts.

6. **(C)** This technique makes books and supplies readily available and reduces administrative and behavioral problems. (A) is incorrect because this process just increases interaction problems between the student monitors and the students they are distributing the books to. (B) is incorrect because every teacher has seen

the pushing and shoving that goes on in this situation, and it wastes time. (D) is incorrect because this approach is an inefficient use of teacher time. Besides, it will not be appropriate when the materials are needed later in the day.

7. **(B)** Peer leaders are much more important to these students than Ms. Zmbui is. Students at this age will follow peer leaders and Ms. Zmbui can harness this developmental trait to help her with discipline. (A) is incorrect because students do not follow rules just because the rules are firm, or because the rules have been posted. Students certainly don't follow rules because they have been asked to memorize them. (C) is incorrect because cooperative learning activities are effective, but using them or not using them will not, themselves, help Ms. Zmbui become a better classroom leader. (D) is incorrect because there is nothing about competition among students that will make Ms. Zmbui a more effective leader, and the practice actually creates problems in the class.

8. **(D)** This choice identifies the approach that Ms. Zmbui should not use. It is improper to discuss individual student achievement with groups of parents. Even if the parents seem to agree to share the results, the practice can only lead to problems. The remaining choices give examples of ways to promote effective communication with parents.

9. **(B)** There is very little in education about which we are absolutely sure—but time on task is one of them. It is well established that students learn more when they spend more time on task. Ms. Zmbui's main goal as a classroom manager is to promote learning, and this is clearly the best choice. The other choices can be effective forms of classroom management, but none of them can even match the proven positive impact of time on task.

10. **(C)** The answer to this is common sense, but it also fits Kounin's definition of what "with-it" teaching means. (A) is incorrect because just being aware of techniques does not mean you use them. (B) is incorrect because this choice means "with-it" in one sense, but it does not describe an approach to teaching. (D) is incorrect because the respect from peers described in this choice is not an approach to teaching.

11. **(B)** Ms. Gonzalez is reactive while the other teacher is proactive. Generally speaking, proactive teachers are the best classroom managers. (A) is incorrect because Ms. Gonzalez is not proactive. (C) is incorrect because many teachers don't know parents at the beginning of the school year, and this should not stop a teacher from making contact. (D) is incorrect because the other teacher is proactive, not Ms. Gonzalez.

12. **(A)** Research shows that starting a lecture with a motivation, compared to the other choices, is the most effective way to enhance instruction. (B) is incorrect because it is good to make eye contact with students during a lecture. (C) is incorrect because walking around the room, alone, does not enhance instruction. (D) is incorrect because a topic above students' *ability* level will detract from the effectiveness of a lecture.

13. **(C)** During the first two years of high school students tend to follow peer leaders. By the last two years of high school students are more responsive to adult authority. (A) and (B) are incorrect because they apply as equally to ninth graders as to seniors. (D) is incorrect because teachers who are constructively authoritative are usually best at discipline.

14. **(D)** The school has its own society that must be appreciated and "mastered" by beginning teachers. This is frequently a teacher's first step to success in a school. (A), (B), and (C) are incorrect because the word "society" in this question does not refer to the larger society or the larger community. A school's society is unique to that school.

15. **(B)** Most abused children suffer abuse at the hands of a relative or family member. It is possible that anyone in the other three categories listed might abuse a child, and they cannot simply be ruled out. And child abuse by a teacher or some other public figure tends to be more widely known. However, the likelihood that one of these people will be the abuser is greatly diminished when compared to those listed in choice (B).

16. **(A)** This choice identifies the most inappropriate action for Mr. Ramirez. A teacher does not have the right to search students' lockers without administrative direction and approval. School administrators may direct and oversee a locker search in some circumstances. The other choices represent effective ways to respond to the problems raised by those at the meeting and described in the scenario.

17. **(B)** Studies indicate that, overall, about 70 percent of high school students use illegal drugs other than alcohol. This percentage soars when alcohol, illegal for most high school students, is included. The percentage may vary somewhat from school to school, but overall it typically does not fall as low as (C) 45 percent or (D) 25 percent, nor rise as high as (A) 90 percent.

18. **(C)** The emotional problems caused by child abuse are too severe to respond to an alternative learning environment. It is possible, but not guaranteed, that students who are (A) drug abusers, (B) alcohol abusers, and (D) potential dropouts can be helped by an alternative learning environment.

19. **(C)** Students are least likely to drop out when the school provides extra support and when school officials and teachers find some way to keep the student interested in school. (A) This choice may be effective with some students, but overall, potential dropouts do not respond well to being told what things will be like. (B) is incorrect because just providing statistics about how many students drop out is unlikely to discourage any student from dropping out. (D) is incorrect because parent conferences are a good idea, but will not, themselves, prevent students from dropping out of school.

20. **(A)** Teachers are permitted to criticize school board members and school officials. Of course, this may not always be the wise thing to do, particularly for new

teachers. (B) is incorrect because a teacher may never disclose a student's confidential records for any reason. That does not stop a parent from disclosing that information. (C) is incorrect because it goes without saying that a teacher can't do anything to disrupt the functioning of a school. (D) is incorrect because teachers can't do anything that will interfere with their teaching performance without putting themselves in jeopardy, even if they do it away from school.

21. **(B)** Consider each Roman numeral in turn. Then choose your answer.

   I. Incorrect. Teachers can be sued civilly for job-related activities.
   II. Incorrect. Teachers do not have academic freedom and they must teach the curriculum specified by the school district.
   III. Correct. Teachers have freedom of association, but not necessarily freedom in activities that arise from that association.
   IV. Incorrect. Tenured teachers can be dismissed for cause or as part of a staffing reduction.

   Only III is correct—(B).

22. **(C)** In a sense, a school board is responsible for everything in a district and very little can happen without some sort of approval from the board. In practice, the board has a more limited number of primary responsibilities. Consider each Roman numeral in turn. Then choose your answer.

   I. Correct. This is one of the board's most important responsibilities.
   II. Incorrect. This is primarily an administrative responsibility.
   III. Incorrect. The board may make policy about school assignment, but very rarely actually assigns a student to a school.
   IV. Correct. This is another of the board's most important responsibilities. The board has a responsibility to ensure that the long-term and short-term goals are being met.

   I and IV are correct—(C).

23. **(D)** Note the EXCEPT in the question. Standardized tests are not an *essential* feature of effective schools. But most effective schools use standardized tests in some manner. (A) High expectations, (B) time on task, and (C) strong, effective leadership are incorrect because these are essential features of effective schools.

24. **(D)** School boards cannot remove a book from a school library just because a school official or school board member objects to its content. However, school boards may remove books from school libraries for other reasons. Public libraries are bound by different rules than school libraries. (A) is incorrect because school officials may not, themselves, remove books from a school library. (B) is incorrect because if a school board appropriately removes a book from a school library there is nothing a parent can do to prevent it. But a parent could petition the board to reconsider their decision. (C) is incorrect because teachers may not prevent students from reading books found in a school library.

25. **(B)** Grades remain the primary motivation for students to do work in school. (A) praise (C) privileges, and less so (D), the opportunity to learn, all contribute to a student's motivation. These other choices are but a secondary consideration compared to (B).

26. **(D)** A prerequisite competency refers to some skill or knowledge a *student* must possess to learn a competency. In the sense used here, competency does *not* refer to teachers. (A) is incorrect because a competency refers to what the *student* must learn or do. (B) is incorrect because a prerequisite competency comes before the main objective; it is not a part of the main objective. (C) is incorrect because the term prerequisite competency does not apply to admission or transfer requirements.

27. **(D)** Ms. Johanssen should use this method because it gives students a chance to think about the answer and keeps the answer to a reasonable length, which maintains students' interest. (A) is incorrect because calling on students quickly does not give them adequate time to formulate a response. (B) is incorrect because calling out answers makes for a chaotic process. (C) is incorrect because nothing is gained by forcing students to answer quickly when a few more seconds would permit a full and complete answer.

28. **(B)** Among the choices given, it would be best for Ms. Johanssen to ask questions that will be answered correctly about 70 percent of the time. This provides for a mix of difficult and easier questions. This guideline will foster a range of questions that will not be too frustrating for students and will offer opportunities for discussion. (A) is incorrect because the questions would be too easy if Ms. Johanssen expected all the questions to be answered correctly. (C) and (D) are incorrect because an intended correct answer rate of 50 percent or 25 percent would indicate the questions were too difficult and too frustrating for students.

29. **(C)** Students in cooperative learning groups devise their own plan and work actively together to gather information. Usually, one member of the group reports the group's findings. (A) is incorrect because this kind of cooperation does not describe cooperative learning groups. (B) is incorrect because the teacher gives cooperative learning groups the topic, but group members themselves devise a working plan. (D) is incorrect because a cooperative learning group may do this, but working with Cooperative Extensions does not describe cooperative learning groups.

30. **(D)** The discovery approach proceeds inductively from examples and details to generalizations and conclusions. (A) is incorrect because deductive teaching is like direct teaching where students first learn the generalization and then the details and examples. (B) is incorrect because the discovery approach is most effective for teaching concepts, not skills. (C) is incorrect because some say that discovery teaching goes from the concrete to the abstract, but just the term "concrete" does not identify the discovery approach.

31. **(D)** A summative evaluation sums up what the student has learned in a chapter or lesson, and that is the intent of the test Ms. Echevira is giving. (A) A formative evaluation is used to determine what will be taught in the future. Ms. Echevira's test may help some with that, but it is not the main purpose of the test. (B) and (C) are incorrect because a standardized test and a norm-referenced test serve the same purpose: to compare a student with the performance of many other students. Ms. Echevira's test does not serve that purpose.

32. **(B)** The description says the test is reliable, which means that it is consistent from one administration to the next. (A) is incorrect because the reliability mentioned in the description has nothing to do with shipping. (C) is incorrect because the description says nothing about the tests predicting success in college. (D) is incorrect because there is nothing in the description to indicate the test can be used many times without the likelihood that someone will cheat. Repeated usage of the same test may well compromise its content.

33. **(B)** Test scores that are significantly lower than those from comparable districts are a source of concern. An evaluation of the curriculum and methods used in the school is indicated by these results. (A) is incorrect because some action is indicated, and that action may be revealed by an evaluation of the curriculum and methods. (C) is incorrect because this might be a good idea as a part of the overall evaluation of the school's curriculum and methods. But just reviewing national standards does not address the issue of low test scores. (D) is incorrect because average scores on normed tests are an effective and appropriate way to compare comparable school districts.

34. **(D)** Girls score generally lower on the mathematics section of the PSAT than boys. Even though the gap is narrowing, girls tend to be discriminated against for Merit Scholarships. As recently as a few years ago, girls received about 45 percent of the Merit Scholarships. (A) is incorrect because college success correlates more significantly with high school grades than with PSAT scores. (B) is incorrect because an IQ test, and the resulting score, measure ability, while the PSAT includes sections designed to measure achievement. (C) is incorrect because a projective test is a psychological test to help determine personality traits, and this does not describe the PSAT.

35. **(A)** Overall student achievement in a high school correlates most highly with the overall socioeconomic status (SES) of students in the school. That is, the more wealthy the families in the school, the better students perform overall on tests. (B) is incorrect because individual student achievement may correlate highly with intelligence scores, but overall, the scores of all tests in the school correlate most highly with SES. (C) cooperativeness and (D) motivation, however measured, do not correlate as highly with overall test scores as does SES.

36. **(B)** IQ tests have a mean of 100 and a standard deviation of 10, and IQ scores from 90 to 100 are in the normal range. That means that 97 is in the normal

range, and the other choices are incorrect. There is no evidence from this score that this student is mentally retarded.

37. **(A)** Authentic assessment means a teacher collects and reviews students' actual work or observes students while they are working. (B) and (C) are incorrect because tests are not used in authentic assessment, and there is no process called test authentication. (D) is incorrect because authentic assessment is based on the teacher's own observation and not on the observations or evaluations of students in the class.

38. **(D)** Minority students as a whole are *not* less capable, but as a whole they do have fewer opportunities for learning at home, which tends to lower achievement scores. (A) is incorrect because minority students are not less capable. (B) is incorrect because parents of minority students are as concerned about their student's education as other parents are. (C) is incorrect because Ms. Bisone should not lower learning expectations for her students. High expectations lead to more learning.

39. **(D)** The acceptable approach is for Ms. Bisone to modify the plans to account for the cultural heritage of the students in her class. (A) is incorrect because the topics should be those regularly taught in the school's United States history courses. (B) is incorrect because the objective should be at the same difficulty level, although Ms. Bisone may adapt her teaching approach. (C) is incorrect because it is fine for Ms. Bisone to help her students understand English in the context of learning history. But she should not adapt her objectives to become English objectives.

40. **(A)** Every teacher is a reading teacher. ESL means English as a Second Language, while LEP means Limited English Proficiency. Teaching English as a Second Language includes using context clues to identify words. (B) is incorrect because teaching mathematics in the first language is an example of bilingual education. (C) is incorrect because teaching English as a Second Language does not include instruction in the foreign language. (D) is incorrect because standard spoken English is the goal, and ESL instruction does not encourage regional or local dialects.

41. **(B)** A student will not be helped by permitting him or her to ignore certain classroom rules. Children who have problems in school because of the cultural and linguistic adaptations can benefit from (A) a quiet, private place to work, (C) a flexible schedule, whenever possible, and (D) a warm and supportive atmosphere.

42. **(B)** Children from immigrant families will often not benefit from extensive homework because there may not be help available from parents. (A) is incorrect because lowering expectations does not help these students. (C) is incorrect because teaching in the native language will not help these students, who will need to master English to enjoy viable careers. This is different from helping

children make the transition from their native language to English, which could be helpful. (D) is incorrect because this requirement is not helpful since English proficiency is beyond the capability of most of these students. However, it may be useful to ask students to *make progress* toward English proficiency.

43. **(D)** This choice means that the cultural identities of children have become more pronounced, and this is what has happened in American schools. (A) is incorrect because the academic atmosphere is always affected by students' backgrounds and this is even more noticeable today. (B) is incorrect because recent immigrant groups tend not to be from Europe and so these students are not accustomed to the European atmosphere of American schools. (C) is incorrect because there is even more need to deal with students' cultural differences because students' cultural identities are more pronounced than in the past.

44. **(D)** Parents and families have *the* overwhelming impact on children. School programs, no matter how effective, can never replace the role of parenting. (A) is incorrect because families are and always have been the main influence on children during their early years and nothing has happened to change this. It is just that the American family is different now than it was a few generations ago. (B) is incorrect because the nature of the American family has changed for the worse, particularly where children are concerned. (C) is incorrect because schools have a significant influence on the lives of children, but not the profound influence that families have.

45. **(D)** A clear, structured learning environment is always an effective approach to teaching. This does not mean that structure is rigid, but rather a comfortable and predictable environment for students. (A) is incorrect because it is difficult to imagine being too encouraging, and encouragement does not mean doing work for the students. (B) lowering learning expectations and (C) de-emphasizing mastery are ineffective instructional strategies.

46. **(B)** Ms. Horlieb should observe and evaluate students while they are working. Ms. Horlieb can't give any kind of a test while the lesson is underway. She would not be able to administer the test or the quiz described in the other choices.

47. **(D)** An extrinsic motivation is some sort of overt reward, such as points to be earned. Just discussing those points can be motivating. The other choices do not represent extrinsic motivation, although they might be a good introductory motivation for a lesson, depending on the lesson and on students' interests.

48. **(C)** Students typically learn most when they are supervised by a teacher. (A) is incorrect because some students may learn most when they work independently, but that is not typical. (B) is incorrect because some parents are capable of appropriate supervision, but that is not usually the case. (D) is incorrect because some students may learn most while they complete an appropriate assignment on the computer, but that is not where most successful learning occurs.

49. **(D)** Achievement level refers to what students know, while ability level refers to what they are capable of learning. It is best to teach more than a student already knows, but within their ability to learn. Instruction can be adapted to teach very advanced concepts within a student's ability. (A) and (C) are incorrect because Mr. Joacmen should not teach above students' ability. It will prove too frustrating. (B) is incorrect because Mr. Joacmen should not teach less than what students already know.

50. **(A)** Evaluation is at the sixth and highest level of Bloom's Cognitive Taxonomy. (C) analysis is the fourth level, and (D) application is the third level. (B) comprehension is at the second level on this hierarchy of learning objectives.

51. **(A)** Students learn best when mastery, a thorough understanding of a topic, is expected and all of the class time is used for instruction. (B) Using some class time for noninstructional activities interferes with learning. This is a matter of concern since noninstructional activities can take up a significant portion of class time. (C) and (D) are incorrect because students learn best when the teacher expects mastery, even if mastery is not achieved.

52. **(D)** Ms. Mirandi should consistently ask questions of the entire class to keep every student engaged in the learning process. (A) It is not a bad idea to ask complete questions, but this is not the choice that she should most consistently follow. (B) It is fine to ask some questions of individual students and (C) she should ask difficult questions to challenge students, but none of these choices should be followed as consistently as (D).

53. **(D)** A general overview of a lesson best describes an advanced organizer. (A) is incorrect because an anticipatory set is a brief activity or event at the start of the lesson that engages students and focuses their thoughts on the lesson objective. An anticipatory set does not provide a general overview of the lesson. (B) is incorrect because by using metacognition a teacher would show students how to think about their learning, that is, how to actively monitor and regulate mental processes. (C) is incorrect because in inquiry learning, teachers ask students to "discover" generalizations by working from specific examples to general ideas.

54. **(A)** Ms. Davies should always show a child's record to a natural parent, unless there is a court order preventing it. The scenario mentions no such order. (B) A legal guardian, whether related to the student or not, has the same rights as parents. (C) The parents have the right to request that a minor child see his or her own records. (D) Minor children do not decide whether or not parents see their records.

55. **(C)** It is appropriate for Ms. Davies to help every student in the class. Mr. Keredo would have given the same response if a nonmainstreamed student asked for help. Mr. Keredo has specific responsibilities but that should not interfere with helping all the students in the class. The remaining answer choices represent inappropriate ways for Ms. Davies to respond to the situation.

56. **(B)** The IEP is a legal document and it must be implemented as written. Parents may take action if provisions of an IEP are just ignored. The other choices are incorrect because teachers are not in a position to alter or ignore any of the IEP's provisions. But a teacher should bring problems with an IEP to the attention of the responsible person to see if a revision is possible.

57. **(B)** Public school officials cannot interfere when students use inoffensive speech, which includes spoken words and symbols or words displayed on their person. However, students may not engage in offensive speech or interfere with the operation of the school. (A) and (D) school newspapers are the school's property and school officials can control the content of these papers. (C) students cannot refuse to attend classes.

58. **(C)** Parents have a vital role themselves, and through the Board of Education, in setting the overall goals for the district. However, this group is least knowledgeable about instructional objectives and they are the least appropriate source among those given for instructional objectives. The other choices all represent appropriate sources of instructional objectives.

59. **(D)** An instructional objective is a clear description of a student's knowledge or performance. (A) is incorrect because this choice describes the procedures used to help students reach the objective. (B) is incorrect because this choice describes a normed test result. A criterion-based test would be used to find out whether or not students had learned lesson objectives. (C) is incorrect because this choice describes the learning materials used during a lesson.

60. **(C)** School districts may not employ "reverse discrimination" when removing teachers, although it is permissible to use the practice when hiring teachers. (A) A teacher can't be denied tenure because she is pregnant. However, there is nothing about being pregnant that ensures a teacher will receive tenure. (B) Nontenured teachers have virtually no employment rights, and administrators or the Board of Education need only say they are not pleased with a teacher, or say they think they can do better. (D) Districts are permitted to recruit in this manner.

61. **(A)** This choice is correct because it has to do with listening and *not* reading. Note the word EXCEPT in the item. Difficulty with auditory discrimination does not itself interfere with reading. Early hearing problems can inhibit reading and writing development. However, Lisa writes well and understands verbal directions. The remaining choices could be the cause of Lisa's trouble understanding written directions.

62. **(C)** A student must have an audience and a purpose in mind before writing. (A) is incorrect because the order of presentation is important, but this must come after writers know who they are writing for and why they are writing. Each of these factors may change the order of presentation. (B) and (D) are incorrect because they are things that are done after the writing begins, not before.

63. **(B)** Clicking on a hypertext word reveals a definition or underlying meaning. Hypertext links to word definitions hold tremendous promise for reading instruction. (A) is incorrect because the links do not tie together "hyper" ideas. (C) is incorrect because links do not usually move or vibrate to draw attention. (D) is incorrect because a link may change color when clicked, but that is to let you know you have visited that link before.

64. **(C)** A definite reward schedule, some means of giving rewards (points, paper coupons, plastic tokens), and a means of redeeming tokens or points are the essential ingredients of a token economy. (A) The word "token" in this choice means figurative, and does not mean a real token to be handed out to children.

65. **(C)** Note the word NOT in the item. Assigning an in-class composition, by itself, does not indicate that an ongoing assessment is underway. There must be some evidence that the composition is being assessed. The remaining choices do indicate that an ongoing assessment is underway. (A) is incorrect because observing students as they work is a very effective ongoing assessment approach. (B) is incorrect because the teacher regularly reviews students' daily work. (D) is incorrect because daily performance samples are collected and reviewed.

66. **(D)** The only conclusive information in Rodney's profile is that he appears to do better on authentic assessment. Authentic assessment gives students an opportunity to demonstrate achievement that may not show up on standardized tests. (A) is incorrect because his score of 7.9 is below average for ninth grade. (B) is incorrect because the last sentence says his writing score is above grade level for his class. (C) is incorrect because a score one year below grade level and an above average writing sample do not support the need for intensive help in writing.

67. **(B)** The grade level is based on the entire national group of students who took the test. It is quite common for test scores of a class, of a school, or of a school district to be higher or lower on average than the national average. (A) and (D) are just meaningless statements about test scores. (C) This statement is generally true. More or less half of the students nationally who take a standardized test are below grade level. But this statement does not explain the student's test score situation.

68. **(C)** The least helpful way to find information is to just type in a Web address. Frequently, information about a subject is not found at a Web address with that name. There are many different suffixes (.com, .edu, .gov, .net, and so on). A student would have to choose the correct suffix as well as the correct Web name. (A) is incorrect because using a search engine is the best way to locate information on the Internet. (B) and (D) are incorrect because these can be effective ways to get information on the Internet. They are more effective than just typing in the Web address, but less effective than using a search engine.

69. **(D)** Students may be working on the problem at different times of the day. The best approach is for students to submit written samples of their solutions for the teacher to review. (A) is incorrect because students will not be working on the solution for the entire class, and there will not be enough time to observe all the students. (B) is incorrect because Mr. Siegrist's problems are not part of a standardized test. The teacher presents the problems. (C) is incorrect because cooperative learning is not itself an assessment tool.

70. **(A)** You don't have to know these science concepts to answer the question. It is always best to help students learn science through actual experience. Choices (B), (C), and (D) are incorrect. Each of these choices has value, but none is as good as actual experience.

71. **(D)** This is not an example of positive reinforcement, or of any kind of reinforcement. The remaining choices are all examples of positive reinforcement.

72. **(B)** The Constitution of the United States of America does not specify which governmental entity has the responsibility for education. But the constitution states the responsibilities not specifically assigned shall be the province of the states. In every state, including New York, the state has the responsibility for education. The State of New York may assign some of its responsibilities to (C) and (D) school boards and local town governments.

73. **(B)** This is exactly the situation in which cooperative learning groups excel. Students learn from interaction in the group, from the presentation made by other groups, and from your reaction and other's reactions to the presentations. (A) is incorrect because working independently is one of the least effective approaches to reading comprehension because it lacks interaction with teachers and other students. (C) and (D) are incorrect because the approach involves direct instruction in which the teacher just provides the information.

74. **(B)** Formative evaluation helps a teacher plan future lessons for a student. Samples of a student's writing best furthers that goal. (A) is incorrect because a discussion with a student may help a teacher, particularly if the discussion follows a review of the student's writing. But a discussion is not the best opportunity. (C) is incorrect because the Iowa Test of Basic Skills is more useful when standardized scores are indicated. (D) is incorrect because an end of unit test is also more useful as a summative evaluation of writing skills, but not as an evaluation of a student's writing.

75. **(D)** The student's writing contains several verb tense shifts. In the first sentence "sat" is past tense, while "play" is present tense. In the second sentence, "saw" is past tense, while "sit" is present tense. (A) and (B) are incorrect because the nouns and pronouns are used correctly. (C) is incorrect because the only spelling error is in the last sentence.

76. **(A)** A reasonable answer to a problem usually means to a computation problem. This is the best example because students frequently make key entry errors when they use a calculator. A student can tell if the answer is reasonable if he or she estimates first. (B), (C), and (D) are incorrect because estimation in these measurement examples does not ensure that an answer is reasonable.

77. **(D)** In authentic assessment the students summarize the results of their cooperative work. Choices (A), (B), and (C) are incorrect. All of these choices are characteristics of cooperative learning groups.

78. **(A)** Gardner's theory of multiple intelligences supports the use of interdisciplinary units. Gardner says that students have many intelligences and interdisciplinary units promote simultaneous use of these intelligences. (B) is incorrect because Gardner does not say that students should know about the intelligences. (C) and (D) are incorrect because Gardner's theory does not support the elimination of assessments or of students establishing the criteria for quality.

79. **(C)** It is during these grades that students turn most to peer groups and are most resistant to authority. The activity that one sees in the early grades and the maturity later in high school typically present fewer discipline problems than (C).

80. **(A)** A weekly plan allocates available time to lessons. (B) is incorrect because the plan descriptions are reversed in this choice. (C) is incorrect because the first part is correct but the second part is not practical because not enough is known at the beginning of the year to prepare these plans. (D) is incorrect because it is usually just the opposite. Teachers usually hand in plan books containing weekly plans.

Constructed Response

Show your essay to a professor of education. Ask that person to rate your essay from 1–4 using this scale.

4 A well developed, complete written assignment.
Shows a thorough response to all parts of the topic.
Clear explanations that are well supported.
An assignment that is free of significant grammatical, punctuation, or spelling errors.

3 A fairly well developed, complete written assignment.
It may not thoroughly respond to all parts of the topic.
Fairly clear explanations that may not be well supported.
It may contain some significant grammatical, punctuation, or spelling errors.

2 A poorly developed, incomplete written assignment.

It does not thoroughly respond to most parts of the topic.

Contains many poor explanations that are not well supported.

It may contain some significant grammatical, punctuation, or spelling errors.

1 A very poorly developed, incomplete written assignment.

It does not thoroughly respond to the topic.

Contains only poor, unsupported explanations.

Contains numerous significant grammatical, punctuation, or spelling errors.

ATS-W—Secondary Essay Scoring

Your goal is to write an essay with a score in the upper half. Score your essay using the scale above and the sample essay that follows. Scoring your own essay can be difficult. Showing your essay to a scoring expert will probably help you evaluate your performance.

Sample Essay

This essay would likely receive a total score in the upper half. The essay addresses all the specific points in the essay prompt. The writer explains why it is important to integrate technology with the school subjects. The explanation includes how technology integration will help students learn the school subjects and will help apply this integration to the real world. The essay includes two effective strategies—building teams to implement technology integration and providing expert technical support. Finally, the essay convincingly explains why this plan will be effective.

The length of this essay also indicates that it is worthy of a score in the upper half. The number of words itself is not enough to earn a high score. However, an essay of about this length will likely be required for a high score.

Integrating Technology in the Classroom

Technology is found throughout our society. Every subject taught in school today can be enhanced through the use of instructional technology. For some reason though, technology is used in a limited way and frequently used inappropriately in schools. The term "instructional technology" does not apply just to computers or the Internet. Every aspect of life either is or soon will be technology based or technology enhanced. Since school subjects are increasingly aligned with the real world, students must learn technology skills in high school in order to succeed in that world.

Assume that I am the technology coordinator for a school and that my job is to help classroom teachers integrate technology with the subject they are teaching. My first strategy would be to meet with the faculty from individual departments. I would want all of them to be a part of this technology integration. We would discuss how they currently use technology in their classrooms. Many good ideas would certainly be generated from this discussion. I would then try to bring those ideas together with other approaches to form a preliminary technology integration plan. One of the guiding principles of the plan would be "technology second." This phrase means that teachers and students would not use a technology just because it exists. Technology would be used if it meets the needs of the individual subjects.

My second strategy would be to provide expert support for faculty as they integrate technology. One example might be using Excel in the different subjects. Excel has many capabilities that people are unaware of. People know it is a spreadsheet that can be used for business. However, they may not realize that it has wonderful graphing capabilities that are very useful in social science and science classes. It can also work with equations and functions, which makes Excel ideal for many high school classes. This one program can be used in many different ways and successfully integrated across subject areas.

Once a plan is drawn up, I would help individual faculty members implement the plan. We would meet as a group every 6 weeks to assess the progress of the plan and suggest modifications.

I would expect the plan to be successful because it is tailored to the individual needs of faculty members and to the specific needs of their disciplines. The faculty would have ownership of the plan and be involved in its assessment and adjustment. I also expect the plan to be successful because expert help would assist in implementing the technology. The software itself should hold tremendous interest for both faculty and the students, and both groups would be expertly guided in its use.

See pages 59–68 at *http://www.nystce.nesinc.com/PDFs/NY_fld091_prepguide.pdf* for a scoring guide and additional samples of weak and strong Secondary ATS-W essays.

PART 4

CST PREPARATION

CST: Multiple Subjects Objectives

CHAPTER 12

> ### TEST INFO BOX
>
> The following pages contain the official list of objectives for the CST: Multiple Subjects. Review these objectives to develop a full understanding of the topics on this test.
>
> Following your review of these objectives, complete the CST Preparation Guide in Chapter 13 on page 351 to further prepare for the test. Finally, take the Practice CST: Multiple Subjects in Chapter 14 on page 363.
>
> ### SUBAREAS
> ### SELECTED RESPONSE
>
> I. English Language Arts
>
> II. Mathematics
>
> III. Science and Technology
>
> IV. Social Studies
>
> V. The Fine Arts
>
> VI. Health and Fitness
>
> VII. Family and Consumer Science
>
> ### CONSTRUCTED RESPONSE
>
> VIII. Foundations of Reading

Objectives

SUBAREA I—ENGLISH LANGUAGE ARTS

1. Understand the Foundations of Reading Development

EXAMPLES

- Demonstrate knowledge of the developmental progression from prereading to conventional literacy, with individual variations, and analyze how literacy develops in multiple contexts through reading, writing, and oral language experiences.

- Define phonological awareness and phonemic awareness, and analyze their role in reading development.

- Demonstrate knowledge of concepts about print (e.g., book-handling skills, awareness that print carries meaning, recognition of directionality, ability to track print, ability to recognize and name letters).

- Demonstrate knowledge of the alphabetic principle and analyze how emergent readers use this principle to master letter-sound correspondence and to decode simple words.

- Demonstrate knowledge of a variety of word identification strategies, including use of phonics, use of semantics and syntactic cues, context clues, syllabication, analysis of word structure (e.g., roots, prefixes, suffixes), and sight-word recognition,

- Analyze factors that affect a reader's ability to construct meaning from texts (e.g., word recognition, reading fluency, vocabulary development, context clues, visual cues, prior knowledge and experience).

2. Understand skills and strategies involved in reading comprehension.

EXAMPLES

- Demonstrate knowledge of literal comprehension skills (e.g., the ability to identify the sequence of events in a text, the ability to identify explicitly stated main ideas, details, and cause-and-effect patterns in a text).

- Demonstrate knowledge of inferential comprehension skills (e.g., the ability to draw conclusions or generalizations from a text, the ability to infer ideas, details, and cause-and-effect relationships that are not explicitly stated in a text).

- Demonstrate knowledge of evaluative comprehension skills (e.g., the ability to distinguish between fact and opinions in a text, the ability to detect faulty reasoning in a text, the ability to detect bias and propaganda in a text.

- Apply knowledge of strategies to use before, during, and after reading to enhance comprehension (e.g. developing and activating prior knowledge, connecting texts to personal experience, previewing a text, making predictions about a text, using K-W-L charts and other graphic organizers, taking notes on a text, discussing text).

- Demonstrate knowledge of methods for helping readers to monitor their own comprehension as they read (e.g., think-alouds, self-questioning strategies).

- Demonstrate knowledge of various methods for assessing comprehension of text (e.g., questioning the reader, having the reader give an oral or written retelling, asking the reader to identify the theme(s) or to paraphrase or summarize the main idea).

3. Understand and apply reading skills and strategies for various purposes (including information and understanding, critical analysis and evaluation, literary response, and social interaction).

EXAMPLES

- Recognize how to vary reading strategies for different text and purposes (e.g., skimming, scanning, in-depth reading, rereading) and for different types of genres of written communication (e.g., fiction, nonfiction, poetry).

- Apply knowledge of techniques for gathering, interpreting, and synthesizing information when reading a variety of printed texts and electronic sources.

- Recognize how to analyze and assess a writer's credibility or objectivity when reading printed and electronic texts.

- Analyze and interpret information from texts containing tables, charts, graphs, maps, and other illustrations.

- Demonstrate knowledge of strategies to promote literary response skills (e.g., connecting the text to personal experience and prior knowledge, citing evidence from a text to support an interpretation, using reading logs or guided reading techniques).

- Identify effective ways of modeling independent reading for enjoyment and encourage participation in a community of readers (e.g., book clubs, literature circles).

4. Understand processes for generating, developing, revising, editing, and presenting/publishing written texts.

EXAMPLES

- Analyze knowledge of prewriting strategies (e.g., brainstorming, prioritizing and selecting topics including clustering and other graphic organizers).

- Identify effective techniques of note taking, outlining, and drafting.

- Revise written texts to improve unity and logical organization (e.g., formulating topic sentences, reordering paragraphs or sentences, adding transition words and phrases, eliminating distracting sentences).

- Edit written work to ensure conformity to conventions of standard English usage (e.g., eliminating misplaced or dangling modifiers, eliminating sentence fragments, correcting errors in subject-verb agreement and pronoun-antecedent agreement).

- Edit and proofread written work to correct misspelling and eliminate errors in punctuation and capitalization.

- Apply knowledge of the uses of technology to plan, create, revise, edit, and present/publish written texts and multimedia works.

5. Understand and apply writing skills and strategies for various purposes (including information and understanding, critical analysis and evaluation, literary response and personal expression, and social interaction).

EXAMPLES

- Analyze factors a writer should consider when writing for a variety of audiences and purposes (e.g., informative, persuasive, expressive), including factors related to selection of topics and mode of written expression.

- Recognize how to incorporate graphic representation (e.g., diagrams, graphs, time lines) into writing for various purposes.

- Apply knowledge of skills involved in writing a research paper (e.g., generating ideas and questions, posing problems, evaluating and summarizing data from a variety of print and nonprint sources).

- Identify techniques for expressing point of view, using logical organization, and avoiding bias in writing for critical analysis, evaluation, or persuasion.

- Demonstrate knowledge of strategies for writing a response to a literary selection by referring to the text, to other works, and to personal experience.

- Demonstrate awareness of voice in writing for personal expression and social interaction.

6. Understand skills and strategies involved in listening and speaking for various purposes (including information and understanding, critical analysis and evaluation, literary response and expression, and social interaction).

EXAMPLES

- Recognize appropriate listening strategies for given texts and purposes (e.g., interpreting and analyzing information that is presented orally, appreciating literary texts that are read aloud, understanding small-group and large-group discussions).

- Analyze factors that affect the ability to listen effectively and to construct meaning from oral messages in various listening situations (e.g., using prior knowledge, recognizing transitions, interpreting nonverbal cues, using notetaking and outlining), and apply measures of effective listening (e.g., the ability to repeat instructions, the ability to retell stories).

- Analyze how features of spoken language (e.g., word choice, rate, pitch, tone, volume) and nonverbal cues (e.g., body language, visual aids, facial expressions) affect a speaker's ability to communicate effectively in given situations.

- Recognize how to vary speaking strategies for different audiences, purposes, and occasions (e.g., providing instructions, participating in group discussions, persuading or entertaining an audience, giving an oral presentation or interpretation of a literary work).

- Recognize the effective use of oral communication skills and nonverbal communication skills in situations involving people of different ages, genders, cultures, and other personal characteristics.

- Apply knowledge of oral language conventions appropriate to a variety of social situations (e.g., informal conversations, job interviews).

7. Understand and apply techniques of literary analysis to works of fiction, drama, poetry, and nonfiction.

EXAMPLES

- Analyze similarities and differences between fiction and nonfiction.

- Demonstrate knowledge of story elements in works of fiction (e.g., plot, character, setting, theme, mood).

- Apply knowledge of drama to analyze dramatic structure (e.g., introduction, rising action, climax, falling action, conclusion) and identify common dramatic devices (e.g., soliloquy, aside).

- Apply knowledge of various types of nonfiction (e.g., informational texts, newspaper articles, essays, biographies, memoirs, letters, journals).

- Analyze the use of language to convey style, tone, and point of view in works of fiction and nonfiction.

- Recognize the formal elements of a poetic text (e.g., meter, rhyme scheme, stanza structure, alliteration, assonance, onomatopoeia, figurative language) and analyze their relationship to the meaning of the text.

8. Demonstrate knowledge of literature, including literature from diverse cultures and literature for children/adolescents.

EXAMPLES

- Demonstrate awareness of ways in which literary texts reflect the time and place in which they were written.

- Demonstrate awareness of the ways in which literary works reflect and express cultural values and ideas.

- Recognize major themes and characteristics of works written by well-known authors.

- Demonstrate knowledge of important works and authors of literature for children and adolescents.

- Analyze themes and elements of traditional and contemporary literature for children and adolescents.

SUBAREA II—MATHEMATICS

9. Understand formal and informal reasoning processes, including logic and simple proofs, and apply problem-solving techniques and strategies in a variety of contexts.

EXAMPLES

- Use models, facts, patterns, and relationships to draw conclusions about mathematical problems or situations.

- Judge the validity or logic of mathematical arguments.

- Draw a valid conclusion based on the stated conditions and evaluate conclusions involving simple and compound sentences.

- Apply inductive reasoning to make mathematical conjectures.

- Use a variety of problem-solving strategies to model and solve problems, and evaluate the appropriateness of a problem-solving strategy (e.g., estimation, mental math, working backward, pattern recognition) in a given situation.

- Analyze the usefulness of a specific model or mental math procedure for exploring a given mathematical, scientific, or technological idea or problem.

10. Use mathematical terminology and symbols to interpret, represent, and communicate mathematical ideas and information.

EXAMPLES

- Use mathematical notation to represent a given relationship.

- Use appropriate models, diagrams, and symbols to represent mathematical concepts.

- Use appropriate vocabulary to express given mathematical ideas and relationships.

- Relate the language of ordinary experiences to mathematical language and symbols.

- Translate among graphic, numeric, symbolic, and verbal representations of mathematical relationships and concepts.

- Use mathematical representations to model and interpret physical, social, and mathematical phenomena.

11. Understand skills and concepts related to number and numeration, and apply these concepts to real-world situations.

EXAMPLES

- Select the appropriate computational and operational method to solve given mathematical problems.

- Demonstrate an understanding of the commutative, distributive, and associative properties.

- Use ratios, proportions, and percents to model and solve problems.

- Compare and order fractions, decimals, and percents.

- Solve problems using equivalent forms of numbers (e.g., integer, fraction, decimal, percent, exponential and scientific notation), and problems involving number theory (e.g., primes, factors, multiples).

- Analyze the number properties used in operational algorithms (e.g., multiplication, long division).

- Analyze number properties to manipulate and simplify algebraic expressions.

  12. Understand patterns and apply the principles and properties of linear algebraic relations and functions.

EXAMPLES

- Recognize and describe mathematical relationships.

- Use a variety of representations (e.g., manipulatives, figures, numbers, calculators) to recognize and extend patterns.

- Analyze mathematical relationships and patterns using tables, verbal rules, equations, and graphs.

- Derive an algebraic expression or function to represent a relationship or pattern from the physical or social world.

- Use algebraic functions to describe given graphs, to plot points, and to determine slopes.

- Perform algebraic operations to solve equations and inequalities.

- Analyze how changing one variable changes the other variable for linear and nonlinear functions.

  13. Understand the principles and properties of geometry and trigonometry, and apply them to model and solve problems.

EXAMPLES

- Identify relationships among two- and three-dimensional geometric shapes.

- Apply knowledge of basic geometric figures to solve real-world problems involving more complex patterns (e.g., area, perimeter of composite figures).

- Apply the concepts of similarity and congruence to model and solve problems.

- Apply inductive and deductive reasoning to solve problems in geometry.

- Use coordinate geometry to represent and analyze properties of geometric figures.

- Apply transformations (e.g., reflections, rotations, dilations) and symmetry to analyze properties of geometric figures.

14. Understand concepts, principles, skills, and procedures related to the customary and metric systems of measurement.

EXAMPLES

- Demonstrate knowledge of fundamental units of customary and metric measurement.

- Select an appropriate unit to express measures of length, area, capacity, weight, volume, time, temperature, and angle.

- Estimate and convert measurements using standard and nonstandard measurement units within customary and metric systems.

- Develop and use formulas to determine the perimeter and area of two-dimensional shapes and the surface area and volume of three-dimensional shapes.

- Solve measurement problems involving derived measurements (e.g., velocity, density).

- Apply the Pythagorean theorem and right triangle trigonometry to solve measurement problems.

15. Understand concepts and skills related to data analysis, probability, and statistics, and apply this understanding to evaluate and interpret data and to solve problems.

EXAMPLES

- Demonstrate the ability to collect, organize, and analyze data using appropriate graphic and nongraphic representations.

- Display and interpret data in a variety of different formats (e.g., frequency histograms, tables, pie charts, box-and-whisker plots, stem-and-leaf plots, scatterplots).

- Compute probabilities using a variety of methods (e.g., ratio and proportion, tree diagrams, tables of data, area models).

- Use simulations (e.g., spinners, multisided die, random number generators) to estimate probabilities.

- Apply measures of central tendency (mean, median, mode) and spread (e.g., range, percentiles, variance) to analyze data in graphic or nongraphic form.

- Formulate and design statistical experiments to collect, analyze, and interpret data.

- Identify patterns and trends in data and make predictions based on those trends.

SUBAREA III—SCIENCE AND TECHNOLOGY

16. Understand and apply the principles and processes of scientific inquiry and investigation.

EXAMPLES

- Formulate hypotheses based on reasoning and preliminary results or information.

- Evaluate the soundness and feasibility of a proposed scientific investigation.

- Apply mathematical rules or formulas (including basic statistics) to analyze given experimental or observational data.

- Interpret data presented in one or more graphs, charts, or tables to determine patterns or relationships.

- Evaluate the validity of a scientific conclusion in a given situation.

- Apply procedures for the safe and appropriate use of equipment and the care and humane treatment of animals in the laboratory.

17. Understand and apply concepts, principles, and theories pertaining to the physical setting (including earth science, chemistry, and physics).

EXAMPLES

- Analyze interactions among the earth, moon, and the sun (e.g., seasonal changes, the phases of the moon).

- Analyze the effects of interactions among components of air, water, and land (e.g., weather, volcanism, erosion).

- Distinguish between physical and chemical properties of matter and between physical and chemical changes in matter.

- Distinguish among forms of energy and identify the transformations of energy observed in everyday life.

- Analyze the effects of forces on objects in given situations.

- Infer the physical science principle (e.g., effects of common forces, conservation of energy) illustrated in a given situation.

18. Understand and apply concepts, principles and theories pertaining to the living environment.

EXAMPLES

- Recognize the characteristics of living things and common life processes.

- Analyze processes that contribute to the continuity of life (e.g., reproduction and development, inheritance of genetic information).

- Analyze the factors that contribute to change in organisms and species over time.

- Compare the ways a variety of organisms carry out basic life functions and maintain dynamic equilibrium (e.g., obtaining nutrients, maintaining water balance).

- Analyze the effects of environmental conditions (e.g., temperature, availability of water and sunlight) on living organisms and the relationships between plants and animals within the community.

- Infer the life science principle (e.g., adaptation, homeostasis) illustrated in a given situation.

19. Apply knowledge of technology and the principles of engineering design.

EXAMPLES

- Demonstrate an understanding of technological systems (e.g., transportation system) and the principles on which the technological systems are constructed (e.g., the use of component subsystems).

- Analyze the roles of modeling and optimization in the engineering design process.

- Evaluate a proposed technological solution to a given problem or need.

- Apply criteria for selecting tools, materials, and other resources to design and construct a technological product or service.

- Recognize appropriate tests of a given technological solution.

- Analyze the positive and negative effects of technology on individuals, society, and the environment.

20. Understand the relationships among and common themes that connect mathematics, science, and technology, and the application of knowledge and skills in these disciplines to other areas of learning.

EXAMPLES

- Make connections among the common themes of mathematics, science, and technology (e.g., systems, models, magnitude and scale, equilibrium and stability, patterns of change).

- Apply principles of mathematics, science, and technology to model a given situation (e.g., the movement of energy and nutrients between a food chain and the physical environment).

- Apply principles of mathematics, science, and technology to explore phenomena from other areas of learning (e.g., applying statistical methodologies to examine census data).

- Design solutions to problems in the physical and social worlds using mathematical, scientific, and technological reasoning and procedures.

- Analyze the effects of human activities (e.g., burning fossil fuels, clear-cutting forests) on the environment and evaluate the use of science and technology in solving problems related to these effects.

Subarea IV—Social Studies

21. Understand major ideas, eras, themes, developments, and turning points in the history of New York State, the United States, and the world.

EXAMPLES

- Define important conceptual terms (e.g., racism, nation-state, nationalism, feudalism) and use them to analyze general historical phenomena and specific historical events.

- Analyze the social effects of major developments in human history (e.g., the agricultural revolution, the scientific revolution, the industrial revolution, the information revolution).

- Understand major political, social, economic, and geographic characteristics of ancient civilizations and the connections and interactions among these civilizations.

- Examine reasons for organizing periods of history in different ways and compare alternative interpretations of key events and issues on New York State, U.S., and world history.

- Analyze the effects of European contact with indigenous cultures and the effects of European settlements on New York State and the Northeast.

- Analyze how the role and contributions of individuals and groups helped shape U.S. social, political, economic, cultural, and religious life.

22. Understand geographic concepts and phenomena and analyze the interrelationships of geography, society, and culture in the development of New York State, the United States, and the world.

EXAMPLES

- Define important geographic terms and concepts (e.g., habitat, resource, cultural diffusion, ecology) and use them to analyze various geographic issues, problems, and phenomena.

- Demonstrate an understanding of the six essential elements of geography: the world in spatial terms, places and regions, physical settings, human systems, environment and society, and the use of geography.

- Recognize physical characteristics of the earth's surface and the continual reshaping of it by physical processes (e.g., how weather, climate, and the water cycle influence different regions).

- Analyze the development and interaction of social, political, cultural, and religious systems in different regions of New York State, the United States, and the world.

- Examine ways in which economic, environmental, and cultural factors influence demographic change, and interpret geographic relationships, such as population density and special distribution patterns.

- Analyze the impact of human activity on the physical environment (e.g., industrial development, population growth, deforestation).

23. Understand concepts and phenomena related to human development and interactions (including anthropological, psychological, and sociological concepts).

EXAMPLES

- Use concepts, theories, and modes of inquiry drawn from anthropology, psychology, and sociology to examine general social phenomena and issues related to intercultural understanding.

- Evaluate factors that contribute to personal identity (e.g., family, group, affiliations, socialization processes).

- Recognize how language, literature, the arts, media, architecture, traditions, beliefs, values, and behaviors influence and/or reflect the development and transmission of culture.

- Analyze the roles and functions of social groups and institutions in the United States (e.g., ethnic groups, schools, religions) and their influence on individual and group interactions.

- Analyze why individuals and groups hold different or competing points of view on issues, events, or historical developments.

- Understand the processes of social and cultural change.

24. Understand economic and political principles, concepts, and systems, and relate this knowledge to historical and contemporary developments in New York State, the United States, and the world.

EXAMPLES

- Define important economic and political terms and concepts (e.g., scarcity, opportunity cost, supply and demand, productivity, power, natural rights, checks and balances) and use them to analyze general phenomena and specific issues.

- Analyze the basic structure, fundamental ideas, accomplishments, and problems of the U.S. economic system.

- Recognize and compare basic characteristics of major models of economic organization (e.g., traditional, marker, command) and various governmental systems (e.g., democratic, authoritarian).

- Analyze values, principles, concepts, and key features of American constitutional democracy (e.g., individual freedom, separation of powers, due process, federalism).

- Compare different perspectives regarding economic and political issues and policies in New York State and the United States (e.g., taxing and spending decisions).

- Analyze ways in which the United States has influenced other nations (e.g., in the development of democratic principles and human rights) and how other nations have influenced U.S. politics and culture.

25. Understand the roles, rights, and responsibilities of citizens in the United States and the skills, knowledge, and attitudes necessary for successful participation in civic life.

EXAMPLES

- Analyze the personal and political rights guaranteed in the Declaration of Independence, the U.S. Constitution, the Constitution of the State of New York, and major civil rights legislation.

- Recognize the core values of the U.S. democratic system (e.g., justice, honesty, the rule of law, self-discipline, due process, equality, majority rule, respect for minority rights).

- Demonstrate an understanding of the U.S. election process and the roles of political parties, pressure groups, and special interests in the U.S. political system.

- Explain what citizenship means in a democratic society and analyze the ways in which citizens participate in and influence the political process in the United States (e.g., the role of public opinion and citizen action groups in shaping public policy).

- Examine the rights, responsibilities, and privileges of individuals in relation to family, social group, career, community, and nation.

- Analyze factors that have expanded or limited the role of the individual in U.S. political life during the twentieth century (e.g., female suffrage, Jim Crow laws, growth of presidential primaries, role of the media in political elections).

26. Understand and apply skills related to social studies, including gathering, organizing, mapping, evaluating, interpreting, and displaying information.

EXAMPLES

- Evaluate the appropriateness of various resources and research methods for meeting specified information needs (e.g., atlas, bibliography, almanac, database, survey, poll) and apply procedures for retrieving information using traditional resources and current technologies (e.g., CD-ROM, the Internet).

- Demonstrate an understanding of concepts, tools, and technologies for mapping information about the spatial distribution of people, places, and environments (e.g., mapping grids, latitude and longitude, the advantages and limitation of different types of maps and map projections).

- Analyze information in social studies materials (e.g., identify central themes in important historical speeches or documents, distinguishing fact from opinion, evaluating multiple points of view in policy debates).

- Interpret information presented in one or more graphic representations (e.g., graph, table, map) and translate written or graphic information from one form to the other.

- Summarize the purpose or point of view of a historical narrative.

SUBAREA V—THE FINE ARTS

27. Understand the concepts, techniques, and materials of the visual arts; analyze works of visual art; and understand the cultural dimensions and contributions of the visual arts.

EXAMPLES

- Identify basic elements (e.g., line, color) and principles (e.g., unity, balance) of art, and recognize how they are used to communicate meaning in works of art.

- Analyze two-dimensional and three-dimensional works of art in terms of their visual and sensory characteristics.

- Apply knowledge of the characteristics of various art media (e.g., two-dimensional, three-dimensional, electronic) to select a medium appropriate for a given artistic purpose or intent.

- Apply knowledge of basic tools and techniques for working with various materials (e.g., clay, textiles, wood).

- Analyze how works of art reflect the cultures in which they were produced (e.g., materials or techniques used, subject matter, style).

- Compare works of art of different cultures, eras, and artists in terms of characteristics such as theme, imagery, and style.

28. Understand concepts, techniques, and materials for producing, listening to, and responding to music; analyze works of music; and understand the cultural dimensions and contributions of music.

EXAMPLES

- Compare various types of instruments (e.g., strings, percussion, woodwind, brass, electronic) in terms of the sounds they produce.

- Define and apply common musical terms (e.g., pitch, tempo).

- Use basic scientific concepts to explain how music-related sound is produced, transmitted through air, and received by listeners.

- Relate characteristics of music (e.g., rhythm, beat) to musical effects produced.

- Recognize basic technical skills that musicians must develop to produce an aesthetically acceptable performance (e.g., manual dexterity, breathing techniques, knowledge of musical notation).

- Analyze how different cultures have created music reflective of their histories and societies (e.g., call-and-response songs, ballads, work songs, folksongs).

29. Understand concepts, techniques, and materials related to theater and dance; analyze works of drama and dance; and understand the cultural dimensions and contributions of drama and dance.

EXAMPLES

- Compare dramatic and theatrical forms and their characteristics (e.g., pantomime, improvisation).

- Relate types of dance (e.g., ballet, folk, modern) to their characteristic forms of movement, expressive qualities, and cultural origins.

- Analyze how technical aspects of performance (e.g., costumes, props, lighting) affect the message or overall impression created by a performance.

- Recognize how language, voice, gesture, and movement are used to develop character and create interaction among performers in theatrical productions.

- Analyze ways in which different cultures have used drama and dance (e.g., to teach moral lessons, to preserve cultural traditions, to affirm the sense of community, to entertain).

SUBAREA VI—HEALTH AND FITNESS

30. Understand basic principles and practices of personal, interpersonal, and community health and safety; and apply related knowledge and skills (e.g., decision making, problem solving) to promote personal well-being.

EXAMPLES

- Identify common health problems and explain how they can be prevented, detected, and treated.

- Recognize the basic knowledge and skills necessary to support positive health choices and behaviors.

- Apply decision-making and problem-solving skills and procedures in individual and group situations (e.g., situations related to personal well-being, self-esteem, and interpersonal relationships).

- Recognize basic principles of good nutrition and use them to plan a diet that accommodates nutritional needs, activity level, and optimal weight.

- Analyze contemporary health-related issues (e.g., HIV, teenage pregnancy, suicide, substance abuse) in terms of their causes, effects, and significance for individuals, families, and society and evaluate strategies for their prevention.

- Interpret advertising claims for health-care products and services and distinguish between valid and invalid health information.

- Analyze environmental conditions and their impact upon personal and community health and safety.

31. Understand physical education concepts and practices related to the development of personal living skills.

EXAMPLES

- Recognize sequences and characteristics of physical development throughout the various developmental levels.

- Demonstrate knowledge of activities that promote the development of motor skills (e.g., locomotor, manipulative, body mechanics) and perceptual awareness skills (e.g., body awareness, spatial and directional awareness).

- Apply safe concepts and practices associated with physical activities (e.g., doing warm-up exercises, wearing protective equipment).

- Understand skills necessary for successful participation in given sports and activities (e.g., spatial orientation, eye-hand coordination, movement).

- Analyze ways in which participation in individual or group sports or physical activities can promote personal living skills (e.g., self-discipline, respect for self and others, resource management) and interpersonal skills (e.g., cooperation, sportsmanship, leadership, teamwork, communication).

32. Understand health-related physical fitness concepts and practices.

EXAMPLES

- Recognize components, functions, and common disorders of the major body systems.

- Demonstrate knowledge of basic components of physical fitness (e.g., strength, endurance, flexibility) and apply principles of training.

- Apply strategies for developing a personal fitness plan based in self-assessment, goal setting, and an understanding of physiological changes that result from training.

- Analyze the relationship between life-long physical activity and the prevention of illness, disease, and premature death.

- Apply knowledge of principles and activities for developing and maintaining cardiorespiratory endurance, muscular strength, and flexibility, and levels of body composition that promote good health.

SUBAREA VII—FAMILY AND CONSUMER SCIENCE AND CAREER DEVELOPMENT

33. Understand concepts and practices related to child development and care and apply knowledge of family and interpersonal relationships.

EXAMPLES

- Recognize stages and characteristics of physical, cognitive, social, and emotional development during infancy, childhood, and adolescence.

- Demonstrate knowledge of children's physical, dietary, and hygienic needs (e.g., nutritional guidelines, dental care, proper washing procedures) and apply developmentally appropriate methods for promoting self-care during childhood.

- Identify causes of common childhood accidents and health care emergencies and apply physical care and safety guidelines for caregivers of infants, toddlers, and preschool and school-age children.

- Analyze factors that affect decisions about whether and when to have children and recognize ways to prepare for the responsibilities of parenthood.

- Demonstrate knowledge of family structure (e.g., extended, blended, single parent, dual career), roles and responsibilities of family members, and the functions of families in society.

- Recognize the types and characteristics of interpersonal relationships and analyze decision-making processes related to interpersonal relationships.

- Examine social and cultural influences on interpersonal communication and analyze factors affecting the formation of positive relationships in the family, workplace, and community.

34. Understand skills and procedures related to consumer economics and personal resource management.

EXAMPLES

- Recognize rights and responsibilities of consumers in various purchasing situations (e.g., rights in relation to product and service warranties and guarantees).

- Demonstrate knowledge of types and characteristics of consumer fraud and apply procedures for seeking redress and registering customer complaints.

- Apply knowledge of procedures for making major purchases (e.g., comparison shopping, negotiation, interpreting labels or contract terminology).

- Analyze considerations involved in selecting and maintaining housing and motor vehicles, obtaining credit and insurance, and making investments.

- Examine steps and considerations involved in planning and maintaining a person or family budget and apply money management guidelines appropriate for various situations.

- Demonstrate knowledge of personal and family resources (e.g., time, skills, energy) and apply decision-making and goal-setting procedures for managing personal and family resources in various situations.

35. Understand basic principles of career development; apply processes and skills for seeking and maintaining employment; and demonstrate knowledge of workplace skills, behaviors, and responsibilities.

EXAMPLES

- Demonstrate knowledge of the relationship of person interests, skills, and abilities to successful employment and recognize the relationship between the changing nature of work and educational requirements.

- Recognize factors to consider when evaluating careers and applying procedures for conducting career research.

- Demonstrate knowledge of steps involved in searching for a job and recognize factors affecting the success of a job search (e.g., writing an effective letter of application, résumé preparation).

- Apply skills and procedures for job interviews (e.g., personal appearance and demeanor, communicating effectively during an interview).

- Apply knowledge of effective communication principles, work etiquette, interpersonal skills, and techniques for handling stress or conflict in the workplace.

- Recognize rights and responsibilities in relation to employment (e.g., protection from harassment and discrimination, employer's performance expectations).

SUBAREA VIII—FOUNDATIONS OF READING: CONSTRUCTED-RESPONSE ASSIGNMENT

The content to be addressed by the constructed-response assignment is described in Subarea I, Objectives 1 and 2.

CST: Multiple Subjects Preparation Guide

CHAPTER 13

TEST INFO BOX

The CST Multiple Subjects has 90 selected-response items and one constructed-response item.

The test is based on eight subareas. The first seven subareas are assessed by selected-response items. The seventh subarea is assessed by the content area assignment.

Selected-Response 90% of Score	**Approximate Number of Selected-Response Items**
I. English Language Arts	21
II. Mathematics	18
III. Science and Technology	13
IV. Social Studies	15
V. The Fine Arts	8
VI. Health and Fitness	8
VII. Family and Consumer Science and Career Development	7

Constructed Response 10% of Score

VIII. Foundations of Reading:	10% Constructed-Response Assignment

Consider these suggested Steps to prepare for the CST: Multiple Subjects

---

Preparation Steps

I. Visit the CST: Multiple Subjects Test Preparation Website

(*http://www.nystce.nesinc.com/PDFs/NY_fld002_prepguide.pdf*)

- Review the Selected-Choice questions and answers.
- Review the Sample Constructed-Response Item and scored essays.

II. Take a Related Practice Test

Pearson creates the CST: Multiple Subjects Test for New York. Pearson also creates a similar Multiple Subjects test called the CSET: Multiple Subjects. The names are quite similar.

The CST: Multiple Subjects is a different test, but there are strong subject matter similarities. The CSET: Multiple Subjects has selected-response items in the following areas.

CSET: MULTIPLE SUBJECTS	
Reading, Language	History and Social Science
Literature	Science
Mathematics	Human Development
Physical Education	Visual and Performing Arts

You can see the strong similarities. There is a complete CSET: Multiple Subjects practice test online. Many students report the CSET: Multiple Subjects practice test helped them prepare for the question types on the CST: Multiple Subjects.

Here is the link to the CSET: Multiple Subjects practice test. Follow the instructions and try the test. *http://www.cset.nesinc.com/CS_viewPT_opener.asp*

Use the CSET Practice Test Results to identify possible opportunities for further study in areas covered on the CST. Do not answer the CSET constructed-response items because these items are not like the CST constructed-response item.

III. Review Steps from this Book

Step 1: Review the test-taking strategies on pages 9–18

Step 2: Review Chapter 5 in this book for help answering Reading Comprehension Questions

Step 3: Review Chapter 6 in this book for an English and writing review.

IV. Additional Review

Many additional Resources are available to review subjects appropriate for elementary school teachers. Here are some suggestions that students have found helpful. You should use those resources that you believe will increase your CST: Multiple Subjects scores.

READING INSTRUCTION

This link takes you to a summary of the most up to date information about reading instruction.

Summary of the National Reading Panel
www.nichd.nih.gov/publications/nrp/upload/smallbook_pdf.pdf

MATHEMATICS

IXL Mathematics is a math website for elementary students, but it has proven useful for elementary teachers as well. The site is organized by grade level. Fourth, fifth, and sixth grade is a good choice for you.

Click on a grade and a topic. You will be given a series of problems. Answer correctly, and you move on to a more difficult problem. If you answer incorrectly, there is an explanation of the correct answer. This process of trying problems is a good way to master mathematics skills.

IXL Mathematics
www.ixl.com/

UNITED STATES HISTORY

This succinct online review covers all aspects of United States History. Links in the article take you to opportunities for further study.

Wikipedia US History
en.wikipedia.org/wiki/History_of_the_United_States

WORLD HISTORY

This site gives a quick overview of World History. Links in the article offer opportunities for further study.

Wikipedia History of the World
en.wikipedia.org/wiki/History_of_the_world

TECHNOLOGY

Here is a good list of nontechnical technology terms that might help on the test.

Pennsylvania Education Association
www.psea.org/general.aspx?id=830

This link takes you to a dictionary of more technical terms.

Dictionary of Technology Terms
www.scsb.org/glossary.html

SCIENCE

Here is a list of about 100 science terms to support and augment your science review.

Science Terms

altimeter An instrument that uses air pressure to record height, such as the height of a plane.

anemometer An instrument to measure wind speed.

angiosperm A group of plants that produce seeds enclosed within an ovary, which may mature into a fruit.

annuals Plants that die after one growing season.

asexual reproduction Reproduction involving only one parent.

atmosphere The Earth's atmosphere is primarily nitrogen and oxygen. The atroposphere extends from the surface to about 10 km; the stratosphere from 10 km to 50 km; the mesosphere from 50 km to 80 km; and the thermosphere is the atmosphere beyond 80 km.

aurora borealis (northern lights) Light emission from the upper atmosphere that appear in many shapes and colors.

bacillus A rod-shaped bacteria.

blood Fluid that circulates throughout the body of an animal, distributing nutrients, and usually oxygen.

canopy A layer of tree branches and other vegetation elevated above the ground.

carbon dioxide (CO$_2$) A colorless, odorless gas that is important in the Earth's atmospheric greenhouse effect. Frozen CO$_2$ is dry ice.

carcinogen A substance that can lead to cancer.

carcinoma A malignant tumor, which forms in the skin and outside of internal organs.

carnivore An organism that eats meat, which includes animals, fungi, and plants.

ceilometer An instrument that measures cloud height.

cell The fundamental unit of all life. The cell consists of an outer plasma membrane, the cytoplasm, and genetic material (DNA).

celsius A temperature scale in which water freezes at 0 degrees and boils at 100 degrees.

chemotherapy A cancer treatment that includes chemicals toxic to malignant cells.

chinook wind A warm, dry wind on the eastern side of the Rocky Mountains.

chlorophyll The green substance that absorbs light during photosynthesis.

chromosome A single DNA molecule, a tightly coiled strand of DNA, condensed into a compact structure.

clone An identical copy of an organism.

cloud A visible group of water or ice particles in the atmosphere.

commensalism A relationship between dissimilar organisms that is advantageous to one and doesn't affect the other.

continental divide In the United States, the part of the western mountains that separates water flowing toward opposite sides of the country.

convection The movement up in the atmosphere of heated moisture. Thunderstorms are often caused by convection.

core The portion of Earth from beneath the mantle to the Earth's center.

cross-pollination Fertilization of one plant by pollen from a different plant species.

diabetes A disease related to lowered levels of insulin.

diploid cell A cell with two copies of each chromosome.

DNA (deoxyribonucleic acid) This primary component of chromosomes carries an organism's genetic code.

double helix A term used to describe the coiling strands of DNA molecule that resembles a spiral staircase.

ecology The study of the interactions of organisms with their environment and with each other.

ecosystem All the organisms in an area and the environment in which they live.

El Nino Warming of Pacific Ocean seawater along the coast of South America that leads to significant weather changes in the United States.

embryo The stage of cellular divisions that develops from a zygote.

enzyme A protein that aids biochemical reactions.

epicenter The place on the surface of the Earth immediately above the *focus* of an earthquake.

esophagus The part of the gut that connects the pharynx and stomach.

estuary A place where fresh water and seawater mix.

flower The reproductive parts of flowering plants.

fossil Evidence of past life.

fruit The part of flowering plants that contains seeds.

gamete Reproductive haploid cells that combine to create a zygote.

genus The level of plant and animal between the species and the family.

germination The process by which seeds develop into seedlings.

gill The tissues aquatic animals use to breathe in water.

glucose A simple sugar and a product of photosynthesis.

gut That part of the body cavity between the mouth and anus including in most animals the mouth, pharynx, esophagus, stomach, intestine, and the anus.

haploid cell A cell with one set of chromosomes, which is half the regular (diploid) number.

heart A muscle that pumps to circulate the blood.

herbivore An organism that relies primarily on plants for food.

hypothesis A preliminary proposition that can be tested through scientific study.

insulin A hormone needed to transport glucose to cells.

interferon Small proteins that stimulate viral resistance in cells.

intestine The digestive tract between the stomach and anus where most nutrients are absorbed.

isotope Atoms of the same chemical element with a different number of neutrons but the same number of protons. Isotopes of an element have the same atomic number but may not have the same mass.

jet stream Strong upper wind currents in a narrow stream that flow west to east in the United States. Weather patterns are related to the position of the jet stream, which changes often.

kelvin A temperature scale in which 1° Kelvin equals 1° C. 0° Kelvin is about −273° C. 0° Kelvin is called absolute zero because there is no movement of molecules.

knot One nautical mile per hour or about 1.15 miles per hour.

larva In the metamorphosis of insects, the larva becomes a pupa before it becomes an adult.

lenticular cloud An almond-shaped cloud usually seen on windy days.

lipids Compounds that are fats and oils.

magma Molten rock formed in the Earth that may appear on the surface.

mantle The part of Earth located between the crust and the core.

marsupial A mammal whose young crawl into its mother's pouch to complete development.

meiosis The process in which a diploid cell divides to form haploid cells.

metamorphosis In most amphibians, a process in which larva goes through significant changes, perhaps including a pupa stage, before becoming an adult.

mirage The phenomenon when refraction of light makes objects appear where they are not.

mitosis Cell division consisting of prophase, metaphase, anaphase, and telophase, that usually creates in two new nuclei, each with a full set of chromosomes.

moraine Material deposited by a glacier and often marking a glacier's furthest advance.

nebula An interstellar cloud of dust and gas.

nerve A bundle of neurons, or nerve cells.

neuron A cell that reacts to stimuli and transmits impulses consisting of a body with a nucleus and dendrites to receive and axons to transmit impulses.

niche An organism's unique place in the environment.

nimbostratus A dark cloud, but not a thundercloud, that frequently produces rain.

nucleus An organelle in a cell that contains chromosomes.

nymph The larval stage of an aquatic insect.

paleontology Study and interpretation of fossils.

parasitism A relationship between organisms in which one organism benefits and the other does not die, even though the second organism may be harmed.

perennials Plants that live through more than one growing season.

permafrost Soil beneath the earth's surface that stays frozen throughout the year.

phloem The tissue in plants that conducts nutrients.

phylum A level of plant and animal classification between class and kingdom.

placenta A tissue in the uterus through which nutrients pass from the mother to the fetus.

plankton Floating aquatic plants (phytoplankton) and animals (zooplankton).

plate tectonics The movement of plates and the interaction across the Earth's surface to form land masses.

pollination Movement of pollen to a plant egg cell, often by wind, bees, or other animals.

pupa In metamorphosis, the stage between the larva and adult.

radiocarbon dating A way to date organic substances based on the carbon-14 remaining.

rainbow Light refracted through raindrops to form colors of a spectrum from red to blue.

reef A ridge built in water by organisms such as coral.

seed In plants, a seed includes the embryo.

sonic boom A loud noise caused by a shock wave when an object exceeds the speed of sound.

summer solstice When the sun is highest in the sky and directly above the Tropic of Cancer 23½° North Latitude. This date usually falls on June 22.

tree rings Rings that show how many years a tree has been growing. The thickness of the rings may reveal other information about climatic conditions.

vernal equinox When the sun is directly over the equator. This date usually occurs on March 20.

virga Precipitation that evaporates before it reaches the Earth's surface.

weathering The physical, chemical, and biological processes by which rock is broken down into smaller pieces.

wind chill The combined cooling effect of wind and temperature. Higher wind chills indicate that a body will cool more quickly to the air temperature.

FINE ARTS

Here is brief section about analyzing art with a glossary of art terms.

Analyzing Art

Art appears in many incarnations, including paintings, photographs, prints, carvings, sculpture, and architecture. When asked to analyze any work of art, you can comment on the content, the form, the style, and the method used by the artist.

The *content* is what actually appears in a work of art. It is the subject matter of the art. Don't take the obvious subject matter for granted when considering your analysis. Choose descriptive words as you search for ways to capture the content of the image in front of you. For example, a landscape may contain peaceful blue skies, a raging river, cows and horses grazing, or seemingly endless grassy fields. A portrait may show a happy person or someone filled with concern or worry. A sculpture may show a smoothly muscled athlete. A building may have cascading stairs or a series of columns that thrust upward to the ceiling.

The *form* of a work of art is the order imposed by the artist. Form is the design of the work regardless of the content. A painting or photograph may show strong horizontal or vertical orientation. Perhaps the work is symmetrical, with one part a mirror image of the other. Some works may be tilted or asymmetrical.

The *style* refers to the artist's way of expressing ideas including formal styles such as gothic, high renaissance, baroque, or impressionist. In a painting or picture you can notice how the artist uses color. The colors may blend or clash. There may be an overall dark tone to the picture, or it may be light and airy. Perhaps the artist used dots of paint to produce the image.

The *method* is the medium used by the artist to create the work. It may be an oil painting or a watercolor. Perhaps the artist created prints or an etching. A three-dimensional work of art may have been sculpted, cast, carved, molded, or turned on a potter's wheel.

Keep these elements of content, form, style, and method in mind as you respond to the questions on the CST.

Glossary of Art Terms

allegory Art that represents or symbolizes some idea or quality.

amphora An egg-shaped Grecian urn.

ankh An Egyptian hieroglyph that represents life. See illustration.

Ankh

annealing Softening by heating glass or metal that has become hardened.

arch A curved span. See illustration.

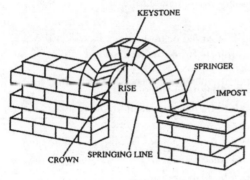

Arch

arebesque Very intricate designs based on plant forms.

atrium An open rectangular-shaped court, often in front of a church.

avant-garde Art considered ahead of its time.

baluster A small curved post or pillar.

balustrade A railing usually supported by balusters.

batten Strips of wood used as a base for plastering or for attaching tile.

bevel To round off a sharp edge.

biscuit Unglazed porcelain.

bust A sculpture showing the head and shoulders.

calligraphy Decorative writing.

canopy A fabric covering.

casement A vertically hinged window frame.

ceramics All porcelain and pottery.

chalice An ornamental cup often used in religious services.

chancel The part of a church reserved for clergy.

collage Art created by pasting together many media including newspaper, fabric, and wood. A collage may also include paintings or drawings.

colors Many colors can be created by combining the primary colors. See illustration.

Color Wheel

column A free-standing, circular pillar. Several different styles exist. See illustration.

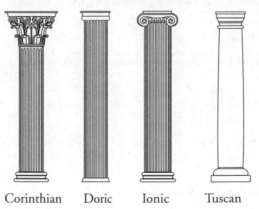

Corinthian   Doric   Ionic   Tuscan

course A row of bricks or stones.

cuneiform Wedge-shaped writing associated with Babylonians and Sumerians.

decoupage Cutting out designs to be used in a collage.

eclectic Drawing on many styles.

enamel Powdered glass bonded to a metal surface by firing.

engraving Inscribing a design on glass, metal, or some other hard surface.

etching Designs created on metal plates by applying acid to initial scratchings and the prints made from these plates.

filigree Gold or silver soldered to create elaborate, delicate patterns.

focal point The place on a work of art to which the eye is drawn.

foreshortened Objects painted or drawn as though they were seen from an angle projecting into space.

fresco A painting applied to wet plaster.

genre The type of painting—portrait, landscape, etc.

golden ratio The proportion of approximately 1.6 to 1, which is said to represent the most pleasing artistic proportion. For example, a window 3 feet wide would meet this proportion by being 4.8 feet high.

hieroglyphics Egyptian symbols representing letters or words.

illustration An idea or scene represented in art.

kiosk A small booth with a roof and open sides.

linear A way of representing three-dimensional space in two dimensions.

macrame Artwork made of knotted fabrics.

monolith A figure sculpted or carved from a single block of stone.

mural A painting made on or attached to a wall.

niche A wall recess.

obelisk A rectangular block of stone, often with a pyramidal top.

papier maché Paper (newspaper) soaked with water and flour and shaped into figures.

parquet A floor made of wooden tile.

perspective Representing three dimensions on a flat surface.

pigment The material used to color paint.

plaster Limestone and sand or gypsum mixed with water, which can be shaped and then hardened. Plaster can also be carved and is often used to finish walls and ceilings.

projection The techniques of representing buildings on a flat surface.

quarry tile Unglazed tile.

relief Carved or molded art in which the art projects from the background.

sarcophagus A stone coffin.

scale The relative size of an object, such as the scale was one inch to one foot.

sizing Gluelike material used to stiffen paper or to seal a wall or canvas.

stipple Dab on paint.

tapestry Fabric woven from silk by hand.

tempera A type of painting that binds the pigment with a mixture of egg and water or egg and oil.

uppercase Capital letters.

vihara A Buddhist monastery.

warp In weaving, the thick, fixed threads.

weft In weaving, the thin threads that are actually woven.

HEALTH AND FITNESS FAMILY AND CONSUMER SCIENCES

TIP

This link to the New York State Health, Physical Education, Family and Consumer Sciences website is an excellent source of information.

> www.emsc.nysed.gov/sss/schoolhealth/schoolhealtheducation/healthPEFACS
> LearningStandards.pdf

CAREER DEVELOPMENT

This link takes you to several documents about New York State Career Development

> www.emsc.nysed.gov/cte/cdlearn/cdosresourceguide.html

Final Step

Take and Score the Practice CST: Multiple Subjects on the following page.

One Last Reminder

The CST: Multiple Subjects is a content-based test. You will not know the answer to a number of questions. Don't let that bother you. Don't start doubting yourself. Make your best guess and move on.

CST: Multiple Subjects Practice Test

CHAPTER 14

TEST INFO BOX

This full-length practice test includes the types of items you will find on a real CST test. The distribution of test items and the difficulty of a test varies from one administration to the other. The test you take will likely be of a somewhat different difficulty level than his test.

You have 4 hours to answer the 90 selected-response items and to complete the constructed-response essay. Take the test in a realistic timed setting. Remember that many people do better on a practice test than they do on the real test.

When the test is complete, review the answer and explanation for each item. Compare your constructed response to the sample at the end of the selected-response answers.

When you are ready, turn the page and begin.

Answer Sheet
CST: MULTIPLE SUBJECTS

1 Ⓐ Ⓑ Ⓒ Ⓓ	21 Ⓐ Ⓑ Ⓒ Ⓓ	41 Ⓐ Ⓑ Ⓒ Ⓓ	61 Ⓐ Ⓑ Ⓒ Ⓓ
2 Ⓐ Ⓑ Ⓒ Ⓓ	22 Ⓐ Ⓑ Ⓒ Ⓓ	42 Ⓐ Ⓑ Ⓒ Ⓓ	62 Ⓐ Ⓑ Ⓒ Ⓓ
3 Ⓐ Ⓑ Ⓒ Ⓓ	23 Ⓐ Ⓑ Ⓒ Ⓓ	43 Ⓐ Ⓑ Ⓒ Ⓓ	63 Ⓐ Ⓑ Ⓒ Ⓓ
4 Ⓐ Ⓑ Ⓒ Ⓓ	24 Ⓐ Ⓑ Ⓒ Ⓓ	44 Ⓐ Ⓑ Ⓒ Ⓓ	64 Ⓐ Ⓑ Ⓒ Ⓓ
5 Ⓐ Ⓑ Ⓒ Ⓓ	25 Ⓐ Ⓑ Ⓒ Ⓓ	45 Ⓐ Ⓑ Ⓒ Ⓓ	65 Ⓐ Ⓑ Ⓒ Ⓓ
6 Ⓐ Ⓑ Ⓒ Ⓓ	26 Ⓐ Ⓑ Ⓒ Ⓓ	46 Ⓐ Ⓑ Ⓒ Ⓓ	66 Ⓐ Ⓑ Ⓒ Ⓓ
7 Ⓐ Ⓑ Ⓒ Ⓓ	27 Ⓐ Ⓑ Ⓒ Ⓓ	47 Ⓐ Ⓑ Ⓒ Ⓓ	67 Ⓐ Ⓑ Ⓒ Ⓓ
8 Ⓐ Ⓑ Ⓒ Ⓓ	28 Ⓐ Ⓑ Ⓒ Ⓓ	48 Ⓐ Ⓑ Ⓒ Ⓓ	68 Ⓐ Ⓑ Ⓒ Ⓓ
9 Ⓐ Ⓑ Ⓒ Ⓓ	29 Ⓐ Ⓑ Ⓒ Ⓓ	49 Ⓐ Ⓑ Ⓒ Ⓓ	69 Ⓐ Ⓑ Ⓒ Ⓓ
10 Ⓐ Ⓑ Ⓒ Ⓓ	30 Ⓐ Ⓑ Ⓒ Ⓓ	50 Ⓐ Ⓑ Ⓒ Ⓓ	70 Ⓐ Ⓑ Ⓒ Ⓓ
11 Ⓐ Ⓑ Ⓒ Ⓓ	31 Ⓐ Ⓑ Ⓒ Ⓓ	51 Ⓐ Ⓑ Ⓒ Ⓓ	71 Ⓐ Ⓑ Ⓒ Ⓓ
12 Ⓐ Ⓑ Ⓒ Ⓓ	32 Ⓐ Ⓑ Ⓒ Ⓓ	52 Ⓐ Ⓑ Ⓒ Ⓓ	72 Ⓐ Ⓑ Ⓒ Ⓓ
13 Ⓐ Ⓑ Ⓒ Ⓓ	33 Ⓐ Ⓑ Ⓒ Ⓓ	53 Ⓐ Ⓑ Ⓒ Ⓓ	73 Ⓐ Ⓑ Ⓒ Ⓓ
14 Ⓐ Ⓑ Ⓒ Ⓓ	34 Ⓐ Ⓑ Ⓒ Ⓓ	54 Ⓐ Ⓑ Ⓒ Ⓓ	74 Ⓐ Ⓑ Ⓒ Ⓓ
15 Ⓐ Ⓑ Ⓒ Ⓓ	35 Ⓐ Ⓑ Ⓒ Ⓓ	55 Ⓐ Ⓑ Ⓒ Ⓓ	75 Ⓐ Ⓑ Ⓒ Ⓓ
16 Ⓐ Ⓑ Ⓒ Ⓓ	36 Ⓐ Ⓑ Ⓒ Ⓓ	56 Ⓐ Ⓑ Ⓒ Ⓓ	76 Ⓐ Ⓑ Ⓒ Ⓓ
17 Ⓐ Ⓑ Ⓒ Ⓓ	37 Ⓐ Ⓑ Ⓒ Ⓓ	57 Ⓐ Ⓑ Ⓒ Ⓓ	77 Ⓐ Ⓑ Ⓒ Ⓓ
18 Ⓐ Ⓑ Ⓒ Ⓓ	38 Ⓐ Ⓑ Ⓒ Ⓓ	58 Ⓐ Ⓑ Ⓒ Ⓓ	78 Ⓐ Ⓑ Ⓒ Ⓓ
19 Ⓐ Ⓑ Ⓒ Ⓓ	39 Ⓐ Ⓑ Ⓒ Ⓓ	59 Ⓐ Ⓑ Ⓒ Ⓓ	79 Ⓐ Ⓑ Ⓒ Ⓓ
20 Ⓐ Ⓑ Ⓒ Ⓓ	40 Ⓐ Ⓑ Ⓒ Ⓓ	60 Ⓐ Ⓑ Ⓒ Ⓓ	80 Ⓐ Ⓑ Ⓒ Ⓓ
81 Ⓐ Ⓑ Ⓒ Ⓓ	86 Ⓐ Ⓑ Ⓒ Ⓓ		
82 Ⓐ Ⓑ Ⓒ Ⓓ	87 Ⓐ Ⓑ Ⓒ Ⓓ		
83 Ⓐ Ⓑ Ⓒ Ⓓ	88 Ⓐ Ⓑ Ⓒ Ⓓ		
84 Ⓐ Ⓑ Ⓒ Ⓓ	89 Ⓐ Ⓑ Ⓒ Ⓓ		
85 Ⓐ Ⓑ Ⓒ Ⓓ	90 Ⓐ Ⓑ Ⓒ Ⓓ		

Answer Sheet

Practice CST: Multiple Subjects

Directions: Each item on this test includes four answer choices. Select the best choice for each item and mark the letter on the answer sheet.

1. Phonemic awareness instruction is most effective with children when

   (A) it focuses on many different types of phoneme manipulation.
   (B) it is taught as phonological awareness.
   (C) they learn the sounds along with the phonemes.
   (D) the children understand that phonemic awareness is the same as phonics.

2. Which of the following sentences is grammatically incorrect because of the irregular nature of the English verb construction?

   (A) Blaire bringed the car to the mechanic.
   (B) Blaire hopped happily down the street.
   (C) Blaire were practicing a play.
   (D) Blaire speak to her friend yesterday.

3. Based on recent findings, silent independent reading

   (A) has not been shown to improve reading achievement.
   (B) has been shown to improve reading achievement but not fluency.
   (C) has not been shown to improve reading achievement but has been proven to improve reading fluency.
   (D) has been shown to improve both reading achievement and fluency.

4. Which of the following is the best example of the phonemic awareness skill of phoneme identity?

   (A) A child recognizes the sound of "w" in the word was.
   (B) A child recognizes the sound of the word was.

   (C) A child recognizes that the sound of "w" is the same in the words was and want.
   (D) A child substitutes the sound of "w" in was with the sound of "h" to form the new word has.

5. When we talk about teaching onsets and rhymes to young children, we are talking about

   (A) written language that matches each syllable.
   (B) spoken language smaller than syllables but larger than phonemes.
   (C) written language found at the very beginning or the very end of a poem.
   (D) spoken language units smaller than a phoneme that combine to make up individual phonemes.

6 In which of the following sentences is the underlined word used correctly?

   (A) The ropes helped the mountain climber with her ascent.
   (B) The runner assented the winner's platform.
   (C) The diver ascended to the lowest depths of the ocean.
   (D) The tree limb stood in the way of the cat's assent up the old oak tree,

Use the passage below to answer items 8–9.

(1) Choosing educational practices sometimes seems like choosing fashions. (2) Fashion is driven by whims, tastes, and the zeitgeist of the current day. (3) The education system should not be driven by these same forces. (4) Three decades ago, teachers were told to use manipulative

materials to teach mathematics. (5) However, consider the way mathematics is taught. (6) In the intervening years, the emphasis was on drill and practice. (7) Now teachers are again told to use manipulative materials. (8) Even so, every teacher has the ultimate capacity to determine his or her teaching practices.

7. Which of the following revised sentences would be most likely to improve the style of the passage?

   (A) Sentence 1—The choice of educational practices sometimes seems like choosing fashions.
   (B) Sentence 3—The education system should not have to react to these forces.
   (C) Sentence 5—However, consider mathematics and the way it is taught.
   (D) Sentence 8—Even so, every teacher can determine his or her teaching practices.

8. Which of the following describes the best way to rearrange sentences to improve the organization of the passage?

   (A) Move sentence 2 before sentence 1.
   (B) Move sentence 4 before sentence 3.
   (C) Move sentence 5 before sentence 4.
   (D) Move sentence 6 before sentence 5.

9. Most people feel at least some stage fright, particularly at the beginning of an oral presentation. The best strategy for handling this stage fright is to

   (A) begin with a well thought-out introduction.
   (B) explain your nervousness to your audience.
   (C) make extra use of hand and arm movements.
   (D) use the whole stage and move actively to maintain your comfort.

Base your answers to items 10–11 on this excerpt from an oral presentation.

(1) Jean Piaget is world famous for his research on child development. (2) According to Piaget's research, children are at the concrete operational stage of development for most of their elementary school years. (3) However, in the early school years, students are usually in the preoperational stage. (4) During the preoperational stage of development, students do not grasp many fundamental concepts. (5) Helping children make the transition from preoperational to concrete operational stages means striking a balance between not teaching a concept and teaching the concept with concrete materials.

10. Which of the following best characterizes this presentation?

    (A) It is primarily a narration.
    (B) It is primarily an opinion.
    (C) It is primarily an exposition.
    (D) It is primarily a reflection.

11. Which of the following sentences, when added as the second sentence to the presentation, would make it primarily a persuasive presentation?

    (A) "Piaget conducted most of his developmental research on just a few children."
    (B) "Children may not be best served if instruction is not based on Piaget's stages."
    (C) "Primary teachers are most likely to encounter students who are at the preoperational stage."
    (D) "Piaget frequently collaborated with Barbel Inhelder."

12. Which of the following is usually the focus of an epic?

    (A) Profound feelings or ideas
    (B) Love and chivalry
    (C) Political ideas
    (D) A single mythological figure

Use this map to answer item 13.

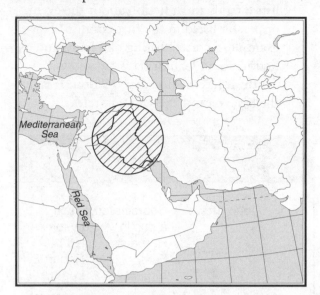

13. The lined area on the map shown above best represents the location of which of the following ancient civilizations?

   (A) Egypt New Kingdom
   (B) Hellenistic Greece
   (C) Kush Kingdom
   (D) Mesopotamia

Use this list to answer item 14.

Civilization began on an island
Home to the Mycenaeans and the Minoans
Invaded by the Dorians
Location of Sparta

14. The description given above best describes which of the following ancient civilizations?

   (A) Assyria
   (B) Egypt
   (C) Greece
   (D) Phoenicia

15. When Christopher Columbus sailed, he

   (A) never returned to Europe from his explorations.
   (B) first established a settlement in what is now the state of North Carolina.
   (C) never reached the mainland of North America.
   (D) first established a settlement in what is now the state of Virginia.

16. Which line in the table below correctly matches a description with the name of an event leading up to the Revolutionary War?

Line	Event	Description
1	Sugar Act	This act put a limit on the amount of sugar that the colonies could import.
2	Stamp Act	This act placed a tax on each legal document prepared in the colonies.
3	Boston Massacre	Several dozen colonial militia, including Crispus Attucks, were killed without provocation in Boston Square.
4	Boston Tea Party	A thousand colonists, dressed as Native Americans, attacked ships bearing tea to the main tea warehouses in Boston Harbor and threw the cases of tea into the water.

   (A) Line 1
   (B) Line 2
   (C) Line 3
   (D) Line 4

Use this excerpt from the United States Constitution to answer item 17.

Article II.

[Section 1.] The executive Power shall be vested in a President of the United States of America. He shall hold his Office during the Term of four Years, and, together with the Vice President, chosen for the same Term, be elected, as follows:

Each State shall appoint, in such Manner as the Legislature thereof may direct, a Number of Electors, equal to the whole Number of Senators and Representatives to which the State may be entitled in the Congress: but no Senator or Representative, or Person holding an Office of Trust or Profit under the United States, shall be appointed an Elector.

17. What is the impact of Article II, Section 1 on the election of the President of the United States of America?

   (A) The President of the United States is elected directly by the people of the United States.
   (B) The President of the United States is elected by a majority of the states.
   (C) The President of the United States can be elected by less than a majority of the voters.
   (D) The number of presidential electors equals the number of representatives.

18. In the table below, which line correctly lists a truth and a fiction about the event or person listed in the first column? For example, a correct listing of a truth and a fiction about California is as follows. Truth: It has earthquakes. Fiction: It is on the east coast of the United States.

Line	Event or Person	Truth	Fiction
1	John Brown	Coordinated a raid in Harpers Ferry, Virginia	Captured by forces led by Robert E. Lee
2	Abraham Lincoln	Spoke against slavery	Spoke in favor of slavery
3	Dred Scott Case	Dred Scott has no standing in court	Dred Scott is property and not a citizen
4	Emancipation Proclamation	Issued by President Lincoln	Freed all slaves

   (A) Line 1
   (B) Line 2
   (C) Line 3
   (D) Line 4

19. Which of the following stages of skiing represents potential energy?

   (A) The skier is going to the top of the hill on a ski lift.
   (B) The skier is waiting at the top of the hill.
   (C) The skier pushes off from the top of the hill.
   (D) The skier is skiing down the hill.

Use this summarized portion of the periodic table to answer item 20.

6	7	8
C	**N**	**O**
12	14	16

14	15	16
Si	**P**	**S**
28	31	32

32	33	34
Ge	**As**	**Se**
73	75	79

50	51	52
Sn	**Sb**	**Te**
111	122	128

20. Which of these elements has 16 neutrons?

(A) C
(B) P
(C) Se
(D) Sn

21. When written as a formula, Newton's second law of motion is $F = ma$, where F is force, m is mass, and a is acceleration. Which of the following is the best explanation of this law?

(A) Something heavier will move slower than something lighter.
(B) It is easier to move something if it has less mass.
(C) The more the acceleration you apply, the less mass the object has.
(D) The more mass the object has means more force is applied to it.

22. Which of the following best illustrates heat transfer through conduction?

(A) People feel heat when they stand near an electric stove.
(B) People feel heat when they stand in the sunlight.

(C) People feel heat when they stand in front of a hot air blower.
(D) People feel heat when they touch a steam radiator.

23. A green plant is placed in a terrarium and subjected to continuous light and to watering. Which of the following will happen as a result of photosynthesis?

(A) The plant will produce oxygen.
(B) The plant will produce carbon dioxide.
(C) The plant will produce water.
(D) The plant will produce carbon monoxide.

24. In most cases, a plant must be pollinated before it can bear any fruit. Pollination is important because it provides

(A) sperm to fertilize the plant.
(B) a rich culture in which seeds and fruits can develop.
(C) the medium in which plant fertilization takes place.
(D) a way to attract bees.

Use this diagram to answer item 25.

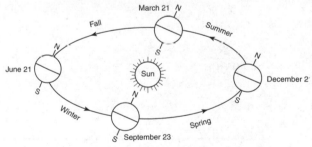

Seasons in the Southern Hemisphere

25. The diagram above demonstrates that seasons on Earth are due to

(A) Earth's rotation.
(B) the distance from Earth to the sun.
(C) Earth's tilt.
(D) Earth's revolution.

26. A weather observer would use a hygrometer to measure which of the following?

    (A) Rainfall
    (B) Humidity
    (C) Wind speed
    (D) Air pressure

27. Two types of elevators travel up and down inside a very tall building. One elevator starts at the first floor and stops every x floors. Another elevator starts at the first floor and stops every y floors. Which of the following is the best way to find at which floors both elevators stop?

    (A) Find the common multiples of x and y.
    (B) Find the common factors of x and y.
    (C) Find the prime factors of x and y.
    (D) Find the divisors of x and y.

28. What is the value of the 7 in 1.37×10^{-2}?

    (A) $\dfrac{7}{10}$

    (B) $\dfrac{7}{100}$

    (C) $\dfrac{7}{1000}$

    (D) $\dfrac{7}{10,000}$

Use this number line to answer item 27.

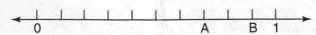

29. Which of the following could *not* be found on the number line between Point A and Point B?

    (A) $\dfrac{27}{34}$

    (B) $\dfrac{79}{86}$

    (C) $\dfrac{81}{91}$

    (D) $\dfrac{38}{54}$

30. Which of the following best describes the arithmetic expression $1\frac{1}{4} \times 1\frac{1}{3}$?

    (A) There are $1\frac{1}{4}$ pounds of clay, and we want to find an equal share for 3 people.

    (B) Each of three people has $1\frac{1}{4}$ pounds of clay, and we want to find out how much clay there is altogether.

    (C) There are $1\frac{1}{4}$ pound of clay, and we want to find $\frac{1}{3}$ more than that amount.

    (D) There are $1\frac{1}{4}$ pounds of clay, and we want to find how much clay to take away to make $\frac{1}{3}$ pound.

31. The landscaper recommended a mix of $3\frac{1}{2}$ pounds of rye grass seed per $\frac{3}{4}$ pound of blue grass seed. If the lawn needs $5\frac{1}{4}$ pounds of rye grass seed, how many pounds of blue grass seed would be needed?

    (A) $\dfrac{3}{8}$ pounds

    (B) $1\frac{1}{8}$ pounds

    (C) $1\frac{1}{2}$ pounds

    (D) $4\frac{1}{3}$ pounds

32. This multiplication problem is missing many digits. Each missing digit is represented by a $\square$, although every $\square$ does not represent the same number.

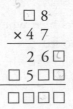

Which digit is in the tens place in the product of the two numbers?

(A) 5
(B) 6
(C) 7
(D) 8

Use this coordinate grid to answer item 33.

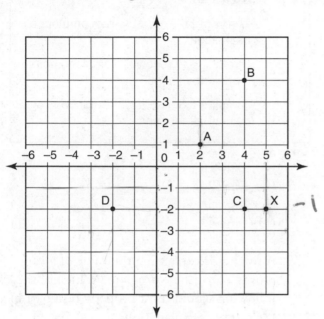

33. Point *X* is on a line with a slope of −1. Which of the other points is also on that line?

(A) *A*
(B) *B*
(C) *C*
(D) *D*

34. A phone company has a rate plan of $0.29 per call (*c*) and $0.04 per minute (*m*). Which of the following expressions could be used to find the cost of a call?

(A) (0.29 + 0.04)
(B) 0.04*m* + 0.29
(C) 0.29*m* + 0.04
(D) *m*(0.29 + 0.04)

Use this diagram to answer item 35.

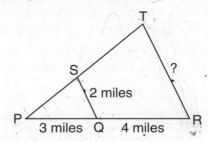

35. Engineers are building two bridges to span a deep canyon. They arranged the roads and bridges to form two similar triangles. △*PQS* is similar to △*PRT*. If the bridge from *Q* to *S* is 2 miles long, how long is the bridge from *R* to *T*?

(A) 3.0 miles
(B) 3.66 miles
(C) 4.66 miles
(D) 9.33 miles

Use this diagram to answer item 36.

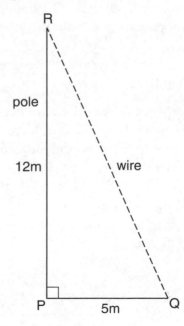

36. A 12-meter pole is at a right angle to the ground. Construction workers want to attach a wire at the top of the pole and then to a point on the ground 5 meters from the pole. How long will the wire be?

    (A) $\sqrt{17}$ m
    (B) $\sqrt{60}$ m
    (C) 13 m
    (D) 17 m

37. An elementary school teacher engages students in the following physical education activity.

    > Students walk continuously around the gym floor.
    >
    > Then students walk around the floor, stopping for 5 seconds every 3 steps.
    >
    > Students walk backward continuously around the gym floor.
    >
    > Then students walk backward around the floor, stopping for 5 seconds every 3 steps.

    This activity is most likely designed to help students

    (A) experience the difference between backward and forward locomotion.
    (B) develop time-movement locomotor awareness.
    (C) experience the difference between free flow and bound flow
    (D) warm up for subsequent physical activities.

38. Which of the lines in the table shown below correctly pairs a physical activity with the type of skill?

Line	Activity	Description
1	Jumping up toward a basketball backboard	Manipulative
2	Throwing a basketball	Locomotor
3	Stretching to receive a basketball pass	Nonlocomotor
4	Jumping to catch a basketball rebound	Balance

    (A) Line 1
    (B) Line 2
    (C) Line 3
    (D) Line 4

39. A teacher is explaining the value of a cardiovascular fitness program. Which of the following would most properly be a part of the teacher's explanation?

    (A) Lowers HDL cholesterol
    (B) Raises LDL cholesterol
    (C) Raises muscle strength
    (D) Lowers heart rate

40. Which of the following is the most appropriate way to monitor the impact of exercise on children?

    (A) Monitor the children's pulse rates.
    (B) Observe how "hard" children are breathing.
    (C) Take note of how much the children's eyes are dilated.
    (D) Feel the children's foreheads to detect elevated body temperatures.

41. Which of the lines in the table shown below correctly pairs a physical term and the definition of that term?

Line	Event	Description
1	Shape	Relative position of different parts of the body
2	Middle space activities	Activities performed when kneeling
3	Arhythmic movement	Movements performed to a steady beat
4	Force	Distance moved during a locomotor activity

(A) Line 1
(B) Line 2
(C) Line 3
(D) Line 4

42. Lisa sees Rita defending herself by fighting back after another student hit Rita with a book. Which of the following responses by Lisa would indicate the most advanced stage of moral development when compared with the other responses?

(A) Lisa mentions to Rita that what she did was morally correct but against the school rules.
(B) Lisa tells Rita that she should be careful because Rita might be punished for her actions.
(C) Lisa finds a teacher and tells the teacher about what she observed.
(D) Lisa tells Rita that Rita's parents would not approve of the fighting.

43. Children's tendency to ignore warnings about the dangers of drug abuse is most likely a result of

(A) a desire to be included in a group of friends.
(B) an inability to conceptualize the real impact of drug abuse.
(C) an insatiable desire for the euphoria caused by drugs.
(D) a need to escape from an oppressed reality or a depressed life.

44. Sex-based differences in the physical growth of boys and girls is best characterized by which of the following choices?

(A) Boys enter a period of steady growth around age 10.
(B) Girls enter a period of steady growth around age 8.
(C) Boys enter adolescence at about age 10.
(D) Girls enter adolescence at about age 10.

45. Of the following choices, which is most indicative that a child is at the preoperational stage of development?

(A) The child demonstrates egocentric thinking.
(B) The child is able to add and subtract numbers using manipulatives.
(C) The child believes that a hidden object cannot be found.
(D) The child can conserve number.

46. A student's life is most influenced by his or her family. Which choice least accurately characterizes most American families?

(A) A majority of families have mothers who work.
(B) An increasing number of children are latchkey children
(C) Less than 10 percent of American families have a mother as a homemaker, a father as the sole breadwinner, and children.
(D) Families are groups of people living together who are related to one another.

47. Elementary school students frequently learn vicariously, meaning that the students

(A) learn by doing.
(B) learn through a wide variety of activities.
(C) learn if there is a clear structure.
(D) learn from others' experiences.

48. Which of the activities listed below would be most likely to help elementary school students develop an aesthetic perception, an appreciation, of dance?

(A) Ask students to view a dance performance and to identify the time and space elements in the performance.
(B) Ask students to view a dance performance and to identify the cultural style of the performance.
(C) Ask students to view a dance performance and to interpret the meaning found in the performance.
(D) Ask students to view a dance performance and to interpret the history of the dance form.

Use the following picture to answer item 49.

49. Which best describes the picture above?

(A) A bucolic scene
(B) An active scene
(C) A morning scene
(D) A languid scene

50. As part of a theater activity, an upper elementary teacher partitions the class into groups of three or four students. The teacher has a set of index cards that describes general situations. The teacher hands one of the cards to a group. The group has a few minutes to come up with a skit, which they then act out in front of the class. Which form of professional acting does this activity most closely resemble?

(A) Stand-up
(B) Pantomime
(C) Comedy
(D) Improv

51. In a class, students will have the opportunity to produce and direct a brief dramatic work. Which of the following would best help distinguish one student's role as producer from another student's role as director?

(A) The producer is responsible for planning and writing a performance, while the director is actually responsible for implementing the producer's overall scheme.
(B) The producer follows the director's lead and makes arrangements for stage sets and props.
(C) The producer is responsible once the performance begins, while the director is responsible for everything leading up to the actual performance.
(D) The producer has overall administrative responsibility for the dramatic work, while the director has creative responsibility for the work.

52. A person viewing the visual art technique called a fresco is most likely viewing it

(A) on a canvas.
(B) in a church.
(C) on a wall.
(D) on a board or a piece of wood.

Use the following passage to answer item 53.

Music consists of pitch, the actual frequency of a sound or note, and duration. A tone has a specific pitch and duration. Different tones occurring simultaneously are called chords. A melody is the tones that produce the distinctive sound of the music. Harmony is chords with duration. Pitches separated by a specific interval are called a scale. Most music is based on the C major diatonic scale found on the piano's white keys (C, D, E, F, G, A, B). The C chromatic scale includes the seven notes of the diatonic scale plus the five sharps and flats corresponding to the black keys on the piano.

53. According to the passage, the C chromatic scale:

(A) corresponds to the white keys on the piano.
(B) is contained in the C major diatonic scale.
(C) can be played on only the piano.
(D) includes notes corresponding to the first seven letters of the alphabet.

54. A teacher using phoneme deletion activities promotes phonemic awareness by

(A) breaking a word into separate sounds and saying each sound.
(B) recognizing the sounds in a word that do not match the sounds in another word.
(C) recognizing the word remaining when a phoneme is removed from a longer word.
(D) substituting one phoneme for another to make a new word.

55. Phonics is the predictable relationship between graphemes and phonemes. What do experts generally say about phonics?

(A) Systematic and explicit phonics instruction is the essential element of early-grade reading programs.
(B) Literature-based instruction that emphasizes reading and writing is the essential element of early-grade reading programs.
(C) Sight-word programs are the essential element in early-grade reading programs.
(D) Basal programs that focus on whole word or meaning-based activities are the essential element of early-grade reading programs.

56. A teacher incorporating recent research findings will most likely use which of the following approaches to improve a student's reading fluency?

(A) Round-robin reading in which students take turns reading a passage
(B) Monitored oral reading
(C) Silent independent reading
(D) Hearing models of fluent reading

57. A teacher uses semantic organizers because this approach is most likely to help students

(A) understand the meaning of words, expressions, and sentences in relation to reference and truth.
(B) identify the underlying structure of a story.
(C) relate pictures and diagrams in the text to the text itself.
(D) identify related ideas and concepts in a text.

58. Which of the following would indicate to a teacher that a student is using a metacognitive approach to reading comprehension?

   (A) A student grasps the overall structure of a story.
   (B) A student summarizes the essence of a story.
   (C) A student adjusts his or her reading speed.
   (D) A student works cooperatively with others to comprehend a story.

59. A child has most likely learned the meaning of a word

   (A) indirectly, through context clues.
   (B) directly, through phonics learning experiences.
   (C) indirectly, through everyday experiences.
   (D) directly, through phonemic learning experiences.

Use this passage to answer item 60.

The computers in the college dormitories are actually more sophisticated than the computers in the college computer labs. In addition, the dorm computers cost less. The person who bought the dormitory computers obviously shopped around until he or she found powerful computers at a low price. The person who runs the computer labs simply bought the computers offered by the regular supplier.

60. Which choice best states the main idea of this paragraph?

   (A) It is better to use the computers in the dorms.
   (B) Since the computers in the dorms are always in use, it is better to use the computers in the labs for most purposes.
   (C) It is better to shop around before you buy.
   (D) Wholesale prices are usually better than retail prices.

61. A class is studying an epic, meaning that the work under study might be:

   (A) *King Arthur and the Knights of the Round Table*
   (B) *Gulliver's Travels*
   (C) *The Odyssey*
   (D) *Paul Bunyan*

62. *Alice in Wonderland*

   (A) is based on a real character.
   (B) is categorized as an epic by English scholars.
   (C) includes primarily realistic characters.
   (D) was written to soothe children at a time when many children died at a young age.

63. Which of the following is most closely associated with the early development of civilization?

   (A) The Upper Nile River and the Lower Nile River
   (B) The Tigris River and the Euphrates River
   (C) The Mediterranean Sea and the Red Sea
   (D) The Caspian Sea and the Black Sea

64. A teacher is planning to review events in American History. Which of the following is the teacher most likely to review first?

   (A) The writing of the Decleration of Independence
   (B) The writing of the Constitution of the United States
   (C) The First Continental Congress
   (D) The Stamp Act

65. Most historians would agree that the event that marked the beginning of the Reformation

   (A) was when Mary I of England killed many Protestants during her reign.
   (B) occurred in Italy during the time of the Renaissance.
   (C) when Puritans sailed for the New World.
   (D) when Martin Luther nailed his 95 theses to a church door in Germany.

66. Which line in the table given below correctly matches an early American colony or colonizer with events related to that colony?

Line	Colony/ Colonizer	Description
1	Christopher Columbus	Columbus established a small settlement before returning to Europe.
2	The Lost Colony	John Smith established this colony near Roanoke, Virginia.
3	Jamestown Colony	Sir Walter Raleigh established this colony that came to rely on slaves for tobacco production.
4	The Pilgrims	The Pilgrims established a colony at Plymouth and drew up the Mayflower Compact.

   (A) Line 1
   (B) Line 2
   (C) Line 3
   (D) Line 4

Use this map to answer item 67.

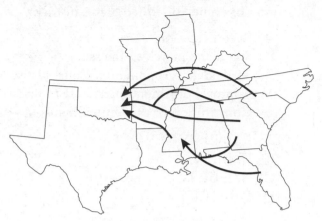

67. The map above best shows which events between the Revolutionary and Civil Wars?

   (A) The migration of settlers from the east coast toward California.
   (B) The forced removal of Native Americans to Oklahoma.
   (C) The establishment of railroads from the east to the Midwest.
   (D) The first wagon train trails to jumping-off points in the Midwest.

68. Which line in the table given below *does not* correctly match a person or people in the War of 1812 with a description of what that person or people did?

Line	Event	Description
1	Francis Scott Key	Wrote the "Star-Spangled Banner"
2	British Troops	Sacked and burned Washington, DC
3	Andrew Jackson	Fought the Battle of New Orleans
4	Commodore Perry	Fought the British in Baltimore Harbor

   (A) Line 1
   (B) Line 2
   (C) Line 3
   (D) Line 4

69. Which of the following shows the correct order of events in United States history?

    I. Reconstruction
    II. Sherman's march to the sea
    III. Surrender at Appomattox Court House
    IV. Approval of Amendment XIII to the Constitution of the United States

    (A) I, II, III, IV
    (B) II, III, IV, I
    (C) II, I, III, IV
    (D) IV, II, III, I

Use this passage to answer item 70.

NOW, THEREFORE, by virtue of the authority vested in me as President of the United States, and Commander in Chief of the Army and Navy, I hereby authorize and direct the Secretary of War, and the Military Commanders whom he may from time to time designate, whenever he or any designated Commander deems such actions necessary or desirable, to prescribe military areas in such places and of such extent as he or the appropriate Military Commanders may determine, from which any or all persons may be excluded, and with such respect to which, the right of any person to enter, remain in, or leave shall be subject to whatever restrictions the Secretary of War or the appropriate Military Commander may impose in his discretion.

70. What was the purpose of this passage?

    (A) It established secret flight test areas in California that eventually helped in the development of the stealth bomber.
    (B) It established Japanese internment camps during WWII.
    (C) It established a military defense zone at the United States-Mexico border.
    (D) It created exclusion zones in San Francisco shortly after the San Francisco earthquake of 1906.

71. Which of the following involves changing the electrical charge of an object?

    (A) Rubbing a glass rod with a silk cloth
    (B) Using a 12-volt battery in place of a 6-volt battery
    (C) Using a 20-amp fuse instead of a 10-amp fuse
    (D) Turning off the switch to an electric heater

72. When white light is refracted through a prism, it splits into many colors, like the colors of a rainbow. What does this phenomenon show?

    (A) The colors appear only when light is refracted through a triangular object.
    (B) The prism has a colored filter that separates these colors.
    (C) White light is formed by a combination of all these colors.
    (D) If all these colors were refracted through a prism, white light would be visible.

73. Which of the following best describes a function of the nose and the mouth in the respiratory system?

    (A) Filter out oxygen
    (B) Exhale carbon dioxide
    (C) Heating air
    (D) Expectoration

74. You are floating on a lake in a boat about 100 yards from the shore. You can hear someone talking at the shoreline. What is the best way to explain this phenomenon?

    (A) Sound travels faster through air.
    (B) Sound travels faster through water.
    (C) Sound travels from the shore because of the materials that make up the boat.
    (D) You hear the sound because of an echo.

75. A primary objective of a school mathematics program is to teach students to estimate first to be sure a calculation is reasonable. Which of the following instructions best meets that objective?

    (A) Estimate the answer to 6,294 + 7,892 before you find the answer with a calculator.
    (B) Estimate the answer to 900 + 9 before you find the answer with paper and pencil.
    (C) Estimate the number of beans in the jar before you count the beans.
    (D) Estimate the distance from your desk to the door before you measure the distance.

76. Which of the following powers of 10 would you multiply by 3.74 to get 374,000,000?

    (A) 10^6
    (B) 10^7
    (C) 10^8
    (D) 10^9

77. Cutting through a cylinder could produce all of the figures below except which one?

    (A)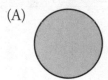

    (B)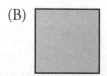

    (C)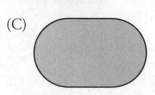

    (D)

78. These are examples of a student's work.

    $$6\overline{)520} = 86.4 \qquad 9\overline{)736} = 81.7 \qquad 8\overline{)150} = 18.6$$

    The student continues to make the same type of error. Which of the following would be the student's answer to 124 divided by 5?

    (A) 2.2
    (B) 20.2
    (C) 22.5
    (D) 24.4

79. During a second-grade mathematics lesson, the teacher presents this problem.

    "There are 43 people on the camping trip. If 5 people can fit in a tent, what is the least number of tents needed?"

    Which of the following is the best strategy to solve this problem?

    (A) Guess and check
    (B) Interpret the remainder
    (C) Make an organized list
    (D) Choose the operation

80. Deena finished the school run in 52.8 seconds. Lisa's time was 1.3 seconds faster. What was Lisa's time?

    (A) 51.5 seconds
    (B) 54.1 seconds
    (C) 53.11 seconds
    (D) 65.8 seconds

Use the following flowchart to answer item 81.

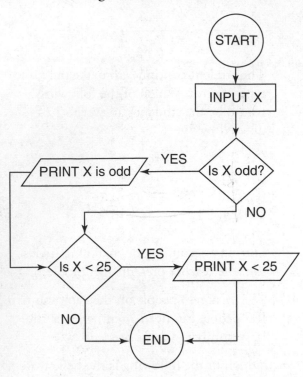

81. One of these numbers was put through the flowchart shown above, and no answer was printed. Which number was put through?

(A) 25
(B) 18
(C) 13
(D) 38

82. Three pieces of wood measure $\frac{1}{2}$ foot, $\frac{2}{3}$ foot, and $\frac{5}{12}$ foot. What is the average length of these pieces of wood?

(A) $\frac{19}{12}$ foot

(B) $\frac{19}{24}$ foot

(C) $\frac{19}{36}$ foot

(D) $\frac{19}{44}$ foot

83. Which of the following would be the most appropriate way to improve the eye-hand coordination of a young student?

(A) Provide numerous highly organized team activities
(B) Provide for numerous pyramid-building activities
(C) Provide many different-sized objects for the student to juggle
(D) Provide many different-sized balls for the student to throw, catch, and kick

Use the activity described in the box below to answer item 84.

Moonball

Everyone stands in a circle.

Get a beach ball or a balloon with a cloth cover.

Toss the ball into the circle.

Keep hitting the ball into the air.

Keep the ball in the air as long as possible.

Count the number of hits aloud as you go.

Start again if the ball hits the ground.

---

84. This game is best described as a

(A) competitive game.
(B) cooperative game.
(C) locomotor game.
(D) a nonlocomotor game.

85. In general, a learning-disabled student is characterized by

(A) achievement scores significantly below intelligence scores.
(B) intelligence scores significantly below achievement scores.
(C) IQ scores below 90.
(D) achievement scores in the lower quartile.

86. Which color results from mixing two complementary colors?

   (A) A supplementary color
   (B) Reddish brown
   (C) Gray
   (D) A primary color

87. James Fenimore Cooper lived much of his life in Cooperstown, New York, a town named after his father. James Fenimore Cooper is best known for authoring which of the following books?

   (A) *Baseball's Hall of Fame—Cooperstown*
   (B) *The Last of the Mohicans*
   (C) *The Adventures of Huckleberry Finn*
   (D) *The Legend of Sleepy Hollow*

88. An elementary school is planning a career day. A committee of teachers is deciding which careers should be represented among people who will briefly visit each class in the school. Which is the best principle to guide the committee's choices?

   (A) Invite people from the lowest-paying careers to the highest-paying careers to give students the widest possible range of choices.
   (B) Invite people who represent the range of careers representative of the community to expose students to the types of careers students are most likely to pursue.
   (C) Invite people who represent the highest-paying or most prestigious careers to communicate to students that they too can achieve.
   (D) Invite the working parents of students in the school to help the students develop pride in their families and emphasize the place of each family in the community.

89. Which is the best approach when integrating a school subject with technology?

   (A) Focus on the most current cutting-edge technology and its role in society.
   (B) Use technology to the extent that it supports the subject matter's objective.
   (C) Ensure that technology is fairly and equitably available to all students.
   (D) Use technology to the greatest extent possible, without any limits on students' experiences.

90. Major John André was captured as a British spy during the Revolutionary War in 1780 at Tarrytown, New York. Andre was carrying notes from Benedict Arnold. At that time, Benedict Arnold was

   (A) a civilian, having left the army.
   (B) commandant of West Point.
   (C) in command of the British forces in the United States.
   (D) in England.

CONSTRUCTED RESPONSE

A teacher is observing two students as they carry on a discussion about everyday events. The teacher is paying particular attention to Jeanie. The teacher's purpose is to detect any issues with English grammar or usage. The following is a transcript of part of the conversation between Quinn and Jeanie.

Quinn—What are you going to do this weekend?

Jeanie—I are going shopping.

Quinn—What store?

Jeanie—It's the store down by the school.

Quinn—I guess your brother is going.

Jeanie—That is what he say.

Quinn—What do you think you'll buy?

Jeanie—I ain't sure.

Quinn—Take a guess.

Jeanie—I are not sure.

Quinn—It was crowded the last time I went there.

Jeanie—I hope it is not when I went there this weekend.

Quinn—See you later.

Jeanie—Just keep it among us.

Task

Use your knowledge of English grammar to write an essay in response to the items below. Write a single essay that incorporates your response to both tasks.

Identify one of Jeanie's issues with grammar, particularly subjects and verbs. Describe how you identified these issues from the discussion above, and give two specific examples to support your conclusion.

Identify one of Jeanie's issues with grammar, particularly with tense. Describe how you identified these issues from the discussion above, and give two specific examples to support your conclusion.

Answer Key

PRACTICE CST: MULTIPLE SUBJECTS

1. C	24. A	47. D	70. B
2. A	25. C	48. A	71. A
3. A	26. B	49. D	72. C
4. C	27. A	50. D	73. B
5. B	28. D	51. D	74. D
6. A	29. B	52. C	75. A
7. D	30. A	53. D	76. C
8. C	31. B	54. C	77. C
9. A	32. D	55. A	78. D
10. C	33. A	56. B	79. B
11. B	34. B	57. D	80. A
12. D	35. C	58. C	81. D
13. D	36. C	59. C	82. C
14. C	37. C	60. C	83. D
15. C	38. C	61. C	84. B
16. B	39. D	62. A	85. A
17. C	40. A	63. B	86. C
18. D	41. A	64. D	87. B
19. B	42. A	65. D	88. A
20. B	43. B	66. D	89. B
21. B	44. D	67. B	90. B
22. D	45. A	68. D	
23. A	46. D	69. B	

Answers Explanations

1. **(C)** Phonemic awareness is the ability to hear, identify, and manipulate phonemes in spoken words. (A) is incorrect because phoneme manipulation is just one part of phonemic awareness. (B) is incorrect because phonological awareness includes phonemic awareness but also includes words and syllables. Including words and syllables with phonemic awareness is not effective. (D) is incorrect because phonemic awareness is not the same as phonics.

2. **(A)** Substitute *brought* for *bringed.* The word *bringed* is not appropriate because of the irregular nature of the English verb construction. (B) is incorrect because the verb *hopped* is used correctly. (C) and (D) are incorrect because although *were* and *speak* are not used correctly, these problems are not caused by the irregular nature of English verb construction.

3. **(A)** Studies have consistently failed to confirm that silent independent reading helps students become better readers. (B), (C), and (D) are all incorrect because research does not show that silent independent reading improves either reading achievement or reading fluency.

4. **(C)** Phoneme identity means to recognize the same sound in different words. (A) is incorrect because it is an example of phoneme isolation. (B) is incorrect because it is an example of phoneme blending. (D) is incorrect because it is an example of phoneme substitution.

5. **(B)** This choice gives the definition of onsets and rhymes. (A) is incorrect because onsets and rhymes are often smaller than syllables. (C) is incorrect because onsets and rhymes are not directly related to poetry. (D) is incorrect because onsets and rhymes are often larger than phonemes.

6. **(A)** *Ascent* means "the process of going upward," which is what the mountain climber is doing. (B) is incorrect because *assented* means "agreed" and it does not make sense for the runner to agree the winner's platform. (C) is incorrect because *ascended* means "to go up," but the diver is going down. (D) *Assent* means "to agree" and it does not make sense for a cat to agree up the old oak.

7. **(D)** This sentence is too wordy. Replace the wordy "has the ultimate capacity to" with "can" to improve the style of the passage. (A) is incorrect because this change removes the parallel structure of the original sentence. (B) is incorrect because changing the words "driven by" to "react to" changes the meaning of the sentence and does not improve the style. (C) is incorrect because it alters the meaning from "consider the way mathematics is taught" to "consider mathematics," which is a different idea, and does not improve the style of the passage.

8. **(C)** The thought expressed in sentence 5 naturally comes before the thought expressed in sentence 4. (A), (B), and (D) are all incorrect because the sentences referred to in these choices are correct as placed in the paragraph.

9. **(A)** The best strategy among those listed for handling stage fright is being prepared for the introductory part of your presentation. (B) is incorrect because you should never share your stage fright or uncertainty with an audience. (C) and (D) are incorrect because these techniques are not likely to alleviate stage fright.

10. **(C)** The main purpose of an expository presentation is to explain. This presentation explains about Piaget and his operational stages. (A) is incorrect because a narration tells either a factual or a fictional story (B) is incorrect because the presentation conveys only facts about Piaget's research and does not include any opinions. (D) is incorrect because a reflection describes a scene, a person, or an emotion.

11. **(B)** The intent of a persuasive presentation is to convince the audience of a particular point of view. This sentence seeks to convince audience members to incorporate Piaget's ideas in their teaching. It does not matter if the audience agrees with the sentence. (A), (C), and (D) are all incorrect because they just continue the explanation, which is the hallmark of an expository presentation, not a persuasive presentation.

12. **(D)** An epic focuses on a single mythological figure. (A) is incorrect because a lyric is most closely associated with profound feelings or ideas. (B) is incorrect because this theme is most closely associated with a novel. (C) is incorrect because this theme is most closely associated with a romance.

13. **(D)** The lined area east of the Mediterranean and east of the Red Sea corresponds to Mesopotamia. This region contains the Tigris and Euphrates Rivers. Historians often identify Mesopotamia as the birthplace of civilization. (A) is incorrect because Egypt is located south of the Mediterranean and west of the Red Sea. (B) is incorrect because Greece is located on the northern shore of the Mediterranean. (C) is incorrect because the Kush Kingdom is located south of Egypt and west of the Red Sea.

14. **(C)** Greek civilization began on the island of Crete, which was home to both the Minoans about 3000–1400 B.C. The Mycenaeans lived in Greece about 1600–1100 B.C. Greece was invaded by the Dorians about 1100–800 B.C. Sparta is located in Greece. None of the other choices can claim these elements. (A) is incorrect because Assyria was essentially landlocked in Mesopotamia. (B) is incorrect because Egyptian civilization developed along the northern Nile River. (D) is incorrect because Phonecian civilization developed along the eastern coast of the Mediterranean.

15. **(C)** Columbus sailed the Caribbean and landed in what is now the Dominican Republic and the island of Hispaniola. He never reached the mainland of North America. (A) is incorrect because Columbus did return to Europe during his explorations. (B) is incorrect because Sir Walter Raleigh established a settlement in North Carolina. (D) is incorrect because John Smith established the Jamestown Colony in Virginia.

16. **(B)** This line includes an accurate description of the Stamp Act, which required a tax stamp for each legal document. (A) is incorrect because the Sugar Act limited the export of other commodities. (C) is incorrect because although Crispus Attucks was killed in the Boston Massacre, five colonists, not several dozen, were killed. Additionally, the massacre occurred with provocation. (D) is incorrect because far fewer than a hundred colonists boarded ships and dumped tea into the harbor, not a thousand.

17. **(C)** This article of the Constitution establishes the Electoral College. The popular vote chooses electors, not the president. The electors then vote for the president. In recent presidential elections, a candidate received a majority of the electoral votes but did not receive a majority of the popular vote. (A) is incorrect because this article says that the people of the United States do not directly elect the president. (B) is incorrect because states do not elect presidents. A candidate can prevail in a majority of states but not win the majority of the electoral votes. (D) is incorrect because as the article says, the number of electors is equal to the number of senators and representatives combined.

18. **(D)** For a choice to be correct, the truth must be true and the fiction must be false. Only (D) shows a combination of a true statement and a false statement. Read the explanations in the table.

Line	Event or Person	Truth	Fiction
1	John Brown	This statement is true.	This statement is true. Robert E. Lee led the forces that captured John Brown at Harpers Ferry.
2	Abraham Lincoln	This statement is true.	This statement is true. Lincoln spoke in favor of slavery while he was in Illinois.
3	Dred Scott Case	This statement is true.	This statement is true.
4	Emancipation Proclamation	This statement is true.	This statement is false. The Emancipation Proclamation freed slaves in Confederate States.

19. **(B)** Energy is the ability to do work. The skier at the top of the hill has the most potential to create kinetic energy by skiing down the hill. (A) is incorrect because this choice does not represent any energy potential since there is no way to activate it. (C) is incorrect because a skier pushing off the top of the hill represents kinetic energy, which is the energy of movement. (D) is incorrect because the skier skiing down the hill represents kinetic energy.

20. **(B)** To find the number of neutrons, subtract the atomic number (number of protons) shown at the top of each cell and the atomic mass shown at the bottom of each cell. Among the elements listed as choices, element P (phosphorus) has 31 − 15 = 16 neutrons. Other elements have 16 neutrons, but none of these elements are an answer choice. (A) Element C (carbon) has 12 − 6 = 6 neutrons. (C) Element Se (selenium) has 79 − 34 = 45 neutrons. (D) Element Sn (tin) has 111 − 50 = 61 neutrons.

21. **(B)** This formula means the more mass there is, the more force you need to accelerate it. Less mass means you need less force. A commonsense example of a heavy airplane moving faster than a lighter bicycle explains why answer (A) is incorrect. (C) is incorrect because making something go faster does not reduce its mass. (D) is incorrect because more mass does not mean more force will be applied to it.

22. **(D)** Conduction means heat transfer by direct contact. (A) and (B) are incorrect because these choices give examples of heat transfer by radiation (no physical contact). (C) is incorrect because this choice gives an example of heat transfer by convection (moving air).

23. **(A)** Photosynthesis by a green plant produces oxygen and carbohydrates (sugar and starch). (B) is incorrect because photosynthesis uses, but does not produce, carbon dioxide. (C) is incorrect because photosynthesis uses, but does not produce, water. (D) is incorrect because photosynthesis neither uses nor produces carbon monoxide.

24. **(A)** Pollen contains the sperm that fertilizes the egg cells found in the plant. (B) and (C) are incorrect because pollen provides neither a rich culture nor a medium for either plant development or fertilization. (D) is incorrect because pollination does not attract bees, although flowers on some plants attract bees to their pollen.

25. **(C)** Summer occurs in the Southern Hemisphere when that hemisphere tilts toward the sun. Summer occurs in the northern hemisphere when that hemisphere tilts toward the sun. (A) is incorrect because Earth's rotation creates periods of daytime and nighttime. (B) and (D) are incorrect because the distance from Earth to the sun, created by Earth's revolution around the sun, does not create seasons.

26. **(B)** A hygrometer measures humidity. (A) is incorrect because a rain gauge measures rainfall. (C) is incorrect because an anemometer measures wind speed. (D) is incorrect because a barometer measures air pressure.

27. **(A)** The common multiples of x and y will reveal at which floors each elevator stops. Find the common multiples to find the floors at which both elevators stop. For example, the multiples of 2 are 2, 4, 6, 8, 10, and so on. The multiples of 3 are 3, 6, 9, 12, 15, and so on. Since 6 is a common multiple, both elevators stop at the sixth floor. (B), (C), and (D) are all incorrect because

the factors of a number are the same as the divisors of that number. Prime factors are factors that are also prime numbers. Divisors do not show at which floors elevators stop. The largest divisor of a number is the number itself.

28. **(D)** Begin by rewriting this expression; 10^{-2} means move the decimal point two places to the left. $1.37 \times 10^{-2} = 0.0137$.

    The 7 is in the ten-thousandths place. It has a value of $\dfrac{7}{10,000}$. (A), (B), and (C) are all incorrect because these choices do not show this answer.

29. **(B)** The number line shows 0 to 1 with a mark every $0.1 \left(\dfrac{1}{10}\right)$. *A* is located at $0.7 \left(\dfrac{7}{10}\right)$. *B* is located at $0.9 \left(\dfrac{9}{10}\right)$. Find the decimal value of each fraction.

    A. $\dfrac{27}{34} = 0.79$ YES

    B. $\dfrac{79}{86} = 0.92$ NO

    C. $\dfrac{81}{91} = 0.89$ YES

    D. $\dfrac{38}{54} = 0.703$ YES

    Only choice B is not between Point A and Point B.

30. **(A)** Equal shares usually means division. However, multiplying by $\dfrac{1}{3}$ is the same as dividing by 3. This answer best matches the expression. (B) The expression is $1\dfrac{1}{4} \times 3$. (C) The expression is $1\dfrac{1}{4} + \dfrac{1}{3}$. (D) The expression is $1\dfrac{1}{4} - \dfrac{1}{3}$.

31. **(B)** This is a proportion problem and can be approached in a few ways. This is the more classic approach and uses decimals, which is easier than using fractions. Write a fraction for what you know about the grass seed mix: $\dfrac{3.5 \text{ rye grass}}{0.75 \text{ blue grass}}$. Now write a fraction with an unknown for the total amount of seed: $\dfrac{5.25 \text{ rye grass}}{b \text{ blue grass}}$. Write a proportion and cross multiply.

$$\frac{3.5}{0.75} = \frac{5.25}{b}$$
$$3.5b = 3.9375$$
$$b = \frac{3.9375}{3.5}$$
$$b = 1.125$$

The decimal 1.125 is the fraction $1\dfrac{1}{8}$.

Answer Explanations

32. **(D)** Enough information is given to complete the entire problem.

$$
\begin{array}{r}
3\ 8 \\
\times\ 4\ 7 \\
\hline
2\ 6\ 6 \\
1\ 5\ 2\ 0 \\
\hline
1\ 7\ 8\ 6
\end{array}
$$

An 8 is in the tens place in the product.

33. **(A)** A slope of –1 means the line goes from the upper left to the lower right on the grid, which eliminates *B*, *C*, and *D*. A slope of –1 means move right 1 square every time you move down 1 square. A line through *A* and *X* follows that pattern and has a slope of –1.

34. **(B)** This expression correctly shows multiplying $0.04 times the number of minutes plus the general charge of $0.29. (A), (C), and (D) are all incorrect because these choices do not show this answer.

35. **(C)** Corresponding side of similar triangles are proportional. Write a proportion, cross multiply, and divide to find the length of *RT*.

$$\frac{RT}{PR} = \frac{QS}{PQ}$$

$$\frac{RT}{7} = \frac{2}{3}$$

$$RT = \frac{7 \times 2}{3}$$

$$RT = \frac{14}{3}$$

$$\frac{14}{3} = 4.66$$

Side *RT* is 4.66 miles long.

36. **(C)** Use the Pythagorean theorem, $a^2 + b^2 = c^2$, where *c* is the length of the wire.

$$5^2 + 12^2 = c^2$$
$$25 + 144 = c^2$$
$$c^2 = 169$$
$$c = 13$$

The wire will be 13 feet long.

37. **(C)** The hesitation between movements introduces students to the idea of bound flow, while the uninterrupted movement introduces students to free flow. (A) is incorrect because of the 5-second hesitation in the activity. (B) is incorrect because the movement time is the time required to complete a movement. (D) is incorrect because the activity has a specific objective; it is not just a warm up.

38. **(C)** Stretching does not involve moving the legs and so it is a nonlocomotor task. (A) is incorrect because jumping is a locomotor task. (B) is incorrect

because throwing is a manipulative task. (D) is incorrect because jumping is a locomotor activity.

39. **(D)** Generally speaking, regular cardiovascular activity lowers heart rate. (A) is incorrect because HDL cholesterol is "good" cholesterol that may be raised by cardiovascular activity. (B) is incorrect because LDL cholesterol is "bad" cholesterol that may be lowered by cardiovascular activity. (C) is incorrect because cardiovascular activity itself does not increase muscle strength.

40. **(A)** Pulse rate is the best way to determine if an exercise has become too demanding. (B) is incorrect because hard breathing is not as effective as pulse rate at determining the impact of exercise. (C) and (D) are incorrect because these choices do not include an effective way to determine the impact of exercise.

41. **(A)** This is the correct match of term and definition. (B) is incorrect because middle space activities are performed while standing. (C) is incorrect because arhythmic activities occur at irregular intervals. (D) is incorrect because force refers to the body tension that accompanies an activity.

42. **(A)** People at the most advanced stage of morality distinguish between legality and morality. (B), (C), and (D) are all incorrect because these descriptions are associated with earlier stages of morality in which students associate with teachers, parents, and other authority figures.

43. **(B)** Children have little appreciation for their own mortality or their own vulnerability. They have great difficulty understanding the consequences of drug abuse. (A), (C), and (D) are all incorrect because these choices give reasons for using drugs but not the most likely reason that children ignore warnings about the dangers of drug abuse.

44. **(D)** Typically, girls enter adolescence about age 10 while boys enter adolescence a few years later. (A) and (B) are incorrect because the period of steady growth begins about at age 6 for both boys and girls. (C) is incorrect because boys enter adolescence at about age 12.

45. **(A)** A student's thinking is very egocentric during the preoperational stage, which extends from approximately 18 months to 7 years of age. (B) is incorrect because this trait indicates that a student is at the concrete operational stage, which extends from approximately 7 to 12 years of age. (C) is incorrect because this trait indicates the student is at the sensorimotor stage, which extends from birth to approximately 18 months of age. (D) is incorrect because this trait indicates the student is at the concrete operational stage, which extends from 7 to 12 years of age.

46. **(D)** This choice least accurately characterizes most American families. This choice is sometimes accurate. However, it is not as accurate as the other choices. (A), (B), and (C) are all incorrect because these choices are the three most accurate characterizations of American families among the choices given.

Answer Explanations

47. **(D)** Vicarious learning means to learn through others' experiences. (A), (B), and (C) are all incorrect because these choices do not accurately describe vicarious learning.

48. **(A)** Only this choice is related to an appreciation of dance and dance elements. (B) is incorrect because this choice is related to the cultural style of a dance. (C) is incorrect because this choice is related to the underlying meaning of dance and not the dance itself. (D) is incorrect because this choice is related to the history of dance.

49. **(D)** *Languid* means "without animation," which this picture certainly represents. (A) is incorrect because *bucolic* means an "idealized country life," which this painting does not portray. (B) is incorrect because this is not an active scene. (D) is incorrect because nothing about this picture suggests that this is a morning scene.

50. **(D)** The students must improvise their acting using the general description on the card. (A) is incorrect because stand-up is a rehearsed comedic form. (B) is incorrect because pantomime uses only body movements. (C) is incorrect because the students do not have to create a comedic improvisation.

51. **(D)** The student's role as director is to create the performance. The producer has overall administrative responsibility. (A), (B), and (C) are all incorrect because these choices do not show the correct roles of director and producer.

52. **(C)** A fresco is created in wet plaster on a wall. (B) is incorrect because although a fresco may be present in some churches, that is not the most likely place to find a fresco. (A) and (D) are incorrect because these choices do not indicate where a fresco would appear.

53. **(D)** The C chromatic scale includes the C major diatonic scale. That C major diatonic scale includes notes corresponding to the first seven letters in the alphabet. That means that the chromatic scale also includes notes corresponding to the first seven letters of the alphabet.

54. **(C)** Phoneme deletion means to remove a phoneme from one word and to leave another word for students to identify. In an easy example, remove the /s/ from stack to form tack. (A) is incorrect because phoneme segmentation involves recognizing or counting each phoneme in a word. (B) is incorrect because phoneme categorization involves recognizing a sound not found in another word or words. (D) is incorrect because phoneme substitution is the technique of substituting one phoneme for another to make a new word.

55. **(A)** Early-grade students need systematic and explicit phonics instruction to become good readers. This approach is not the only approach that could be included; however, it is the only approach that must be included. Choices (B), (C), and (D) are all incorrect because they are examples of nonsystematic phonics approaches. The evidence is clear that these nonsystematic approaches are not as effective in early grades as systematic phonics approaches.

56. **(B)** Fluency is the ability to read accurately and quickly. Monitored oral reading that includes feedback from the teacher is the most effective way to help a student achieve fluency. (A) is incorrect because round-robin reading does not increase fluency, probably because each student reads a relatively small part of the passage. (C) is incorrect because no current evidence indicates that silent independent reading improves fluency or reading comprehension, although no final proof shows that it does not help. (D) is incorrect because although students need to hear models of fluent reading, this approach is less likely to improve fluency than choice (B).

57. **(D)** Semantic organizers are a special type of graphic organizer that may look like a spiderweb and help students identify related events and concepts in a text. (A) is incorrect because semantic organizers are not related to the linguistic study of semantics described in this choice. (B) and (C) are incorrect because they describe some types of graphic organizers but not semantic organizers.

58. **(C)** Metacognition means thinking about thinking. In this case, it means thinking about reading. A student who adjusts his or her reading speed is thinking about the reading process and reacting appropriately. (A) is incorrect because understanding story structure is an effective comprehension technique but is not metacognition. (B) is incorrect because summarizing a story is another effective comprehension strategy that is not metacognition. (D) is incorrect because although cooperative learning can be an effective way to learn comprehension strategies, it is neither an approach to reading comprehension nor a metacognitive strategy.

59. **(C)** Children are surrounded by a world of words. They learn most words by talking with others, overhearing conversations, and reading. (A) is incorrect because context clues are an important way for children to learn word meanings but are just a part of the indirect experiences that lead to understanding a word's meaning. (B) and (D) are incorrect because explicit phonics instruction and phonemic awareness instruction are essential elements of reading instruction but are not the way children learn the meaning of most words.

60. **(C)** Most of this paragraph is devoted to a discussion of buying computers, not using computers. The person buying the dorm computers got a better deal because he or she shopped around. (A) is incorrect because the paragraph does not say that the dorm computers are better to use, just that they are more sophisticated. (B) is incorrect because nothing in the paragraph indicates that the dorm computers are always in use. (D) is incorrect because nothing in the paragraph indicates that either set of computers were bought wholesale. Even though this statement is generally true, it does not flow from the paragraph.

61. **(C)** *The Odyssey* is an epic. It is a long narrative poem of grand sweep that focuses on a single heroic person who represents an entire nation. (A) is incorrect because *King Arthur and the Knights of the Round Table* is a legend. (B) is incorrect because *Gulliver's Travels* is a satire in which the characters mocked and ridiculed leaders in England. (D) is incorrect because Paul Bunyan is a legend.

62. **(A)** This book is based on a real girl Alice Liddell. (B) is incorrect because *Alice in Wonderland* lacks the broad sweep and the heroic nature of an epic. (C) is incorrect because most of the characters in *Alice in Wonderland* are not realistic. (D) is incorrect because *Alice in Wonderland* was written around 1865, well after the time referred to in this choice.

63. **(B)** Civilization is usually associated with a written language, which was most likely invented by the Sumerians about 5000 years ago near the confluence of the Tigris and Euphrates rivers. (A) is incorrect because the Nile River is certainly the center of important civilizations but is not where written language first appeared. (C) and (D) are incorrect because civilization did develop around the seas mentioned in the choices, but they are not the birthplace of civilization.

64. **(D)** These events occurred over about two decades. The English government instituted the Stamp Act in 1765. The Stamp Act required every legal document to carry a tax stamp. Choice (A), the Decleration of Independence, was written in 1776. Choice (B), the Constitution, was written in 1787. Choice (C), the First Continental Congress, met in 1774.

65. **(D)** The Reformation began about 1513 when Luther nailed his 95 theses to a church door. (A) is incorrect because Mary I of England was born a few years after the Reformation began. (B) is incorrect because the Renaissance began hundreds of years before Luther's rebellious act. (C) is incorrect because the Puritans sailed for the United States in the early 1600s.

66. **(D)** This line in the table accurately describes the Pilgrims and the colony they established in New England. (A) is incorrect because Columbus never landed in America. He did establish a colony in what is now the Dominican Republic. (B) is incorrect because Sir Walter Raleigh founded the Lost Colony. (C) is incorrect because John Smith founded the Jamestown Colony.

67. **(B)** The lines on this map represent the Trail of Tears, the forced removal of southern Native Americans to the Indian Territory, which is now Oklahoma. (A), (C), and (D) are all incorrect because the arrows begin only in southern states. So they could not represent the westward movement of settlers, railroads, or wagon trains from the east coast.

68. **(D)** Perry was in charge of a small American fleet on Lake Erie. (A), (B), and (C) are all incorrect because they are accurate matches of a person or people with events during the War of 1812.

69. **(B)** This choice shows the correct time order. Sherman's March to the Sea was during the Civil War. Everything else came either near the very end of the Civil War or after the Civil War. The correct answer will show I after II, so eliminate choice (A) and choice (D). The Surrender at Appomatox Courthouse was before Reconstruction, so eliminate choice (C). That leaves only choice (B), which is correct. Amendment XIII was ratified in 1865, before Reconstruction began in 1866.

70. **(B)** This text is from Executive Order No. 9066, signed by Franklin Roosevelt, which established military areas. The document does not mention Japanese, referring instead to "any or all persons." However, the intent of this text and the rest of the document was clear to all. (A), (C), and (D) are all incorrect because the wording is innocuous enough that it might refer to any of these choices, but it does not. The secrecy of test flight areas are secured by other orders. No official military defense zone is at the Mexican border. The federal government did not issue exclusion decrees after the San Francisco earthquake.

71. **(A)** Rubbing a glass rod with a silk cloth removes electrons and creates a negative electrical charge. (B), (C), and (D) are all incorrect because the electrical charge of an object refers to whether the charge is positive or negative. None of these actions has any impact on the charge of an object.

72. **(C)** The prism separates all of the colors that make up white light. (A) is incorrect because the colors of a rainbow appear when light is refracted through raindrops, not just triangular objects. (B) is incorrect because a prism does not have a colored filter. However, the shape of the prism does help create the effect. (D) is incorrect because a prism separates colors, not combine them.

73. **(B)** The nose and the mouth serve two important respiratory functions. They inhale air, which contains oxygen, and exhale carbon dioxide. The second of these functions is the only one listed. (A) is incorrect because the lungs filter out oxygen, not the nose and mouth. (C) is incorrect because the mouth and nose do heat air, but this is not a part of the respiratory system. (D) is incorrect because the mouth expectorates, but this is not a part of the respiratory system.

74. **(D)** Echoes frequently enhance sound production around bodies of water. (A) is incorrect because scientists report that sound travels faster through water than through air. (B) is incorrect because although sound does travel faster through water, this fact does not alter the volume. Additionally, the person is not listening through the water. (C) is incorrect because the materials the boat is constructed from, which are not described here, have no impact on how loud the voices are.

75. **(A)** Students frequently make key entry errors when they use a calculator. If a student estimates first, he or she can tell if the answer is reasonable. (B) is incorrect because the answer is obvious and estimation is not nearly as important as in choice (A). (C) and (D) are incorrect because no calculation is required to take these measurements.

76. **(C)** Move the decimal point 8 places to the right to get from 3.74 to 374,000,000. To accomplish this, multiply 3.74 by 10^8. (A) is incorrect because $3.74 \times 10^5 = 374,000$. (B) is incorrect because $3.74 \times 10^7 = 37,400,000$. (D) is incorrect because $3.74 \times 10^9 = 3,740,000,000$.

77. **(C)** There is no way to cut through a cylinder and produce rounded ends and straight sides. Cutting parallel to its base creates shape (A). Cutting perpendi-

cular to the bottom creates shape (C). Cutting diagonally through the cylinder creates shape (D).

78. **(D)** This student divides correctly but writes the remainder as a decimal. The correct answer to 124 divided by 5 is 24 R 4. (A), (B), and (C) are all incorrect because these choices do not show the error pattern.

79. **(B)** The answer to the division example is 8 R 3. In order to solve this problem, the student must interpret the remainder of 3 to mean that an extra tent is needed. In other words, at least 9 tents are needed for the camping trip. (A), (C), and (D) are all incorrect because these choices do not show the correct strategy to solve the problem.

80. **(A)** Smaller numbers represent faster times. Subtract, 52.8 − 1.3 to find Lisa's time. (B), (C), and (D) are all incorrect because these choices do not show Lisa's time.

81. **(D)** Trace the numbers as they move through the flowchart to see that the flowchart only prints numbers that are odd or less than 25. Choice (D), 38, is the only number that is neither odd nor less than 25.

82. **(C)** To find the average, add the lengths and then divide by the number of wood pieces, 3.

$$\frac{1}{2} = \frac{6}{12}; \quad \frac{2}{3} = \frac{8}{12}; \quad \frac{5}{12} = \frac{5}{12}$$

$$\frac{6}{12} + \frac{8}{12} + \frac{5}{12} = \frac{19}{12}$$

$$\frac{19}{12} \div 3 = \frac{19}{12} \cdot \frac{1}{3}$$

$$\frac{19}{12} \times \frac{1}{3} = \frac{19}{36}$$

The average length is $\frac{19}{36}$ foot.

83. **(D)** Eye-hand coordination is not fully developed in young children. The activities described in this choice help develop that skill. However, (A), (B), and (C) are not the best ways for a young student to develop eye-hand coordination.

84. **(B)** In moonball, all the students have the same goal, which is to keep the ball in the air. (A) is incorrect because moonball is not a competitive game. All students have the same goal. (C) and (D) are incorrect because moonball involves both locomotor and nonlocomotor skills. So it cannot be classified in either category.

85. **(A)** This answer is the definition of learning disabled. The measure of a student's learning is below the level predicted by the measure of a student's intelligence. (B), (C), and (D) are incorrect because the particular IQ or achievement score alone does not identify a learning-disabled student.

86. **(C)** Complementary colors are opposing colors on the color wheel. Mixing complementary colors produces gray. (A), (B), and (D) are all incorrect because mixing complimentary colors does not produce the colors listed.

87 **(B)** James Fenimore Cooper (1789–1851) is best known for authoring *The Last of the Mohicans*, which has been further popularized in television and movie adaptations. (A) is incorrect because although the Baseball Hall of Fame is located in Cooperstown, New York, Cooper did not author any books about baseball. (C) is incorrect because Mark Twain wrote *The Adventures of Huckleberry Finn*. (D) is incorrect because *The Adventures of Sleepy Hollow* was authored by Washington Irving, another New York writer.

88. **(A)** Students should be exposed to the widest-possible range of careers. The goal of the career day should be to let students know their options. (B) seems a tempting choice but is too limiting, regardless of the level of achievement in the community. (C) is another tempting choice. It shows students the best. However, it is too limiting. The vast majority of students in any school will not pursue those careers. (D) has the emotional appeal since it involves families. However, the choice is too limiting. It will inevitably create problems and draw unnecessary attention to students with family issues.

89. **(B)** The correct approach is to use technology in a way that supports the objective. Not all technology is good for every subject. (A) is incorrect because the most cutting-edge technology does not integrate well with many subject's objectives. (C) is incorrect because it does not address the issue of subject matter integration. (D) is incorrect because technology should be used to the extent that it supports integration with the subject's objectives.

90. **(B)** At that time, Benedict Arnold was in command of West Point, an American fort before the United States Military Academy was established there in 1802. The other choices are incorrect. Arnold escaped from West Point, down the Hudson River on a British ship, after hearing of André's capture. Arnold switched sides and served in the British Army in the United States, although he never commanded the forces. He settled in England some years later and died there.

Constructed Response

1. Read and Understand the Task

Two students are talking. The teacher is paying attention to Jeanie to identify errors she may make in spoken English grammar. The task specifically asks about grammatical errors that Jeanie made with subjects and verbs and with tense. Concentrate on Jeanie as you read the dialog.

2. Mark the Dialog

For this type of question, mark each error that Jeanie makes. Mark right on the dialog. Mark all the errors, not just the ones mentioned in the task.

Just put "SV" next to examples of subject-verb errors and "T" next to tense errors.

Quinn—What is going on this weekend?

Jeanie—I are going shopping.

(SV—Singular subject and plural verb. Change *are* to *is*.)

Quinn—What store?

Jeanie—It's the store down by the school.

Quinn—I guess your brother is going.

Jeanie—That is what he say.

(T—Wrong tense. Change present tense *say* to past tense *said*.)

Quinn—What do you think you'll buy?

Jeanie—I ain't sure.

(Usage error—Never use *ain't*. It is not standard English.)

Quinn—Take a guess.

Jeanie—I are not sure.

(SV—singular subject and plural verb. Change *are* to *is*.)

Quinn—It was crowded the last time I went there.

Jeanie—I hope it is not when I went there this weekend.

(T—The past tense *went* is used to describe something that will occur in the near future. Change *went* to *go*.)

Quinn—See you later.

Jeanie—Just keep it among us.

(Usage error—The word *among* refers to more than two people. (Change *among* to *between*.)

3. Identify the Error Patterns

Respond to all the points raised in the task.

Do not focus on the word usage errors in the dialog. They are important, but the task asks about only subject-verb and tense errors. Concentrate on those.

SUBJECT-VERB ERRORS

In this dialog, Jeanie incorrectly uses plural verbs with singular subjects in "I are going shopping" and "I are not sure." Jeanie may make other subject-verb errors, but they are not evident in the dialog.

TENSE ERRORS

In this dialog, Jeanie has problems with past and present tense in "That is what he say" and "I hope it is not when I went there this weekend."

4. Write the Essay

You have spent your time preparing to write the essay. You have identified Jeanie's grammatical mistakes, and you have specific examples. The test makers want to see that you can explain all this in a brief essay.

If you write a high-scoring essay, you will have to answer fewer multiple-choice items correctly to pass the exam.

Show your essay to a professor of education. Ask that a person to rate your essay from 1–4 using this scale.

4 A well developed, complete written assignment.

Shows a thorough response to all parts of the topic.

Clear explanations that are well supported.

An assignment that is free of significant grammatical, punctuation, or spelling errors.

3 A fairly well developed, complete written assignment.

It may not thoroughly respond to all parts of the topic.

Fairly clear explanations that may not be well supported.

It may contain some significant grammatical, punctuation, or spelling errors.

2 A poorly developed, incomplete written assignment.

It does not thoroughly respond to most parts of the topic.

Contains many poor explanations that are not well supported.

It may contain some significant grammatical, punctuation, or spelling errors.

1 A very poorly developed, incomplete written assignment.

It does not thoroughly respond to the topic.

Contains only poor, unsupported explanations.

Contains numerous significant grammatical, punctuation, or spelling errors.

For this assignment you should,

- demonstrate that you have identified the problems Jeanie has with subjects and verbs and with tense.
- identify and discuss specific examples of these problems.
- convey that you understand about subject-verb agreement and verb tense and understand the importance of these grammatical skills in a child's life.

Try to earn a score of 3 or 4. You should write two paragraphs, one for each error type. The first sentence in each paragraph should describe the error type. The subsequent sentences in each paragraph should give the two examples of each error type and some additional details.

Since you have done the planning, now take the time to write well. You should always reread and edit your essay. You can erase or cross out and replace words, as long as your essay is legible. You will find more help about writing essays on pages 113–126.

Many test makers say writing well is not that important as long as your essay can be understood. Do not believe them. A well-written essay will almost always earn a higher score. Additionally, a longer, well-written essay usually earns higher scores than a shorter, well-written essay. The test makers recommend an essay of 150 to 300 words. We recommend that you write at least 250 to 275 useful words. Write legibly. If you write 12 words on a line, your essay will be about 21 to 23 lines long.

Sample Essay

The following essay would earn a score in the upper half.

The transcript of Jeanie's conversation reveals that Jeanie has difficulty with subject-verb agreement. This difficulty occurs when Jeanie uses a singular subject and a plural verb. In the first example, Jeanie said, "I are going shopping." Instead she should have said, "I am going shopping." In the second example, she said, "I ain't sure." Instead she should have said, "I am not sure." Jeanie needs help identifying the correct singular verb to accompany a singular subject. Jeanie probably also has difficulty matching plural verbs to plural subjects. However, that difficulty is not present in the dialog.

The transcript of Jeanie's conversation also reveals that Jeanie had problems with verb tense. In the first example, Jeanie said, "That is what he say." She should have said, "That is that he said." She used the present tense say when she should have used the past tense said. In the second example, Jeanie said, "I hope it is not when I went there this weekend." She should have said, "I hope it is not. . . when I go there this weekend." In this example, she incorrectly used the past tense. This example may be a little harder to notice because "when I went there this weekend" sound perfectly fine on its own. The teacher has to notice from the introductory words "I hope" that the sentence does not refer to a past event. In social situations, subject-verb disagreement and using the incorrect tense can also create problems. In fact, Jeanie also used the wrong words at times. Her difficulties should be addressed immediately.

PART 5

JOB SEARCH

Finding a Teaching Job

How Can I Find a Job?

Before discussing this question, let's talk about rejection. Remember, you need only one teaching job. If you are interested in 100 jobs, you should be extremely happy with a success rate of 1 percent. A success rate of 2 percent is more than you need, and a very high success rate of 5 percent will just make it too hard to decide which job to take.

Rejection and failure are part of the job search process. Be ready; everyone goes through it.

Okay, I'm Ready to Begin. How Do I Find a Job?

Begin by deciding on the kind of teaching jobs you want and the geographic areas you are willing to teach in. There is no sense pursuing jobs you don't want in places you don't want to go.

Write your choices here.

These are the kind of teaching positions I'm interested in.

_____   _____
_____   _____

These are the counties, towns, places, areas, or locales I'm willing to teach in.

_____   _____
_____   _____

You can change your mind as often as you like. But limit your job search to these choices.

Follow the guidelines presented below. You must actually do the things outlined here. Reading, talking, and thinking about them will not help.

> - Make and use personal contacts (network)
> - Find out about every appropriate teaching position
> - Apply for every appropriate teaching position—go to every interview
> - Develop a good resume
> - Develop a portfolio
> - Use the placement office

Make and Use Personal Contacts (Network)

You will not be surprised to learn that many, if not most, jobs are found through personal contacts. You must make personal contacts to maximize your chances of finding the job you want. Take things easy, one step at a time, and try to meet at least one new person each week.

Find a way to get introduced to teachers, school administrators, board of education members, and others who will know about teaching jobs and may influence hiring decisions. The more people you meet and talk to, the better chance you will have of getting the job you want.

Get a mentor. Get to know a superintendent or principal near where you want to teach, and ask that person to be your mentor. Tell them immediately that you are not asking for a job in their district. (That will not stop them from offering you one if they want to.) Explain that you are just beginning your teaching career and that you need help learning about teaching jobs in surrounding communities and about teaching in general. Ask your mentors to keep their eyes and ears open for any openings for which you are qualified. You can have several mentors if you want to. Listen to their advice.

You already have a lot of contacts through your friends and relatives. Talk to them all. Tell them you are looking for a teaching job and ask them to be alert for any possibilities. Ask them to mention your name and your interest in a teaching position to everyone they know.

Find Out About Every Appropriate Teaching Position

The contacts you have and are making each week will help you keep abreast of some teaching opportunities. Follow these additional steps. Look in every paper every day distributed in the places you want to teach. Don't forget about weekly papers.

Call all the school districts where you want to teach. Ask the administrative assistant or secretary in the superintendent's or principal's office if there are current or anticipated job openings in the district. If you are in college or a recent graduate, visit or contact the placement office every week and ask your professors if they know about any teaching opportunities.

Apply for Every Appropriate Teaching Position— Go to Every Interview

Apply for every teaching position that is of the type and in the location(s) you listed. No exceptions! Direct application for a listed position is probably the second most effective way to get a job. The more appropriate jobs you apply for, the more likely you are to get one. It is not unusual for someone to apply for more than 100 teaching positions.

Go to every interview you are invited to. Going to interviews increases your chances of getting a job. If you don't get the job, it was worth going just for the practice.

Your application should include a brief cover letter and a one-page resume. The cover letter should follow this format: The first brief paragraph should identify the job you are applying for. The second brief paragraph should be used to mention a skill or ability you have that matches a district need. The third brief paragraph should indicate an interest in a personal interview. Every cover letter should be addressed to the person responsible for hiring in the school district.

Develop a Good Resume

A good resume is a one-page advertisement. A good resume highlights the things you have done that prospective employers will be interested in. A good resume is not an exhaustive listing of everything you have done. A good resume is not cluttered.

For example, say you worked as a teacher assistant and spent most of your time on lunch duty and about 10 percent of your time conducting whole language lessons. What goes on the resume? The whole language experience.

Your resume should include significant school-related experience. It should also include other employment that lasted longer than a year. Omit noneducation-related short-term employment. Your resume should list special skills, abilities, and interests that make you unique.

An example of a resume using a format that has proven successful appears in this chapter. This resume combines the experience of more than one person and is for demonstration purposes only.

An outline of a resume you can copy, to begin to develop your own resume, is also included in this chapter. If you are interested in two different types of teaching positions, you may have two resumes. Go over your final resume and cover letters with a placement officer or advisor and show them to teachers and school administrators.

Develop a Portfolio

Develop a portfolio to show to potential employers. Choose four or five lesson plans you like. Rewrite them extensively to incorporate all the elements of a good lesson plan. Carefully type them in final form and include them in your portfolio. Include examples of your student's work that you believe will be well received by a principal or superintendent. You may want to take pictures of a classroom you've worked in showing class arrangement and bulletin boards. Include other materials to show your familiarity with current teaching methods.

TIP

Be sure to show your portfolio to your education advisor and a principal before you show it to prospective employers. Make changes in the portfolio as they recommend.

TIP

College placement offices often give seminars on job hunting and interviews. Take advantage of these.

Use the Placement Office

If you are a college student or graduate, use the school's placement office. Set up a placement file that includes recommendation letters from professors, teachers, and supervisors. It's handy to have these references on file. If a potential employer wants this information, you can have it sent out from the placement office instead of running around.

What Time Line Should I Follow?

Let's say you are looking for a job in September and you will be certified three months earlier in June. You should begin working on your personal contacts by September of the previous year. You should start looking for advertisements and tracking down job possibilities during January. Have your placement file set up and a preliminary resume done by February. You can amend them later if you need to. Start applying for jobs in February.

Any Last Advice?

Stick with it. Let people help you. Follow the steps outlined here. Start early and take things one step at a time. Remember the importance of personal contacts. Remember that you need only one teaching position. Let people help you.

Teacher Certification and Job Search Links

Note that all links were active as of press time. However, links can change.

NEW YORK

New York State Teacher Licensing
http://www.highered.nysed.gov/tcert/certificate/

This link takes you to the New York State Office of Teaching home page, where there are further links to certification information, including the TEACH certification system, and other resources.

Northern Westchester/Putnam BOCES Job Search
http://www.olasjobs.org/

This is the best place to start looking for a teaching job outside of New York City. This link takes you to the OLAS job application site at Putnam Northern Westchester BOCES, which includes a current listing of openings and a comprehensive online application system. Use this site to find and apply for most teaching positions in Westchester County, Putnam County, Rockland County, and most other areas of New York State.

NYC Information Portal
http://schools.nyc.gov/TeachNYC/default.htm

This link is the information portal for those interested in teaching in New York City.

Map of New York City School Districts
http://maps.nycboe.net/

New York City School Finder
http://schools.nyc.gov/TeachNYC/teachinnyc/OurSchoolsOurStudents/SchoolMaps.htm

This site gives detailed information, including accurate mapping, of all schools in New York City.

CONNECTICUT

Connecticut Teacher Certification
http://www.sde.ct.gov/sde/cwp/view.asp?a=2613&Q=321230

Connecticut Job Search
http://www.ctreap.net/

Partial List of Connecticut Teacher Openings
http://www.cea.org/jobs/vacancies.cfm

NEW JERSEY

New Jersey Teacher Certification
http://www.state.nj.us/njded/educators/license/

NJ Hire
http://www.njhire.com/MainTemp.cfm?page=mainpage.cfm&UserType=1&CFID=3855468&CFTOKEN=332ec93-e3225c93-7f22-4861-b73a-7fefa6540bf8

This site contains state-sponsored job links with other useful New Jersey certification information.

PENNSYLVANIA

Pennsylvania Teacher Certification
http://www.teaching.state.pa.us/

Pennsylvania Department of Education Job Search System
https://www.tcs.ed.state.pa.us/jobsearch/doorway.asp

NATIONAL

NY Times/*Monster.com* Teacher Jobs
http://jobmarket.nytimes.com/jobs/category/education-training-jobs

There are many categories to check.

School Spring Teacher Jobs
http://www.schoolspring.com/searchForm.cfm?&

This is an extensive list of teacher job openings for many states taken from many sources. There is significant duplication of BOCES.

All School Districts in a State
http://en.wikipedia.org/wiki/Lists_of_school_districts_in_the_United_States

This link shows all school districts in each state. If a district has a website, you can access it through this link.

From Barron's—Teacher Certification Exams

To order visit us at
www.barronseduc.com
or your local book store

Barron's Educational Series, Inc.
250 Wireless Blvd.
Hauppauge, N.Y. 11788
Order toll-free: 1-800-645-3476

In Canada:
Georgetown Book Warehouse
34 Armstrong Ave.
Georgetown, Ontario L7G 4R9
Canadian orders: 1-800-247-7160

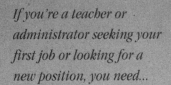